THE NEW MIDDLE AGES

BONNIE WHEELER, *Series Editor*

The New Middle Ages is a series dedicated to transdisciplinary studies of medieval cultures, with particular emphasis on recuperating women's history and on feminist and gender analyses. This peer-reviewed series includes both scholarly monographs and essay collections.

PUBLISHED BY PALGRAVE:

Women in the Medieval Islamic World:
Power, Patronage, and Piety
   edited by Gavin R. G. Hambly

The Ethics of Nature in the Middle Ages:
On Boccaccio's Poetaphysics
   by Gregory B. Stone

Presence and Presentation: Women in the
Chinese Literati Tradition
   by Sherry J. Mou

The Lost Love Letters of Heloise and Abelard:
Perceptions of Dialogue in Twelfth-Century
France
   by Constant J. Mews

Understanding Scholastic Thought with Foucault
   by Philipp W. Rosemann

For Her Good Estate: The Life of Elizabeth
de Burgh
   by Frances A. Underhill

Constructions of Widowhood and Virginity
in the Middle Ages
   edited by Cindy L. Carlson and Angela
Jane Weisl

Motherhood and Mothering in Anglo-Saxon
England
   by Mary Dockray-Miller

Listening to Heloise:
The Voice of a Twelfth-Century Woman
   edited by Bonnie Wheeler

The Postcolonial Middle Ages
   edited by Jeffrey Jerome Cohen

Chaucer's Pardoner and Gender Theory: Bodies
of Discourse
   by Robert S. Sturges

Crossing the Bridge: Comparative Essays on
Medieval European and Heian Japanese
Women Writers
   edited by Barbara Stevenson and
Cynthia Ho

Engaging Words: The Culture of Reading in
the Later Middle Ages
   by Laurel Amtower

Robes and Honor: The Medieval World of
Investiture
   edited by Stewart Gordon

Representing Rape in Medieval and Early
Modern Literature
   edited by Elizabeth Robertson and
Christine M. Rose

Same Sex Love and Desire Among Women
in the Middle Ages
   edited by Francesca Canadé Sautman
and Pamela Sheingorn

Sight and Embodiment in the Middle Ages:
Ocular Desires
   by Suzannah Biernoff

Listen, Daughter: The Speculum Virginum
and the Formation of Religious Women in
the Middle Ages
   edited by Constant J. Mews

Science, the Singular, and the Question of
Theology
   by Richard A. Lee, Jr.

Gender in Debate from the Early Middle
Ages to the Renaissance
   edited by Thelma S. Fenster and
Clare A. Lees

Malory's Morte Darthur: *Remaking Arthurian Tradition*
   by Catherine Batt

The Vernacular Spirit: Essays on Medieval Religious Literature
   edited by Renate Blumenfeld-Kosinski, Duncan Robertson, and Nancy Warren

Popular Piety and Art in the Late Middle Ages: Image Worship and Idolatry in England 1350–1500
   by Kathleen Kamerick

Absent Narratives, Manuscript Textuality, and Literary Structure in Late Medieval England
   by Elizabeth Scala

Creating Community with Food and Drink in Merovingian Gaul
   by Bonnie Effros

Representations of Early Byzantine Empresses: Image and Empire
   by Anne McClanan

Encountering Medieval Textiles and Dress: Objects, Texts, Images
   edited by Désirée G. Koslin and Janet Snyder

Eleanor of Aquitaine: Lord and Lady
   edited by Bonnie Wheeler and John Carmi Parsons

Isabel La Católica, Queen of Castile: Critical Essays
   edited by David A. Boruchoff

Homoeroticism and Chivalry: Discourses of Male Same-Sex Desire in the Fourteenth Century
   by Richard Zeikowitz

Portraits of Medieval Women: Family, Marriage, and Politics in England 1225–1350
   by Linda E. Mitchell

Eloquent Virgins: From Thecla to Joan of Arc
   by Maud Burnett McInerney

The Persistence of Medievalism: Narrative Adventures in Contemporary Culture
   by Angela Jane Weisl

Capetian Women
   edited by Kathleen Nolan

Joan of Arc and Spirituality
   edited by Ann W. Astell and Bonnie Wheeler

The Texture of Society: Medieval Women in the Southern Low Countries
   edited by Ellen E. Kittell and Mary A. Suydam

Charlemagne's Mustache: And Other Cultural Clusters of a Dark Age
   by Paul Edward Dutton

Troubled Vision: Gender, Sexuality, and Sight in Medieval Text and Image
   edited by Emma Campbell and Robert Mills

Queering Medieval Genres
   by Tison Pugh

Sacred Place in Early Medieval Neoplatonism
   by L. Michael Harrington

The Middle Ages at Work
   edited by Kellie Robertson and Michael Uebel

Chaucer's Jobs
   by David R. Carlson

Medievalism and Orientalism: Three Essays on Literature, Architecture and Cultural Identity
   by John M. Ganim

Queer Love in the Middle Ages
   by Anna Klosowska Roberts

Performing Women: Sex, Gender and the Medieval Iberian Lyric
   by Denise K. Filios

NECESSARY CONJUNCTIONS: THE SOCIAL SELF IN MEDIEVAL ENGLAND

David Gary Shaw

NECESSARY CONJUNCTIONS
© David Gary Shaw, 2005.

First published in 2005 by
PALGRAVE MACMILLAN™
175 Fifth Avenue, New York, N.Y. 10010 and
Houndmills, Basingstoke, Hampshire, England RG21 6XS
Companies and representatives throughout the world.

PALGRAVE MACMILLAN is the global academic imprint of the Palgrave Macmillan division of St. Martin's Press, LLC and of Palgrave Macmillan Ltd. Macmillan® is a registered trademark in the United States, United Kingdom and other countries. Palgrave is a registered trademark in the European Union and other countries.

Library of Congress Cataloging-in-Publication Data

Shaw, David Gary.
   Necessary conjunctions : the social self in medieval England / David Gary Shaw.
      p. cm. — (The new Middle Ages)
   Includes bibliographical references and index.
   ISBN 1–4039–6689–3 (hc. : alk. paper)
    1. England—Social life and customs—1066–1485. 2. Community life—England—History—To 1500. 3. Group identity—England—History—To 1500. 4. Community—England—History—To 1500. 5. England—Social conditions—1066–1485. I. Title. II. New Middle Ages (Palgrave Macmillan (Firm))

DA185.S47 2005
307′.0942′0902—dc22   2004059352

A catalogue record for this book is available from the British Library.

Design by Newgen Imaging Systems (P) Ltd., Chennai, India.

First edition: March 2005

10 9 8 7 6 5 4 3 2 1

Printed in the United States of America.

In Memory of
Iva Beck Smith and David A. T. Peterson

CONTENTS

List of Figures and Tables   ix

Preface   xi

Abbreviations   xiii

1.   Introduction: The Self in Social History   1

2.   Master Values of Town Life   21

3.   *E Pluribus Unum:* Peer Pressures   47

4.   The Marriage of Self and Structure   69

5.   Friends, Enemies, Patrons   93

6.   Battles at the Boundary of the Self   121

7.   Self-Possession   145

8.   A World of Individuals   165

9.   Conclusion: The Shape of the Social Self   197

Notes   207

Bibliography   259

Index   281

LIST OF FIGURES AND TABLES

Figures

4.1	Use of arbitration in lawsuits	74
4.2	Arbitration by sociopolitical group	83
4.3	Commons' arbitration partners	88
5.1	Basic network illustration	118

Tables

4.1	Commons' use of arbitration	79
4.2	Middling and petty arbitration according to opponents' status	79
4.3	Shares of arbitration by sociopolitical status	82
4.4	Trespass arbitration by sociopolitical status	86
4.5	Commons' arbitration partners	87
5.1	Inner and outer circle of contacts by political grouping	101
5.2	Network density and intensity	119

PREFACE

This book flows from my earlier work on urban communities and remains poised between the corporate and the personal, which it seeks to connect. It ends with biographies that are the result of social–historical engagements with ideas, structures, social networks and the permeable boundaries of the self. In its essence, one of my necessary conjunctions is that between the methods and manners of social history and those of cultural history. This methodological fusion is no less important than the engagement with self and society.

Unsurprisingly, this book owes much to social and cultural historians and social scientists around the world, whose works have greatly enriched me; their names are in the notes and bibliography, but the thanks are real. Certain individuals have been kind and tolerant in listening to me talk about my ideas and reading and commenting on what I had done. More-over, some anonymous readers have come to be iconic professionals for me. Closer to home I have benefited from the work ethic of my Wesleyan University history department colleagues, who read the manuscript, some-times as part of their responsibilities, and have offered advice, encourage-ment, reading suggestions, or a kind word, which is never hard to accept. Sharp readers they are and not easily pleased: I particularly thank Bruce Masters, Vijay Pinch, Phil Pomper, Rick Elphick, Vera Schwarcz, Nat Greene, and Ann Wightman. Outside readers who have improved the man-uscript or my mind include Nancy Partner and Derek Neal at McGill University and Gabrielle Spiegel of the University of California at Los Angeles, as well as Bonnie Wheeler at Southern Methodist University. I must also thank my Wesleyan sociology colleague Robert Rosenthal, who very generously provided me with his extensive reading notes on social network theory, the use of which helped me to write Chapter Five. Need-less to say, all errors are my responsibility.

The research for this book goes back many, many years, to moments long before it was conceived. I must therefore thank many librarians and archivists who often silently supported me by pretty consistent competence and kindness, at the Wells Town Hall, the Wells Cathedral Library, Lambeth

Palace Library, the Public Record Office (now the National Archives), the Somerset Records Office, the Bodleian Library, Balliol College Library, the Borthwick Institute of History at the University of York, Acadia University, Killam Library (Dalhousie University), McLennan Library at McGill University, the National Library of Scotland, Edinburgh University Library, and of course Wesleyan University's libraries, especially Olin. I thank David Perry for assistance with the relational database behind parts of chapters four and five, as well as the Ford Foundation which helped to fund his work several years ago. The preparation of the manuscript has been aided by my editors and the staff at Palgrave. I thank Bonnie Wheeler again, Melissa Nosal, the copy-editing team at Newgen, and William Fain. I also thank Elizabeth Jones for her help in completing the extensive references and Manolis Kaparakis and John Hammond for help with the figures and tables.

A book about small groups and the bonds that connect individuals is understandably haunted by many people, living and dead; the excellent little community of the Wesleyan History Department is one simulacrum of the medieval, as are my families, especially the Smiths of Nova Scotia, strange sources for past times perhaps, but effective and intriguing models.

Nearer and more conventionally, I must thank my near, most dear family. We are fairly undemonstrative even in private, so on the page I should leave it at this: I am constantly grateful for Sheila and Sarah, without whom this book would have been finished long ago, but much less happily.

ABBREVIATIONS

AH	Wells, Wells Cathedral Library, Almshouse Document
Cal. Pat. R.	*Calendar of Patent Rolls.* Henry III–Henry VIII. 45 vols. HMSO, 1891–1916.
CB	Wells, Wells Town Hall, Convocation Book
Chaucer	Chaucer, Geoffrey. *Riverside Chaucer.* Ed. Larry Dean Benson. Boston: Houghton Mifflin, Co., 1987.
Creation of a Community	David Gary Shaw, *The Creation of a Community. The City of Wells in the Middle Ages.* Oxford: Oxford University Press, 1993.
CS	Camden Society
EETS	Early English Text Society
LPL	London, Lambeth Palace Library
Mr Goodall's Book	Wells, Wells Town Hall, "Mr Goodall's Book"
RS	Rolls Series
Serel	Serel, Thomas. *Historical Notes on the Church of St Cuthbert in Wells, etc.* Wells: J.M. Atkins, 1875.
SMW	*Somerset Medieval Wills 1383–1500.* 3 volumes. Ed. F. W. Weaver. Somerset Record Society, 1901–05.
SRS	Somerset Record Society
WCaCH	Wells, Wells Cathedral Library, Wells Cathedral Charters
Wells Cath. Reg.	Wells, Wells Cathedral Library, Register
Wells City Ch.	Wells, Wells Town Hall, Wells City Charters

CHAPTER 1

INTRODUCTION: THE SELF IN SOCIAL HISTORY

The Bishop Orders His Tomb at St. Andrew's

In March 1850, a hole five feet deep and ten feet wide was opened in the south aisle of the Cathedral Church of St. Andrew, Wells. It was found, like most historical ventures, to be in a "very dry state." "It contained one skeleton only, and a few handfuls of dark mould. . . .What remained of the bones was of a dark chocolate colour."[1] Such were the remains of Thomas Beckyngton, eminent historical object, former secretary to Henry VI, and bishop of Bath and Wells. What most impressed the nineteenth-century physician who presided at the disinterment was the skull, which he evaluated with the science of comparative phrenology in mind. Beckyngton had "good frontal development," and good occipital development for that matter: the cranial circumference a solid twenty-two and one-eighth inches at the ear. Inevitably, we give our times and ourselves away.

What most impressed me, however, was the fact, which Dr. Boyd probably did not know, that this broken mass of darkness had so wanted to be there. Beckyngton was now the bottom layer of a gruesome cake of sensible, imagined self-representation, dreamed up long before. Beckyngton's death, if not his dying, was a thoughtful and well-planned affair. He died in January 1465, about 400 years before Dr. Boyd took a look, but he had devised his own death at least fifteen years earlier. Like all medieval people, he had to worry about where he would lie, but privilege allowed him to choose a prominent place within a major church, the symbol of his county. He opted for a spot not too far from the choir. He built the tomb with a chapel nearby where priests would sing for his soul and those of his friends, as well as all the faithful Christian dead.

The tomb communicates a complex message. Without question, Beckyngton himself was at the center of this display in life as well as in death. He is one of the few fifteenth-century inhabitants of Wells whom we could pick out on the street were he to walk again as if in life. His top layer effigy is realistic, apparently mimetic since it conforms roughly to the manuscript portraits of him that exist in Oxford and Cambridge libraries.[2] They are strong statements for a renaissance interest in personal details. He was sculpted in his full episcopal regalia, once brightly painted, and still showing some good color. Lying beneath the well-dressed bishop as member of the world is the middle layer, set just above the floor. This is the sculpture of his cadaver. Naked, grey, it was never painted so that it would heighten the contrast to the top layer's frosting. The bones press through wasting skin. This rendition of a popular English monumental effigy style passionately captured powerful cultural reflections on death, when life's "peinted trouth was turned to gile."[3] A contemplation of death, the end of the earthly life, was often interpreted in medieval culture as a kind of narrative pivot—a great, sure fact upon which men and women could concentrate their minds, and sometimes convert them, giving themselves more fully to the Christian life and its powerful moral narratives. That Christian story saw a great advantage in death after a well-led life: death itself was another fraught pivot for paradise. As the *dies irae* puts it: "Death and nature will be struck dumb, when the body reawakens to face God's judgment."[4] There was so much to lose: "When the turuf is thy tour, and thy put [pit] is thy bour, thy wel and they white throte shulen wormes to note, what helpet thee thenne, all the worilde wenne?"[5] Humbled by design, the bishop expressed without embarrassment his appreciation of these theological truths.

Beckyngton himself consecrated the chapel in 1452 when he led a requiem mass for the souls of the bishops of Wells, his parents, and all souls. He looked down upon his own English face, his rich robes, his jowls, but also upon the naked husk. He had been born humbly in Somerset, traveled far in the world as a royal emissary, an influential national figure, but had wisely withdrawn from an increasingly dangerous politics. As his pension, he did not seek the rich diocese of Salisbury that others had always preferred, but rather his home diocese and the city of Wells. This was probably one of the market towns his weaving father would have traveled to and sold wool in when Thomas was a child.[6] He had reached home, and chosen the hole that he wanted to lie in, "watching God made and eaten all day long."

There is a sharp contrast between the merely physical aspect of the tomb, cloaked in its otherworldly and deeply religious cloth, and the essentially social character of such a grand case of medieval death. Looking at the artwork alone, knowing that the body was underfoot, can encourage us to abstract his art into a uniquely personal statement, even a private one that seems representative of purely internal hopes, repentance, and fears—a piece of poetry and prayer: "Timor mortis conturbat me," (I am agonized by the fear of death).[7] Perhaps he was. And while the tomb and the knowledge of the man underneath *are* poetry, they were consecrated and created in a powerfully social milieu, in the center lane of a spiritual highway. Beckyngton initiated prayers that were violated only by the reformation, prayers that he hoped would be offered by the many visitors who would visit Wells Cathedral and come round the choir and see him in glory and hope, lying there thrice, till the end of history. They prayed, and maybe some still do when they see him. Art persuades.

The record itself, however, tells us that Beckyngton worked his faith through his multiple communities, his individuality entangled at every turn with others. He had many friends, but here I think especially of the throng of people—hierarchically noted in the text—which turned out to watch him consecrate his holy place. He led the mass "in the presence of the dean and some canons of the cathedral, and very many other men and women."[8] A quick social hierarchy is indicated, one that emphasizes that the civic community turned out along with the ecclesiastical. The mention of women is a sure sign of the presence and interest of regular, if devout, townspeople drawn there by Beckyngton. The bishop was like that. On another occasion, he gave the town easy access to his good, and possibly holy, water supply, and asked the city dignitaries to visit him at his tomb every year as a corporate statement.[9] He wanted the recognition and the continuity. They visited, and still do.[10] So this figure at the center of a busy church was a man of high status who wanted to be home amidst people who would honor him and help him through purgatory. Ambitious and driven though he was, his dreams and schemes, like everyone's, arrived at meaning only in this inevitably social context that he anticipated and benignly manipulated. Thomas Beckyngton left us no interesting personal writings,[11] little that bears on his soul as revealingly as these showy physical remains—monuments and mould—which speak at every point of his connections and relations, of the worldly context of his self, of the necessary conjunction of self and surroundings.

I think I can hear the low thud of Bishop Beckyngton, the particular quality of his social self, but to hear similar sounds from quieter, more common people is one way to express the aim of this book. Another is to give an account of the nature of late medieval human agency in the context of its social life. I borrow the term *social self* to gesture at the notion of an embedded agency or an individuality in which the social group—the air that sustains the free agent—proves as crucial as the particular person.[12] I want to argue that the social self is a category that can unlock crucial features of medieval personhood. It can encompass the person as an essential social being as well as a thoughtful, feeling agent. It can show how different similar lives can be. I return to develop the notion of the social self later in this chapter.

The geographic framework for my examination is England, with a local focus on the small cloth-making cathedral city of Wells. A town of a few fairs a year, regular markets, but a stagnant economy overall in the fifteenth century, it contained two powerful communities: the cathedral church and the Borough Community of citizens and their families.[13] (Beckyngton was as a comet to both of these.) Community can mean many things, but membership in these two communities inevitably indicates some privilege and status. Those outside these two select groups included that half of the population who worked for small wages or begged. They were members of the parochial community but not the political, and they were in no sense powerful or influential in the city, similar though their material milieux and aspirations probably were.

Much of the study relies on a close interpretation of the citizens' social relations after the arrival of plague and before the Reformation (particularly 1375–1520). This small West Country town is plainly no microcosm of the universe, beautiful as both are. But Wells provides a convenient particular social context against which to develop the possibilities for a social self's existence. Moreover, it is important that I can draw on the details of Wells's economic, political, social, and ideological history to construct a plausible account of a much more difficult and revealing set of questions, which focus on how the individual self is developed through interaction with social ideas, social networks, groups of friends, and enemies. The support of the certainties that previous study of Wells has provided is crucial. More important, the proper understanding of individuality, of friendship, and of small groups requires observation in situ; like the better journalist we must go to the place. If any general criticism deserves to be made of the considerable and impressive work of literary scholars on topics of medieval identity, it is that for many, even some who show considerable commitment to social concepts, their work often lacks adequate social anchorage, however well textually, theoretically, and ideologically centered it is. On the other hand, Wells materials are imperfect to be sure, but the success of this study should be measured in part by its stimulus to others who find the methods and conclusions an incitement to modification, revision, and rebuttal in the best tradition of social history.

Still, this is not a book about Wells but about medieval possibility, and to address the need to fill the common mind with ideas and perspectives, we draw considerably on whatever other evidence later medieval England can supply. In moving further afield for motifs, insight, and examples we shall, however, continue to show a preference for the urban source and the vernacular. I hope we can perceive a quite common kind of life—lived often in parallel to Bishop Beckyngton's, only sometimes converging with his—and this goal recommends that we generalize from materials that are akin to our people, urban more than rural, English speakers and thinkers more than Latin. We sin enough in having to favor literacy over talk, but that at least is a sin of the trade rather than of my choice.

Self and Society in Medieval History

The study of medieval urban social history has largely been consumed by the question of community, which has developed considerable nuance under the simultaneous pressure of skeptical inquiry and close attention to detail. For some, that question meant more than the consideration of where *real* community was located and how strongly it might exist, or whether it was a pure tool of class or group interests. It has raised the question of the relationship that held between the group and the individual, society, and its selves. In realizing that communities aren't as smooth and easy as the anthropologists once thought, medieval historians have seen how much they may contain and mask other interests, other forces.[14] Our question now does not start with individualism, but by asking what kind of self can be seen and believed when we drop our tone—if not our sights—and face the social world of an English provincial town and ask about people more generally, including those humbler than Bishop Beckyngton but perhaps not radically different from him. With few exceptions, the approach to such people across Europe has been muted, tentative, sometimes acknowledged as impossible.[15] It is certainly difficult and in examining them, we must put aside such classic questions as the nature of their humanism, the dignity of man, and usually the nature of their personal psyches. Furthermore, this is only partly because, as Montaigne and Natalie Davis suggest, those fighting for a living have little time for such depths.[16]

I would argue that the medieval social self must be understood by taking small groups and individual agency into more focused account. Our historiographical approach must be bottom up in the sense of first bracketing the generalization of class and society and scrutinizing the nature of community, while we get to work on the concrete reality of selves and their interaction in small groups. Not possessing the kind of rich material that inquisitor's records have elsewhere provided, or the detailed personal narratives that might play the same role, has the silver lining of forcing us to see the individual working within the social world in all his or her ordinariness. Eager for details, historians sometimes rely too much on the extraordinary survival.[17] The hope of this book is to find ideas, rhetoric, and methodology to see the self *in* society rather than conceiving a sharp break between individual and society.

On this latter point, medieval social historians would surely agree. Indeed, social historians have had a striking tendency to make the self and even individual agency seem quite irrelevant, giving all our answers to a variety of weakly individualized social forces.[18] This has been easy to do because as mentioned above, we possess relatively few of the kinds of evidence, such as personal letters and diaries, which would *force* us to see a particular modest self in a straightforward way. Furthermore, the Burckhardtian truth intervenes: the possibilities for self-expression in the Middle Ages do seem limited even at the intellectual top; they were certainly different. The self-conscious, voluble, 'self fashioning' that Stephen Greenblatt long ago made famous has a most un-medieval quality to it.[19] The relentless Margery Kempe *can* seem too strange to be a guide to anyone but herself.

Others ask whether the self or agency should matter anyway? Perhaps Pierre Bourdieu was correct when he wrote that, "the history of the individual is never anything other than a certain specification of the collective history of his group or class. . ."[20] This too is a deep, partly true view, worth considering. The question is: *How* certain a 'specification', perhaps he or she is even a unique one? Nevertheless, between the heroism of political atomism, and the swamping of the individual by its universal—the point where Bourdieu and Hegel seem to meet—there is a larger place for understanding how the self develops in social circumstances, than historians have wanted to appreciate. Unsurprisingly for social historians, society and the relation of group to class have mattered more.[21]

Nevertheless, social historians should acknowledge that their unwillingness to address the question of the self is an interpretive prejudice, an implicit *decision* that itself limits the effective reality of actors in history. It is not enough to rely on the view, a kind of methodological individualism, that the implicit assumption is that all actions are by agents rather than groups or society as a whole, if one's written work and imaginary don't show it. At best, this condition blocks our querying the matter more closely and understanding the hidden possibilities of social agency. Moreover, this is the correct decision only if we believe that a better understanding of self and agency are irrelevant or unrecoverable. Social historians have not, however, sufficiently investigated the matter, although other medievalists have never stopped writing persuasively about recognizably active individuals and social history has certainly become more aware of the appeal of the individual if not always of the self.[22] At times like this, a bit of theory is a useful tool to help produce the space for writing about social agency and that is part of what this chapter provides.

It is certainly a timely venture. In the exciting and grand *Cambridge Urban History of Britain's* medieval volume there are twenty-four chapters, none of which engage these questions directly, although several of them reflect the surge of interest in questions of culture and attitude.[23] Yet, a much slighter recent survey has virtually nothing to say of culture, let alone self or agency.[24] Clearly, a case needs to be made for the self and a map sketched so that a distinctly social historical advance on this front becomes possible.

It is all the more timely because there is a distinct interest in individuals among historians these days. Publishers aren't alone in feeling that readers, especially beyond academic specialists, want a full and familiar world, and that requires the individual to play an important role. It must be said, however, that the conceptual place of the individual has remained distinctly subservient to working out or exemplifying the facts of the larger social class or grouping rather than telling us about the ways of the self. Nevertheless, Judith Bennett's recent, effective textbook manages to make the peasant Cecilia Penifader into an individual who made choices, even as she is an example of a type. In this case, social history does embrace social agency as much as it makes social history go down more easily.[25] In a somewhat similar way, Robert Tittler has focused on a world of individuals to display experience of the material and the broader culture after the Reformation, and this too leaves us hungry to think harder about the structure of self and agency lying underneath, characterized by social interaction.[26] By contrast, it is possible to focus on individuals and provide very little detail about what mattered to people as opposed to what they did. Medieval biographies tend in this direction and even when they are massively better, as in Colin Richmond's account of the Pastons or Sir John Hopton, they aren't meant to bend to the audience of social history.[27] Nevertheless, even the conventional method of contextualization of an individual helps to raise the deeper questions of the self and its social life.

There are other hopeful directions within social history. It has always been true that the way that some historians have dealt with their subjects has naturally provided scope for the self and agency, even without thematizing it. P.J.P. Goldberg's work on marriage, for instance, has this quality.[28] Much rural work has circled the question of the individual because it is a natural correlative to the peasant 'community'.[29] But Sherri Olson's study of village life comes close to articulating questions of social agency when she makes her target understanding "the culture of shared interests. . .and the villager's understanding of these interests," all conceived "beneath the institutions of village government."[30] Her conclusions are equally directed to the individual, as she claims that in the post-plague period "individuals made families important" rather than the reverse.[31] Marjorie Keniston McIntosh has not engaged the self, but has clearly put agency back in by focusing at various points in her study of social regulation on the "the discretionary agency of the. . .jurors," rather regular people with their fingers on small but significant levers of power.[32] In a different manner,

Barbara Hanawalt has consistently kept the question of how social life mattered to the people involved very close to the surface of her work, even when addressing the urban milieu. Her work is fundamentally empathetic. For instance, *Growing up in Medieval London* represents a rather bold, even experimental attempt to render the significance of lives constituted through their particular social interactions, imaginatively writing semifictional but historically anchored accounts of crucial moments along a life's way.[33] Most systematic in the urban context is Jenny Kermode's rich study of merchant communities in northern England. By thinking on the basis of individual lives, Kermode turns often to the question of motivations, and can force questions of the meaning of agency rather close to the surface: "As to why men sought public office, one can only conclude it was a desire to be at the center of things and to savor the consequent respect and status. Hierarchical systems of government create oligarchy and stimulate ambition, particularly in fluid times."[34] The study of the social self begins, in effect, by moving further along Kermode's line of inquiry.

The question of the self has flickered intermittently since the 1970s "discovery of the Individual," and its surrounding debates mainly concerned with rather special and prominent 'high' cultural figures such as Abelard and Anselm. For present purposes, however, the end of that line of dispute is perhaps most apposite. Historians have sometimes advanced a place for the self, but it has not been a central theme for a long time. The earlier work that seems most useful starts not with Alan Macfarlane's narrow polemics on English individualism, but when Caroline Bynum modified the strongly individualist claims of the 1970s made by Colin Morris and others.[35] She argued that it was the new emphasis on the *external* self that made the development of the *internal* self possible and pressing.[36] Group and individual claims grew together in the twelfth and thirteenth centuries. The virtue of her critique was to synthesize the two poles and reconcile, logically, what might otherwise seem strict and ruling opposites, but she was the first historian, I think, onto this necessary conjunction.[37] Another historian who has theorized well to see beyond the individual versus community model is Ronald Weissman. He invoked the theoretical usefulness of symbolic interactionism, the social philosophy beginning with George Mead, originator of the term 'social self', as a means of revising renaissance historiography. On Weissman's account too, social relations are the real social players that are constitutive of individual selves and of larger social groupings, to a greater degree than my conception, although Weissman's individual never loses the ability to manipulate his or her situation.[38] Mead's ideas also inspired Richard D. Logan's retrospective examination of the scholarship of the emergent self, leading him to see instead different kinds of selves emerging, especially that of the "autonomous observing viewpoint."[39]

More recently, Nancy Partner has developed a psychoanalytic account that also lays emphasis on the social milieu, a sometimes-dormant feature of Freud's own thought. Furthermore, she has constructed arguments and found examples that suggest that the individual element, the role of the agent, is critical to understanding history, as crucial as the sociocultural context. Naturally, this becomes more obvious when one focuses on particular lives and the choices people make to work the socially given matter into a particular life.[40] To this extent, at least, there are similarities to those postmodern theories, such as in some of Miri Rubin's work, that make a space of variable size for people to negotiate and manipulate the social situation, without requiring it to dominate them.[41] Even the most recent revivalist of the old question of individualism is conceptually alive to the fusion of self and world, using the notion of personality to find more in the medieval period than was heretofore supposed, and to find it earlier, for personality is, "an inalienable quality of any human being living in society."[42] All of these client approaches seek to recover a place for the social agent without denying the power of culture or social relations.

To some extent, such questions force us toward thinking about medieval experience, a word prominent in Tittler's subtitle above. It is an evocative term, somewhat controversial in theoretical quarters but it has the virtue of asserting the relevance of our sympathetic understanding of the past.[43] We must do more, however, than merely to evoke the past; we need to engage past selves in a serious and analytic way.

Meaning, Experience, and Emotion

The reading of meaning into past selves has often been declared problematic for historians. The ability to make an interesting guess at this, however, *is* one of this book's goals. "The idea that imputing passionate and complex inner lives to persons we know through historical sources is an insult to them seems astonishing to me. . ."[44] That the reaction of many historians *is* still to worry about such an imputation is my justification for this section, but historians would not always have been so worried. On one reading, Collingwood thought the pinnacle of the historian's art was to achieve so full an understanding of a situation as to re-create the mind of a past subject.[45] More pertinently perhaps, the ability to read such feelings was to the early days of serious modern history, not only a possibility but also a necessity. This is quite clear in Hume, who was quick and confident in commenting on the states of minds of his subjects: character was crucial, predictable within its limits, and even susceptible of a science of its own.[46] The realities of sensory life and of human nature were fundamental and significantly constant; they provided a baseline of assumptions upon which the historian could calculate the externalities. That other enlightenment man Freud is the same: beneath the multiple melodies of custom and history is the basso continuo of the psychoanalytic self.[47] Whatever the contingencies and customs, reason was able to make sense of human action and observed phenomena. These shared elements of humanity provided us with our access to the minds and feelings of the past, once we were armed with the evidence. The problem today is in knowing where the project of history as construction is, once we become doubtful of the human nature upon which both enlightenment and romantic historians agreed.

We could change our minds, and turn back to nature: "A long time ago I seriously set myself the task of experimentally demonstrating, from an historical standpoint, the non-existence of human nature; twenty-five years later I find myself supporting a diametrically opposed theory. . .At a certain point my research was transformed into a reflection on the limits of historical knowledge. . ."[48] Thus Carlo Ginzburg, hot on the trail of a wild historical image—the witches' Sabbath—was led by the night hunt and the desire for answers to undergo a conversion, and to shift the problem of history from ontology back to epistemology.[49] Regardless of human nature, however, our breaks with the past are rarely inscrutable. Furthermore, our ability to fashion meanings acceptable to a wide variety of our contemporaries is almost as unimpaired as it was for Hume. Because of skepticism or disagreement, we have sometimes exaggerated the difficulty in recovering the mentality of the past.[50] As historians know, the mentality of the past was expressed in social and cultural life, whose relics we study. It was not hidden away in minds long gone, not all of it. Furthermore, we do not have to worry about recovering the fourteenth century unobserved, pristine. This is impossible. Understanding as an act of self is fixed in a particular consciousness and a particular historical moment. Meaning for us, even if about them, is still *our* meaning about them. It is produced, however, in acts of understanding that stretch from our prejudices to embrace the information in their documentary "evidence."

Thus, if medieval social life has often been depicted in a dry and dammed way, it is in part because of a failure of interpretation and imagination. Social history needs to employ cultural and literary techniques to recover medieval ways of thought and practice following methods and insights that some literary and philosophical theories have encouraged. Both the assumptions of philosophical hermeneutics and the practice of reader-response criticism, for instance, point us toward the necessity and the possibility of constructing a context of assumptions held by our historical subjects.[51] These assumptions will themselves become the object of debate and dispute among us, but they should not be shunted to the side as inadmissible forays into private minds or hidden feelings. It is not merely a question of imagination, but of bringing into the play of social history more of the interpretive techniques of cultural and literary history. Fundamentally, we must continue to read different kinds of texts and to make them enlighten each other. Later medieval literature and art can help in positioning us to interpret more fully the possibilities of peoples' dispositions. We will rarely be confident saying what an individual thought, but we should know what the possibilities were. Without question, the advances in this quarter in the last few years have been significant. A signal achievement is *Fifteenth-Century Attitudes,* which provides a considerable array of notions to help historians interpret their people.[52] Scholars are advancing rapidly on these fronts and should soon be able, I hope, to engage each other better on these matters.[53] But let us not leave the self out of our framework.

Indeed, the social self is a crucial category for understanding later medieval life and a useful one for all historical moments. Furthermore, the characteristic shape and significance of the later medieval urban social self forces us to make more of how people comprise groups. Perhaps, it is the group that is the oddity within social history.[54] In order to explain my approach fully and prepare my argument, I want to outline the self and social self somewhat abstractly, but with an eye to the lines of research this book takes. The detailed historical character of the medieval social self will only appear through the subsequent chapters. Through them I hope to show not only the utility of the concept but how the social self of the later Middle Ages, especially in its urban guise, was a supple and flexible thing, dependent on both the personal resources of individuals and their interaction with close family, friends, and enemies. It varied wildly within groups of equals, and yet it was the ruler by which political and social achievement could be measured by others and calculated by the self. Touched constantly by ideas, by memories, by hopes, the social self was the fluid person underneath the heavy structures of 'society' and 'culture'. As such, it was in many ways subordinate to them, but it was inevitably closer to the meaning of both social and private life.

From Self to Social Self

What follows is some philosophy and some theory to orient the reader to my approach and to show why it is advantageous to proceed through the social self. In perhaps the most significant theoretical engagement by a medievalist in medieval social theory—omitting Hayden White, who was not acting as medievalist—Stephen Rigby argued, "The choice confronting us is not whether to be theoretical or not, but whether or not we wish to become aware of the theories which we cannot avoid employing."[55] Others have recently argued as vociferously that nontheoretical historians need to use theory to defend their lines of communication and supply.[56] Rigby's use of the fascinating closure theory provides important ideas for conceiving of social groups such as the citizens of medieval towns, a key 'systact' in his terminology.[57] It may in fact be complementary to the social self. The general notion of the social self needs articulation first, for it may be said to underlie the distinctive groups whose power relations, whose exclusions, Rigby's theories imagine.

Here is how I understand self and social self. To start from a minimal condition, the self seems to be a highly localized site of awareness.[58] People need not have consciousness or understanding; selves do. The self is bound, at least for this worldly life, to a body. An important corollary of this principle is that the self identifies with its body and expresses itself by its body. This was probably more obvious to the pre-Cartesian medieval world than to us. They not only knew that their bodies would rise again, but they believed, in St. Bonaventure's words, that "The rational soul, because it is a soul. . .has an inclination towards the body."[59] Body and soul were more companionable then than now, and we must pay attention to the body's language fully to understand the medieval self.[60]

Hume provided a sharp and useful hint for conceiving the self: in his famous formulation, we are each "a bundle or collection of different perceptions, which succeed each other with an inconceivable rapidity."[61] On his minimalist account these perceptions are, like the perceptions of any thing, separate items that are sewn together by an act of mind. For Hume, this latter action is of less importance than the perceptions themselves: they do not authorize unifying themselves into an identity—an object—unless they are actually observed as unvarying. From a useful start, however, Hume's mistake is to downplay this relational act of the imagination. The current of perceptions and impressions is strong, but the imagining and organizing thing is the self, which interprets their procession in complex and variable ways and was always there. The perceptions are immediately tied—as Kant was to argue in extending and revising Hume—to concepts, to ideas, and dispositions of language in a more modern idiom. The essential aspect of this for our story is the *interpretive* nature of this meeting of self and perceptions, later the person and his or her social world.

The self develops through the dialogic action of living in the world.[62] At every moment, we are reacting to patterns and possibilities that have been established in advance by the world. We only come to know what we are by reflection upon social intercourse and our own attempts at action and reflection. We develop our understanding of words themselves in this ongoing way. We are rarely the simple observer, but are always encased in prejudices and predispositions, which historians can discover.[63] Perceptions are always caught in an inescapable interpretive framework[64] that is dominated by customs and habits. History's weight on us is constant and immense, and it is composed mainly of language and custom. We do not originate these, but we enter them as into a house, well furnished both with goods and routines. This is perhaps the dominant and convergent lesson of Heidegger, Wittgenstein, Giddens, and so many others.[65] This is also the fact of life that should encourage historians to outline social ideas and practices. It should be stressed, however, that the self is not constructed solely by its environment, but also by the interpretive action that means not only suffering the world but also coming to understand it and your place within it. There is room here for a self to innovate and try to transform that place by thought or action.[66] The particular way a self or groups of selves do so is the actual subject of history.

The question of self and society focuses, then, on the nature of the self's agency when each individual emerges slowly into a world already so well appointed. It is not only that you grow inside a particular language such as English. That is the baldest part. It is that you are born into a particular historical situation, into a family with a known social standing, a reputation, and a level of wealth, and its own quirky traditions. There is, furthermore, a host of other relevant social and cultural conditions that vary according to stage of life, geography, and historical vicissitude, but each of which has its own linguistic and symbolic protocols. Thus on Pierre Bourdieu's account, the sense of agency is grander than the reality just because the limitations and dominance bequeathed by milieu, by the *habitus* (custom), are deemed decisive.[67]

Typically, however, in matters of social life, most people mainly run along well-enough-worn paths, and some eras, the medieval perhaps, hold powerful and re-enforced prejudices that discourage claims of invention or innovation, ideological, mechanical, or otherwise. It does at least seem that here Burckhardt was right:[68] the Middle Ages loaded its values less on egocentric self-expression than have later periods. Its interwoven literary and religious culture limited and channeled egotistical expression. One of the great problems that Margery Kempe's contemporaries had with the mystic was that she seemed all too showy and exhibitionist, longing for approval and attention in a suspiciously unsaintly way. She was too much of an original, touched by pride. Strikingly, her supporters, however, countered this by adducing her similarities to St. Bridget and other pious souls who cried and screamed under the guidance of the Holy Spirit.[69] In other words, to be something real and admirable was still *not* to be an original.

"I remember an old scholastic aphorism, which says, 'that the man who lives wholly detached from others, must be either an angel or a devil.' When I see in any of these detached gentlemen of our times the angelic purity, power, and beneficence, I shall admit them to be angels. In the meantime we are born only to be men."[70] The end of contemplating the relation of group and individual is a recognition of their interpenetrating, mutually constituting reality, their necessary conjunction. The terminology is for convenience; the challenge is to demonstrate which options were available in the historical place into which these people were thrown, and from which they could never fully extricate themselves. People opt rather delicately for choices in circumstances only partly of their making and even less a matter of their explicit design. Beckyngton did not invent the model of his death, but he fully appropriated it and showed every sign of investing it with value: it was an act both personal and yet powerfully imbued with tradition. It was not merely a private statement but one understood across his culture.

The world always arrives already interpreted, seen through historically contingent categories, prejudices that are revealing and inevitable.[71] Beckyngton worked with his world, its possibilities, the knowledge and aspirations of masons and painters, the poetry in his head that others had written, but that he liked. We do the same, at least with the traces the fifteenth century has left us. As Beckyngton engaged, cajoled, and interpreted his symbolic inheritance, so do we in writing our history. As Nelson Goodman has argued, new worlds are made out of old.[72]

It is strangely difficult today to give a convincing theoretical account of the self and its agency. Some seem unwilling to credit the significance of agency that people seem to feel and that they include in their self-descriptions, rare though these were in the Middle Ages.[73] The power of the socioeconomic situation has been well established by social historians and theorists from Marx to Giddens. Plainly, however, even according to Bourdieu, the habitus is never enough to let one *know* what an individual would do in a given situation.[74] Rather it sets parameters for agency. Agents cannot build the instrument they are set at, but once set there, some improvise, while others prefer to play only old tunes, and a few make revolutions from their inheritance. In any age, the surprising strength of well-chosen words is the most deceptively powerful form of worldmaking.

The sense of self does not exist in a vacuum. It is built from the narrative of its interaction with the world in a language—not purely verbal but ritual, gestural, and customary—that is given full-blown to the ego by that very world. Limited by environment, but never fixed by it. The open and contingent quality of these predispositions is clear: history changes, and does so greatly by surprising syntheses of newly organized ideas and institutions. Without question, however, the tendency to conformity (inertia) is massive at any time, and especially in an age such as the late medieval which valued conformity *per se*. Obviously, the self fashions its story under seductive constraints.[75] Nevertheless, the self is always, as Charles Taylor has argued, pre-eminently a self-interpreting animal. If culture can dominate and constrain a person, if the subjective identity is a necessary part of understanding how power relations work,[76] it is because the core of the self is an interpreter who can only be controlled by trying to put a blindfold or blinkers on its creative narrative. Although parts of everybody's account of life are plagiarized, this does not prove that his or her stories cannot be significantly original. Some social historians might not think that these narrative or hermeneutical idiosyncrasies add up to much, but if one is as interested in meaning as in causation, then God *is* in the details.

A shift from self to social self is a useful and workable transition for the social historian. The private self, the full self, can be proved in only a few medieval cases. But the self is fundamentally a self in society, in a culture. We do not have to extract selfhood from isolation. Much of the self is already on display in its dialogue with the world. Even in Margery Kempe's case what is at least partly a revelation of a private self serves well to display her social self—what her agency and understanding in the world consisted in. If Hume was on to something when he defined identity as a bundle of perceptions, I think we can similarly approach the social self. It is a bundle of perceptions held about an individual by a social world.[77] There is certainly no *real* and unchanging substance here, a set and simple identity—whatever our opinion about the reality of private self or soul. There is a constant back and forth, a multifaceted, multiparty exchange of perceptions and interpretations of who someone is. Critically, that person, as the one typically most concerned about his standing and identity, is the one most likely to try to manage and fashion his social self in the public domain by advancing and acting in accordance with his private self and his self-interpretation. His companions or compatriots may disagree with him or among themselves about his identity, so the social self is more fragmentary, perhaps more "protean" than the private.[78] For the social self is more likely to be created from the inherited public types than created *de novo* from private narratives or innovative language. It will be very difficult at this level to innovate radically without loss of sanity or status. The embedded nature of the self should, however, make us confident that in tracking the social self we track the individual in the context in which he or she acted and interpreted.

Within this context, however, I stress the historical and the hermeneutical. The weight of social meanings is as critical as the nature and structure of social relations in defining the meaning of the self. The impact of language, habitus, the personal history of the participants, their negotiation of their socially determined roles provides a context for the social actions that form relationships. Furthermore, as I have argued, the self remains in dialogue—an ongoing historical process—with cultural representations, perceptions of its own life story, possibilities, and the meanings offered by friends and social groups. From out of the maze of structured social life and antecedent ideas, unique lives emerge from the common world, but never so individual as to be incomprehensible to the people who live alongside. The uniqueness of life grows from the creativity that is possible whenever you drop a new person into an old ritual, an old ritual into a fraught time, a familiar emblematic color against a revolutionizing background. The self in history is mainly the social self, for it is perhaps all that is left of human nature to say that a person's nature is to fashion herself out of tools she does not own, in the context of a world that she did not initiate, and cannot ignore.

The Method for Capturing the Social Self

To find the specific shape of the social self is first to find a group of categories that existed within a community and a country. The concepts that a social and moral world was made out of need elaboration, as does the typical social dynamic and the relevant structures of association in which people lived. Perhaps oddly, interpreting the social self is only secondarily about the recovery of particular individuals and groupings of individuals, although this is part of the goal. The pursuit of the later medieval social self first requires sensitivity to the prevailing scales of values that were dominant in a town. We need to know *their* conceptual framework, what mattered among their cultural detritus, their inheritance. It means optimally examining people in action as they contend for status by trying to substantiate their self-interpretations in the public domain. If my account of the self were at all correct it would be a serious mistake to restrict ourselves to literary reflections of the self, for this would certainly invest pure concepts and their manipulation under mainly generic constraints and artistic conventions with too much authority. This is why social history *in situ* remains necessary for discerning the popular social self: it has the tools to capture and dissect the significance of anonymous acts, structured acts that reach us silently, like the fragmented frames of films from which the soundtrack has long since disappeared. The social self is not a purely verbal creature.

How shall we corral our bundles of public perceptions in such a way that we can know what they mean? Certainly, we need to examine a public forum and to learn its pronouncements, rituals, and social life. Again, this recommends rooting the project in a particular locale and its records. There is little so well suited as the records of petty dispute, which I exploit in detail. If I am successful, the many records that exist for other places present ample evidence for similar kinds of discussions. Disputes also reflect desires in an unusually concise way. Other than records of purchases, few documents speak so directly of what someone thought was worth having, worth fighting for, or just worth denying to someone else. The Wells court records have another advantage, however, because they are notes of very minor disputes as measured by money or power. There were no lawyers involved, no professionals, and the participation of members of the community was put at a premium. There are disadvantages to be sure, lacunae in the records, but the parameters for self-conception and the defense of self can be made out well, with the mix of evidence at Wells, augmented by published records from across England. Despite the insular quality of some of the evidence, Wells burgesses were part of other communities, not only their "freemen community" but also sometimes a broader "merchant community" to use some of Kermode's categories.[79]

Much of my evidence and analysis in parts two and three comes from the petty court of the citizens of the town. The kinds of issues that will lead us toward our interpretation of the common social self in a later medieval town will be initially somewhat institutional, dependent on the dispute settlement processes of the burgesses' guild. We must fix the extent to which the pressure of the local guild and the weight of general guild ideas of fraternity, obedience, and hierarchy, for instance, provided a further limiting context for the citizen's range of action and self-expression. For citizens to excel, they would have to learn to do so according to the guild's conventions and ideas. Similarly, if, for example, the cathedral officials of Wells had been violently determined by custom or animosity against burying bishops within the church, then Beckyngton's dream-burial might have been forced into an exterior grave-yard, a new chapel, an ugly confrontation with the cathedral's masters, or some other innovation to consummate his hopes. In the lay world of Wells this court represented the burgesses, and reflected their collective interests and authority, which must have channeled and limited some individual interests. A study of the court's methods of dispute settlement will highlight the way the larger group's special interests were brought to bear in the resolutions of small, mainly private matters, a subject to which Marjorie McKintosh among others has recently contributed much.[80]

Restraint could more explicitly give way to channeling and opening up realms of possibilities for the exercise of public and showy power in the town. Without question, it is difficult to evaluate the battle of selves in a community without knowing enough of their precise, personal motivation, of their private selves. We can describe, however, how institutions could be clearing houses for social and political advancement, for the building of oligarchic aspirations, and the exercise of public virtue. A close study of how judicial power was devolved to individuals via the process of arbitration will illuminate these issues. Figuring out how power bore down on some and was shared among others in the community brings out the way that people were differentiated within the local hierarchies. This examination in chapter 4 will show the possibility for ambition and publicly validated pride under the constraints of community. Here one had to be creative within the institutional context.[81]

Within all these court-reflected interactions, the townspeople were always acting in relation to others. This was of course theoretically predictable: what else is social life? The patterns of interactions, however, can themselves be analyzed by recourse to the study of small and informal groups. These social networks illustrate the mesh of social relations and can blaze the path toward individual lives. They reveal the typical placement of different kinds of people within the town's various social cliques, as well as demonstrating the role of these cliques themselves. If ideas and institutions constitute the ongoing cultural forces that limited all burgesses, the specific social networks (clusters of interactions) in which they moved are a little more likely to reveal the particular character of individuals and their associations. Social self and pattern of life begin to come together.[82]

For many the main business of the court was purely the defense of their honor and interests—here things get most personal even as they reveal groupwide assumptions. Examining the use of this public forum as a place to fight for your good name displays this clearly. While almost any case was to some extent about the protection of self and reputation, these were most centrally at issue in cases of slander and petty violence. The different kinds of selves held by different elements of the town emerge when blows and lies were passed out in public and then recounted in court. Such evidence shows the disparity among social selves, and how their social inequality affected their treatment by others. The hierarchies of the household and the town combined to produce different magnitudes of social selves for masters and servants, for husbands and wives. The limited kind of public self available to servants and wives becomes as obvious as the unusually rich and growing social self possessed by prominent heads of households and civic officers.[83]

These court discussions will lay out, I hope, the kind of interactions that burgesses had with each other. They will also gesture at the meaning that such relationships had for the group and for the individuals. Self-expression took other forms that need discussion. The materiality of even a poor culture such as the medieval is arresting and revealing. Later medieval English people tried to express their social standing in their goods and clothing, and they were sharper than we are, at reading social meaning from the cut of the cloth. Before turning to biographical accounts, we shall describe from Wells and other urban material, the trappings of the self that people used as emblems of their identity. This will mean focusing on how their patterns of consumption communicated their standing in the world. Food, entertainment, and other small comforts also became zones for social self-expression. The apparent growth in later medieval English disposable incomes helped to generate a rich rhetoric of consumption that was expressive enough of people's aspirations to be alarming both to moralists and the national political elite.[84]

The strongest case for the individual perspective is best made, however, not from the isolated moment or by simple reference to the possibilities for expression, but in the context of a life. The lure of social biography is usually a fishing lure—one to be resisted. It is my hope, however, that this can be overcome. By chapter 7, we shall have mapped out the structure of social networks, the way that power and identity were constructed and reflected in group activities, the extent of the social self, and the ethical expectations of this social world. Furthermore, select biographies will follow that will rely on the more richly documented individuals whose lives can give us a stronger appreciation of the variety of social selves who lived together in Wells, sharing social space with Bishop Beckyngton.[85]

All told, what follows in this book is an interpretation of social life based on a variety of techniques that derive from many academic traditions. The methods brought to bear are mainly those of social history and social science. The insights and orientation of anthropology and sociology are particularly useful, especially in thinking about groups, reciprocity, and honor in the context of dispute settlement. Social network theory provides a method of assessing the otherwise bewildering evidence of social interactions outside of formal groupings. The skills needed to make the social and personal biographies work are more purely those of integrating the foregoing discussions into a kind of narrative prose that will convince the reader of the worthiness of the entire project. The biographies come at the end. It seems to me that cultural history, prosopographical techniques, sociological and anthropological insights, and the uses of biography itself all make more sense and better arguments if they can be combined, overlaid. Evidence that is partial and merely suggestive on its own can recover a fuller argumentative coherence when the truths born of multiple perspectives and diverse techniques are employed.[86]

This leaves us on the edge of our question, if not of our seats. Before we begin the social history, however, it is first necessary to make an argument for the overwhelming importance of a cluster of concepts by which later medieval English townspeople interpreted their public lives. These intertwining master values of public life were fidelity (trustworthiness), honor (worship), and hierarchy (degree). The first speaks to the virtue of standing by people and things you respect; the second speaks of standing for yourself and fighting for your identity in the press of social life; and the third speaks of the need for the first two—and everything else—to conform to and reflect the related cosmic and social orders. Where a self fits into that hierarchy at any given moment was greatly determined, especially in urban life, by the public assessment of her fidelity and honor. Chapter 2 shows the importance of these notions and their range of meaning; the subsequent chapters try to use them coherently to interpret the self in its social life. It is a task with both methodological and writing challenges, but as with Beckyngton's tomb, so with this book: it is built from layers, method laid upon method, perspective upon perspective, in the hope that in the end there will be sufficient density for the thud of reality to sound.

CHAPTER 2

MASTER VALUES OF TOWN LIFE

In social history, actors without ideas are empty, just as ideas without actors are blind. This chapter tries to construct some of the cultural assumptions of the later medieval town in order to fill up some of its actors and give sight to its ideas. This attempt to examine part of the cultural habitus, to extract the common mind from nonlocal sources, requires only a little justification, for while we can never be sure without examination that 'elite' ideas have a direct and large impact on popular notions, historians have for a long time made important use of such materials. The social self demands it, for this is the concrete acknowledgment that consciousness matters, that people have ideas upon which they draw when making their decisions. This does not mean that there are not considerable difficulties in trying to determine what the sources tell us and how far we repeat the goals of the dominant in repeating their texts. But from Sylvia Thrupp through Rodney Hilton and Philippa Maddern to *Fifteenth-Century Attitudes* and Marjorie McIntosh's *Controlling Misbehavior in England,* medieval historians have helped to display the mind of the matter in ways that allow us to see better what it all meant.[1]

Without question, the gap between philosopher's idea and commoner's action could be especially large. Moreover, the goals of control, of shaping rather than reflecting what people were like and what they were doing, are a typical and treacherous characteristic of fiction and advice literatures, of moralists and philosophers. At the same time, however, such literature grows from a world, and typically reflects the successes, of the powers that have dominated the scene.[2] As such, dominant literature, almost by definition, reflects and strengthens the fundamental terms of discussion, the parameters of thought. Resistance may not be futile, but it will typically be reactionary. In other words, for it or against it, people will fight their battles on the hegemony's ground, its agenda. It is because the hegemony made so much of the theory of kings that one day kings' heads would fall ceremoniously in a torrent of reasons: revolution is reaction.

More pertinent, however, is the problem of selecting the correct venue for our discussion of social selves: which are the sources that are most likely to have connections with our people? First, we should rely on the growing body of English texts rather than the 'high' cultural, Latin source. Naturally, we favor those that have either a proven or plausible popularity, orientation to the urban situation, or whose textual intention or form assumes a popular audience.[3] Works aimed at Christians generally, especially sermons and pastoral manuals, but including a wide variety of nonfiction, will have pride of place. In addition, less didactic works can help, such as letter collections, the records of guilds elsewhere, and whatever of relevance other towns' printed administrative sources provide. There is much help also in such literary productions as the mystery plays and lyric verse, whose audiences were varied. Any kind of source might help and the coordination of a wide variety of sources strengthens our conclusions.

Historians can no longer doubt the deep penetration of literary culture throughout later medieval England, but especially in the towns. Of course, most people read very little even when they could read at all, but they heard much and were intelligent and assiduous listeners. They heard texts and spoke to those who had read them, especially the many dozen clerics who milled about the taverns of Wells and met the citizens in the cathedral nave or the Vicars Close.[4] The middling sort of people who were Wells citizens or burgesses were just the kind to receive the maximum exposure to clerical culture and its productions.[5] Margery Kempe could not read, but she used her access to the priests, friars, and monks of Lynn to build up a formidable and sometimes precise knowledge of a wide range of 'texts' and their ideas, somewhat sidestepping the problem of women's general illiteracy.[6] Marjorie McIntosh has noted the surprisingly close congruence between rather arcane ideas of order in literature and the notions of functionally illiterate jurymen across England.[7] The task in this chapter is assessing how ideas existed for integration into the social fabric of life. I make no evaluation of the significance of the literary sources under discussion except to argue here that the chief naivety historians should eschew is that of thinking that ideas are separate from experience, that ideas are written merely to establish control, rather than written to reflect a view that asserts control through its admiration of order or the like. No one is more bound to the tyranny of a hegemonic idea than the hegemon, be he or she prince, prelate or academic.

Perhaps even more critically, however, while part of most major thinkers' works consists in the kind of rush of logic and invention that is theirs alone, most of what even the Ockhams and Wyclifs wrote and all of what lesser writers produced reflected and drew on the broader world: they work from a common and oddly commonplace pith of insight. Their work frequently grew from perceptions and concerns that were themselves more public than private, more common than the fantasy of genius. Thinkers' social selves affect and limit their unique geniuses too. Much of my cultural evidence exists only because men of serious moral outlook or high moral office looked hard at the world and sought to correct townspeople's abuses. In so doing, they traced, in a tone determined by their cultural medium, the outline of that world, the world we need to understand. Strangely, in that world it was *not* absurd for Margery Kempe to lecture to bishops and doctors of divinity, sometimes while dining with them.[8]

This chapter can only be considered an illustration of its argument rather than a proof, for I display here the 'literary' side of what I see within the social dynamic of smalltown life. It is really less abstracted from that life than it seems. Nevertheless, the argument must be clear and it is that fidelity, honor, and hierarchy are the central social values of town life. Consciously or not, people used them to guide and assess their actions and those of others. They were the values worth worshipping or subverting, sites of control and resistance both. The tougher and related argument is that they are the kind of spine of ideas that urban actors had to have if their recorded actions are to make sense. I don't claim, of course, that any particular person in Wells had these particular ideas at a certain moment, but rather that townspeople lived and operated in a world in which such ideas shaped and defined discourse and practice, that they were in effect part of the furniture of social consciousness. It is something of an axiom of this chapter that there is a partially common if indeterminate culture, shared and comprehensible across the country, but certain features of this culture matter more in some minds and in some social situations. Here we track the secular urban forms. If I do not believe, as some postmodern authors might, that this discourse was separate from action, I do believe that the formation of values that guided actions occurred in part beyond the intentions and knowledge of the people of a provincial town. The discourse of value I want to analyze 'structurated' (Giddens) or 'prejudiced' (Gadamer) people's possible actions and identities.[9] These master values were those that all townspeople as social selves had to work with or work against, and which they probably would have recognized.

That recognition sets them aside from questions of gender, which in many respects would have seemed to fifteenth-century people as too straightforward to need comment and wholly irrelevant to social action, fundamental as it was to social identity. Christine de Pisan was not incomprehensible to her fellows, but her points were not taken in whole.[10] In what follows, gender will flicker often, and I have chosen my examples in ways that bring women and men into the picture together, typically through the family. This is important because in some important sense what follows in this chapter and this book represents the affirmation of the proposition that men and women cannot be taken apart in this period and that women's *social* selves suffered as a consequence. If this social world was a system, it was one in which women counted much less as a group than they did as individual—important but subordinated, even sublimated— parts of a complex social person, headed by the father, patriarchy one supposes. In many respects the unit of social identity varied; it was not necessarily or even typically the atomistic ego of our modern imagination. Having said this, there is no question that we learn more about the public face of masculinity and the social selves of men.[11]

Trustworthy Wights

No concept captures the ambivalence of self in society so well as trust or fidelity. Trust so often grows from doubt, and with worry, as the internal eye educated by precept and experience, by parents and malicious peers, assesses the other person, the prospective object of trust. Sometimes we all must act out a faithfulness about which we remain seriously skeptical. "The mouth seith ane, the hert thinketh another."[12] Caught in social life, we must trust and rely on each other. But in the Middle Ages, and in any age of less government and ineffective policing than we now assume, the burden of assessing the trustworthiness of people was mainly individual. While each person did not create the dominant value, he or she applied it under pressure and learnt its consequences by experience. Reputations were known and made by public discussion; rumors circulated among clique and community but were grounded in the suspicions and experiences of individuals.[13] If a great deal that follows in this book makes much of the exterior person, the clothes it wore and the gestures it carefully articulated and interpreted, it is partly because of this atmosphere of constantly charged evaluation.[14] Yet this critical gaze could never be capricious, for those you doubted might soon become instrumental to your business or your personal ambitions.[15] One needed to be careful not to malign them, or dishonor them lightly or unintentionally. Social memory was strong because so many eyes and ears made it. Even if, as Richard Firth Green has argued, the meaning of truth as fidelity was at this time challenged by the intellectual notion of truth as correspondence to reality, fidelity remained the great moral engine of urban social life.[16] In the medieval world faith and fidelity were never truth's lackeys.

Fidelity was the great relational value. It was the virtue that connected people and provided the basis for evaluating the good of any relationship. It was the conceptual anchor of 'service', which has been called "the dominant ethic of the middle ages."[17] If we have started to discuss it on a negative footing, it is because like all values and ideals it often thrives as a prescriptive concept because of the perceived success of its opposite in daily affairs. Fidelity worked to define the good person, the well-tended relationship, but most often showed up in the negative discriminations of morality. In later medieval urban society commerce was a great venue of practical fidelity and one of the richest in disappointed trust. Crucial and ubiquitous as commercial and religious trusts were, I give the most space to elaborating the emotional source for so much of the language of trust and mistrust, the family. Husband and wife, brother and brother were powerfully operative in literature and reality in constituting the meaning of archetypically good and bad relationships. Although the faith in God was philosophically superior, everyday life and personal experience gave such a primacy to parents, to children, to spouses, and to siblings that the understanding of God was itself often clothed in family relationships.[18]

Medieval people lived a life illuminated by the possibilities and pitfalls of faith. The moralists were eager to make clear to people how the little things they did in life added up to sins against God, but they had little expectation that any but the odd Lollard or contemplative would actually lose faith for long. Trust in God was often expressed under strain, when fear and necessity bred prayer. At such moments people spoke directly to the "Trusty king and trewe in trone [heaven]."[19] As knowledge, religious trust—faith—was partial. According to Aquinas, "Faith is a certain foretaste of that knowledge which will make us happy in the life to come."[20] Beautiful as the whiff was, the knowledge and its certainty were beyond the earthly pale. Extreme situations and fear drove people fully and explicitly to God. Travelers were especially nervous in setting out, so they might pray with the affirmation that, "In Jesus Criste is all my trust."[21] The greatest affirmation of this supreme faith is the well-known story of the sacrifice of Isaac. This was one of the set pieces of medieval culture, known from sermons and a moving part of the mystery plays from which townspeople honed their knowledge and sensibility.[22]

An ambiguous story, the near sacrifice of Isaac by his father brought two powerful claims of trust and loyalty into apparent conflict: the claim of God and the claim of family, especially of a child and son, who was himself a miracle by virtue of his birth to an elderly Sarah, and who says to Abraham, "I luf you mekill, fader dere."[23] But what God seeks and hopes for and perhaps despairs of in people is no different than a burgess's hope and is clearly articulated in the Wakefield "Abraham":

> *Deus:* I will help Adam and his kynde,
> Might I luf and lewte [loyalty] fynde;
> Wold thay to me be trew, and blyn [give up]

> Of thare pride and of thare syn:
> My servand I will found and frast [test],
> Abraham, if he be trast [trustworthy];
> On certan wise I will hym proue,
> If he to me be trew of louf.[24]

While the rest of the play is a highly moving drama about the love existing within the nuclear family (Abraham at one point worrying "What shal I to his moder say? / For 'where is he' tyte [quickly] will she spyr [inquire],")[25] and about the intense zone of fidelity that could exist there, the overwhelming trust was due to God, and offered willingly by Abraham—fathers and children. While Margery Kempe seemed little concerned with her children, the strength of bond to her father endured: "I am of Lynne in Norfolk, a good mannys dowtyr of the same Lynne, which hath ben meyr five tymes of that worshipful burwgh."[26] Moreover, she admired the faithful support of her traumatized husband too.

If it could be a challenge for the greater father God to get his faithful dues, it's no surprise to see how fidelity fared in the public domain and in commercial life.[27] Broken contract can be read simply as an annotation of a court of law, but more productively it should be understood as the violation of a *social* relationship of faith that had been developed with care and worry. Business lived under faith, in effect a brave, accommodating, hopeful and perilous way. In Wells' courts as elsewhere the broken agreement remained one of the acknowledged pleas peeved burgesses could bring against each other. Implicit in every one of these cases is the breach of trust. What the man had committed himself to by word was not undertaken. This opened him up to a number of incendiary remarks, of the type his reputation could not easily take. If he had sworn an oath to support his word, then the charge of perjury, a trespass but also a religious crime, was also available to his opponent.[28] As Craig Muldrew has argued for early modern England, "The moral language of people's credit and honesty, of plain dealing and keeping of promises, dominated the way in which market relations were conceived."[29]

To the traditional moralist, say the clergyman scanning the urban world, the specialized vices of the craftsman or shopkeeper were fixated on acts of deception and faithlessness. It seemed that urban life was made of men particularly prone to untrustworthiness and to lying.[30] The *Book of Vices and Virtues* provided an entire branch of avarice for that of merchandise, and deceit was its core-wood. The sins noted included the intention of selling as high as possible and buying as low, of deceiving buyers as to the quality of goods by keeping the lighting high to enhance what was actually fine but elsewhere low enough to obscure blemishes, and by making the top of the grain pile of finer quality than what was hidden underneath. Townspeople no doubt could have warmed to these charges and to the concern which that same morality text shows for the manipulation of weights, an act clearly undermining a universal trust. However, perhaps most deeply at issue in all these examples was the claim that commerce made a person especially prone "to lye, to swere and to swere false." These sins of statement point up the urban propensity to employ things of supposed certainty with an eye to deceiving that reliability, even to use and abuse the oath to God for what were vain undertakings from a spiritual point of view.[31] Urbanity produced avarice, and avarice cultivated faithlessness and deceit.

Abusing swearing was particularly egregious because it extended the violation of fidelity from the merely human to the divine. The merchants may not have done this with any disrespect. Indeed, except when they were thorough sinners indeed, the wide use of oaths in late medieval England was part of a broad attempt to try to secure trustworthiness in times that made it difficult even for the honest always to deliver on their word. To swear on what was worthy and venerable—the Gospels, relics, the name of God—was to add a guarantor of unimpeachable integrity. We can see how trust bends toward the question of honor. Trust both reflects and helps to create an individual's honor and status in a community.

If the relationship to God was the one deserving of utter trust and therefore truly a paradigm of fidelity, it was at the same time never to be construed as a relationship of equality. What God gives is by grace, the wonderful ultimate for the individual in a Christian dispensation. The loyalty and devotion offered to Him, however, are unable to guarantee grace in and of themselves. That is why when earthly clothes were given to the Godly relation, He was most often the father, and urban fathers benefited from the high uses of their mundane family position. We have already seen that in the mystery tales Isaac was utterly loving and almost willing to die simply on account of his father's willing it. The translation of key relationships into the rhetoric of the family is *nearly* timeless; it was certainly prevalent in the medieval period. In that time at least the function of the translation was partly normative. Expectations and hierarchies were inscribed onto the relationships, characterizing those relationships as necessary and having an especially strong and hierarchical variety of faithfulness. Their naturalness and universality were assumed, and they were very widely employed metaphorical and allegorical forms. Just as with God, one was to honor father and husband, love children, protect wives, stick by brothers. But the possibilities of infidelity lurked behind every affirmation and hope, and these possibilities were very richly explored. Since the centrality of the father-centered family and the fictional brotherhood of the guild of citizens were overwhelming in Wells and elsewhere it will be especially helpful to develop the nature of trust and faithfulness in the context of the social uses of the rhetoric of family.

The Necessary Link: The Rhetoric of Family as Fidelity Displayed

We know nothing more vivid and suggestive about Wells families than this moment—did it last five minutes?—in Curteys family history. The Curteys family was one that survived in Wells' records for several generations, though with no particularly great social or political distinction. In the late 1350s Richard, a brother in a now fatherless family, was struck by a mental illness of an alarming sort, called a frenzy. We can see it as a sort of essential state of violence, albeit of vague scope and unclear intentions. In 1363, after living with his family—brother and mother—for four years, he suffered an awful breakdown. There had been many small moments of threat and violence and fear, the business of living with a psychotic, which ended quietly. This time it was otherwise, as Richard ran amuck in their two-story house. He chased his mother, who must have been deep within medieval middle age, and after a struggle threw her out of the solar, the upstairs room which often overhung the street. His rage at her was obviously deep. Unsatisfied with throwing her into the street, he found a knife, and then ran after her, stabbing her where she lay. After going back inside, he met his brother, Henry, who had presumably shared the burden of caring for his insanity. It seems Henry had heard his mother's cries. A tussle followed in which "Henry would have taken the knife from [Richard's] hand," but in pulling it away, Richard "struck himself in the body," and died.

Plainly, here, we see the end of a long series of violent, petty, if fraught, moments, which for reasons we cannot know, and need not guess at, were converted to serious and lethal violence. Henry was arrested, for the document comes to us as a royal pardon, noting that it was self-defense.[32] Things in Wells as elsewhere could get very serious, very fast, and the line between petty and serious is partly in the eye of the beholder, partly in the human agent's intention, partly in the realm of luck. We can see from this extraordinary case the kind of animosities that took place in the somewhat more private world of the family, with its wells of significant emotion. Aquinas had said that the "particular good of each individual person cannot be attained without domestic prudence, i.e. without the proper administration of the household."[33] We see here some things that the community's sensibility would have curdled at: the murderous attack on a mother violates primary devotion; the violation of brotherhood, the mythic substance of the guild of burgesses. But if the final tragedy is clear enough, it should also be clear that this was possible only because of the domineering importance that motherhood and brotherhood, and missing fatherhood, signified in that culture.

To call someone father signifies, says a moralist, that he is "lord of the hous," "chyveteyn [chieftain] and begynnere and welle," "ordenour and governour and purveyour of his meyne, and namely of his children."[34]

This is spoken of God, but is conveyed in the language of social and family life. The relationship of child to father thus captures an essential and, in the hierarchical outlook of the age, beneficial and appropriate subordination. When the patriarch of the Cely family, Richard the elder, addresses his letters to a son, he writes simply, for instance, "To Jorge Cely at Caleys," and no address in the hundreds of letters in their correspondence expresses less deference. But when George Cely, a mature and accomplished merchant himself, writes in reply, it is "Unto my ryght whorschyppffull ffadyr Richard Cely. . ."[35] Deeply bound to each other as they both were—the father is plainly solicitous whenever danger of disease or rough seas threatens his son—the quality of the loyalty was sharply uneven.[36] As cause, fathers were God-like creators, but they were also, as Adam "our foremost fader" the source of the bitter legacy "to be borne in sekenes, forto lyven yn travalyle, and forto dye yn drede."[37] Grandly good, deeply bad, a father simply was, the great *object* of fidelity.

Yet, for all the importance that the father had in later medieval culture, and that the men of Wells enjoyed as masters of their houses, it was brotherhood that was the more often invoked ideal relationship within public life. No wonder, really, for the society of burgesses was a group of men—families attendant in the background at best—who were nominally legal and social equals, neither serfs, nor lords. The old imperatives of urban life had meant that while social diversity was crucial, the dominant ideologies allowed individuals to rank wherever their current fortunes placed them. There were few official signs of where one stood. Brotherhood in the towns can most fruitfully be discussed in terms of membership in societies such as the burgesses or citizens guilds. But craft associations and connections that are more casual were also subsumed by the ethics of the brothers. Again, the form of the Cely letters bears this out. John Dalton, business associate to George Cely, addressed him as "Intierly beluffyd brother," just as his natural brother Richard Jr. did.[38] It was not just that they were both members of the Calais wool monopoly (the Staple) either, for the gentleman Robert Radclyff (among others) also addressed these merchants as his brothers.[39] It is not far-fetched to see this as drawing on assumptions of closeness and reliability that were part of the cultural connotation of the brother. That is part of what makes for the sense of special tragedy amidst the Curteys family's deaths.

Indeed, what is striking about this most common, imagined relationship is its rich ambivalence. More than the parental terms, brotherhood was often depicted as abused. Without the benefit of clearly structured subordination (i.e., father to son) to provide order and restraint, men who were fictitiously or naturally brothers were found with lamentable frequency to be at each other's throats or at least in powerful and potentially angry connection. And yet, brothers still were such, and might be called back to peace and amity on that very ground. As the mystery plays showed, notwithstanding the theft by deceit of a birthright, Isaac was willing to return and Esau was willing to forgive. However, that play followed the bleaker story of the slaying of Abel in a resentment that could only be familiar and familial.

Such complex representations immediately recover the sense from which we started. Trust set up expectations, hopes, justifications, but it was in the world of legally equal burgesses—as with legally equal aristocrats—as much a pronouncement of a virtuous ideal as an attempt to describe fallen reality. Fraternity was an operative ideal, embedded in institutions and ideas, in the habitus of the medieval town stretching to connect men and women both, but it was placed there because of a defect of the world's current ordering:

> Sometyme the world was so steadfast and stable
> That mannes word was obligacioun;
> And now it is so fals and deceivable
> That word and deed, as in conclusioun,
> Ben nothing lyk, for turned up-so-doun
> Is all this world for mede and wilfulnesse,
> That al is lost for lak of stedfastnesse.[40]

It was in the face of such a lack of trustworthiness that the ritualized language and institution of brotherhood flourished, most especially in the towns where the destabilizing influence of commerce, and the constant agreements implied by it, flourished. The fraternity was a rich zone of constructed intimacy, which created expectations and set constraints on behavior. Medieval towns were quilted all over into collections of guilds and fraternities for ruling elites, entire citizenries, parochial fraternities, joining individuals in devotion and charity, as well as the robust mercantile companies of London, which blended their business fellowships with the institutions that typified guilds everywhere. They all tended to share occasions for common worship, a means of private and amicable dispute settlement, and the chance to eat or drink together in a ritual way.[41] Aliens and strangers were the terms used for those outside the structure of guilds and citizen-corporations that dominated towns. The process of becoming a burgess or guild-brother or sister was to be naturalized, as we still say. It was to become a kind of social intimate, someone with whom one could be seen to eat and drink without embarrassment, shame or fear.[42]

But notional brotherhood also acknowledged the parity in status that allowed for the frank exchange of words and accusations that brothers can manage most powerfully, especially when unrestrained by the figure of their father. Is this paternal strength the difference between the story of Cain and Abel and that of Jacob and Esau? Absent Adam's weakened honor cannot restrain Cain, whereas Isaac, even if old and feeble, limits the violence and recrimination of his sons. They were forced toward subtlety, and cunning thrives under such civilizing restraints. This fatherly role was supplied, as we shall see, by the Borough Community of Wells as a whole and by community associations everywhere. The devotion required by the group was similar to the respect expected of a father, and it could be steely and exacting, literally humiliating. It was pure discipline. A prominent London merchant, a governor of the Mercers company, who had started out defending his actions against the company, "alle hawty and Roaily, full of pride [and] disdeyn[ing] to stond bare hed," found himself about two weeks later "knelyng on his kne" and ritually "knowlege[d] hym selff gyltie." He sought forgiveness.[43] The harsh and domineering fatherhood of the group was brought to bear to negotiate the claims and self-evaluations of the brothers, necessarily, emotionally, but not easily, bound together. The moral bond was fidelity; and the language of family provided it with the awe-inspiring certainty and naturalness of family. One could not speak or act against fidelity and remain as impressive a person as one had been.[44]

Worthy of Worship

Honor is the rich and reciprocating concept that will help us to understand how those who were trustworthy and generally virtuous received their social reward. Honor is, however, a word that opens up the divide in master values between the later medieval town and the modern world. Trust we still value; but honor has gone underground. Its meaning needs some preliminary discussion before we suggest its importance to the social self of the Middle Ages, especially as honor was the lynchpin of that self.

Hobbes is the philosopher who seemed to have most esteemed the concept and his account takes us immediately into the English ways of honor, apparently different from the Mediterranean world on which much useful anthropological theory was based.[45] He wrote in what appears to be honor's English hay-day[46] and shrewdly noticed that honor is the *public recognition* of the power that a person is thought to have. "Honor consisteth in the inward thought, and opinion of the Power, and Goodness of another. . . ." The "external signs" of that esteem were "worship."[47] Moreover, this conceptualization is perfectly medieval, unlocking their language for us, even though Hobbes worked in an otherwise seriously changed and changing England. Both Hobbes and the most prominent modern thinker on honor, Julian Pitt-Rivers, see it as not simply a vague term of praise but as having a "general structure. . .particular to a given culture."[48] This is in part because the world of honor is not a metaphysical or mystic system but one tightly rooted in social life, less theorized on than recognized and demanded, even as a kind of right.[49] For more than Hobbes' definition shows, honor is demanded by virtue of the evaluation a person gives or expects of himself. This is not an independent evaluation, solely simple self-assessment. Rather it is a judgment that works best when it is plausible, rooted in experience and shared by the rest of the relevant social community. For Hobbes was certainly correct to say that "let a man (as most men do), rate themselves [*sic*] as the highest Value they can; yet their true Value is no more than it is esteemed by others."[50]

Whereas fidelity represented the powerful grip of social relations, a guiding ideal for medieval people, honor was a dynamic and two-way pressure system reflecting, with the day-to-day, moment-to-moment shifts of a stock market, the worth of an individual in the common eye of the community. It is less an ideal than an active social criterion. This is why an act or an insult that is given in front of others—the more the worse—was a gesture of greater magnitude than whatever might go on, face to face, alone. As Pierre Bourdieu puts it, acting for one's honor is "defending, cost what it may, a certain public image of oneself."[51] Such are some of the convergent views on this subject, drawn from more recent theorists, although Hobbes was plainly still living in an England where this was the dominant, if not the typical, material for philosophical speculation. His insights are virtually later medieval.

As such, we should note the wise generality of his formulation, which leaves open some of the questions upon which scholars have recently concentrated, such as what exactly characterized honor in the later medieval and early modern scenes. Scholarly discussions have made plain that a wide variety of content filled up honor. Some believe that honor was in transition as older, 'chivalric' or bastard feudal notions gave way to a more moralistic, conscience-centered quality.[52] Others, Cynthia Herrup for instance, see the early modern scene at any rate as characterized not by transition but by "multivocity, even self-contradiction."[53] While others believe that it was more systematic, fundamentally fused to the entire cultural system of gender and language.[54] While the latter view seems correct in its suggestion of the universality of honor and related notions, all scholars seem to agree at least that "honour came in many forms,"[55] of which the most relevant to the urban scene need to be discussed here in their dynamic and general forms, in later chapters in terms of their content.

Perhaps more than other historians, I find it useful to consider English honor as a process, manifest in acts and words, in gestures.

Q: But what things are necessary to genuine honor?
A. . . .good manners and behavior.

Good name and repute *follow* the doing. [56] In the later medieval urban landscape of fluid statuses and structure without rigidity, honor thrived. Here a man could "sore *labour* for worship and renown [my emphasis]."[57] One might act out one's honor, but it existed sycophantically—dependent upon one and yet not one's to command—and could be gauged by the degree to which other people upheld a social self by rendering it *worship*. Honor is not about the entire system of social estimation—the hierarchical ordering—but about people *acting* to acknowledge your status. As Pierre Bourdieu has observed: "The ethos of honour is fundamentally opposed to a universal and formal morality which affirms the equality in dignity of all men and consequently the equality of their rights and duties."[58] It would be as well to say that once we are all nearly equal, there's little room left for honor to be *acted*. Yet it could thrive in a world where the social distinctions were small and legal equality the rule; if it began among the warriors and aristocracy it was effectively translated, albeit full of multivocity, to the urban landscape of legal equals.[59]

Moreover, where there is honor there is the self. There are many ways to illuminate this notion, but I have chosen to work out its conceptualization through an analysis of worshipfulness, the state of being worshipful and inducing the respect of others, which they act out through words and gestures toward you. Again, we can start with God, the most sublime and obvious object of worship. It may seem startling to us today to realize how much there was a continuum of honor that reached from the irrelevant, little-esteemed pauper woman of Wells, through the eccentric Margery and John Kempe, through the local, county, and national elites, through royalty, to God. It was all a matter of due esteem and appropriate comportment. To offer and to sacrifice are the extravagant acts "longyn only to God," to whom people give so much because He is the "yevere of grace and makere of holynesse, sauyour and foryeuere of sin."[60] It is a feature of all honorable commerce that the one who is worth the most is the only one who can give graciously. No counter-gift could compensate such a gift. The unevenness of the transaction sharpens the gap between the honorableness of the two parties. It is this extraordinary worshipfulness that God represents and that gave the story of the Magi special significance for the medieval audience.[61] Kings were in the usual order of things above all others and their gifts to people were used to show *their* importance and not that of the recipient, who was in fact marked as less honorable than the monarch by being a proper object of a gracious gift. Ironically, then, the three kings go to worship the child, to give him offerings to reflect *his* power not theirs.

To ordinary men too, however, there was high worship due, and rightfully so, morally so. It was marked by the bent body, by kneeling, bowing, falling to the ground, raising hands in supplication, all before the worthier person, the same gestures that some urban plays imagined Mary would give the angels.[62] A churchman was eager to remind people that such marks of worship were only allowed to people, "aungel, man and womman," (in most likely order of worth), when they had the touch of sovereignty in them by virtue of their office or position, when, in other words, they revealed the image of God in them, like the stolen blue that the sea shows.[63] Still, it is clear that both men and women could be worshipped. Taken to its most Christian limits, this was always a sovereignty ladled out by God. It meant: honor all people, "meen and wymmen."

Honor is freshest and most real in the act of worship. The need to draw such reverence toward you and to retain that level to which you were accustomed were of the greatest importance and it is worth stressing that this was true of women as much as men, even though the nature of woman's honor was simpler, more awful than that which surrounded a man, but interdependent with his honor. A suitor was a worshipper, however, and his attentions made a girl or woman's value known to her and the world.[64] Indeed, in creating her social value, he announced and confirmed it. But she had achieved it by inducing his interest. As the fictional mother counseled, ". . .be of fair beerynge and of good tunge:/ thorugh thi fair beerynge/thi worschip hath encresynge. . ."[65] It was how you carried yourself—the perfect phrase to capture the fact that you had the possibility to affect your social identity regardless of the hierarchical rank the world had served you. Kings worshipped babies; and boys worshipped girls. There was a known, if limited, power in the objectivized position.

Fundamentally, there was something unnatural and wonderful in being honorable. It was a miracle of social life. The natural state was humility, low-liness, "buxumnes," a graciousness in religion but a horror in day-to-day social life. The cultivation of pride and fortune ended this wasteland and sowed the fertile social self. Social substance—you are a well known "some-body"—brought you worship and developed pride further, the first achievement as delicious as the second was dangerous. "When thi better spekes to the, / Do offe thi cape (cap) & bow thi kne."[66] "Unto thi betere evermore thou bowe."[67] To bow and remove one's hat was honor and men in England acted easily to give honor, marking a certain comfortable civility and a desire not to offend over small matters. An Italian visitor of about 1500 noted that the English would hold their hats in hand for the duration of a conversation, odd and remarkable to Mediterranean eyes.[68] Social success was getting other people to act out your honor.

Take off your hat, bow, and then speak, and in that speaking was honor also marked: "Dere lady" "Goode sir," "Syrs," "Lordynges." People were referred to by their rank, which was often sweetened civilly with a touch of presumptive praise.[69] In letters, the same was true. The later Middle Ages was innovating our accustomed and rigid epistolary forms, but theirs remained highly honor-inflected. To the "especyall goode masters" was added "Ryght worschyppffull syrs" and "reverent masters," and these used for the Celys, mere merchants of London. Brothers were less worshipful with each other and more affectionate. Gentry would write to burgesses politely and pleasantly but again without stooping to suggest worshipfulness. When the King wrote to the city of Coventry, inevitably seeking cash, he referred to them as "trusty and well-beloved," crucial adjectives of society as we have seen, but not terms of worship.[70] Nevertheless, this is just to underline that the small gesture and the formal word, common as they were, were acts of worship calibrated to the speaker and hearer. The social self and its honor were balanced by the receipts of worshipfulness. When courtly lovers spoke or wrote to their ladyloves, it might be "To you, hie worschip & magnificence."[71]

In the sometimes moving poem of spurned love "La Belle Dame sans Merci," the lady of the title chastises her inflamed and persistent lover that "To hym that longeth honneur and noblesse, upon non othir schuld not he awayte."[72] Honor is your own and you must look after it. The person that spends too much time in worship of others, minimizes himself. The great exception was when someone else's honor was also your own: families and clients might profitably work this way.

We shall see that honor was very unevenly distributed, but it is worth stressing that sex fundamentally affected honor. Indeed, given the "multivocity" of honor, this is no surprise; some early modernists have even seen male and female honor on divergent trajectories, and everyone agrees to an honor differential between the genders.[73] Nevertheless, we should see that women were susceptible of the same kind of honor as men, reflected by parallel models of worship such as I have been discussing. Their social worthiness was publicly marked by acts of deference, for instance, but this was possible only assuming the highly gendered core of her honorableness, her sexual chastity. Women's honor had a component of pure state to it, whereas men's was almost wholly mobile.[74] As Laura Gowing puts it, "Women's relationship to standards of sexual behavior was radically different from that of men, not just in the scale of capability, but in the very terms in which it was constructed."[75] Today chastity has paled into a comment on sexual activity alone, but in the later Middle Ages it spoke of containing one's sexuality, indeed one's personality, within the proper social bounds. For a wife, it was to be a sexual woman only with her husband; for a widow or an unmarried woman, it was to be wholly continent. A woman's dangerous predicament was that this status could be a dominant feature of her social self, a kind of vicious trump of manifold virtues. Of course, this can easily be exaggerated, for it was to some extent to the benefit of men to make this seem so, especially in a world where the realities meant that adultery was no basis for divorce. Male fears manifest in morality and comedy are easy to find, *The Canterbury Tales* being the central exhibit.

More pertinently, a woman's risk was not so much a matter of her actions as of her reputation: "And even if the gossip [renommée] is false, it can never be erased."[76] While much could be lost at a stroke, your honor could be won only by assiduous good words and works, a variety of them for a man, one perpetual one for a woman. As they reasoned, "He that in youthe no vertu will yowes,/ In age all honor shall him refuse."[77] Crucially, however, the concern for honor was thought to emerge from a fear for shame, for the rapid collapse of one's social standing. The psychological fact was tightly related to the social reality and the appropriate personal response. A woman subordinated herself so as not to shame herself by desiring too much. "The bigynnynge of thi worchip, is to drede schame."[78] Women's dread was larger for the risks they felt were fundamental and with little enough nuance, for it was "women's sexual misconduct [that] damages the household honour."[79] Such was the world in which their agency operated, tightly intertwined and subordinated to the fortunes of others.

To act shamefully was to produce your own dishonor. "She went away all shamed and confused in herself, seeing his stableness and her own unstableness."[80] Margery Kempe's sense of humiliation in these lines nicely links shame and confusion, and indirectly honor and fidelity. Her dishonor was in offering herself into adultery and the news would probably spread, she knew, hurting herself and her husband and her father too. To conclude here, however, we need only stress how the master values were intertwined and how they propped each other up, almost systematically. Steadfastness affected honor; and as we have glimpsed and shall now see in greater detail, honor helped to order hierarchy, which fidelity and worship welded into a world.[81]

Status and Hierarchy

Social history has never doubted the importance of hierarchy, and the later medieval world was perhaps the most stratified in European history. Hierarchy is no less the cultural than the social skeleton of the later medieval world, even in its somewhat less class-inflected urban form. In a model sermon of the early fifteenth century, it was explained that God arranged marriage in response to Adam's loneliness, but that for it to work "a man schal takon a wyf *lyke* of age, *lyk* of condiciouns, and *lyk* of burth; for thereos these ben acordyng, it is *lyk* to fare wel, and ellys not [my emphases]." In likeness is distinction. To be appropriate, a wife who would be buried deep within a man's social self—*suttee* for the self—should be like the man. If allowed into a marriage, the difference in status, the fundamental gap among people with which the world operated, would corrode and destroy the union. There would be no home. Even people of closely proximate status, say Margery and John Kempe, could feel the strain of the relatively small superiority of her father to her husband.[82] Outside that bond of private subordination lay the structure of social difference in the public world. The hierarchy of husband over wife was reordered by the couple, mainly according to the man's status, but tinted with his wife's standing. Degrees of status were fundamental to the later Middle Ages and they were the grounds of contention, anxiety, and even disruption.[83]

Nothing is better known than that the universal ideal of medieval life was a world well ordered, even radicals tended to see the right world as one in good balance, whatever they thought of the present one. It would be well into the sixteenth century before other models of less harmonious vision would prevail.[84] Each kind of ordered vision shared the understanding that in this world and the next, people were ordered by ranks and kinds, hierarchically conceived. Even when underlying equalities were being asserted— for instance, that death will overcome us all and level us—the importance of differences could be underlined. Everyone, from angels to infidels, had his or her place. The greatest of townsmen, Dante, painted an otherworldly hierarchy of sin and beneficence, in which the true (i.e., eternal) meaning of worldly actions organized people in the afterlife, where truth was manifest. Their worldly social status pales in the afterworld and they are situated geographically and morally according to their sins (or virtues). The lustful stand there; the proud here. Mortally so in hell; penitent in Purgatory.

Dante was more bold than typical, and there was an order of power that ran close to his vision like an old highway shadowing a new, occasionally intersecting. It focused on death's leveling function, on the way that one kind of power and hierarchy would be transmogrified, often horribly, by eternity's judgment. Beckyngton's tomb also spoke to this theme: that those powerful on earth would be laid low, turned to worm castings as much as the rest of us. This older and more popular imaginary form actually strengthened the worldly assumptions of hierarchy.[85] Thus, an interesting antidote to Dante is to look at the *The Dance of Death.* The English version of this poem was probably produced by 1440 and its themes were already well known in iconography.[86] It rung a peal that people immediately took notice of and preferred. The poem was an attempt to rouse Christians, to get their attention, even when they would hide behind their worldly status:

> Oh yee folkes harde herted as a stone
> Which to the world have al our advertence. . .
> Where ys youre witte, where ys youre providence

To see a-forne the sodeyne vyolence
Of cruel dethe?. . .
Dethe spareth not low ne hye degree.[87]

But to awaken people to the crisis of death and the future was to focus on their *degree* and estate itself rather than to deny these. The pope goes first, he who was "sette moste hye yn dygnite/ Of al estatis."[88] The poem's hierarchical vision is foremost, for even if the pope is reduced by death to equality with all Christians and realizes, in his response to Death, that "al honoure. . .is litel worthe," (71–72), it behoves him "this daunce for to lede" (65). Emperor, cardinal, king, and patriarch follow. They are all cast down in their worldly order and are all festooned in the honorable phrases of nobility to which they were accustomed. Death may be ironic, but he remains polite and particular about worldly class. The contrast to Dante is clear. Dante is only deferential to saints, friends, and authors.

The hierarchical assumptions of life are complicated in this later medieval vision by the sheer variety of statuses imagined. The old world of the three orders of clergy, knights, and peasants is gone and apparently forgotten.[89] Instead, two ranked societies—the ecclesiastical and the lay—are interwoven. The one integrated structure has thirty-one ranks—only three of women—in one version and thirty-four in the other manuscript. There is great social subtlety seeded within a fairly rigid conceptual hierarchy, whose concepts were themselves types. That there were so few ways to imagine women shows in itself the limits placed on their social selves' independent potential.[90] The male imagination rarely thought of them and did so in a very limited way when they were not subsumed within their husbands' or fathers' identity and ranked accordingly, although given more practical contexts more nuance could be found, as Cordelia Beattie has argued, and as the later, French all-women's dance of death proves.[91] This patriarchal imagination, however, reflected and strengthened key features of social life.

Dealing explicitly with men, however, there was great variety. Even upon the urban stage there were several distinctions, which lived alongside fraternal notions. The first purely urban figure death found is the mayor, but only one of the two versions has him. The Landsdowne manuscript version places him after the squire, before regular canons and abbots. Somewhat later is the bailiff, a figure of the town as well as the country, followed by the burgess and the cathedral canon, the merchant, the craftsman, the usurer, the man of law, the minstrel, the parson, the laborer, the friar and the child. There is a rough hierarchy displayed and although the two versions differ about which categories to include and where to include them, the principle is certain and sure. Life is so ordered. The Christian vision is well buried in the day-to-day and even the religious agitator did not usually argue for egalitarianism, a barely comprehensible idea for most.

The most characteristic urban types do point up some of the prevalent assumptions about town life. The burgess is characterized by avarice. It is for him "grete displesauns / To leve al this. . . .houses, rentes, tresoure & sub-stauns."[92] The mayor must give up his "power. . .notable in substaunce," and cannot escape by recourse to "richesse or force of officeres."[93] Nor do all the merchant's travels and vainglorious focus on "lucre and wynnyge" help him. His "labour" fails him, just at the craftsman's cleverness cannot get round death. Neither his "subtilite," "coriouste," nor "cunnyng of fressh devise" can help.[94] Only the laborer among possibly urban types has thought about death before, for "in this world here ther is reste noon [for him]."[95] He has no earthly abilities relevant to power, nothing to stake that anyone could imagine being persuasive or seductive.

The elements of urban power identified in the poem turn out, however, to ring true enough within the limits of such stereotyping. They identify degree and power with substance, which is both a matter of money and social prestige. Avarice and vainglory drove the urban successes. We could call them the pursuit of wealth and honor if we seek non-pejorative terms. At any rate, hard work and cunning dealing won these 'goods'. We shall see all these factors at play later, for these were the tools by which a man's—but not a woman's—fundamental position was attained and maintained within the values of town life.

The Dance of Death can be an introduction to the hierarchical assumption of daily social life, the prescribed ideas by which the powerful and power-less tended to think of themselves and of others. The social self was itself made partly by the powerful cultural and social forces that produced these terms. Similarly, the later medieval terminology of social identity was not simple, nor was the difference between craftsman or merchant, merchant or mayor, bailiff or mayor, merchant or gentleman always clear. The differences between overlapping categories and adjacent groups had to be worked out in isolation from systematic discussions. The judgment about who was who in substance, as opposed to the question of what you did for a living, could not always be made as simply as a hegemonic hierarchical system would have liked. Even that system shows plenty of signs of doubt or breakdown as reflected in prescriptive literature.

Medieval hierarchy was undergoing a revolution in the later Middle Ages. Upon the solid continuity of the gender hierarchy that assumed men and women were governed by two different kinds of virtues and then were governed by their other social identifications, there was a sharpening and sometimes unwelcome realization that the upper classes were in flux and that the lower classes were more complex than earlier theories had recognized.[96] Town eyes had started to convey their sight into ideology. To see a party united by the common cause of pilgrimage was, for Chaucer's narrator, to see and to tell of what united them briefly but what divided them in detail, to "tell yow al the condicioun / Of ech of hem so at seemed to me, / And which they weren, and of what degree, / and eek in what array that they were inne."[97] He found many kinds of people between knight and prioress and for the most part, they were known for the jobs that they did. This does not mean that the great estate differences were moot, but that there was a social imagination that could also focus on your occupation and on perceived success within the world you inhabited. When at home in a small town, this was the social vision that mattered.

Part of the reason why Chaucer is so destabilizing is that his characters interact. Since, as Stephen Rigby has argued, within town society itself, "gradation may offer a better image of urban stratification" than anything with sharp borders,[98] it is not surprising that status could be negotiated and that this was often done at a personal level, affected by the way people understood each other. In *The Canterbury Tales'* imaginary, people could defend themselves, explain themselves, and perhaps amend other people's evaluation of their positions. The Wife of Bath and the Pardoner do this. Stories are told to discipline companions and to counter their accounts and who they are. The knight is so silent because he can contribute so little to the unruly and all too common group of estates with whom he finds himself. Savvy to the urban scene, Chaucer shows the country elite as distant to most townspeople. The different estates function rather equally and can spar over marginal superiorities, always within limits. By contrast, *The Dance of Death* gives a simple, dreamy account, actually quite comfortable with the worldly system of honor and encouraging nothing *socially* destabilizing. Burghers will be burghers; bishops will be bishops. Interaction is beyond its schema.[99]

Howard Kaminsky has drawn attention to how tightly individuality and living one's estate were connected. Property, pedigree and pretension required corresponding action and living. To be a knight was to have a claim and to be able to act it out, to perform your status in the world.[100] This was part of the projection of honor that I have already discussed. But Kaminsky's insights—although focused on the noble estate—are easily transportable to the urban milieu and indeed across the society's social imagination. Chapter 6 examines this issue closely, but the point here is that the social self would perform itself publicly, at which moments hierarchy and degree were supposed to be and expected to be manifest. For this reason, Chaucer knew it worthwhile to record what people wore and knew too that it was still all a *seeming,* yet one that people usually took to be an honest sign of real social status. No wonder that Joan of Arc was so bewildering: she acted all wrong and dressed all wrong.

All people needed to act *their* estate and not someone else's. Hoccleve said of Humphrey, Duke of Gloucester: "His lust and desir, Is, as it well sit to his hy degree."[101] God "created never thynge, but that gaf to it such vertue as it ought to have."[102] Living high could be a sign of your essential condition, not just your aesthetic pretensions. Here hierarchy's potential rigidity, the skeleton under the skin of honor, protrudes, explaining the anger and contempt some felt with the nouveaux riches and other aspirants to higher status. A tailor with a side-street shop in Wells *should* act differently, dream differently. This is why we have those peculiar, characteristic, impractical later medieval documents, the sumptuary laws. Three times in the fourteenth and fifteenth centuries Parliament passed laws prescribing clothing according to status. The idea was simple: to restrain people from dressing over their proper station in life. Rich merchants were respectable figures, but for everyone clothes were supposed to show who you were, to exhibit estate, a crucial part of the social self. They were not to show who you wanted to be. The idea of regulating clothing was to protect the value of traditional social hierarchy and the need for the social sign to match the accepted reality.[103]

Rank was heavily inflected with type or estate. Thus, Chaucer's use of the word degree seems ambiguous. However, when he completed his catalogue of companions, which included, among others, minor church officials, guildsmen, and manorial officers, he pronounced that he had told "th'estaat" of each and had fulfilled the literary sociologist's role.[104] There were plenty of estates whose hierarchical position with respect to each other was unclear or underdetermined. Indeed, we might say that Chaucer often acknowledged difference of estate where there was a kind of equality. A scholar is not simply below a nun's priest, nor a pardoner obviously subordinate to a summoner, but each is conceived as significantly distinct in habit and mind because of their social identities. They fight and bicker, use wit, charm, and pique to advance their social selves on the assumption that they are equal in class but seeking to be superior in honor. This is the typical kind of advantage that one burgess may hold over another. Within the stricter and limited hierarchy of nobility and commonality, varieties of subtly presented selves exploded, to which we, like Chaucer and even the Dance of Death, must be attentive. In all kinds of moments, the culture marked social distinction, for whether they were focusing on the large distance between king and laborer, or the fine grades between mayor and merchant they saw, sang, and even dined by degrees.

People watched people by degrees, expecting status to be reflected by position in a painting or a procession. Processions and the diverse views of them unite in suggesting they were an occasion to mark the current, relevant differences among the individuals of the group or the subgroups

within the community. Knowing the man in front of you mattered therefore. When walking with "a wordyer mon," "lette thy Ryght sholdur folow
his bakke." And don't interrupt him when he's speaking.[105] A town such as
Coventry arranged its Corpus Christi processions–ridings—according to
crafts, which would shortly perform the plays. First the fishers and cooks,
then the baxters and milners, and so on.[106] The processions at York were
simply described in 1425 as consisting of "a multitude of priests dressed in
surplices, followed by the mayor and citizens of York, along with a great
crowd of other people following."[107] But elsewhere the fact that sociopolitical
substance, sheer degree, organized people within these groupings was made
clear. Wells' rules stipulated that within the unity of the burgesses mono-
chromatic and orchestrated procession, each burgess was to ride or walk
"after his degree."[108] Honor rendered into hierarchy.

But it was not just a matter of ceremonial occasions. More nerve-wracking
were the social occasions such as dinner parties to which the fourteenth and
fifteenth century were attaching complex manners and expectations. At the
table you could see at glance who was who, who was rising, who falling,
all by their deportment toward each other. How high up in the hall did
you sit? How freely did the wine flow or was the food shared? Not all
were equal guests: "The[e] the next degre loke thou wisely / To do hem
Reverence by an by." You should "suffre hym fyrste to towche the mete,"
even when it was your favorite.[109] However, if in doubt, treat a man as an
equal. In fact, at the grandest of occasions, you were unlikely to get a chance
to taste the best morsel, however good your manners. Rare as they were, the
lavish royal or ducal feast set the hegemonic standard and reflected the
embedded assumptions of hierarchical degree. John Russell, arbiter elegan-
tiae of Humphrey, Duke of Gloucester in the first half of the fifteenth
century, wrote the book on these matters. From an initial remark that the
pope has no peere and presumably dines alone at a table, he works through
respectable society. Each type of person is assigned to a group according to
dignity and their menus were most likely to reflect the assignation. The
good host helped people to live according to their rank and you helped
them to *know* that rank:

    For the baliffes of a Cite purvey ye must a space
    A yeman of the crowne
    Sargaunt of Armes with mace,
    A herrowd of Armes as gret a dygnyte has
    Specially kynge harrawd
    Must have the principalle place;
    Worshipfulle merchaundes and riche artyficeris,
    Gentilmen welle nurtured & of good maneris,

> With gentilwommen
> And namely lordes nurieris,
> Alle these may sit at a table of good squyeris.[110]

Politely as this is written, this was the last table to be mentioned, the lowest table discriminated. Beneath this were people of scant society and little substance. They could be overlooked because they were taken to be too small. What the theoretician might consider briefly, the poor at the bottom of the system,[111] the practical man could overlook.

They were the people famously fed on the leftover trenchers from the feast. But even within the feasting hall the food presented might vary depending on who you were and where you sat. Rather than choose a menu fixe, it chose you. Rank determined how many dishes a guest received and how many people shared a "mess." John Russell noted that earls and bishops could sit at a double helping of two messes, whereas barons, the mayor of London, or chief justices would sit with each other sharing a mess for every two or three men. Others were sat three or four to the mess with the likes of burgesses and squires certainly receiving only a mess for every four diners.[112] The quality of the bread you received would similarly reflect your overall standing: how important were you? How fresh, how white was your bread?[113]

The whiter your bread, the earlier a scribe would set your name in a series of witnesses to a document. From Bishop Beckyngton's archive: "Witnessed by John Godwyn, master of the city of Wells, John Sadler and Richard Vicarye, constables there, John Sholer, John Chew the elder, and many others."[114] What does all this mean? That people of all kinds were practiced in discriminating by degree and occupation. They *saw* in categories and looked for signs to help them interpret ambiguities. A marshal and usher must have had a special calling for this. As Russell noted, before a feast, you needed to "demeene [consider] what estates shalle sitte in the hall, than reson with youre self. . . . Thus shalle ye to any state / do ronge ne preiudice, to sette every persone accordynge. . .as aftur the birthe, livelode, dignite. . . ."[115] It was a form of social perception that everyone shared and that dominated life. In the vision of hierarchy, one's honor found its proper level and meaning.[116]

Conclusion

The importance of concepts of degree and hierarchy to the later Middle Ages are easily beyond doubt. Historians long ago identified this aspect of the period. Similarly, they have more recently thought about honor in a discrete way. The large place I've given to fidelity also shouldn't surprise anyone, given my concern with the social self. The claim, is, however, stronger: these are the key values through which the actions and selves of medieval townspeople become richly comprehensible for us, as for them.

Before going on, however, we do need to emphasize the status of these values and the ways in which they fit together, for surely they were highly inflected with each other and yet were in important ways not quite commensurate. Degree or hierarchy seems to speak of a system, honor of the quality of an individual, and fidelity a virtuous, even emotional, attachment to others. These meanings are accurate enough, albeit simplifications, but my suggestion is that it is useful to see them acting as a kind of ethical system or complex for social action and social understanding. I use the word system with some hesitation because I don't want to suggest that everything is easily explained by these terms, but to stress the interconnected quality they have, even as they operate at different levels. The most salient feature is to recall the argument from chapter 1 that people are socially made in groups, by others' dialogue with self. Given that fact, fidelity has a special preciousness as the model value—covering a variety of model behaviors and words—by which people felt the most personal and compelling bonds between them. It often operates as a family value; it is most often cast in an emotive quasi-familial language. It seems even to be insulated against the judgments based solely on honor or indeed on Christian ethics. The dream of beautiful fidelity is Paolo and Francesca, loyal and loving, to their dishonor and damnation.[117]

Honor is the hope of successful fidelity. It is the estimation of the world: a person's reputation, a man's market value. Because of this, it turns fidelity outward, generalizing it. A happy effect of friends and family will be to spread your name abroad and well, to build honor up from the facts and fruits of fidelity. It seems very close to degree and to hierarchy, but the crucial difference is that hierarchy and degree refer to a systemic appreciation that statuses and social types order the world. Everyone fits in somewhere on a schedule of degrees and honorableness. This schedule, however, is not the product of a flow of information and reputation between self and friends and community. Generally, it is more abstract, a way of thinking about people and society that says three things: everyone is a *kind* of person (formed by sex, lineage, and calling); people can be judged as good or ill according to their kind; and kinds of people can be ranked in terms of social prestige, although it was not necessary to do so at all moments.

The actual content of honor, the appropriately faithful action, is determined in part by the particular culture's sense of society, the degree of stratification, the sharpness of social class. The perpetual doubt around matters of status within a town, especially a modest town such as Wells or King's Lynn, may have given them a particular version of social selves, which were engaged in the upper half of the secular social body in rather close and almost academic rivalries, mixing friendliness and resentment. It is difficult to assert standing confidently where there was no clear status to determine precedence, just fickle money and occasional office.

Nevertheless, while an individual's honor and fidelity might be called into doubt, people generally could *not* call into doubt these concepts themselves, and even less often did it occur to someone to doubt the orders of men and women, even so bewildering a radical as John Ball. "When Adam delved and Eve span, who was then the gentleman?" is a question that makes much better sense to us than it did to almost anyone in the year 1381 but gender distinction remained unquestionable.[118] At the end, it is right to say that the social air described in this chapter has a masculine conceptual face, that the medieval urban social self was determinately male-centered. We should argue at the same time, however, that the model of the male face, a father's face, *required* a subordinate body, whose members were male and female, hierarchically ordered, interdependent, but notionally appendages to the dominant man. To embody these ideas and reveal their full force, we must now proceed to concrete social circumstances, which pressed heavily on individual social selves and joined with ideas to provide the constraints, or tools, which developed social selves, even within the small and relatively homogeneous environment of the English town.

CHAPTER 3

E PLURIBUS UNUM: PEER PRESSURES

And if at any time any differences arose or offenses broke out (as it can not be but sometimes there will, even amongst the best of men) they were ever so met with or nipped in the head betimes, or otherwise so well composed as still love, peace, and communion was continued. Or else the church purged off those that were incorrigible when, after much patience used, no other means would serve, which seldom came to pass.

William Bradford, Of Plimoth Plantation

"You were very right to tell me then," said Isabel. "I don't understand it, but I am very glad to know it."
"I shall always tell you," her aunt answered, "Whenever I see you taking what seems to be too much liberty."
"Pray do—but I don't say I shall always think your remonstrance just."
"Very likely not. You are too fond of liberty."
"Yes, I think I am fond of it. But I always want to know the things one shouldn't do."
"So as to do them?" asked her aunt.
"So as to choose," said Isabel.

Henry James, The Portrait of a Lady

Much more than we can imagine today, medieval people were almost overwhelmed by a social world that rarely left them alone. Every individual faced an idiosyncratic collection of social pressures. Medieval townspeople had no fewer social pressures than peasants in their village communities. For the privileged urban burgesses or citizens—those men who had chosen to enroll in the Borough Community of their town or city, to pay its taxes and have its privileges—their fraternity was an important high-pressure and high profile glass tank. It is a very good one through which to see the mingling of group and individual. But since the game to which people subscribe was, like language, not of their own creation, this chapter tries to show how such groups might press upon their members, bending them all, if breaking only a few.[1] It did so at every step by invoking and strengthening the master values of fidelity, honor, and hierarchical order upon which the justification for social action and social control rested.

The question of social regulation and its growth in medieval England has lately become a central concern of historians. It is difficult given the nature of medieval urban records, to deny the importance of the subject, but as has not always been made clear, some form of ethical social control is virtually co-terminus with the existence of civic records; legislation for the "whole moral environment" is "as old as the civic idea itself."[2] The recent work of Marjorie McIntosh would seem, in fact, to be noting not so much the *origin* of the rise of social control but the *extension* of social control toward often marginal people and a somewhat, only somewhat, different kind of violation.[3] Of course, the possibility that the decline of traditional community may have encouraged a regulatory over a cooperative mentality of control needs even more discussion.[4] Moreover, social regulation need not always take the form of government rules but, as it does so often today, through judicially acknowledged sanctions developed in law cases and the kind of business that courts encourage. In other words, boroughs, from the first, were keen to impose ethics to solve disputes and control misbehavior in commerce, in nuisances (street soiling and the like), but also on matters of honor such as defamation. By 1370 rather extensive modes of regulating behavior were already in place across England.

The evidence of this chapter highlights another aspect of later medieval social and ethical control by displaying how among the relatively advantaged burgesses there was a considerable attempt to keep members well-ordered and under the communal grip. Much of the impetus for the changes that McIntosh describes emerges from the sensibility of group ethical dominance that confraternal associations exerted, including those associations that were part and parcel of urban governance, such as the Borough Community of Wells, the Trinity Guild of Coventry, or the University of Oxford. If this is so, then it is the extension of the *targets* of social control rather than the very idea that was the distinctive feature of fifteenth- and sixteenth-century social domination. Moreover, its impetus may well have been religious, an awakening in advance of Protestantism, but possibly related, to the need to bring the ethical discipline already exerted on elites and friends to the broader communities.

The regulating of communities and fraternities was, therefore, ubiquitous in medieval towns, but the particular local situation gave special features to every group's forms of control. In Wells, upon which we shall concentrate, the Borough Community—the citizens' or burgesses' collective as it were—represented the socially superior and generally richer half of the population of the town. Moreover, it had—from at least the thirteenth century—wanted to attain full lordship, that is, full political and economic control of the city. This was the kind of privilege the king had given to similar borough organizations in his royal cities as early as the twelfth century. It made such burgesses virtual lords of their town, somewhat vulnerable small players even in royal and national affairs as Lorraine Attreed has recently emphasized.[5] For Wells as for many towns, however, such vistas were radically foreshortened.[6] While their Borough Community had some royal sanction because of a rather empty royal charter of 1201, the town was the possession of the Bishop of Bath and Wells, who did not want to give up his prerogative, profits, and what little honor went with them. The later fourteenth-century burgesses knew this; some, still alive, when their continuous records began in the later 1370s, had experienced the upheaval of 1343 when the burgesses had foolishly and futilely tried to free themselves of the bishop. The Borough Community was the organization that conserved the burgesses' civic importance under the color of a sworn and endowed fraternity. By 1370 they ran a court for their own members, had stopped coveting the bishops' property, and had won by his acquiescence numerous other powers and privileges in the town.[7] From certain angles, they looked almost like a free and fully privileged city, but their fraternal ethos, for good and ill, was marked by its origins in suspicion and collusion, in the tight, fraught institution of guilds and fraternity. Perhaps during the time on which we are focused some of these historical reasons were forgotten, and inertia, custom, and private ambition were providing as much of the critical momentum for the Community's activities.

The goal in this chapter is not to give a politics of the medieval town, but rather to demonstrate the nature of one critical venue of group pressure on individuals and their social selves before we advance to take a more egocentric approach to those selves. We need, in other words, to fix the authoritarian and social framework of later medieval social selves. The chapter falls clearly in the realm of Stephen Rigby's questions of 'exclusionary closure' in two related ways. On the one hand, we focus on how men were threatened with social degradation that threatened to lose them membership in a privileged group; but on the other, we shall see in action a broad elite, whose existence as the whole body of the town was a fiction the force of which was first to separate and second to empower its membership even under adverse circumstances.[8] Such processes were ubiquitous in medieval towns, but I focus on the men who were citizens or burgesses of Wells. They came to that position by either purchasing or inheriting the right to join the Community.

The Borough Community was not itself fundamentally unlike the corporations or communities of most other English towns. But the limited jurisdiction of its court, and its development within the institutional and cultural structure of the guild or fraternity then sweeping English urban society, opened a rather different sort of law and equity to the citizens of Wells. The political conviction bequeathed to and shared by the burgesses in the late fourteenth and fifteenth centuries was that their collective worth was bound up with the integrity of this fraternity and the vitality of its court. They shored their political position up by voluntarily joining the guild and then by binding themselves to this slightly subversive, impressively effective institution. By the late fourteenth century, when we can make a detailed analysis of its proceedings and practices, the tensions that had created it were waning, but its sheer usefulness was to guarantee its relative prosperity. As in Margery Kempe's Lynn, civic corporation and socioreligious fraternity had blended nearly perfectly: within their convocations—as the burgesses called their meetings—they chose officers with official status in the town as constables, and churchwardens; they chose their leaders, and their pig-catchers, their members of parliament and their tax-collectors.[9] They administered property; passed ordinances binding on their membership; drank and ate together, and held a court overseen by the master of the guild.[10]

But while the guild certainly reflected and created community identity, it also reveals practices, "officializing strategies," that transformed the personal interest into the collective.[11] The social world is ever a harness, sometimes a chafing one. An institution such as the burgesses' fraternity was a taut combination of honor-raising, peacemaking, and ego-suppressing language and rituals. It promised to make a man more of a citizen if only he would respect *it* as the collective super lord, the benevolent mother—lest it show its other side, the correcting, if loving, father.

Eschatology: The Meaning of the End of Things

While there are many ways to examine the effect of the Burgesses' Court and fraternity upon its members' sense of their own place in the social world, few will reveal so much with due economy of space as an examination of the ways court cases were ended. The cases did not differ much from other local franchise and borough courts, except that only burgesses and their households owed suit there. People accused each other of poor workmanship in the cloth trade, battery and defamation, and withholding money owed. But the final stages of a case were treated with a different emphasis from a court with sure and coercive power, such as the one that the Bishop of Bath and Wells held for his tenants, or that the Mayor of Bristol held in that borough. In sum, the Wells way emphasized the fundamental ambiguities of the social self—creature of the group, governed by the individual. The conclusions to cases gesture at group identity, show a sometimes fraternal tenderness, and other times an anger that is most like that of brothers—pent up, showy, tinged with a sense of betrayal—typically shortlived, but ever lurking. The issues were complicated by social and personal concerns, community needs, as well as the obvious and essential dispute among individuals. The community as a whole was thought to be at stake, as well as that part of the self that was created and sustained in the public view; and this was an immense part of the urban self in medieval England. The group lived off of its members, a kind of super parasite that offered improvement, strength and support, even as it took away a quantity of your individuality. Such feelings and concerns existed everywhere but are more evident in the fraternal court context of a place like the Burgesses' Court.

Any subculture's ability to dominate individuals is limited by that culture's direct coercive capacity. Weak coercive power leads to a more cunning variety of domination. In Wells, the coercive deficiencies of the Burgesses' Court created its subtle and almost friendly forms of control. The Court and community's authority was rooted in its members, not in an overlord armed with the authoritarian techniques of the central government or of his own policing powers, retainers and thugs lurking at his side. The burgesses of Wells were in a difficult position because they needed their local guild court to provide them with at least some collective authority and political stature in their own town. Their royal charter gave them a mere form of recognition, but no power, no distinct jurisdiction. They could not by law make their standing manifest by the display of royally provided swords of authority such as York, Bristol, or Coventry could parade.[12] They could not dispute in their own court against uncomfortable ecclesiastical corporations—the Cathedral, the local hospital, or the Vicars Choral, for example—as these other boroughs did. The situation was delicate and yet the corporate group needed nevertheless to apply social coercion to its membership, to structure and discipline them. But as the troubles of the 1340s were long dead and a *modus vivendi* had been achieved, the burgesses were also eager that their court was effective in dealing with their disputes, not just their collective business. It had to remain a boon for private business, for status, maybe even for friendship. But as a voluntary organization, the economic benefits of which were vague at best and really little more than a matter of working local commercial and social networks, there was neither the coercion of market nor of force to support the regime.[13] To an impressive extent, the court ran because of collective, communitarian feeling, and because sharp, calculating business-people saw its strength in building civic virtue and lubricating business. The authoritarian core of the court was almost a vacuum, but vacuums have, after all, a kind of power.

To keep this within the broader framework of English towns, we should note that everywhere authority was created by traditions, the continuity of ideologies and rites that formed all new members' identities partly in congruence with that of the existent burgesses as a whole. The seriousness of membership and the meaning of initiation into the citizenship are worth pausing to consider because they are the interpretational context for much of every town's disciplinary sanctions against its privileged burgesses. There was almost always, as at Wells, a clearly marked, fairly consistent rite of institution,[14] which brought men (and to a certain extent their families) into the Borough Community. In the Wells case, some new members had an antecedent claim based on paternity, apprenticeship, or marriage into a burgess' family (to his daughter or his widow); others came without such a credence, but either way the transformation from outsider to insider, from commoner to consecrated—to follow Pierre Bourdieu's *bon mot*—was effected with an invitation to the private meetings of the group. The private quality is somewhat more distinctive at Wells, for it was the burgesses' public capacity that was defective. They made the most of the ambiguously private quality of their group: in a convocation meeting, the initiate became the focus of a ceremony, the effect of which was to weld the improved individual— improved by the addition of the mark of citizenship being conferred—to the community. The transformation was fertilized by the mingling of ritual gifts and ritual pleasures. The new member was the focus of attention—an honor and a moment of vulnerability in itself, standing in every one's sight so that his standing in their estimation would rise. He offered the first gift, and it was a decisive one—his word, a sign of his self, solemnly sworn, to obey the rules and practices of the fraternity, its leadership, and never to act against its interests.[15] The group demanded fidelity, and extracted an oath to bind self to that group. After this, he continued to act his faith through symbolic gifts. These were some combination of money, gloves, wax, and wine.[16] Membership's high value was established by the very seriousness of the ritual, by the one-sidedness of the physical gifts and by the fees paid. The fruits of the fraternity were obvious, immediate, and indelible. Once you were raised to the status of burgess you were in principle forever the ritual brother of the group. You were bound by their rules and responsibilities as well as their privileges. The community grew stronger by assigning its honor to its new member, and it is the cultural power created by the integration of individual to group that had much to do with providing this jurisdictionally weak court structure with the essential commitment of its members, who knew the charm of their status as burgesses as well as their inability to walk easily away from its procedures and powers. This may seem to adopt the group's domineering perspective, and it is: for the point of these practices was to make men in a certain form. But this book is about the ways that such a ritual-making is only a part of the story, a part of the pressure, that made social selves. We need not go so far as some who have argued that all ceremony is implicit violence, to see that by such means, the group came to matter and to play the role of arbiter of social virtues and master values for its members.[17]

Liminal Sanctions I: Discipline

Every court's effectiveness and manners was determined in part by its real coercive powers. The burgesses of Wells never received letters from the king, urging them to be vigilant about sedition, to be the keepers of order, such as the mayor and aldermen of York received in 1457.[18] Nor could they respond as the York mayor did, once the royal letter was "heard and understood." He invoked an earlier York statute which threatened any citizens who supported rebellious lords. York mayors were themselves threatened with fines of £20 for failing to enforce the rule. Royal power flowed immediately to properly constituted civic authority. The citizens of York were threatened with the loss of their rights, of their civic membership, for aiding anyone of rebellious spirit.[19] Small cost compared with what the King would exact, we might think, but this still makes clear how the line of coercive power moved *through* the citizens of York and their officers. Their Wells counterparts would have been bypassed here, and would have to work their smaller power, both disciplinary and punitive, more lightly.

The Wells regime and court was effective, however, just because it appreciated the weakness of its position no less than its strengths. It set out to draw lines of discipline around its membership, but needed to be careful in picking its fights with its members. The loss of the Wells franchise was more easily borne than that of York or London, Bristol or Norwich; business might survive. In the matter of routine disputes, for instance, the fraternity required that all burgesses sue in its court, but the Wells Court chose to take on few cases that were supposed to go to a royal court according to the Statute of Gloucester.[20] It was wiser to stay within their modest bounds, knowing that to exceed them would be to attract attention to the Burgesses' Court's anomalous nature. It was a realistic position.

The potential for pent up forces of animosity and frustration was large, and much of the genius of the group was in its appreciation of how to retain its status without exhausting its members' patience. Do this, and you discipline your members, make of them a whole that might be wielded and managed by the group or its elite in times of trouble. Discipline might, however, be the management of your weaknesses. The burgesses required that members use its court, even in cases and conditions where the court's effective power was inadequate. When insurmountable difficulties arose, the burgesses required that their members get a license in order to take a dispute to another court, generally a royal court.[21] Between 1377 and 1429,

114 cases ended with a license allowing the case to pass to another jurisdiction, a small proportion of cases and evidence itself of effective discipline. Of those that can be firmly identified according to type of suit, 75 percent were cases of debt, and about 10 percent each were trespass and disputes over chattel.[22] Plainly the pressure was greatest when it involved money; or, to take a different perspective: what this court solved best and most surely were non-monetary issues, especially those that affected a member's status, integrity, or feelings.[23] The key point here, however, is that even when the court's power was deemed ineffective, the Burgesses' Court itself was able to control the kind of matter involved and to preserve its grip on its members by making them beg for what they might otherwise have simply taken: their day in the King's Courts. The effect was to allow the grip of the group to be preserved by the very transgression of its conventions under the community's own authority. From its graciousness, it allowed its boundaries to be broken. All it required was that the path beyond its boundaries was ritualized and real, that is, according to borough rules, and for borough reasons. Members would pass through a narrow and approved doorway to the outside or risk a breach with the group.

The wisdom of adapting to changing conditions and the facts of a tenuous influence was one of the crucial characteristics that this community exhibited. It was not always easy, and sometimes it required altering the traditional rules of the guild. Indeed, towns across England were in flux in the fifteenth century, civic cohesion under pressure.[24] Moreover, there was a tendency for defendants to test the system, under whichever regime they lived. Providing disciplinary order in lawsuits, especially touching on debt, was ubiquitous. We find a fully enfranchised borough such as Southampton, for instance, issuing an elaborate regulation, specifying that inhabitants of that town might miss three court dates, before being hit with significant and escalating fines.[25] The spring of 1404 was a defining moment for the Wells Guild, since it was then that they addressed directly their traditional rules on the subject of issuing licenses to sue in another court on matters of debt. Until then, an individual had to miss three summonses to the court before a license to sue elsewhere could be granted to the plaintiff. An obviously lively discussion—it consumed three meetings—took place over whether to reduce the number of failed appearances to one, in the case of debt suits. Typical of these records, no details of the points of view expressed were recorded, but we can certainly see that practical considerations would have vied with communal concerns. Some would have spoken for tradition, a key value in their culture that tended to affirm the group; others, for the dangers of the court's seeming like an inhibitor of equity rather than a maker of it; perhaps some even worried about the potential of the court's authority and efficacy weakening in the wake of its failure to take a clear stand and to enforce its own rules. The upshot was nevertheless clear. In cases of debt a single failure to appear would be enough to warrant the granting of the license to prosecute at the common law.[26] Different as the details of their powers were, elites and commons in towns as diverse as Wells and Southampton had to face the problem of disciplining their people to preserve business and local authority.

At Wells, the provision of such a license was never taken lightly. But there was clearly more pressure from the early fifteenth century to find a quicker solution when money was involved. Failure to reply was more common in debt cases both before and after this by-law, but the reform at least allowed the brotherhood to keep a degree of effectiveness in its jurisdiction.[27] The recovery of debt was always the largest category of business the court was asked to deal with, but without a means for allowing plaintiffs to go elsewhere the Burgesses' Court would have become an obstacle both to commerce and dispute settlement. The court and the fraternity would have seemed moribund or worthless if membership made it harder rather than simpler to do business and to uphold one's credit and honor.[28] The conduit to royal authority could be seen as a loss of jurisdiction, but it was actually a retrenchment by which the community was able to sustain its own legitimacy. It was a shrewd step. The collectivity preserved its own symbolic authority, even at the expense of some amount of jurisdiction. It maintained discipline in its ranks.[29] It must be stressed that even here, the fraternity made an important distinction: it did not allow its overlord the Bishop of Bath and Wells' courts to be the court of next recourse. This highlights the fact that the autonomy of the group was to be preserved against him, that individual desires could not be given free rein. Royal power was no threat, but the seigneurial was.

Ultimately, the fraternity remained principled but pragmatic in directing and disciplining its members. This had always been its approach to licenses. Even before this 1404 ruling the Borough Community had mainly issued licenses when cash was at stake because other concerns were less critical to real social survival. Licenses were generally granted whenever the creation of peace was wilfully thwarted. In other words, the Community issued licences to prosecute as a means of extending discipline against the recalcitrant and delinquent men in its midst. This included some cases other than those of refusal to answer a charge. In 1422 Thomas Galwey and Thomas Chynnok were in court arguing over detained chattel, very probably cloths or dyes, considering their involvement in cloth-making and selling. Chynnok answered the charges directly; arbitrators were appointed, but were unable to agree on a remedy. It was the failure of the arbitration to work, very possibly because Chynnok refused after all to abide by it, that led the community to license Galwey.[30] In another case in 1392, the arbitrators simply could not reach a consensus, and both the litigants were given the right to sue elsewhere.[31] Very few arbitration cases broke down, but when they did, the community was prone to throwing the matter beyond its limits.[32] This relieved any pressure on the failure of its court to resolve the dispute.

Other considerations arose. William Belle was licensed in 1379 to pursue John Coterel at the common law for 3s., which the court had determined were owed but which had not yet been paid.[33] Sometimes contempt of the court led to harsher action—ejection from the guild—but frequently the involvement of a royal writ was all that was needed to encourage repayment. The power to go to a royal court was sometimes included in the court's original decision. If the defendant didn't pay on time or pay the correct amount, the plaintiff was allowed to proceed to get a writ without waiting for a new session of the Burgesses' Court.[34] When in 1411 William Trewe wanted to recover for chattels that Thomas Broun held, the court quickly licensed him because Broun was no longer resident in the town. But they limited their license to the pursuit of moveable goods only.[35] There was a fair amount of nuance and judgment employed by the court as it attempted to balance practical concerns with the deeper collective need to have the court remain an effective judicial forum, underpinning the sociopolitical mission of the fraternity. Even moving away, as Thomas Broun had, did not break the bond of subordination to the group. Occasionally, the community was forced to remind the membership as a whole that they were bound to sue first in the Burgesses' Court. On other occasions, individuals were specifically charged with doing otherwise. The aim was hardly rigidity. It was rather the hope of balancing the membership's commitment to the community, the belief in a general system of justice, and their satisfaction with the pursuit of their private legal disputes. Lacking the weapons of arbitrary authority, the Burgesses' Court wisely steered clear of most of the pretensions of grand prerogative, but the effect nevertheless was group power and corporate integrity against the individual member.

Liminal Sanctions II: Punish

The most extreme act available to English Borough Communities and citizens' guilds, however, was serious, and rather stark: expulsion. This was the effective cutting away of member from the body, from ritual, from friends, but not of course from the world. While it involved no set rite of institution—no tearing of epaulettes and breaking of sword—no physical manifestation beyond the denial of future entry to the guildhall, it did reverse the act of admission. If the initiation established a promise, an exchange of cultural and material goods, this removal symbolized the breaking of promise, oath, and friendship. If admission built up a sense of identity in the community, of honor, ejection tore part of that identity away, and the nimble, hardened soul had the option of defining himself against the group that formerly helped to define him, or of seeking reconciliation. A person's ability to do business in Wells was not controlled by the burgesses guild and we can only guess whether there would have been an accompanying blackballing of someone who had been ejected. At any rate, a significant number of those ejected later sought readmission, and ejection was the ultimate punishment in the Wells context. Moreover, it was favored wherever towns had large proportions of enfranchised inhabitants.

Expulsion was always used for manifest dishonoring of the burgesses as a whole. In the previously cited York case, the mayor and council of that city promised to expel from the freedom any citizen who wore the livery of a lord and thereby took on his identity, thus weakening the integrity and identity of the City of York, not to mention endangering public authority.[36] Communities reacted most sharply when an individual resisted a town's mayor or master.[37] The word most often used was *rebellion,* and this brings out nicely the act's proximity to treachery, the ultimate infidelity, from the viewpoint of the fraternity's ideology. Those lawsuits that ended in expulsion were a subset of this genus of rebellion. It was a crime theoretically so contemptible that it required the sort of punishment that sought to reduce the transgressor's honor so that the collective honor could rise with the affirmation of its standards by the removal of the depressing ballast.

The meanings of expulsion and brotherhood can be underlined by considering the place of the second-order citizens of the town, those women who by patrimony or marriage were members of the Borough Community. In Wells, women could not generally become burgesses, as they sometimes did elsewhere.[38] But women who were members of a burgess's household were admitted to the court and also defended their rights there. Widows could actually initiate their own cases, independent of any living man, and thus frequently show up in the court records. They were liable to the sanctions of the court, but they were never expelled with the linguistic ceremony of the male reprobates. Never having been inside the core of the membership, they could not be stripped of much honor. When a woman was removed from the group for failure to comply it happened rather quietly. She just disappeared from the record's gaze. Formal ejection, serious rebellion was available to men just because of their high status.

Not surprisingly, there were many more threats of expulsion than actual purges, although throughout the fifteenth century there continued to be actual expulsions as well. Ejection remained a credible threat.[39] The legitimacy of the fraternity as an orderly, coherent social group, as a community, was partly at issue. For expulsion is inevitably an attempt to remove what contrasts too greatly with the standard, what might in a sense pollute the ideas and air, the loving spirit and the common weal of brotherhood. In the less fraternal rhetoric of York, "anyone who supported any suit or quarrel against the rights and liberties of the said city [should]. . .be ejected from the freedom and all benefits and privileges pertaining to it."[40] To be incorrigible was to be chaotic, for the community required at least formal subordination of the individual member to the group as manifested by its regime and its leadership. In the context of lawsuits, however, the "outrage"[41] was in the attitude toward the court. It is important here to realize that the Wells fraternity was in fact a very moderate, and 'reasonable' society, its very power and prestige sprung from its 'goodness'. It was willing to bend over near backward to encourage reconciliation among members and between the fraternity and individuals. Very often expulsions were of short duration. Nevertheless, those who flouted the regime persistently and in the community's eyes and phrase, *stubbornly,* would be denied. In no circumstances were the honor and worth of the community to suffer. Face would not be lost, for the community was in a worldly sense little more than face—a wise, firm, yet loving face, part mother, part father to its many sons. Opinions were similar, however, even where burgesses had more powers. Coventry would threaten disobedience with "enprisonment."[42]

Most expulsions in Wells connected to lawsuits occurred in one of two ways. In some cases the suit itself brought to light outrageous behavior that the community could not honestly abide; or, in other cases, the solution that the court had imposed in a previous case had not been consummated. The first category generally involved a suit in which the plaintiff charged that the defendant had sued him in another court without the license of the community. To add the requisite sense of pique and scandal—another favorite word of Wells scribes—it was often said that the man had acted "against his burgess' oath": and perjury was to all a moral and religious crime. Thus John Galon was expelled in 1380 for having sued Walter Shorthose in the king's court.[43] The same happened to Thomas Chynnok, in 1437.[44] Higher status seems only to have compounded the offense. A Coventry ordinance stressed the need for all "inhabitauntes of theis Citee [to be] obeydyent to the Meyre for the tyme being." Resistance in that case was concentrated among men who had once held high office. Everyone needed to obey the Mayor and Council, "of what condicion or degree so ever he be of." Rebellious former mayors were singled out for degradation. They were to be kept out of the political "processions, festes and all other assembles," kept from wearing the honorable livery of the town, and were at risk for fines or a prison sentence.[45] At Wells, when John Newmaster, himself a member of the judicial elite of the town, sued John King in the bishop's court and then refused on three occasions to answer the burgesses' summons, he was ejected "by the entire community."[46] Other men similarly suffered this fate. Edward Goodgrom, who had sued John Aunger in the bishop's court "against the custom of the place" and had refused to stay the action, was discommoned and a collective grudge was held against him and his family, a rare show of fraternal loathing on the part of the burgesses. They denied his later application for readmission, and years later his son's.[47] A burgess who chose to sue elsewhere was taking a calculated risk. Often such an action would have accelerated the case and proved his seriousness. After all, it brought his opponent into the court where he wanted him. But those who would not give up the suit or who had sued in the bishop's court received a large helping of opprobrium that could well culminate in ejection, the ultimate civic sanction, and the higher their status the greater the need to punish them to protect the group's integrity.

The other suit-related discommonings occurred when the defendant was unwilling to follow the terms the court had set. It didn't matter at this point whether it was an arbitrated or an adjudicated solution. The integrity of the community had spoken; individuals had spent their time in the collective endeavor; and compliance was expected. This was all the truer because the solutions were very often compromises, especially whenever arbitration had been employed. Threats of ejection certainly outnumbered the acts in this category too, but even they were not standard. The threat was issued only when there had been noncompliance. On April 4, 1451 John Syvier lost a judgment to William Weye after acknowledging a debt, by "spontaneous confession." He was told to pay by September 29 under threat of expulsion. The generous time allotment was probably the reason that the stiffer sanction was conditionally imposed. The next month an additional debt to Weye was similarly given a repayment date for October with a threat of expulsion in the case of failure.[48]

Equally often, actual expulsions from the fraternity occurred when burgesses spurned the court's authority passively, either by failing to answer the summons or by failing to reach or acknowledge a decision. It ejected Thomas Smart in 1388 for failing to reply satisfactorily to James Masson's accusation over a disputed piece of pasture. Smart was expelled, and Masson was licensed to sue elsewhere.[49] Thomas Goldsmith was expelled in 1385 for several "contemptible" failures to answer a summons for a debt against William Hert.[50] It is worth noting that the basic structure of valorized membership and related threat of expulsion for 'insubordination' was a common cultural element of English towns.

Why were some threatened, and some even expelled, while others were simply faced by a license allowing their opponents to sue them elsewhere? Surveying all the expulsions, the prominent place that a bad attitude had cannot be underestimated. Contempt in the court—the opposite of worship—directed at the proceedings or the Master, was a serious aggravation of an already poor situation. Implicit contempt was equally palpable when someone persistently failed to appear to answer a summons. Without question, a consideration of character and reputation, as well as status, must have entered the fraternity's deliberations. An individual's honor, the power of his social self, was recognized and acknowledged when the community acted.

More generally, the recourse to licensing and expulsion as modes of conclusion clearly marks the limits of effective fraternity action. At this point, difficult, all too difficult, cases could be cast out without undue prejudice to the overall efficacy of the court. This meant that the desires and disputes of individual members often extended beyond the grasp or interest of the community as a whole. Practically, the burgesses' far-flung and complex relationships sometimes meant that the Burgesses' Court could not seriously cope with all of them. To have done so would either have cost the court the goodwill of a critical number of its members, who might have left the community, thereby destroying it, or to have cost the community the relatively harmonious and tight-knit ideas and practices that allowed it to retain its authority in the distinctive flavor of a fraternity. This, too, could be seen as a path to the effective destruction of the political force of this guild as a delicate counter-weight to the authority of the lord of Wells. Licensing released these dangers, purged the festering problem and thus strengthened the discipline and cohesion of the membership. The group protected its dominance by determining what was beyond its interests or irrelevant to them. The self-limiting power of groups is too often overlooked, but was crucial here, cutting out individuals to save itself. Again, this is an adaptation of typical urban power to local conditions. Expulsion at York or Bristol had clearer economic consequences. Thus, expulsion at a place such as Wells had clearer social and moral significance.

The harsher and considerably rarer result of the expulsion from the brotherhood was employed when the principle of the fraternity itself was thought to conflict with the rebellious character of an individual. When the regime or the symbolic head of the regime—the Master—was consistently scorned, it was obviously necessary to remove the cause, the oath-breaker, who was revealed to be no brother of theirs. The persistent attack on the master's status was a derogation of the Borough Community's honor in favor of the honor (read pride) of the rebel. Here, too, subtle considerations were employed, many of which we can only see dimly. I have already mentioned that the overall character of the individual had to be assessed. But furthermore, it was important to know that it was an isolated person, not part of a group of any prestige in the community. In cases of judicial expulsion, it never seems to have been so. Unlike some of the threats of discommoning launched at those who refused to be rent collectors or were involved in political spats with the master, there is never a sign of clique or faction. The discommoned men were rogues for the moment. For the moment, because about half of those who were expelled were eventually reconciled after "humble submission," capitulating to the group.[51]

The meaning of ejection was one of degradation in the strictest sense. If the power of the medieval guild was in great part derived from its playing the roles of family and community for urban populations, the symbolic meaning of ejection can become more vivid, almost melodramatic. It is worth noting, however, that such a cutting off, cutting away of what was wayward, malicious, prodigal, captured the quality of cultural debasement at least wished on a member by his former family. Not as severe as the practice of expelling some, say prostitutes, entirely from a town, this is on the same continuum, properly adjusted for superior status.[52] The social world of the medieval town was fundamentally divided into two groups: the citizens, all of whom were members of the civic fraternity (*communitas burgi*), and then the foreigners (*forinseci*). This terminology is pregnant. Alien was used in the later Middle Ages to indicate people from other countries, and they could be *naturalized* by joining the citizenry.[53] Yet regardless of where you were born, anyone without membership in the civic guild was a foreigner—an ultimate outsider. In English the word they would have used was stranger, and only due humility could redeem the prodigal son and brother and restore him from strangeness and strange behavior to family familiarity. For most men the threat was enough. For others expulsion was necessary discipline. For a few it was a means of removing what the community mentality took to be an egomaniacal perjurer whose presence was thought to undermine the stability and the decorous continuity of their institution, a man who had already cast himself beyond the civil confines of their civic family. *His* story would be different, but the community's institutions were designed to give both him and the community an experience and an ideology to counter and restrict his private estimation of his worth, his self righteousness. The group's story was familiar and thereby often constraining on its members. For an individual man to preserve his robust and respectable social self against the group was to keep his account plausible in their ears, but when a man failed to convince them he and his story became socially mad. Civic madness and practical estrangement were the result of going it alone against the group. Ethics without the stamp of an authority or community is ever a lonely road, and for most businessmen in a small town, a foolish one. In London, as in Wells, most often they would climb down, kneeling on the ground, and owning themselves guilty, even a greater man seen humbled.[54] At its harshest, the group could be brutal on someone's social self, which sorely felt its limitations at such moments.

Reciprocity as Soft Power

The cunning power of the weakly coercive community emerges even more clearly when we recognize how well its less drastic peace techniques sustained it. The group entrained the individual by its good works and the individual's participation strengthened the group. The community's other favored dispute settlement procedures, including arbitration, are united by their reciprocal element.[55] Some cases certainly were determined in a straightforward and one-sided way, but the majority in which solutions were specified display more nuanced procedures and outcomes. There was commonly one or another form of exchange involved. Most common were debt cases that gave judgment (and therefore money) to the plaintiff but gave time to the defendant. Of course, in the reality of any court, a bankrupt defendant would often have to be given time to pay, but there were immediate sanctions available and often used in other courts, most commonly the right to seize property and chattel to the value of the judgment. The clarity, decisiveness, and one-sidedness of most judgments was a fact of the law courts. A case from contemporary (1416) York's town court illustrates how a jury's return was decisive and clear: "The court decided that the plaintiff should gain nothing for his accusation, and [he] was placed in mercy for this unjust suit."[56] The city of York was rich in privileges and its burgesses ran their court as a king's court, providing sharp and sure justice as a result, often very unlike the court of the burgesses of Wells, whose gift of time could of course be critical in saving businessmen from disaster. This is all a matter of degree, of course, for arbitration was well known in all English urban contexts, in York too. It also helps to explain why the abuse of failing to answer debt cases needed correction. Too much time could quench commerce.

The amount of time given depended of course on the details of the case: the trustworthiness of the parties, the attitude and need of the creditor, the difficulties of the debtor. Many of these things would have been well known without discussion in a relatively small town such as Wells. Adam Ferrour was required to pay John Pestel a debt of 22s. in late January 1378, but he was given three weeks to do it.[57] A small debt of 14d. was immediately acknowledged by Edward Forbour in 1386 but even for this small sum he was allowed by the court and the debtee Richard Whitfot to forgo payment until the St. Andrew's fair two weeks away.[58] Other cases suggest rather more difficult situations for the defendants. The end of the arbitrated dispute between Richard Barbour and John Ferrers was that the 5s. the plaintiff originally sought were indeed to be paid, but not until the Feast of the Annunciation, three months later.[59] The effect of the arbitration was plainly to buy time so that the defendant could pay and survive, acceptable so long as the plaintiff also could cope while he waited for payment. The case of Edward Forbour gives an example of the instalment arrangement, which was also much used by the court as a technique of giving more rapid satisfaction to the plaintiff while accommodating the difficulties of the often indebted Forbour. On May 23, 1392 after Forbour admitted that he owed 6s. to Thomas Smart the court allowed payment to be made in three equal parts, payable on June 24, September 29, and finally at Christmas (three of the traditional quarter days).[60] There were scores of such cases of weak reciprocity. Even from the typical examples I have cited it is clear that the attitude of the debtor probably had much to do with the court's leniency about the granting of time. Very often, it was those who faithfully acknowledged their debts who received time in exchange. In the greatly competitive business of medieval justice, gentleness may have had some appeal and the court's owner—the community—could benefit in noneconomic ways.

Reciprocity could be considerably more tangible than these rather metaphysical swaps of time and value. And it is these strongly reciprocal settlements that particularly make the fraternal effect plain, and indeed, which help to make more convincing the meaning of time-techniques such as I have been describing. These results were somewhat more likely to arise from disputes that went to arbitration. For example, in late 1398 William Greynton sued Richard Peres for a guarantee he had given to a third party for 40d. The arbitrators required Peres to pay 24d. in money to Greynton, which constituted in effect a remission of the damages sought; but they also required "that they should kiss," and the scribe went on to report "that they did kiss."[61] Little persuasion is needed to see the reciprocal solution here.[62] Its effect is all the more striking. For the solutions determined by the court to be as palatable as possible, as useful for the common weal of the fraternity as for the wronged individual, it was imperative and effective to entangle one man's life with another's—plaintiff and defendant—and to place both men in the debt of the fraternity. The whole of the settlement between John Sprot and William de Boys in a 1380 trespass case over the sale of some pears was the exchange of wine. The defendant was ordered to pay a pottle (two quarts) to the plaintiff and to receive in turn a quart.[63] This sort of solution is vivid enough; it was not a large matter; it was probably not a clear matter, but the arbitrators understood that there was blame on each side, and there was a relationship that needed public and pleasant reanimation. Equity was established, men were subordinated to the group, while gifts forced the men into a positive relationship in which the seductions of wine would wash out the aftertaste of a load of bad pears.[64]

Reciprocal sanctions were often used to display guilt to the community, but as often they were used to compensate the fraternity itself for the disturbance of the harmonious hierarchy it cherished. They included, in other words, huge doses of discipline. Thus when the arbitrators considered the animosity and disruption that John Vykerys and John Heynes generated through sheer anger and insults, they decreed that if they offended one or the other again they were to pay the hefty sum of one mark (13s. 4d.) to the fabric fund of the town church over which the fraternity presided.[65] There were many cases of fines threatened contingent on future behavior. Often there was a reciprocal feature here too, very much in line with the tenor of fraternity. It served justice by making guilt manifest and public, a painful enough step that affected reputation—a chief good in medieval urban values. But it also carried within it the embedded consideration of charity, *caritas,* love. The court asserted that there was something seriously wrong with a brother's behavior, but, for charity's sake, he would not at that time be punished to the full extent of his error. The community often showed "grace," giving to people what they didn't deserve, but that helped to make them willing to accept its jurisdiction and the tangible judgments the court did produce.[66] Honor and emotion bind us to those to whom we owe something, even if we feel we had no choice in the matter. Thus these brothers were bound to the parental Borough Community, which structured their actions and identities according to its ends.

Similarly, when John Crote was told that if he ever again damaged anyone's ditches or hedges he would have to pay the church fabric fund 20s. the community was publicly humiliating and warning him, but when Edward Godtyd, the complainant, left the court, he may not have felt satisfied. He was not awarded any damages, suggesting doubts about his story or his own culpability.[67] In a sense even these one-sided warnings involved a reciprocating judgment by which both men could be taken down a peg by the collectivity. Furthermore, the fraternity itself suggested the sinful nature of the activity in its consistent preference for giving its fines (or at least the threats thereof) to the church, to whom sins could more appropriately be compensated.[68] Such homages added to its strength and every act witnessed or participated in built up the traditions acknowledging the group's wisdom and worthiness. Unlike a secular court, the property and profit of a lord, the Burgesses' Court was ostentatiously unconcerned with judicial revenue. It was a matter of peace, concord, and collective ethics, good things all, but social controls nevertheless.[69]

To Stocks or Stool

There would be something lacking if I did not go beyond the burgesses' records to mention harsher features of social discipline in the medieval town. Both the softness and subtlety of the Borough Community of Wells and the harsh panorama in which it worked would be underestimated. The people of Wells may have had to face some stark and manipulative choices within the court of the burgesses, but within the scene of contemporary English punitive measures the methods used were in fact quite gentle. Since "rituals of exclusion were maximally public and personally humiliating" for the most abhorred townspeople, it is important to show how protective privilege could be.[70] The point here is not that Wells burgesses were nicer, but rather that their privileged social selves can be marked as even more advantaged by the honorable quality of their humiliation. The community's protected were privileged. In the first place the sanctions of the fraternity were private. This is not to say that they were secretive about the results of their deliberations or the penalties imposed. There's no evidence for this. Moreover, since the community in an important sense absorbed the more significant people of the town, it's safe to say that anyone who was anyone knew of the checks administered to the upstarts or the recalcitrant. But they did not let the unprivileged get at you, touch you, or laugh. The point really is that in the continuum of practices that urban people typically faced from authority, the burgesses' measures were quite uplifting and sustaining of the membership. Constructing your own private pool was an insulator for your reputation, a partial protection of your social distinction and as such a defense from other common forms of urban degradation.

These could be public and harsh. Scolds and slanderers of Coventry— plainly women in all cases—were sent to the cuckstool, bound sitting in public view for verbal and other attacks.[71] London found diverse uses for the stool, which really meant dung-stool.[72] For men, there was a different device which is more familiar to us as the New England town stocks (*collistrigium*). It was applied in London for all manner of market infractions, which can all be taken as crimes against the community itself, such as the selling of bad fish and meat. The use of such measures was also increasing by the end of the fifteenth century.[73]

Your suffering here was about you and provided a means of damaging, possibly permanently, your standing in the community. Did a slide to the cuckstool or the stocks lead to reform for some while becoming a way of life for others? Whatever the case, it made it clear what the community sanctioned and how it would mete out respectability accordingly. To each offender was attached some sign underlining his or her crime so all would know. It was not simply rebellion, and so apparently not a direct and over-simplified matter of authority as with the Wells burgesses or other guilds. The sign would proclaim the offence in words or in the rotting fish the culprit had tried to sell tied conspicuously around his neck.

This secular display of error found its counterpart in religious life, where the corporate authority can once again be seen as providing a check to egotism and the rampant self. Public penance must have been a common sight, but it was also a serious sanction. Church courts tended to reserve these public events for serious errors, and they were often part of a more serious charge. The Duchess of Gloucester, Eleanor Cobham, was sentenced not only to permanent house arrest for her participation in antiroyal magic, but was sentenced to march with "a meek and demure countenance" from the Temple Bar to St. Paul's and Christ Church on a different day. She would bear a heavy candle as sign, I suppose, of her reconciliation gift to the church and God.[74] Her nobility saved her another typical feature, which Katherine Love of Wells suffered as a convicted sorceress. *Her* march through the town, from the church that represented the community, was in her underwear. Considering the defining nature of clothes as representing your status, this detail was crucial to emphasizing her debasement before God and community and her degradation. She was then exiled from the city. In 1469 Thomas Wortley paid his penance for shedding blood in Grantham churchyard by administering holy water in his bare feet and legs, and later by marching with candle and beads clad in shirt and breeches. He was then humiliated more publicly, having to perform further penance in Grantham market square.[75]

These techniques worked on self and soul, even as they worked through the body. As Maureen Flynn argues, "lay penitents. . .had difficulty conceiving of an act of sorrow that was entirely unrelated to the life of the body."[76] Similarly, those who punished knew the need to act through the body, and not through words of warning alone. A token of abjectness in the community, the punished felt their humiliation as deeply as was possible and before as many people as their social or religious sin demanded. Even to kneel hurt the self; to die one way rather than another ruined the nobleman more than to be caught. To be ground down through the body could only be made worse by making it so public that every peasant, every beggar or resentful journeyman could spit and yell at the criminal, a well-marked thing of a man, become briefly a self synonymous with a sin.

The hardest question to answer is whether the bitterness and debasement a punished person felt, the constraints of a social self withering around the kernel of his own self-assessment, was merely the epiphenomenon of the public and communal meaning. For the group this man was less a self than an object lesson, a sign for others. Urban realities could be so harsh on the social self that finding ways to insulate yourself from such humiliation were paramount. Status insulated, and part of what the Borough Community and similar groups offered its members in exchange for subordination was protection from society's rowdier elements by returning some of its collective prestige to the individual. Exclusionary closure was not only a tool of domination; it was a tool of defense against a very harsh world.

Court and Community: Concluding Considerations

This chapter has explored the production of a pattern of social pathos in later medieval people that served for the most part the prevailing power of the community, which invoked values to safeguard its own power. It can be seen in part as a kind of social defense mechanism employed to keep the group dominant in its relations with individuals. Every little society will have some similar basis for pressuring and inculcating its members with its power and values. What matters for a particular social self is the local form of such browbeating. The local variation achieved in the Wells borough court was milder than that which prevailed elsewhere, even elsewhere in Wells. But it was similar to the experience of discipline other English town citizens, burgesses, and inhabitants would have faced, especially where the ethos of the fraternal had some sway. Everywhere the group was itself patron and supporter of its members. As such, it honored them even in the measured tones of its punishments and sanctions. The fraternal factor was important: they operated for love, for charity, for cohesion, and that meant for the sake of the person they sanctioned, chastising the person with the love appropriate to a parent. Prodigal children were plentiful, and most did come home.

The special flavor of the fraternity court of Wells endowed dispute settlement with a leavening of social balance and pragmatic moderation. The ambiguous tensions and pressures that socializing created in the community could be drawn on to lead the burgesses toward frequently gentle, frequently reciprocal solutions. If fraternity itself could be a great builder and maintainer of a true sense of community, then the wedding of fraternity and court provided the sort of support, flying buttresses to put it in a Gothic idiom, that allowed the community at Wells to mount even higher than the typical fraternity or locality. There was a cost, but it was to the overweening individual, the person who stepped across the lines of proper fidelity to the group. Most people's lives took the shape and value that the group carefully cultivated. This was without question a kind of social domination, but it was unlike other places, other local courts, and certainly later times in towns and countryside because misbehavior was more often managed than controlled.[77]

Community is an analytic continuum. It helped to provide context in which action and ideas occurred, in which a life was understood. But it is not the opposite of identity or individuality. The business of arbitration and the licenses and expulsions, the kisses of peace and the swaps of wine, were just those techniques of community and fraternity that allowed the relations of individuals with different compositions of identity and commitment to act and think *in a sort* of concert within the Wells Borough Community. In this sense, community allows us to speak not of the powerful unanimity of feeling of medieval people, but of a relative solidarity produced through master values and practices, which were pressed onto the individuals, but were not necessarily against their overall interests or contrary to their conscious desires. This is the savvy and cunning of power: to implicate the patient of its actions, and to make him or her a participant in its ways. Trouble only broke out when the gap between the personal sense of social self or the perception of justice could not be reconciled with the community's notions of right and order.[78] If it is the case that social regulation was rising during this period, it is partly because of the success of a certain kind of community leadership, centered in urban corporations and guilds, whose control of their members provided a springboard for greater kinds of control. It is almost as if the notional village community of the whole was replaced by a somewhat more executive community of the upper half.[79]

Since I go on to show the way in which the individual shaped and negotiated his or her sense of self and the public assessment thereof, it is important to bear in mind that the group had its interests and had ways to impose its sense of decorum and ethics on all individuals. It is part of the charm of well-adjusted social life, however, that it could do so while simultaneously serving the ambitious social selves of its members, and indeed protecting them from the destabilizing disasters of their own anger and willfulness. Institutions sensitive to the social selves of the burgesses allowed for the orderly recognition of both the established reputation of people and their own attempts to alter their status or reinforce their reputation within the community. As we shall now see, far from the sometimes arbitrary power of lordship and the Crown, we can see agency in a riot of perpetual play and riposte, one man against the other, in the eyes of their knowing neighbors, under cover of the disciplining group.

CHAPTER 4

THE MARRIAGE OF SELF AND STRUCTURE

The three shepherds of the Wakefield "First Shepherds Play" are common men with common troubles. They are equals—like the small town and urban people we're studying and who would have watched such plays—and that meant that their relative worth to each other shifted only gradually, but perhaps constantly. By contrast, the clear worthiness of Christ was simple for them, although they could see his surpassing quality in two ways, according to two schedules of honor, the worldly and the eternal. As they enter the stable and behold Him, the First Shepherd exclaims: "Hayll, King I thee call! Hayll, most of myght! Hayll, the worthyst of all. Hayll, duke! Hayll, knyght! Of greatt and small Thou art lorde by right. . ."[1] He speaks in the language of high class and power, of feudal rights, familiar things, precisely the things that shepherds did not have, but felt the butt end of. The Second Shepherd follows, however, with the great Christian irony: that Christ is but a baby and a humble one at that: "Hayll, little tyn' mop, rewarder of mede! Hail, bot oone drop of grace at my nede; Hayll, lytytll mylk sop! Hayll, david sede! Of oure crede thou art crop; hayll, in god hede."[2] Odd as this might be to the canons of power, it is undoubtedly so, and known by all. How challenging a master view this is for social life how-ever. These shepherds must assess the child's status and that means their own relative status. They are given a great advantage: the angels have already explained the situation, but furthermore, Christ is outside their normal domain, from another social circle entirely. From either the spiritual or political perspective He is worthiest and of another kind. Here is class difference of the first magnitude.

When, however, we put aside magnitudes of class and forget about the paradigms of feudalism, the scene suggests the dynamic of judgment by which who a person was socially was calculated and asserted by the people around. The play had begun in a more sombre way. The First Shepherd had lost his sheep and his worldly position looked grim, tormented by the specters of poverty and begging, of acting in a way that would invite people to see him as debased, as falling, a fear of many in his audience. "For after oure play com sorrows unryde."[3] To a king he would always be a peasant, but to another peasant there were grades upon grades through which to descend. "As hevy as a sod I grete with myn eene. . .Now beg I and borow."[4] This is the necessary recourse of those whose stature erodes: to need the help of others and to be able only to offer future payment in recompense—the first public sign of failure. The judgments made within one's class or group are the most crucial and gossip carries them quickly.

This brings us to the issue of this chapter, which seeks to address the question: Where did one fit *within* one's social group and what were the means by which such status was conferred, regulated and transformed? There are a variety of perspectives from which to view this question, but *social standing* is one of the most useful. It is general enough to cover such concerns as political power, wealth, and prestige, indeed for whatever makes for *social substance* in a particular context. It has the advantage, in other words, of sidestepping the question of the relation of these elements or of assuming that one of them, say wealth, is naturally or inevitably preeminent.

It is usually too easy to think of power as originating in institutions, the greater the better, and as if institutions have a simple means of imposing themselves and a simple, single will to impose. Furthermore, there lurks in much social history a personifying tendency, which in turn relies on the model of a simple psychology of a simple will with clear interests. These tendencies combine into notions such as class, which act like people and for similar reasons. Our modern minds too easily make monarchies absolute, emperors more so, and dictators unfettered, and hegemonic ideas irresistible. In urban contexts, the lord's power and that of the oligarchy's interests can seem all too natural and clear. But as Stephen Rigby has argued, "the dominant ideology of late medieval towns turns out to be fractured and in the final analysis not very dominant after all."[5] Dominance was in social terms similarly tenuous, often delicate. Looking at the burgesses of towns within their group will make the limited role of the elite obvious and it will, therefore, make obvious how seriously the individual and their individuality was the basic atom of the social world. The question to ask here is how did the sense of *relative* social clout get asked and answered in the later medieval town, how did stratification among the burgesses work out.

It is fair to say that whatever sharp senses of social distinction existed between aristocrats and serfs, there was a very different and more chaotic sense of standing prevalent *within* groups. There a version of fluid stratification was the rule. Urban groups were perhaps especially prone to the pursuit of honor, which is an evaluation of self made by the members of the group in an ongoing and competitive way. The group sets its own rules, disciplines its membership, educates them to the local standard of virtue and it grants relative honor in light of the overall judgment. Noblemen scorn the talk of money, even as burgesses openly gesture at it as the root of their comparative worshipfulness and worth. Within the social space they inherit, individuals work for their own honor, for the expansion and high estimation of their social selves by the group. Within their estate, they must be vigilant and wise to advance their status, for while much will be determined by their economic success, that material flourishing is itself dependent on their social self, that is, on their reputation and its enhancement. Self grounds material life; wealth roots self, as two trees whose roots, trunks and crowns are fully intertwined, one's branches supporting the other's.

Whereas chapter 3 focuses on the action, sometimes harsh, of the institution or group on the individual, this chapter attempts to demonstrate how the social self worked the institutions that contained it. By focusing not so much on disputes as on the way individuals engaged and challenged each other in order to settle disputes, we shall begin to see how people constructed their social standing, and how they were rewarded for their social virtues while going about the business of arbitration. We shall see the structured whirl of an honor system by which people pitted their self-evaluation against someone else's and how it was that third parties, quite often those already broadly respected, were able to exploit the institutions of peacemaking quietly to aggrandize themselves. The social self will turn out to be highly varied among individuals, even among those of similar official standing. Thus, we shall have to make some room for the true contingency of character: same social circumstance, different history. But just as crucially, we shall be able to see how a group-enhancing institution meshed with the private interests of an ambitious group of men, at the same time friends and competitors. My interest is not so much in the effect of the particular institutions—arbitration and the love-day—but on how these intense patterns of social interaction reveal the desires and self-understandings of medieval English people. Honor in action will be manifest.[6]

The implications I draw will seem perhaps excessive to some, so I should perhaps be explicit about what is a hunch and a belief, but not something easily demonstrated. Far from deciding that in some key way everything is about material life or about financial profit, I would suggest that what we are usually safe in asserting is that every transaction—no matter how much it belongs to the mundane mercantile—is in fact about culture, potentially about the making of someone's identity.[7] Culture is the bedrock of all human life, and even a dispute about—or apparently about—a pure debt, is inevitably personal, potentially hurtful, and necessarily comes to its meaning in the context of social life and the interpretation of value. There was a time before money, when wealth was fully welded to self, and this primordial layer is the soil in which more recent culture is planted.

In my discussion in chapter 3 of the ways in which individual interests were challenged and modulated by the community, I passed lightly over the dispute resolution technique that was popular across later medieval England, but which was characteristic of the Wells Burgesses' court and most commonly used there: arbitration. This chapter pursues its answer through a close examination of arbitration, an institution that casts light on the stresses and structures that contained and sustained the individual actor, even at the risk of exaggerating the close-knit quality of the citizens of Wells.[8]

Customs such as arbitration remained attractive and effective in the later medieval world just because personal relations could be so fraught, so susceptible to anger and resentment, individuals always straining for their advantage.[9] Daily life in small communities was direct and personal. However, the results of the arbitration process were fundamentally complex and reciprocal. As we shall see, arbitration spread some of the prestige of judgment to the politically inferior members of the Borough Community, greatly helping to construct their social selves, at the same time as it strengthened the system of constitutional oligarchy and the particular interests of the most ambitious members of the civic elite. Arbitration worked to bridle, channel, and soothe private anger and private desire without alienating the individual from the community and its individual members. Throughout England and Europe arbitration flourished best among burgesses and merchants, in the world of guilds, and amongst the nobility, in other words, amongst groups of peers, of ideological equals.[10] As we examine its effects, we must recognize it was a common form in the later middle ages but did not everywhere have the great significance it did at Wells. Selves would work themselves out differently in other contexts, depending in great part on the local power arrangements. *How* differently is a good question, which, however, is beyond the scope of this chapter.

In Wells, arbitration was the most common of the several, mainly non-adjudicated techniques of conflict resolution adopted by the court. To do arbitration in the burgesses' court was not to avoid the court or its routines and rituals. It was to be engaged by them. After hearing a particular complaint the Master would ask the two parties each to select two arbitrators from among the burgesses to compose the differences between them.[11] They would agree to the arbitration and to be bound by its results: "they placed themselves on the decision of the trustworthy men,"[12] or "they place themselves under the ordination of the four men."[13]

Arbitration was the favorite route to a solution in the eyes of this court. The Burgesses' Court presided over 1251 annotated cases between late

October 1377 and the end of 1429. Nine hundred and eight of these give some indication of a result or conclusion. Moreover, of these, 520 went to arbitration. This is an impressive 57.3 percent of all results. Furthermore, recourse to arbitration remained stable throughout the period, ranging in a given five-year period between about 20 and 55 percent of all cases presented to the court, including those with no annotated result, but evincing no pattern of growth or decline. Moreover, arbitration in Wells continued beyond the range of my statistical survey, in fact well into the sixteenth century.[14] While cases were settled in other ways too, whether by oath-helping, wager of law or love-days (a technique related to arbitration), arbitration was relatively dominant, especially when compared to the other courts the burgesses would have been familiar with in Wells, in other towns or in the royal court system.[15]

Thus, arbitration was one possibility among several, none of which involved anything like an arbitrary or immediate decision by the Master of the court. The special quality of the burgesses' social selves was formed within this culture of dispute and peacemaking, a culture that was perhaps unusually careful of the social pretensions and vulnerabilities of its members. Cases were dealt with individually and resolved by whichever means seemed, given the circumstances, most appropriate. It is not hard to see that such an approach served human interests more than a more rigid or legalistic one might have, regardless of which might have best served justice. Like many guild tribunals, this court sustained a social space meant to keep the interpersonal issue in sight.[16] Thus, the power of the Master in his court was oddly a power for encouraging peace rather than dispensing justice, and this reflected the court's desire to match a problematic social situation to an appropriate means of solution. The Master had to be politic, savvy about the individuals involved, their status and history, the nature of the dispute, and the relative effectiveness of the different dispute settling techniques available to him. Part of *his* moral and social standing depended on his accurate estimation of individuals. This is perhaps why Masters were mainly men who had long experience of the town, who had grown mature within the bounds of the guild.

The social demands of harmony and the dangers of exploding tempers and animosities had an even larger role to play in the frequent turn to arbitrated settlement. I believe this was so wherever arbitration was used, but that we can see it clearly in Wells. The most decisive factor in determining whether arbitration would be used was the *kind* of dispute at hand. Throughout the period (1377–1429) covered by the statistical analysis trespass cases were considerably more likely to go to arbitration than those of debt, withholding chattels, breaking a contract, or reneging on a guarantee of money (see figure 4.1). Debt cases, the largest category of suit,

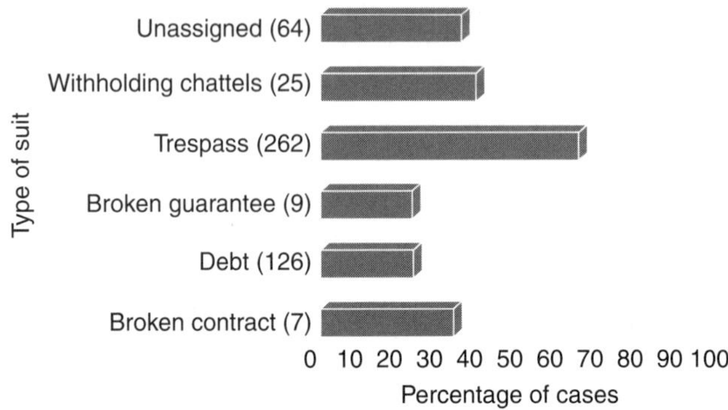

Figure 4.1   Use of arbitration in lawsuits by type of suit (1377–1429)

only ended up decided by arbitration relatively infrequently. 23.5 percent of debt cases were resolved by arbitration, whereas trespass, the second most common suit, went to arbitration in 64.1 percent of the cases. The pattern of suits of broken guarantee was quite like that of debt cases (23.1% went to arbitration), while the pleas of breaking a contract and withholding chattels went to arbitration 33.3 and 39.1 percent of the time, respectively.

Behind the figures is the fact that arbitration was used much more often when an individual's integrity and honor were mainly and directly at issue, his social self. A host of grievances went under the rubric of trespass in Wells, as elsewhere. The cases cannot be statistically calculated with precision because the details are often sparse and fragmentary, but a broad sense of them can easily be conveyed. They generally grew not out of disputes over money, although sometimes money was involved and sometimes it was expected in recompense. Only 8.2 percent of trespass disputes had a precise amount of money noted as sought by the prosecuting party compared to 42.8 percent in cases of debt. This is consistent with the history and nature of trespass. As John Beckerman has shown, the origins of trespass and the essence of its activity in the local courts was rooted in the idea of an injury to honor or integrity (*iniuriae*). Trespass cases need compensation by money not because money was originally at issue but because monetary compensation reflected the damage to the individual over and above the material issue at stake. The core of the complaint was a wound to the self, whether this meant the body, the reputation, or the integrity of your property (especially as defined by the sanctity of the house and its close and surrounding property).[17] The individual was spread across his literal landscape and loomed in the social landscape, enlarged by his ambitions, resented by the envious souls who were "sory of [h]is brotheres profitt."[18]

Thus, prominent among the causes of bad feeling was modern trespass, that is, the violation of the home or the fields. There were also frequent claims of physical injury, especially the public assault that did not draw blood, but stung the pride. (Bloodshed was normally a matter for the royal courts.) Violation of their civic oath was also cited. Typically, this involved such things as supporting a noncitizen against a fellow citizen or perhaps suing a burgess in the bishop's court rather than within the Community court itself. This, too, was plainly an attack on one's honor in the Community, whose oath to God had been taken and was now broken. There was also the wound of slander, *maledictum dixere,* defamation.[19] John Galon seems to have had a sharp tongue—the kind a contemporary preacher expected to be aflame in Hell— and provides a couple of examples.[20] In 1382, John Wood sued him for trespass because he had accused Wood's wife of being a common brawler.[21] About two years later John Taillour charged Galon with falsely calling him a thief.[22] The injury was often not tangible or long-lasting, and the punishment was rarely clear. In the welter of feeling that must have accompanied such complaints, one can tell that the material cause when it existed—the barley that the sheep trampled, or the collapse of the party wall—was only a small part of the problem that had to be solved for real peace to prevail. The strong feelings and the frequent vagueness of the offence that accompanied trespass suits certainly contributed to such cases going so often to arbitration, where the intemperate individuals stepped back to allow others to guard their honor and interests. Arbitration was well suited to this task. Four members of the community, chosen by the litigants but of good reputation, would work out a solution that took facts and social selves into account. Their decision also helped to establish group expectations as well as to curb activities corrosive of the goodwill in the community.[23] This was perhaps especially useful in cases in which the ego of a member was so directly challenged by another. This was after all also the public domain in which virtues were reestablished, as they ever must be, in front of the eyes that would see according to what they learned and often act similarly.

The contrasting case of debt is equally instructive. Debt cases went to arbitration less often partly because the stakes were typically clearer, less often deemed a personal injury or affront. Honor was certainly often at stake, but it was the honor of the *debtor.* The plaintiff's integrity and stature had not been impugned and needed no defense so long as he was not thought to be lying. Indeed, the ability to be a creditor, or to be a little slower to collect your debts, is a variety of generosity indicative of the kind of wealth that was admired in the medieval town. It spoke to the virtues of solidity, wealth, and generosity. More practically, in a debt case the simple presentation of a document might sometimes decide the issue. Often enough, it was simply a matter of modifying the sum demanded in light of goods delivered or services rendered. One could almost say with Richard Firth Green that debt was a plea where the newer notions of truth as correspondence were dominant partly because writing and reckoning had a larger place, whereas trespass was old fashioned and saw truth as a moral virtue.[24] In many debt cases, the argument was really about time. It was a fight to delay paying what was clearly owed, in the hope of first making a gain or a recovery in business. Delay was in fact much more common in cases of debt than in those of trespass.[25] The Court often chose arbitration to treat ambiguity and complexity, especially where two egocentric burgesses were insisting on their own honor.[26]

At every moment, however, a debt case was also about confidence, that the numbers written down, the money loaned or anticipated for business done in good faith, would be properly supported by the custom of the community in accordance with the ethics of honor. In cases of debt, the Master was more likely to call in witnesses to swear on a man's behalf. Fidelity trumped feelings, and thus perhaps feelings were deemed of less use when the matter was mainly financial. The banner of business, the ethos of the urban, was even then faith in commerce, and commerce in good faith. This tended to leave arbitration out of many of the cases.[27] Nevertheless, nearly a quarter of debt cases in the Burgesses' Court did go to arbitration.[28] Often enough social and ethical concerns were more critical than narrow technical expertise in deciding when it was time to appoint *amicabiles compositores,* friendly peacemakers, to seek a settlement.[29] Arbitration was so often employed because it was particularly suited to cope with hot feelings, insults, and attacks on status: a large role in a medieval community, not even behind business in importance.

If it is now clear that arbitration was unusually important in Wells and that it was a potent way for individuals to act socially and politically, we must ask who was able to take greatest advantage from this court regime. Certainly, it is conceivable that arbitration would be strategically deployed as a social weapon. For instance, if only the town elite could act as arbitrators, they would merely be practicing a collective but limited judgship, but retaining their broad collective oversight of the lesser members of the community. Alternatively, perhaps the Master would opt more often for arbitration when lower status burgesses were involved in the lawsuit. A somewhat cynical hypothesis, this proposition assumes that arbitration functioned rather like wardship, or the limited status that married women in the medieval world possessed, even in Wells' court. Married women needed their legally competent overseer to pursue their interests.

By contrast, more frequent, disproportionate recourse to arbitration in cases involving those less prominent might have helped to give these socially less distinguished people a better chance of success, and the community a greater luster of impartiality, of sublime social fairness. This is parallel to the advantage of a person choosing trial by jury rather than by a privileged, unsympathetic judge. This is a more idealistic proposal, but not an outlandish guess in a medieval town such as Wells, where town councilors in 1437 were charged not to show "partialite for dread" or to allow allegiances to others to affect their judgment. The judicial leadership of the town—masters, constables, and councillors—were to "deem and doe evenlye."[30] Thus it is possible that the community's collective clout, expressed by the aid of arbitrators, could have been loaned to its weaker members as a kind of stature-buttress in those times of great personal stress brought on by a dispute with an economic or social superior. The issue is to decide which burgesses were best positioned to improve their sociopolitical position through this institution.

Was there in fact a status-bias when it came to deciding whether arbitration was appropriate? To decide this and many other questions that follow requires that we divide the burgesses according to status. This is a difficult business. We cannot directly consider wealth since we have no suitable records to indicate this. It was a very volatile feature of medieval town life anyway, although a crucial one: "Money makethe the man."[31] Since, however, we are not dealing with the town as a whole, but the Borough Community alone, it is probably best to use their own offices as a rough determinant of status. It is well known that towns were both conscious of status, that they required commensurate "sufficiencee" (substantial wealth) for a burgess to attain high office, and so rewarded wealth with acknowledged status. Indeed, I suspect that wealth can be indirectly tracked via officially conferred status.[32] In Wells, we have a virtually complete record of the annual civic elections from 1377. Furthermore, the offices are presented in order of preeminence that certainly tended to correspond to high visibility in the town's other records. Therefore, I have divided the population of the enfranchised burgesses into four groups of uneven size. Since no burgess ever served in a lower office after having attained a higher, I believe that sociopolitical status once attained was not generally lost (aside from disastrous misfortune perhaps). At the top are the *elite* or judicial leadership, who might also be called the oligarchy. This included those who had attained the status of constable or master, the two judicial offices. The *middling officers* are those who attained the very respectable and important offices of rent collectors (an appointed, unremunerated office in this period) or churchwardens.[33] The *petty* burgesses are those who had attained lower offices but had not yet moved higher up the ladder of honor. These included the two shambles-keepers who oversaw the quality of meat and fish in the market, and the six streetwardens who kept the streets of the town clear of pigs and ran the pound. Those burgesses who had never or had not yet attained any office are classed here as *commoners*. I need only remind the reader again that non-burgesses were excluded from this court. The bottom rank here is hardly the bottom of all Wells society.[34]

The incidence of arbitration among the elite is entirely unremarkable. Of the 125 appearances of the elite in cases, 57 went to arbitration. This is 45.6 percent of the cases, quite close to the corresponding overall arbitration rate (40.5%). The commoners' arbitration rate was almost exactly the same (40.4%). Thus, it is, on the face of it, hard to find any clear patriarchal function in the recourse to arbitration.

The place of equality and a kind of even-handedness is a facet of the Wells fraternity court that is also captured when we examine the twenty-six cases in the period in which one of the official suitors was a woman. All of these women were the widows of burgesses. There were many other cases in which a woman, either wife or daughter of a living burgess, was involved, but those women had no *official* roles. Although the number of such cases is small, there is no large deviation from the general patterns.[35] Fifteen were cases of debt, seven of trespass, two withholding chattels, and two indeterminate. Of these, 9, or 34.6 percent, went to arbitration, 4 of 9 of the trespass cases included. In other words, women were no more likely than lower status burgesses to be "supervised" via arbitration or aided by its intervention. Women were not allowed to act as arbitrators but were apparently not exploited by arbitration. These women, it must be stressed, were taken to be honorary members of the community by virtue of their dead husbands' membership.[36] As far as court cases and the use of arbitration go, they were treated like it, with the one large qualification that the identity enriching benefits of acting as an arbitrator and therefore sharing in the public authority of the group was unavailable to them. Their personal power could neither be developed nor manifested through acting the arbitrator.[37]

Interpretation often rests upon a slight difference in accent. Within the overall "blindness" to status that resorting to arbitration apparently displayed, we can find an interesting pattern. Certain social categories were more likely to have arbitration used when they were involved in a suit as the *prosecuting* party than as the defending. We can discern three distinct groups functioning. First, there were the commoners. They were considerably more likely to have arbitration when they were suing burgesses who had already attained petty or middling offices, that is, marginally superior burgesses. (See table 4.1.) Conversely, they saw somewhat less than average rates of arbitration when they were defending against such higher-status suitors. By contrast, the second group—those who achieved a modestly higher profile in town and guild affairs—displayed a very different profile of arbitration. (See table 4.2.) These petty and middling officers—more regular attendants of the court—were more likely to have arbitration in cases in which they were the defendants than the plaintiffs. And, indeed, these

Table 4.1 Commons' use of arbitration according to opponents' sociopolitical status (as prosecutors and defendants)

Opponents' status	As prosecutors	As defendants
Elite	3 (25%)	16 (33.3%)
Middling	20 (69%)	24 (30%)
Petty	57 (47.9%)	36 (33%)
Commons	167 (40.9%)	167 (40.9%)

Table 4.2 Middling and petty arbitration according to opponents' status (as plaintiffs and defendants)

Opponents' status	As plaintiff (n = 155)	As defendant (n = 68)
Elite	0 (0%)	8 (47.1%)
Middling/petty	9 (18.0%)	4 (25%)
Commons	24 (24.5%)	20 (57.1%)

represent the reverse of the commoners' coin, the cases in which the middling officers' opponents were the humbler burgesses.

The third division included members of the civic elite, who evince no interesting patterns of the kind had by middling and petty burgesses. Arbitration was used somewhat more often when they sued than when they were defending themselves (47.5% or 48/101 and 37.5% or 9/24 respectively). If anything, the elite pattern is closer to that of the common burgesses than the middling and petty.

I must stress that I am identifying a variation here, a tendency that points up some of the meaning embedded throughout arbitration in Wells. I do not intend to obscure the larger fact that in most cases social status just doesn't seem to have been decisive in determining recourse to arbitration. But, these nuances do help us to understand the social dynamic alive in all arbitration cases.

That said, even within the urban middle class a lower-status individual suing his social superior involved the disputants and the Borough Community in a slightly unnatural situation that badly needed naturalizing. The moral acceptability of a social superior's attack on an inferior, even to violence,[38] was clear enough in medieval England, but the reverse can never have been easy. Urban hierarchy was more fluid than rural; urban social relations more varied, partly because of the commercial aspect of life, the constant interchange between buyers and sellers of goods and skills. This meant, however, that the reality of such insubordination would have to be more common in towns, in densely commercial contexts. A debt was, after all, a debt, regardless of social status; and the law and the courts would have to work for equity. Thus, what was unnatural to notions of hierarchy was all too natural and essential to the ideas of urbanity and economy. The potential animosity involved when men of marginally disparate status were disputing sometimes required special treatment to avoid exacerbating the case with the status anxieties of the participants. Thus it is not surprising that when William Crofter, a commoner who never would attain any civic office, sued William Weye, a churchwarden who had only attained his middling status recently, arbitration may well have been invoked with their newly disparate status in mind. The arbitrators were John Cutte, Robert Polglas, Philip Porter, and Thomas Sholere, respectively a constable, a commoner, a churchwarden, and a rent collector. Crofter the commoner chose the elite constable and the other commoner, while the middling man Weye chose two men of similar status to himself, further reflecting a touch of middling-status consciousness.[39] In such a pass, a man might reach out for support to those who were most like him, social simulacra to his own frustrated self, virtual parts of his own identity.

In such cases, the effect of arbitration was as a buffer, holding the worst in men apart. The mediation of the arbitrators helped to soften the possibly insulting nature of the suit itself. The status of the arbitrators—who usually included some higher-status members—and the distance that arbitration established between the two angry parties, provided a space for the solution to emerge with less rancor. The arbitrators palliated the middling status burgess by making his appointed people deal with men who were respected and well honored within the community, possibly even powerful. Here the work of arbitration was to rub off the rough edges of all too obvious urban inequality and to allow men of different status to deal with each other as equals but without dishonoring the burgess who might claim marginal superiority. Rich or poor, brothers remained brothers by virtue of a social institution that made their statuses temporarily moot, rather than by challenging the self worth and honor of the two parties. The social self still could be seeking an expansion of itself, but within limits that place this kind of system far, far away from the feud-arbitration model of some other cultures.[40]

The anxiety over status was strongest among the middling groups, and reflected most when they were legally involved with the humbler burgesses, from whose ranks they had only lately and possibly indistinctly emerged. Relatively few of these middling men would ever make it to the elite of the town. They were in no position to be generous, and were very much those who might resent the accusations, however legal and justified, of their new inferiors. Their identity and position required that attitudes and actions toward them differed from those toward their inferiors. Those at the top of the civic world, however, were surer of their standing, certainly with respect to the commoners. Indeed, the elite's slightly higher use of arbitration is plausibly explained by their willingness to appear secure and generous. There is a whiff here of the sort of reciprocal gift-giving famously discussed by Marcel Mauss.[41] In effect, the strong man, partly to *seem* so, gives up his advantage—that his word is intrinsically and indisputably better than his opponent's—charitably, for love of his brother and of the community. The countergift to the superior burgess was the respect and praise with which the inferior burgess honors him, as well as the growth in his general status in the community. By going to arbitration, the elite citizen actually raises his position by his willingness to affirm the conceptual equality of all burgess-brothers, notwithstanding his own higher status. His character and judgment are publicly seen as rich in the social and moral goods of the fraternity: he rises in the ranks of his equals. Thus the paradoxical world of stratified fraternity—when well ordered and well run—gathers some of its strength from serving its members' private tensions and ambitions.

Plainly, then, arbitration in Wells was sometimes used to assert a collective equality that might easily have been disputed by proud individuals. The kind of case that went to arbitration was determined more by the tension-easing, status-erasing, effects of arbitration than the quality and status of the suitors. Complex cases and irreconcilable accounts also no doubt contributed to its use. The community, armed with the ideology of fraternity, knew all members to be equal in some sense, and intervened with the sweet solution of arbitration. Pitt-Rivers has argued, "A man is answerable for his honor only to his social equals. . .to those with whom he can conceptually compete."[42] If so, then the potential for honor-bound rancor was high among urban burgesses. Arbitration could help by occluding some of the brutal facts of power and influence but also the equally potent forces of willfulness, pride, hope, and desperation that flourish wherever people live together closely and competitively. Thus, it made peace and opened the way for the exercise of virtues. Like the resolution techniques of chapter 3, arbitration disciplined people but it also enabled them.

The Arbitrators

The structure and culture of the arbitration procedure provided a context for the most important aspect of arbitration for the social self: the selection of the actual arbitrators. If we may seriously wonder why the elite should have wanted or allowed a system that contributed to the fraternity's egalitarian tendency rather than as a bulwark to hierarchy, part of the answer is in the way that the practice of arbitration provided significant social, political, and personal advantages not only to those who got to choose their champions but to those who acted as arbitrators. All social selves gained greatly from these practices, which doled out *double* honors.

Arbitration among the nobility in England, Wales, or France all relied on the exclusive use of sufficiently wise or high-status (powerful) people to do the arbitration.[43] How might this model transfer to the low affairs of a middle social group such as the burgesses of Wells? While the diffuse power of the church and community were present in arbitration as an aura around the proceedings, insofar as the church was often the site of arbitraments, it was the arbitrators themselves who provided the key social resources, the goods of personality and wisdom that allowed this non-adjudicating dispute mechanism to thrive and retain the town's collective confidence.[44] To overstate only a little, the arbitrators were the social place where structure and agency met most significantly, where the quality and effect of a social self was prominent and *critical*.

A case of arbitration was a moment of profound nexus for the men of Wells. Like the very disputes it grew from, arbitration involved virtually all kinds of members of the community. About one-third of the burgesses acted at some point in their lives in this high business of mediation, evaluation, appeasement, and performance: 204 burgesses of about 600. It becomes immediately apparent that among those who arbitrated were burgesses of otherwise quite low social position, including many who never held any sort of civic office that reflected prestige or influence. In terms of sociopolitical office, the arbiters were surprisingly broadly distributed, as table 4.3 illustrates.

Perceptions are key in addressing cultural historical questions. Most impressive is the fact that some commoner (not a particular individual but a member of the class) was as likely to *be seen* involved in arbitration as was a member of the constabulary, that dominant component of the city's judicial leadership (26.4% and 28.6% respectively: see figure 4.2). The other groups' shares ranged from 5.5 percent for shambles-keepers to 12.4 percent for the rent collectors.

Table 4.3   Shares of arbitration by sociopolitical status

Offices	*Number (n = 1380)*	*Percentage*	*Per annum*	*Per individual*
Masters	129	9.3	2.5	5.9
Constables	395	28.6	7.6	10.7
Rent collectors	171	12.4	3.3	5.9
Churchwardens	122	8.8	2.4	4.2
Shambles-keepers	82	5.9	1.6	1.5
Streetwardens	117	8.5	2.3	1.2
Commons	364	26.4	7.0	.6

Note: These represent shares or acts of arbitration, not cases. The median whole number of arbitrators per case was four.

Source: Wells Town Hall, Convocation Book I.

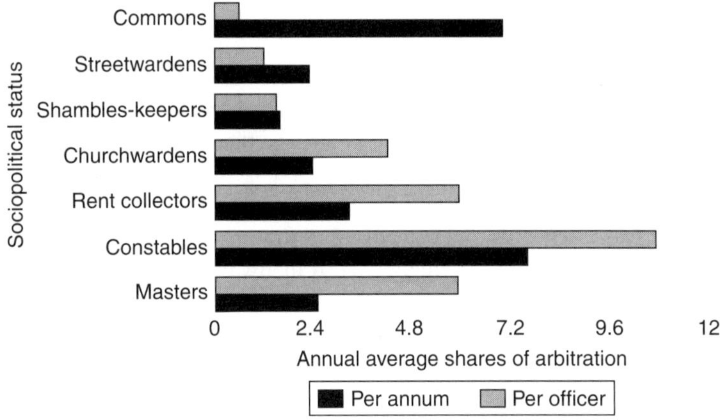

Figure 4.2   The perception of arbitration (sociopolitical status of arbitrators)

It is worth noting that the masters were not the preeminent arbitrators. As a group, the masters did less arbitration than three other categories of burgess. They did no more as individuals (5.9 cases per individual) than did the rent collectors, and did only about half the amount of arbitration as the constables (10.7 cases per individual). This is partly because masters did no arbitration while actually holding magisterial office, and partly because even when they were out of office they continued to play a role of community oversight that apparently encouraged them to arbitrate sparingly so that they could stand up for the broader needs of the Borough Community. In that small number of cases where the Borough Community imposed arbitrators, generally when the Community was itself a party to the dispute, the arbitrators then came from among the judicial elite, especially these former masters.[45]

There is a quiet circumstance that allows us to shade the picture more accurately by understanding the significance that arbitrating had for these men. The fact that the women who were bound to this court for their business could not share in the social goods and graces reflected by acting as arbitrators is indicative of their limited, almost child-like status in the community. Even widows, who in some other respects were treated as equals, could not tap into this power of officially making peace. Like most of the men, but for different reasons, reasons they could by no luck or achievement overcome, Wells women did no arbitration. They were thought *intrinsically* inappropriate to be judges. For male members of the Borough Community, a share of ruling was at least a possibility, and the potential girth of their social selves was all the larger. To play at arbitration and judgment was to play lord for a moment, a manly and powerful image. It was an act that marked an important difference among people.

The high participation of the commons—those who had not yet held a civic office—is, therefore, a powerful proof of the extent of the devolution of authority toward humbler social selves. There were no fewer than sixty-eight arbitrators from the common burgesses, those who had never held any civic office. At the same time, it must be stressed that at the level of the individual the most active arbitrators were drawn from the upper levels of the city, from those who had been rent collectors, constables, or masters. Thus seventy-seven men only once acted as arbitrators (thirty-three of whom were commoners), but seven higher-status men were arbiters in more than fifty cases each, and all did most of this arbitration after having joined the judicial leadership, generally as constables. In other words, arbitration was able to cultivate *both* the guild's democratic tendency and the power needs and expectations of the elite. Honor was proportionately awarded and that meant spread fairly broadly. It reflected its society, and its members' hopes for a share of control and dignity.

In the vast majority of cases, suitors selected their arbitrators. This partly explains why so many kinds of men participated in arbitration. This freedom is itself reflective of the burgesses' eagerness to have a say in their settlements and its attendant prestigious dividends. Yet, legal freedom provides only a weak, limiting force to check other political and economic powers. What other considerations were involved in deciding whom to choose as one's arbitrator? Character, repute, and practicalities needed consideration. Some of these men may have been difficult, perhaps "choleric," "sad and soleynge with heviness in thoght," coveting "right muiche," but even men of such a disposition might be "suttill" enough to chart the path to success. Character was built into reputation.[46] There were, however, also purely practical considerations. Who was in town? Who was willing?

Beyond these issues, however, choosing arbitrators called for concern with at least two broad criteria more closely related to current social standing. A suitor might want to have an individual on his side whose perceived stature within the Community was high. He could tap into such a man's social capital, borrowing his power on credit. The second consideration was as crucial. You had to be confident that the prospective arbitrator would work hard for your interests, and this might well mean—according to his friendship for you. Often enough you want a friend rather than a giant in your corner, but a friend of poor repute, a social brawler, too "bold to fight" as the sanguinary character was reputed to be, or a suspected cheat, would not be very effective.[47] Again, these are values by which men were judged. Part of why medieval women were not allowed—aside from a few countesses perhaps—to judge was that such public action, touched by power, was in a woman a straightforward sign of private vice. And *vir*-tue, etymologically and ethically speaking, was unbecoming in a woman. The Wells arbitrators would work best if their character was consistent with public virtues appropriate to serious sociolegal work such as arbitration. It is no surprise that these virtues overlapped with those acknowledged as essential to community leadership, and helped to make the elite—and especially the constables—the obvious choices for arbitration.

As should now be apparent, the business of concluding a dispute was never merely a private matter, and in the Burgesses' Court it was even more obviously a collective issue with large bearing on people's assessment of social selves. The existence of this court relied on the willing participation of its members. It could not afford to alienate them because there were other games in town in the form of the Bishop of Bath and Wells' courts, not to mention the royal courts hovering hungrily above. At one level this meant that arbitrators would have to be of the right stuff, of "sufficient honor," as contemporaries put it, to inspire confidence in their client's opponent in particular and the community as a whole. There was therefore a double pressure working in favor of those who had already entered or begun to ascend the civic hierarchy. The system needed "discreet" men, and this often meant that the arbitrators would come from a status level not much lower than the *higher* of the two suitors. It would otherwise be an affront to the social self of that man and a little too dangerously democratic. Where honor was at issue, and in some indirect way it always was, the fraternal prejudice of equality was tempered by the reality of a well-ordered hierarchy that also needed to be careful of the interests of individuals.[48]

Late medieval towns were highly conscious of social distinctions, of the varying degrees of reputation and of wealth, occupation and political office.[49] These were well rewarded in official urban status, and unofficial clout. In the broader context of the national and European scene, the later Middle Ages were plainly as conscious of distinctions of status as any period, any place. But, at the same time, it is critical not to see the thicket of qualifications for status and the physical projection of identity in clothing and architecture—the new chimney, glazed window, or the Russian fur—as proof of the rigidity of hierarchy. If, as at Wells, insults against the judicial elite were taken as a form of local *lèse majesté,* it was probably because of the tenuous hold on his status that anyone had. Everywhere in England the signs are the same: of a world in more social flux than it was used to, of every one who was anyone deeply concerned to establish his superior claims in the face of opposition, and always hungry to extend the social self, its honor and power, through associating one ambitious, anxious person with another seemingly more successful one. Great lords were few enough, and everyone else was, if he (or perhaps she) had a chance, on the make, and yet doubting his prospects. The dominant and ostentatious merchants are always the great examples, men savaged by the realities of the wheel of fortune, which first lured them up, and then crushed them underneath. Merchants or their heirs typically disappear from prominence altogether and only occasionally made it safely into the landed gentry. Even within that gentry and county elite, there was the unceasing pursuit of preferment and protection, much discussed in the context of bastard feudal relations and the multiplication of hierarchical alliances.[50]

It was a world in debt, often up to its neck with the weight of favors done, friendship offered. Social capital was repaid in diverse social and cultural ways, helping to determine with whom you would do business, with whom you might ally yourself in Community affairs. At the same time, such a world calls into question the real meaning and role of fraternity. The Borough Community and arbitration were, in fact, a function of fraternity and one does see that the lines of credit were less clearly established here than elsewhere, less certainly a matter of the great social capitalist—the master or constable—lending his prestige and power to lesser men in return for support. There was a little more space for the expansion of the small man.

This emerges even more clearly when we examine the status of the respective suitors and arbitrators. I shall use the trespass cases only. Table 4.4 displays the frequency with which burgesses did arbitration for other burgesses according to their sociopolitical standing. What is most striking is that burgesses of all statuses asked burgesses of all social groups to arbitrate for them. Thus elite members of the guild asked for commoners to arbitrate on 17 occasions, 21.0 percent of the arbitration done for the elite. The commoners were in fact a significant factor in arbitration done for every social category, including of course, their own. Their participation as arbitrators for the middling and elite burgesses serves to re-enforce the element of equity displayed by the Borough Community and the way that the social selves of the modest men found ways to grow within the Community.

Table 4.5 allows us to see more clearly for whom the different social groups did their arbitration. Its most vivid feature is the similarity of the

Table 4.4　Trespass arbitration by sociopolitical status of arbitrators and clients percentage distribution (1377–1429)

Arbitrator's status	Client's status			
	Elite	Middling	Petty	Commons
Elite	51.8	43.6	50.8	31.2
Middling	19.7	27.5	21.2	19.0
Petty	7.4	11.4	6.1	14.6
Commons	21	17.2	21.7	35.1
n	81	87	179	589

Source: Wells Town Hall, Convocation Book I.

Table 4.5   Commons' arbitration partners
according to partners' status

Status	*Occasions (n = 244)*
Elite	91
Middling	57
Petty	51
Commons	45

Source: Wells Town Hall, Convocation Book I.

pattern for all social groups. All did most of their arbitration for commoners, who were the majority of all suitors (64.3%), and less for each social group higher on the ladder of prestige and influence, and smaller in numbers. Remarkably, commoners were not much less involved in all categories of arbitration than those more dominant in the guild. Their main deviation was that they were more often selected by other commoners, somewhat less so favored by their social superiors. But, in fact, all social groups tended to select a little more often, but only a little, from members of their own tier. The tendency again is to confirm the fluidity and equality of a community in which high would sue low, low would sue high, and anyone could be found doing arbitration for anyone else. This is not a nonresult; it suggests a space for character judgments to be made. A key issue in choosing an arbitrator was not just his wealth, but what kind of man he was to you and according to the general report. This also suggests that groups formed across social tiers.

The democratic element of the system is not the entire story. For while it certainly casts into great doubt a view that would take oligarchy, harsh caste-based oligarchy, far too seriously because too rigidly, there are important signs of status and power consciousness revealed in the Wells arbitration system. For as I suggested, if friendship helped to tell men whom to choose to arbitrate, the facts of power and influence were also known to the burgesses and influenced their decision. Part of the social charm of choosing two arbitrators each rather than one was that power and personality could be balanced. Choosing a common burgess of good reputation did not mean having to give up the influence of a higher-status burgess. Significantly, that influence would enhance the power of the elite burgess himself since he was receiving an acknowledgment of his prestige and an occasion to fulfill its potential.

The most popular pairing of arbitrators was, in fact, a high–low combination of constables and commoners. This was used seventy-five times (see figure 4.3). On ninety-one occasions a commoner did his arbitration alongside a member of the civic elite. Commoners were paired with other commoners on 18.4 percent of their arbitration duties. This figure is still a

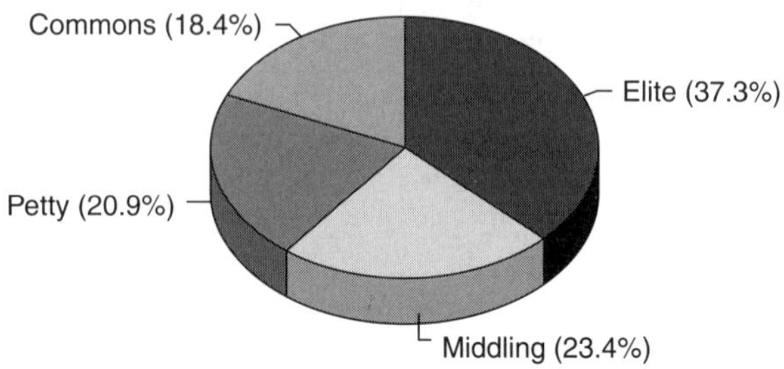

Figure 4.3   Commons' arbitration partners (trespass and debt cases 1377–1429)

sizeable one, showing just how fully the devolution of authority in Wells had gone. At the same time, however, success at law and through arbitration was thought more likely to come with the involvement of higher-status arbitrators, especially in cases where one of the suitors was of relatively high status. Furthermore, the likelihood was that the influence of the elite figure in the arbitration pairing was probably the greater. Everyone would have expected that due deference be paid to the *clearly superior* arbitrator's opinion. Thus without denying the role of the egalitarian—and the real influence this reflected—the elite still could exercise a kind of power through the muddied medium of arbitration and the values of deferential hierarchy, but it was a power that had to remain overtly sensitive to influences from below. All four arbitrators did have to agree, and the rules of consensual committees would have to be followed: cajoling, appeasement, a little anger, but ultimately compromise and at least feigned respect, all around.

The arbitration partnerships in which the elite, middling, and petty burgesses found themselves were almost identical to those of the commoners. The arbitration partnership gave both its members increased prestige, the color of the judicial that was itself tinted with the noble and lordly. But it also points to the existence of frequent, close relationships among burgesses. Just about 40 percent of all arbitrated settlements were decided in part by a commoner, but commoners had exclusive control in only 7.3 percent of all cases. Not bad for people at the bottom of the citizenry, but well tempered by the more powerful men. By the same token, the elite participated in an impressively high 60.8 percent of all arbitration cases, yet they exclusively dominated only 20.6 percent. This is a large figure, except when one realizes that as town judges elsewhere they would have dominated all cases, and remembers the assumptions that some medievalists have made about the character of oligarchy.[51] Among Wells burgesses—that half of the city—four of five arbitrated decisions involved the significant participation, judgment, and potentially special perspectives of those who were in no sense rulers. And while we must recall that most cases of debt did not go to arbitration and that these cases were the most common in the Wells court, there is no doubt that the lines of power and influence are speaking quite clearly in the records of arbitration, and their message is of a rather gentle oligarchy, diffused into the fraternity. Most pertinently, this adds up to a system sensitive to the selves of its many and varied members and able to protect them from what they thought were unfair risks, and also to blandish them with prospects of greater prestige. Within the bounds of hierarchy and the gaze of the collectivity, individuals found in arbitration a place to make, defend, and perform their own honor. Succeed or fail in their drama, they were themselves responsible, and they knew it.

Agent Marries Institution: Both Survive!

The very nature of the arbitrated suits made clear winners and losers rare. Thus the arbitrators frequently expressed relative guilt by assessing different fines in wine to be paid to the opponent, or by differing fines in money, neither ever to be paid because they were remitted by the grace of the "winner," whose gains were thus mainly honorable rather than monetary. The arbitrators might also require the ritual exchange of kisses of peace. It all tallies to a great dance of meaning, where cheques circulated, to appease and please, but never to be cashed. The serious effect of all this was the making of peace. The social system forced its litigants to acknowledge their opponents' integrity, to acknowledge the community and its oversight, and ultimately to know the virtues that arbitration embodied and inscribed on social selves. Frequently, the litigants were said to submit "all debates and quarrels previously existing between them to the ordination of the arbitrators." This habitual expression is important. To a large extent, the ethos and the institution cared little for justice that did not bring peace, founded on some sort of pragmatic and symbolic achievement, firm enough to sustain reconciliation, and commanding the acquiescence of the individuals involved. Therefore, the arbitrators were expected to elicit all pricks to anger and recrimination, so that they could apply a universal salve.

Arbitration throve in the great tangled thicket of later medieval English society, supported by rampant notions of community, hierarchy, fraternity, and individuality—master values—all trained and bent toward the establishment of amicable peace. Where status and violence, whether of the courtroom or the sword, were smoothed away somewhat, there was a breathing space for arbitration. Into this space gifts and consideration, compromise and ritual were poured, and on the whole they were part of an effective system of peacemaking. That peace could be achieved by such techniques does immediately re-enforce our speculation that the practice of arbitration itself works best where there is a degree of equality among the individuals. While we would be surprised to find a king being bound by arbitrators to anyone but another king, it makes sense to find it used among the nobility and encouraged by fraternities. Wells civic guild was certainly not alone in its use.

At Wells, however, we are able to see and indeed to test the reality of the fraternal element in the regime of law and peace. Overall, we have seen that in some subtle but significant ways status did matter when it came to arbitration. The elite certainly did much of the arbitration, but almost startlingly for the Middle Ages, the penetration of the judicial process by men of small status was pronounced. The fraternal ethos of guilds and urban communities no longer seems easily dismissed as idle ideology, platitudes. Further pastel shades can sometimes be added to the tint of oligarchy, once a well-blackened term. At the same time, however, the elite made this institution serve their own claims for prestige and their exercise of power.

Thus we must leave room for hierarchy, for people who could not think calmly of themselves or others except as well ordered, a world that saw honor and status variation as the sinews of that order. Yet, in the later medieval city, status was vague, uncertain, changeable. Legally, all were equal, but financially and politically the burgesses were especially disparate; and almost everyone was at times vulnerable. Furthermore, since Wells' collective political strength depended on the fraternity's continuity, the devolution of honor from Community to its members was natural and encouraged. The honor and burden of judgment undertaken in the community reflected the kind of responsibility individuals had within the collective. Ranged through the combinations of arbitrators chosen by the litigants was a system of sorts, a regime that circulated the goods of status, in which men supported each other for selfish as well as selfless reasons. By such means, the animosities of a world of ambitious "equals"—brothers—were kept in check. And, critically, this could all be done, saving their individual honor.

One might even say that for all this institutional structuring and all the communal good it did, the system worked so well because individuals felt confident calculating and cultivating their own interests, *their* social status within this game. They could play the system for all it was worth. The system played well for men of very different levels of achievement, united perhaps only by the thought they would do better in the future, in the next arbitration, notwithstanding their "fause frends." Can it be that the system and its powerful men flourished even as the individuals processed within the system did too? Only if we bear in mind that the system came with a dominant discourse of honor and stratification and that these worked to reward and sustain certain kinds of achievements over others. We can see, nevertheless, that people did pursue their interests in an independent way, but that this meant dealing with and working through other people. It was true even of the powerful: they could not do it alone, but plainly social selves of all kinds found many moments to assess, act, and take responsibility for themselves and others in this kind of regime. Every town and village had its own institutions and traditions, but those at Wells can help us to see most clearly the breadth of possibility for individual action in intense social circumstances. We see better how a social world, a society, was made of fluid, watchful, eager, and active social selves, moving in and out of alliances. It is to these alliances that we must now turn to understand just how much the company he or she kept defined a person.

CHAPTER 5

FRIENDS, ENEMIES, PATRONS

I thought upon a limerick.
I thought upon a riddle.
I started on a story,
But I stopped it in the middle,
For the story I had started
Was not, you see, the kind
That you tell at a kirk sewaree.

After that time men would stop
For the finish of the story at my
Side-street shop.
My business grew so rapidly
And so did my renown
That soon I was elected to the council of the town,
And they made me the convener of the sewerage committee
For the story I had started at the kirk sewaree.

From "The Kirk Sewaree"

The Significance of Association

The fraught character of premodern social life arose because little, if anything, came to you as your due, as certain, or just a matter of filing the appropriate papers and awaiting the check or the acclaim. People had no social rights. At every moment, the pursuit of legal claims, the establishment of power, and the protection of property was a social business requiring the support of others. Individual status was not certain, nor did a bureaucratic state apparatus neutrally process it. There was no such state, nor any other mechanism to separate the great mass of people from each other. You needed friends; you made enemies; and together these relations helped to define who you were as a social atom in the molecular structure of the town. Your connections to others and interventions on behalf of them were more important than we can easily imagine. We have already seen how complex medieval urban social interactions were. The records of arbitration and dispute settlement that we examine in chapters 3 and 4 start to make clear the extent to which people acted as each other's brokers and abettors. We have seen how the manifold interests of individuals had to be balanced. Who you were in town was determined and reflected by your position in the structures of support that encapsulated your social actions. Nevertheless, certain eyes had a larger share in the creation of any social self. Your own perception was crucial, but also influential were those who watch you and act alongside you most often. Inevitably, the perceptions of the powerful would colonize you and you could rise and fall on their judgment. Whereas if they never saw you, you had almost no sociopolitical existence at all. To be a social being and a political animal was to be a member and a meaning to small groups of judges.

The prickliness and ambitiousness of the social person has been one of the latent themes of chapters 3 and 4. This is another way of understanding the need of the collective to limit and structure the independence of its members. The pursuit of honor, however, is an illustration of the constant pressure produced by conflicting trajectories of individuals that sorely needed to be forced into a sociable shape by arbitration and assumptions of stratification. Kant noticed this feature of human life and called it unsocial sociability. Social rules, orderliness and civility arise through our angers and ambitions, and, oddly, despite us.

The examination of arbitration revealed social standing as a central feature of the later medieval social self, but the context of agency was far richer than that. The individual act of arbitration was part of an ongoing and constantly developing set of patterns that should be understood from at least two relevant perspectives. On the one hand, they are acts and relationships among subsets of the broader community, reflective of small, probably informal and somewhat ephemeral groups, whose core membership and functions need exploring. Such groups are enticing in part because they are elusive, untouched by the heavy ideological over-determination of either medieval or modern assumptions, which have both mainly favored the large group or the individual as their analytic types. The small group is crucial but historically understudied.

On the other hand, however, pursuing the shape of interactions between individuals—the context of the perceptions that make the social self—will lead us to the emergent agent, who rises from the actions made in social life, who comes to his or her social consciousness only in this milieu of activity. This is so, even if our records are partial, as they are, suggestive of possibilities of agency as much as revealing certainties of individual selves. We do, however, know enough about disputes to know that your opponent was often once a close associate, even a friend. A pleasant paradox will emerge: the independence of agency and the vitality of a tightly knit community are both going to get further affirmation, even as community recedes to make way for the emergent self it housed.

The Power of Friendship

A cynicism in historians makes them naturally suspicious of friendship in history. It is the kind of glue of fidelity that could be used to show how cohesive and kind premodern life was: the modernization fallacy. The table-cloth of ideological friendship and community may cover up divisions and antipathies that emerge from the day-to-day realities of power. To allay this fear somewhat I do two things in this chapter: I start with the rough and tumble of daily life, of real disputes complained of by real people, mainly men—unlike the theoretical outlook of chapter 2—and I focus initially on anger and enemies and grudges. I tried in chapter 2 to show that the value of fidelity was not a bland and benighted one, but complex and live to the harsher realities, but now I leave all judgments about the theories of values and virtues to the side. Historians are much happier with the stuff of resentment, and there is no lack of it.[1]

Resentment may well have fuelled the newly articulated doubts of some academic and moralistic medieval people. For the power of friendship was being criticized in the fourteenth century too. No one doubted that there was power in friendship, in preferment, both in the chumminess of equals and the hierarchy of patrons and clients. However, the propriety of these soft and social means of getting ahead and getting things done *was* questioned. If arbitration can stand as an emblem of the burgesses' folkways, it was also considered a social and moral problem that needed reform. Both orthodox moralists like Langland as well as more radical Wycliffite thinkers believed that love-days and arbitration provided a chance for the unreasonable intervention of power and money into the business of justice. They thought, as we mainly do, that justice worked best when it was unattached to social concerns. Justicia is often depicted as blindfolded.[2]

Perhaps the greatest worry about the power of association and patronage came from those who valued it extremely, but feared the power of *other* political and social players. Townsmen's political standing was often simply an effect of their having banded together, so they naturally admired the power of association but knew how effectively other people's social networks could disrupt or destroy their own aspirations. Townspeople, burgesses, were both powerful advocates and creators of close bonds among their members, and greatly troubled by the power of the gentry and nobility to get control of their affairs through the personal link between a burgess and a lord's affinity or retinue. To them, bastard feudalism, the bond of great lord and retainer—the paid friend—was dangerous. Wells's chief constitutional document, redacted in 1437, anxiously sought leaders who would show no "partialite for dread, love, hate or any *affinitye* [my emphasis]."[3] The community needed this, because its members assumed that attachments and personal predispositions were fundamental. The gild of the Lord's Prayer in York warned its members not to abuse their bond: "Also it is forbidden that any brother of the gild shall in the belief that he will have help form his bretheren, be foreward in getting into a lawsuit or quarrel, or in upholding any wrongful cause whatever, upon paoin of losing all hellp and friendship, or any relief, from the guild."[4] Associations made obligations, but left individuals to respond to the awkward, troublesome claims for assistance against people better not disturbed.

These last examples are telling, for civic and religious gilds were themselves the kind of associations that contributed so much to a person's social self. Everyone knew that people could be members of multiple communities and could have diverse and even conflicting allegiances. People cobbled together their complex social selves to pursue their particular ends. Nevertheless, civic associations such as the Wells' burgesses fraternity contributed a chief part of its members' social identity. Public records, contracts, all documents were most likely to declare a man, "John Broun, citizen of Wells," simultaneously to identify and honor him. Furthermore, the community had erected ritual barriers between themselves and others to give formality to this distinction. We have seen in chapter 3 how expulsion from the community was one of the sanctioned conclusions to socially disruptive behavior, as much to say to the shamed man: "*Your* bad behavior ought not to undermine *my* reputation."

While only a few burgesses were forcibly removed from the group, all were admitted and this rite of institution established both a general association with the group and some particular and public connections to specific individuals. To see only the introduction to community, the large-group aspect, is to overlook much that was personal. The new man became a brother, who would show them the due respect and favorable prejudice that he would also deny to outsiders. However, the new burgess never arrived alone. He came recommended by the best referees, other burgesses, his first official friends. These could be symbolic sponsors or flesh-and-blood pledges.[5] Those who were exempt from an admission fee offered no official pledges. *Their* superior right derived from a prior link with the Borough Community, links typical of civic associations across the kingdom. They had either married into a burgess' family by espousing his widow or daughter;

had been born to a burgess; or had, after 1466, been a burgess' apprentice. The bona fides were straightforward here, their identities initially formed by a family connection, as John Broun's son-in-law or Widow Broun's new husband. The majority of burgesses, however, gained admission to the community by fee, and in these cases we usually know who the pledges were. While these were money pledges and I would not want to argue that this relation was of the seriousness of a godfather or sponsor to a modern service club, the association was personal and established the new man's first obligation within the community. Furthermore, these connections sometimes were more significant, the start of a more important friendship.[6]

Friends and Enemies in the Making

Property always helps to constitute identity and the traditional concerns for land ownership excited the social self in a small town such as Wells. Notwithstanding the urban milieu, the country life was a valued component of smalltown existence. The borough of Wells enclosed much land that was underdeveloped, and it bordered on the bishop's manor of Wells. The burgesses often owned or rented small parcels of land all round, using them for gardens, cloth-stretching yards, arable, or pasture for sheep to supply the cloth-making industry of the town. Good fences made good neighbors, but poor hedges enflamed social life and could build on other tensions to make enemies of friends.

An interesting situation focused on Richard Ferrour, the most active burgess in the court record, who died in 1404, an arbitrator on 139 occasions, and John Benet, a prominent man, but one who was not wealthy like Ferrour, nor a member of the oligarchical elite. In September 1385, at the end of his constabular term, Richard Ferrour sued Benet for trespass, and in this case he meant aggravated modern trespass. Ferrour accused Benet of letting his animals eat up Ferrour's standing grain. Ferrour insisted that it had happened "many times."[7] Arbitrators were appointed and they were a high-powered group. The man who would become master in two days, Nicholas Cristesham, was chosen by Ferrour and the man who had been master in 1383, Henry Boudich, was selected by Benet. Each added a substantial lesser man as their seconds, men whose political careers were growing. This suit reveals the Ferrour–Benet relationship at a crossroads, the moment of explosive aggravation that would alter and intensify their public position, but it is also a sign by which to understand their earlier public exchanges, which might otherwise have seemed insignificant.

This was the fourth court case that had brought them together. In 1379, they had met as arbitrators in a case, but worked for opposing sides.[8] February 1380 saw Ferrour's opponent William Davy choose Benet as his second arbitrator.[9] Late that year, in a case between two others, Ferrour and Benet were chosen to lead the opposing arbitration teams once again.[10] Another case can be added: John Benet's first appearance in a court case was in December 1378 and his opponent was Henry Ferrour, Richard's relative perhaps.[11]

It is fair to say that we can make little in particular of this pattern of mild opposition in the records. But the revelation that Ferrour and Benet were unhappy neighbors with long-standing disputes in 1385 makes these traces seem systematic. What is interesting apropos the social self is that their attitude toward each other was well enough known for those who were opposed by Ferrour to think of John Benet as a worthy advocate. In other words, part of their social identity was constructed from their enmity toward each other. Their eventual dispute suggests their ill feelings were rooted in the quality of their neighborliness.

In their own dispute, the arbitrators returned a decision that makes Benet's relative wrong clear. He was ordered to pay compensation of 6s. 8d. to Ferrour, under threat of a 20d. fine to the Borough Community. As a Wells arbitration result, this was a fairly one-sided, clear verdict. It can be seen, in fact, as a decisive collective judgment against Benet in an ongoing dispute and he felt the pique. Knowing the prominence of Ferrour and the careful timing of the case, which came when Ferrour was still constable, Benet may well have felt the judicial elite were attacking him. Realizing that the last official act of the incoming (and presumably already chosen) master was to arbitrate against him may have clinched his suspicion.

One month later Ferrour, the most litigious of all burgesses in the later middle ages, pursued Benet again, apparently for the debt of the 6s. 8d. called for by the past judgment. This is quick reaction in the context of Wells debts, especially since the ability of both men to cope without that amount of money is not in question. Neither was poor. The case was post-poned twice, once because Benet did not appear.[12] Two weeks after this, Ferrour launched another suit, claiming a new trespass, namely that Benet had built a road on Richard's land.[13] Whether this was a new provocation on the part of Benet, or, as is more likely, the old source of anger, from which much else had flowed, Ferrour was plainly trying to exploit the advantages he had gained from the court. Unfortunately, the result of that suit is not recorded.

That men who were warring neighbors would dislike each other and find that well-known dislike translated into part of their public identity is interesting but unsurprising. Of more interest, however, are the practical consequences for third parties. Ferrour and Benet's antipathy was engaged, *counted* on by others, in order to hedge their bets in their own lawsuits. This continued for several years after their suit as well. At harvest time the next year a servant of Robert Horn's trampled and destroyed some of Ferrour's grain, and when the case was sent to arbitration Horn chose Benet.[14] This was perhaps an especially inflammatory decision on Horn's part. When in early 1387 Benet returned to court to sue Thomas Duk for back rent, Duk was quick to select Ferrour as one of his arbitrators.[15] And just to show how such perceptions did linger in the public consciousness, there was the case of Thomas Smart versus James Masson in October 1388. In that case Smart charged Masson with "stealthily creeping onto his land" and trampling it, causing a variety of damage. The landowner chose Ferrour for an arbitrator; the accused trampler, Benet.[16] Benet's reputation had been made. He was the defending arbitrator in another case that year of sheep eating up the fields and garden of a burgess even though Ferrour was not involved.[17]

Small, evanescent, but clearly functional social groups emerged from such well-known personal antipathies. Friendship, in the rich and proper sense that a medieval audience would have acknowledged, was often a contextual relationship: shared antipathy, shared circumstance, led men into each other's camps. People knew: John Benet was honorable, but they also knew that he understood the difficulties of abutting a rich and litigious member of the oligarchy, and would be sympathetic. John Benet would watch out for the ploys and power of Richard Ferrour. We need to extend our analytic techniques to draw out further aspects of social power in the medieval city, to reveal how some social selves were "imperial" selves, dominant and expansive, whereas others were small, isolated, or dependent, prone to suffer colonizing.[18] Based on the records of court contacts, such as chapter 3 makes familiar, I have sampled about one quarter of Wells burgesses of 1377–1429 (and the wives who had court records) in order to map their public social interactions. As source material for social life, this is a rich but obviously flawed source. We cannot follow the patterns of either those sociologists that ask people who their contacts were or those who watch them to see who mattered to them. Nor at this extensive level can we continue to read the pulse of relations such as I have done for Benet, Ferrour, and Smart. Obviously, even in those cases the private self's assessment of which other people mattered and influenced them is beyond us. There are so many relationships that must have thrived and been important, but were never to be recorded in the business of litigation.

The flaws are far from fatal, however. My current intention is not biographical, even if it is concerned with agency. To know the private self from such materials would surely be impossible without understanding the motives and egocentric assessments of the relations reflected—what interviews would show if interviews across the centuries were not an absurdity. The social self, however, is less elusive, for it gathered its substance from its public activity, and while the records are naturally limited for all and distorting of individuals, omitting important parts of their lives, as a basis for analyzing the means by which public selves were constructed and assessed they can be richly illuminating. The social self was affected, structured, even created by the dynamism of social life and its possibilities. To some extent, this should lead us to prioritize the evidence of public, visible dispute and support. Reputations were made quickly and perhaps durably in the more intense light of the guildhall. John Benet has helped to make this vivid.

The evidence from disputes guarantees that the relationships we see were serious. Both disputants and arbitrators knew they were involved in matters with real social and material consequences. With respect to the disputants, one can be sure that the dispute is not an isolated contact, but generally an event that gestures at ongoing previous interactions, often of a more positive sort, typically the kinds of ambivalent relations found between small businessmen and neighbors. Furthermore, for all the individuals cited, whether as disputants or arbitrators, the case was an intensification of the usually weak relationship that membership in the Borough Community had already established. They met together, ate together, acclaimed each other's elections, watched each other's lawsuits. We deal with fragmentary traces, but not with trivial or purely ephemeral ones.

Before beginning an interpretation, there are some important general facts to note. Members of the sample group typically flourished in the community for an average of over seventeen years, probably into their mid-forties, when they declined, but their discernible activity ranged from only a couple of years to over forty.[19] In those years, the median number of court cases they would be involved in was five. On average these sample burgesses arbitrated at four cases each (3.9), but we saw in chapter 4 how complex and various arbitration activity was.[20] While a typical constable had been an arbitrator on ten occasions, a typical commoner arbitrated perhaps once, and many commoners never arbitrated.[21] The middling and petty ranks typically achieved an intermediate level of activity, engaged in a few cases of arbitration during their civic careers.

The social networks of these legally and politically active citizens could vary greatly in size.[22] The average inner circle of contacts (those with whom someone was directly involved in a court case as opposing plaintiff or arbitrator, for example) consisted of 22.5 people, but this figure also hides heavy degrees of variation.[23] The median, for instance—and this necessarily fell among the commoners—was only 14.5 people. The role of court activity in revealing and probably establishing inner circle size is clear. Nothing correlated so closely to inner circle size as the number of cases in which an individual was involved.[24] This is no surprise, although it is worth noting

Table 5.1 Inner and outer circle of contacts by political grouping

	Inner circle size (median)	Outer circle size (median)	Outer: inner circle ratio
Entire sample (98)	14.5	257.5	17.8:1
Oligarchy (7)	56	286	5.1:1
Middling officers (10)	38.5	306	8.0:1
Petty officers (21)	23	300	13.0:1
Commons (60)	9.5	235	24.7:1

that arbitration cases ran second to overall number of cases in correlating to inner circle size. In other words, someone who was, like Richard Ferrour, very active suing and arbitrating came into close contact with the greatest number of people. Perhaps more critically, however, *status* was a very good indicator of activity and inner circle size. The commons alone had a median inner circle of only 9.5 people, whereas the petty burgesses had 23, the middling 38.5, and the judicial leadership an impressively large median of 56 people in their inner circles. (See table 5.1.)

While inner circle contacts meant different things in any individual case, these figures represent an individual's most intense sphere of public activity, reflecting contacts of considerable seriousness, some long-standing, some recent, most significant. Of course we know that everyone had important relations not captured by our record, but the ability of the court system, of the local social world to constitute new relations, is crucial. A high level of public activity developed a man's social and political profile. Arbitrated cases in particular, forged new relationships. The meaning of such relationships is of course one of our key questions, but it is easy to see that arbitrators were moving into other people's business in the respectful and honor-building role of peacemaker. There was social and personal power born of political devolution. The community made space for a social self for whom distinctness if not true autonomy was possible and apparently admirable.

The effect of such activity is in part reflected by the extent of the outer circles recorded. This is an explosive feature. How far can a person's contacts take him/her within a community, once we take into account mediated relationships, that is, the way that B can help A get in touch with C {A>B>C}? Despite wide variation in the number of people you could count in your inner circle of direct contacts, most people who appear in the records at all had *outer circle* contacts of great scope.[25] Via friends, a person could move astonishingly quickly through the entire community. Considering that there were only 150–220 burgesses alive at any time in this period, it is impressive to see that the median outer circle consisted of 258 burgesses. This means that regardless of the size of the more intimate inner circle, every burgess could—by force of friendship or a common acquaintance—reach everyone else in the community.[26] No one had to approach someone as a nonentity, without socially persuasive credentials. This is no doubt part of the meaning of a real and effective fraternity, even though many of the extended links would be in practice unattractive or inoperable because of personal animosity, deaths, and departures.[27] The weak ties of the outer circle were extraordinarily numerous. Some sociologists have also found that weak ties, because of their connecting role, can be particularly potent in helping an individual solve problems and achieve ambitions.[28] Weak ties transformed your social self from the highly charged, dangerous ego to a low-voltage charge of greater reach, safety and effectiveness. Weak ties connected you to other junction boxes in distant social rooms you may only have heard about. You were diffused through the community.

Thus, everyone could reach everyone through a friend or patron. This was good for business, for politics, for dispute settlement. It was a large social fact built up from the conceptual fact of community and social brotherhood: it is the cash value of the rhetoric of fraternity.[29] The community can now be imagined as a structural mode by which a particular kind of social self was produced, a person more passionate about the group because he was practically and culturally well linked to many of the other members. We can conclude that the entire Borough Community was a social network of considerable intensity. These social selves were highly social indeed. We are inflected with others, and smalltown people in medieval England were especially so. But closer examination of individuals proves that all were not equally sociable and the convergence of diffuse community contacts does not demonstrate the full convergence of social selves.

Let's examine two commoners more closely. I choose William Greynton because his social network's significant statistical profile is perhaps the closest thing to a typical burgess among the sample group. Outer circles are so large as to discourage further analysis and even William Greynton, a man who never held any office in the town and who was certainly neither wealthy nor otherwise important, had an outer circle of 340 people. But it is his inner circle contacts that are the crucial ones because these men were his ushers to the broader community. His inner circle consisted of thirty-two members.

Greynton was a member of the community from 1384 till 1407—a longer period than the average. He was in this time a party to eight cases and an arbitrator in a further four. This activity was spread out over time, and notably spread throughout the community. Most striking—but not at all unusual—is the density of his inner circle. Plainly, these thirty-three men knew each other up close and in the fraught context of dispute. They were already burgess brothers, so the contact indicated here was more serious. The second clear feature of this network is exaggerated in Greynton's case, but captures a recurrent feature of commoners' networks: few of his inner circle contacts had repeated official contact with him and only the four men closest to him had multiple contacts.

For the purpose of assessing the importance of such a common burgess, of his social self, it is interesting to consider how little Greynton would stand out in his *own* network if not for our flagging him as central. This was true for almost everyone in the community: that is part of the meaning of the large outer circles. It is a perception sharpened, however, by realizing that in this fairly typical case, about 41 percent of the possible links among members were actualized in the record. Almost half of these men were united within their own networks; their association was not merely a feature of contact with Greynton. In cases mainly independent of him, they came into contact with each other. This leads to a couple of important qualifications of the kind of social networks that a burgess had. A man such as Greynton was less important in his social network than it might at first appear. He was not usually the man who brought everyone together, the man with great clout. In his case, he undertook arbitration and that is a sure sign of some standing and honor, but this cannot easily be built into an argument for his local importance, not yet anyway. His social self was undoubtedly limited by his social role.

A comparison to John Pope will allow us to read the tendency of these social networks better. Similar to Greynton, Pope was a commoner, but he was distinguished by his more frequent arbitration; he arbitrated more than he litigated, a pattern more common among the oligarchical elite than the commoners. Pope's inner circle is like Greynton's, thirty-two people strong, but the shape is somewhat different. Pope had many more repeat contacts than Greynton. Arbitration brought him into relation with some men recurrently. The density of Pope's network was about 49 percent, denser than Greynton's, but not significantly so. Pope was, however, plainly less peripheral and had frequent interaction with a group of about a dozen men who had high and frequent interaction. We might go so far as to say that Pope was part of a clique of interaction that included Thomas Bowyer, Thomas Weye, Ralph Averey, and Philip Porter, and probably others in that central cluster too.[30] Whereas Greynton's main contacts were to two men of considerable activity and importance—Richard Ferrour and Roger Chepman—Pope is less likely to have been marginal or a simple political dependent. By the same token, the level of network density clearly marks Pope as no more crucial a path for other people to pursue power than was Greynton. Pope moved with the modestly influential; he was not exactly one of them.

Elite Networks: Friends in Power

The men who held middle and high office, who were most active within the community, were the men who played their world with the greatest virtuosity. Table 5.1 indicates the features of social networks that are correlated to sociopolitical office. An examination of elite social networks provides a brisk contrast to the William Greyntons of medieval England, for these men's social selves had great reach. To see a big man in the community is not to speak merely metaphorically; in the light of the public interactions of Wells, certain people *were* bigger. This was the concrete reality of their presence in many of their comrades' affairs, sometimes as obstructing litigants, but exceptionally often as facilitating, influence-wielding arbitrators. Social selves are more like bodies than souls, for it is important to see that in every way that mattered, people had different shapes, various bulks and heights, dressed divergently too, and cast different shadows across the social landscape.

An elite burgess and eventual master of the town such as Roger Chepman, who loomed large in Greynton's world, had 3,056 interactions among his inner circle, which included 71 people, that is about five times the size of the sample median. Chepman arbitrated on 26 occasions, and his network density was only 22.61 percent. Richard Gros marks the end of the continuum that suggests that court activity, especially arbitration, produced for some elite people immense social networks in which they were *central* to making contacts. Gros's tremendous inner circle of 129 people had 6,545 contacts among them, yet the network's density was 17.5 percent. Gros was special, active, an arbitrator 66 times, a master of the town.

Plainly, all brothers in an immense family are not equal in all things. The predominance of those like Chepman and Gros who were most active in the court is critical, and much of this activity was as arbitrators, apparently good-spirited official meddlers in others' affairs. They functioned as social mediators, as the *means* by which an individual burgess could reach his outer circle, could find help in the court and, as critically, in his daily commercial and personal life. These were men of influence. They made peace, some of them constantly, and this insinuated them into a great number of small networks, of individual pods. They were the great social bridge-builders, bringing people together or back together, and providing access for future passage between opposing shores. Matthew Arnold wished, "Might our marges meet again." They could only do so with bridges.[31] Here especially we see the oligarchs playing a powerful role for the group and for individuals in need of help, but a role that was richly fertile for developing their own social selves. Placed high in the public eye, a man might make a self upon which political clout and office were hung by those with whom he acted and judged.

Nevertheless, the business of arbitration, which chapter 4 showed helped to foster the power and honor of lesser figures, was at the same time producing power bases for the elite. Those people who were able to arbitrate more were those who were more often honored and trusted in the community. Their good characters as well as their wealth helped to foster good reputations. This in turn provided them with more occasions to insinuate themselves influentially into the affairs of their brother burgesses. To advance by this means, however, a burgess really did have to display the kind of virtuous and influential bearing that helped to make peace for the community without letting his clients down. To later medieval eyes, success within social networks suggested effectiveness within the community because both were based on the practice or possession of honor, fidelity, and social wisdom, a kind of phronesis.

Overlapping though burgesses' social networks were, they show nevertheless that there was a tendency for influence to be built from activity, especially the privilege to arbitrate for someone. While this honorable office was diffused across the community, individual oligarchs and those men on the rise built up richer and more autonomous social profiles than even the more independent commoners. One is struck by the fact that social network analysis, indecisive as it in some ways is, affirms the closeness of this group of dominant men in the town. They developed another kind of friendship, which was built of common interaction, the shared ideological assumption in favor of group unity and responsibility, and of having often to listen to each other and negotiate together. Interest, obligation, and repeated propinquity could breed a kind of institutional friendship. The elite were often friends in power.

The final act of the Benet–Ferrour relationship bears this out. After so much opposition and conflict, these perfect enemies, who spent so much time together at court, in arbitration, witnessing the stewardship of the community's property, had some kind of reconciliation. We cannot say what it meant or how it started, whether it was of their own making or forced upon them by the mediation of the group, but these two influential men show up as arbitrators on the same side of three cases. This constitutes their last contact. At least in the public eye, their social selves were no longer considered a marriage of fire and oil, useful when kept separate, dangerous when brought together.

Benet was influential without quite making it to high office, which may explain the bad feeling that had existed between Ferrour and him since oligarchs rarely showed opposition among themselves. There are moments and exceptions of course, but the weakness of elite factions, if they existed at all, points to the cohesion of this political group, even under the stress of long and frequent interaction. Every one of the network maps I have analyzed shares one thing: the thickness of the lines, the frequency of the interactions that oligarchs had with each other. Over a long career of thirty years, Roger Chepman had three interactions with Henry Maundewar, Richard Peres, Thomas Jay, Thomas Piggesley, and Thomas Weye, four with Henry Sparkford and Thomas Hore, seven with John Newmaster and Richard Gros, nine with Walter Dyer, and fourteen with the omnipresent Richard Ferrour. Five other elite burgesses also figured in his inner circle. These kinds of robust relationships were typical. The center of an elite network diagram was a dense space in which that individual played a large role in concert with his fellows.

This gives only a blunted impression of the ways in which some of these men acted, thought and were symbolized together, as a group. There is something abstract about a group, even a community. However, the way that these chief men embodied the town as its symbols was constant, marked in the paper trail of documents and in the perceptible flesh of public meetings. We could argue long about what kind of friendship they had, but there can be little question that they were structural friends who often became personal friends, that they were socially defined by the prominent company they kept. They met not only at the burgesses' court and at its arbitration sessions, but also as jurors in the bishop's court, in the town council's seats in the parish church, and in the cathedral, where they might appear as lay witnesses, embodiments of the civil town for deeds touching on the common property. There was a high visibility prestige to their association. The pattern of witnessing and presence of burgesses in the cathedral records can be particularly instructive, for it depicts the men whose standing was acknowledged, and therefore reinforced, as high both outside the lay community of the town and within it. Possibly, too, these men could tap most easily into the social networks of the higher clergy with whom they are often associated. This seems especially so, when we see how often the dean and chapter of Wells Cathedral would have the Wells citizen elite witness documents that did not bear on the city at all. They still might conclude, as in a lease touching a parish church in Dorset, "Witnessed by William Vowel, Richard Dier, Thomas Horwode and Thomas Nabbe," four sterling members of the contemporary civic elite.[32]

John Broun and Thomas Tanner were both indisputably influential in the town. Tanner was perhaps the richest man of these years (d. 1401), closely involved in trade from Bristol, so a little less active within the city than Broun and others of similar prestige. They had only three network interactions in the court, but when we cast our research net more broadly, we can see a relationship of frequent contact and trust that combined into an elite friendship. They were arbitrators on two cases together, although as opposing players, one in 1379 and one in 1384.[33] In 1386, John Broun chose Tanner to be his first arbitrator in a suit for debt that he had initiated.[34] At this time, both were already members of the judicial leadership, but Broun did not become a master until 1391. From then on, he shows up in the ceremonial, real, but partial list of witnesses at the foot of so many documents touching on the town's property, when it was thought an important point of validation to have the city's seal and city fathers present and witnessing. Tanner was also often there. They headed the list of witnesses in several charters dated in Wells in the 1390s, images that encapsulate their physical and symbolic nearness.[35] While I have stressed the unity and nonfactional quality of the elite, personal prejudice could certainly coincide with general political aptness, and we can be little surprised that Broun's last act as master in September 1392 was to select Tanner to succeed him. On his next tour of duty in 1395–96, Tanner repaid the compliment by placing Broun in the master's chair once again.[36] Tanner chose Broun as one of the executors of his large estate, last and central proof of the friendship cultivated amidst the pleasures and trials of oligarchy.[37]

It is fair to say that in this case the sense of personal commitment and emotional attachment arises from the post-mortem role Broun played. This final act of friendship, one dying man considering which of the living men was most likely to protect everything that he has been—his goods, his family, his credit, for debts must be paid even in death—was Tanner's last claim on Broun. He accepted the charge. Without it, we should overlook the significance of the early association. With it, we are comfortable in reading their relationship as rich. What limits my entire project is the lack of the clear narrative elements of significance that point up what mattered. In this case, however, we can go beyond structural friendship, friendship in front of the world, social friendship, and leave all adjectives to the side. "Turne to thy freynd, belief not in thy fo."[38] The practice of oligarchy could lead from the art of politics to the pleasures of friendship.

I hazard this, then: it was probably not for sentimental reasons that John Broun asked to be buried next to Henry Bowditch in St. Cuthbert's churchyard.[39] Maybe the spot was near enough a favored icon, a favored view, his accustomed bench. But it seems to me less outrageous now to think that the friendship in life might go so far as to looking forward to reacquaintance on the other side, and that this was part of Broun's motivation.

Before leaving the elite, the place of the sorority of elite women in contributing to the social networks and reach of their husbands and households, has to be acknowledged. It's a darker place in the records, however. The prescriptive literature doesn't recognize any sociopolitical role for urban women, but they must have had one, as other elite women did.[40] When the town council had its annual feast, the master entertained the men, while his wife entertained the women, whose conversation would perhaps be more precious to the historian than that of the men. However, the women's involvement gave greater breadth to the entire community, played auxiliary links among households, but produced a social self for those women that was shadowy, thin, and dependent when compared to those of the men.[41] Still, as a group they had their well-gendered standing. In *Confessio Amantis,* a source wise to London if not sympathetic to the commoner, the poet Gower tells of how a citizen and his wife avenge the dishonor given to her by a lord by trouping to the king's court for judgment. "She goth to pleigne / With many a worthi Citezeine, / And he with many a Citezein. / "[42] Two parallel, apparently influential and coordinated networks work to succor and support the individual who could call upon them.[43] Behind their husbands, some women had networks that extended themselves, but these always worked behind their husbands and quite often for him.

Beyond the Burgesses

If the powerful women must be sketched dimly in the background of the borough's political picture, the numerous clergy of the town are less visible for more complex reasons. They allow us to question, just a little, the issue of social connections beyond the burgesses and their families, the point where the larger social group was left behind. Between clergy and commons there was a greater cultural divide than that which affected men and women within the lay civic community. The records of each—cathedral and city—were shy of the other. Social interaction between the lay elite and the cathedral and its related institutions was another matter. If a picture of autonomy was politically important to the town, especially from the bishop's power, the social and economic realities brought the townsmen into close and sometimes potent contact with the ecclesiastical elite of vicars-choral, canons, and the one parish vicar (selected by the cathedral). Conditions in Wells were particularly ripe. The cathedral was not the town's overlord although it owned much property in the city. It was a secular cathedral of well-paid, well-educated, and somewhat worldly clerks. Furthermore, the cathedral school had long found a significant place for some of the sons of the town. Indeed some prominent fourteenth- and fifteenth-century cathedral officers were from the city.[44] Since the twelfth century the traders in the temple had been a fact and the unsanctified nave was always a convenient place to gossip, to talk business, maybe even to talk about a book or a sermon. Those in the choir did not always appreciate the noisiness of those off-duty clergymen gossiping with the laity, "under color of purchasing goods exposed for sale there."[45]

Similarly, the churchmen went to the town to spend their money and for the company. When a vicar-choral was sanctioned in the fourteenth century for poor behavior it was likely to involve someone in the town. An unusually intrusive and effective bishop furnishes us with a peek into the life of a bad canon, whose better companions must have been similar enough to recognize how close they were to danger. Ralph of Shrewsbury undertook a visitation of the cathedral in the 1330s and much of what he found to complain of repeated the complaints of overly close relations with townspeople that had been more commonly recorded in the thirteenth century.[46] Ralph particularly took on Thomas Haselshaw, a canon resident in the city, who was accused of spending too much time in the wine bars of the town. Haselshaw's answer is rich: he denied it, except for a few breakfasts—perhaps a euphemism for low-alcohol—to which he had been invited by a few "great lords." Perhaps he meant the Earl of Devon or his family, powerful people often enough in the town for recreation and meetings of courts and officials. It is a classic excuse: invited—only three times—great lords. Nevertheless, it betrays other high-level social networks that embraced people. Haselshaw played a card that showed that *any* act could be made more licit if you were doing it with important people. In effect, Haselshaw was invoking common friends and a shared social network, his own greater importance, to resist the accusations of the bishop and other canons.[47]

At the same meeting a vicar, one step lower on the church hierarchy, was charged with "incontinence" with Christina Coteners. Although he successfully defended the claim, the woman was not from among the upper half of the town's social community and the little case points up the opposite of the Haselshaw defense: the interaction between laity and clergy that was barren of powerful pay-off, although very useful in its own right. To get food, friends, and the things that make the good time at the good price relies heavily on tapping into networks of good cheer. There was also large scope for secret and deliberately limited interaction where clergy and sexual relations were involved. Thus another woman who made no other mark on the town records also turned up a few times in the cathedral's: Cecily Pontefract, whose social self was neatly and classically marked by the phrase "of evil repute." Several canons needed to give excuses for their close relations with her and all were forbidden to let her into their houses.[48] Prostitutes no doubt filled a social as well as a sexual role. Adultery or fornication among the burgesses' families and within their world of interlocking networks would be terribly disruptive of town–gown relations. Rare among these and other cathedral city records are fornications between vicars and burgesses' daughters or wives. That kind of meddling was meddling not only with a woman but with a world: the poor, a prostitute, were those cut off from the potent networks of privilege and therefore exploitable by all of them.[49] These were people whose social selves were tiny and morally simple from the public point of view: whore. A little damage would be done to the clergyman but none to any respectable burgess or his family.

Of course many friendships that developed between clergyman and townsperson were quite different, playing on the exchanges sought by men of ambition, some education, and a good deal of pretension on both town and gown sides. This was so, for instance, when John Welshot and his uncle Canon Thomas Cornish worked together, cultivating and co-coordinating town and gown networks.[50] Such links, familial or not, could help to develop a man's social self beyond the local, toward county society. The gentlemen burgesses of these years were men who managed to connect with clergymen of importance as well as country gentry to expand their social selves to the point of leaving the town behind. Richard Vowell, master of the town, was only a sometime resident, trying to keep his local networks in Wells but seeking new and more exclusive associations. He never engaged in trade and was literate and even learned, a history fancier who shared what he knew and the documents he possessed with the scholar William Worcester.[51] A burgess' networks could be far flung and socially significant.

When townspeople and cathedral officials mingled in the city, the question of status based on group, of class, must often have arisen. The canons would have had little convivial social contact with any but the oligarchs, and the vicars-choral were probably the same. Our traces of even these relationships are relatively meager. This does not mean they did not exploit each other for support and friendship. It takes little imagination to see that good relations with a man of the first order (clergy) must always have been elevating, a badge of honor that could be worn socially. If Haselshaw grew by his associating with great secular lords, some secular people liked to subsidize a clergyman to round out their drinking group and raise their status. With serious matters, it was the same. Before burgess William Gascoigne made his generous contribution to help Bishop Bubwith's establishment of the town's almshouse, many sociable occasions must have been passed with the bishop's influential executors, who included a knight and two members of the ecclesiastical administration.[52] Another burgess, John Austell, had been there to witness the bishop's will.[53]

For most burgesses, however, such interactions were more clearly outgrowths of business, which crossed a line that ordination, education, and—so far as anyone knew—God's greater purposes, had placed: it was the kind of social line that did not exist among the burgesses themselves. Thus, it marks both the weakening of their networks at the point where they touched the broader society and the integrity of their own small, interlocked worlds. Strong as their selves were at home, to the superior orders of clergy and the gentlefolk, few burgesses were people to reckon with seriously. At that point, a starker hierarchy overwhelmed all but a few men. The context changed and so did one's self. Gascoigne and Austell had country property and connections and might walk the line but for most burgesses interaction with ecclesiastical dignitaries and country gentry and knighthood were businesslike. Whatever feelings we might imagine to arise in this kind of relationship, we need to note the class difference that made a great burgess of London, let alone of Wells, a questionably humble commoner to the grand eyes of the privileged.[54]

Similar considerations arise when the confessor–burgess relation is considered. Most often, one's confessor was a necessary friend and an unequal one.[55] Full of knowledge, he must be thought a potential social force, unevenly applied in practice. When John Welshot was locked in a bitter dispute with the town and its master in 1501 he had his confessor (and uncle) Thomas Cornish, intercede.[56] He was a cathedral canon, the parish vicar, a suffragan bishop and an Oxford official. Cornish intervened threateningly, invoking not only his own status, but saying he would have the case taken before the king's council no less. In this case, the triple power of family connection, spiritual overlordship, and connection to lords and lawyers near the crown were all being brought to bear. No doubt, the master of the town had some allies to interpose too. Inside the town or beyond, networks could be loyal armies.

Networks of the Modest

The theme of this chapter has been the social self as power network. Whatever people felt about friendship and the faith that it called from them, they deployed their social links for dominance, albeit of a subtle kind. For other people, association brought prestige, simply because you rubbed shoulders with the dominant, whether in guild hall, ale house, or parish church. The most powerful looked to expand themselves by cavorting with canons and county gentlemen. Looking away from the most prominent, however, this theme does not disappear, but retreats so that we can see social clusters that are simpler, the product of less ambitious social lives that saw protection in solidarity and were less able to dream of sowing themselves in distant corners. These are citizens sometimes closer in their ways to the unenfranchised craftsmen and laborers of the town.

Even within the small urban world all manner of exploitative and therefore reductive actions occurred—reductive because they shrunk and degraded your social self. Journeymen suffered at the hands of masters and the small social selves at the hands of the greater ones. As we have seen, the later medieval world saw through typological eyes, often organized by trades: some tradesmen were more vulnerable than others to the influence of the rich and important. Nevertheless, people used the occupational categories as social markers. "Thieving millers and bakers" were satirically imagined to have their own guild and chapel.[57] Women were even more vulnerable since their identities, even when they were skilled, were summed up by the designation 'wife' inflected by her husband's social type and her moral worth. "The Wryght's Chaste Wyf" says it all in its title, and carries this through in its plot, which reveals the nature of the vulnerability of the isolated humbler tradesman and his wife.

In that story a woman's beauty becomes the test of her virtue, when a procession of worthies—the lord, the steward, and the proctor—attempt to gain sexual favors while her husband is away. She locks them all in a dungeon she has handy and makes them work at women's tasks for their food. We can see here how a woman's virtue and a man's virtue were interconnected but quite different, but as importantly, we see what rights men of superior standing felt they had over the wright—a lowly carpenter—and his wife. A carpenter could never amount to enough socially to make him a person of great standing or worth the fullest social respect. Indeed, worries about his ability to protect/curtail the sexual life of any wife had kept this carpenter single for many years. The immoral but socially plausible disdain of the elite imperiled both the wright and his wife. How could they protect themselves? It is with such people, somewhat more common than those focused on so far, that I want to conclude the chapter. This will mean assessing their social networks and finding out both how their social profiles differed from those of the more influential and how they were related to them.

While trade organizations didn't exist in medieval Wells, the association of men by occupation was important for some and provided an immediate milieu of personal and social identity.[58] One trade can serve as a start: bakers. Bakers were by no means typically poor, but if we look to markers of political success—the attainment of political rank in the town—there were no bakers to be found among the medieval Masters of Wells until 1512. The best of them occasionally attained middling rank, maybe a rent collector or a churchwarden, but never a member of the elite.[59] They tended to succeed less than merchants, tailors, or dyers. But they could earn a good living, even in the flat demographic times of the later Middle Ages. According to a 1382 record, there were at least five bakeries in the town, serving a population of about 2,000.[60] That means there were at least five or six master bakers with shops, probably more, and perhaps as many journeymen working for them, not counting apprentices.

Examining the bakers reveals a quite different kind of social interaction from that which we found among the elite. Perhaps surprisingly, bakers do constitute a small group. They show up in each other's inner circles as litigants, arbitrators, supporters in difficult moments, even though it isn't actually clear from the work they did that they *need* have been close. Their customers were probably different, if occasionally overlapping, but they were often in the same market for goods and labor, competing for grain and employees. Sometimes needing skilled help brought them nastily together as they vied to hire the same journeyman. They must also have jostled at the assize of bread held in the town, where they went through the routine fining that amounted to licensing.

Small as the group was they moved in a common social air. When a baker got into a dispute, odds were good that another baker would be nearby. Of the twelve bakers in the network study fifteen had direct legal action with other burgesses. As usual, we should judge this as interaction more than as vigorous enmity. However, that probably crept in too. When John Newton sued Martin Baker for abducting a servant, we can be sure that lines of amity had been crossed and that bitterness had found a home.[61] Nevertheless, many of the interactions also involved arbitration. When faced with the prospect of finding arbitrators the bakers frequently turned to each other. This was a pattern common to the more modest trades. There is a kind of in-grown quality to their social networks. They moved together and identified themselves together, perhaps in distinction to the broader group or the elite against whom some insulation may have been desired. This kind of feeling may well be the social root of the unity that had elsewhere taken on the formal aspect of the craft guild, and that was available for economic, social, and religious purposes. As is well known, the great plays of medieval England, the cycles of mystery plays performed in the larger towns, were in the main productions of various guilds of craftsmen such as these.[62] Similarly, the processions of the crafts also helped to reflect the individual's identification with his occupation, the concept under which the body politic watched him.[63] From the peripheries of power too we can see the ways that your cocoon of friends was both the appearance of your social personality and the thing around which social definition, social dissent, faction and party could grow—if it came to that.

The bakers of the later fourteenth century were not wholly cut off from power and the establishment. They were not an out-group. Bakers were a fully respectable trade, cheat though they sometimes did. What the later fourteenth-century evidence reveals, however, is a kind of line of hierarchy that separated the regular bakers from their patron and leader, John Stoke. He shows up in several of their networks, but his contacts are limited and special. Typically, he was their guarantor at time of their admission to the citizenry.[64] His own career showed considerably more variety than that of contemporary bakers. Shortly after his admission in 1381, he was chosen as streetwarden, the lowest position within the town's civic duties, but a rung most men who advanced had first to touch. He did move on too. He was the kind of burgess whom all kinds of people asked to arbitrate for them. Never really near the elite in wealth or authority—the highest office he held was the middling position of churchwarden[65]—he advanced into the respectable middle and produced a network of contacts richer and broader than his baker buddies, for indeed, every baker who became a burgess in the mid 1380s used Stoke as a pledge. He was not so much their brother as their father, and certainly a patron. Very possibly he was their master, the man who had played father figure to them while they were apprentices, working as his nearly indentured servants, their ambitions tied to his good opinion and preferment.[66]

Stephen Skinner played a similar role among the small group of skinners in the same period. They were as closely knit as the bakers were. Like Stoke, Skinner was a middle-ranking burgess appearing often as an arbitrator from 1378 to 1385. He had a rich network across the community, but he played a large role in the interactions involving other skinners, frequently an arbitrator of their disputes. It has been said that arbitration was often left to those with adequate professional and technical knowledge, such as tradesmen of the same craft.[67] No doubt this is true, but what I would suggest is that Skinner's social skills within the craft may explain his presence at such crucial moments more than his knowledge of how to tan a hide. Skinner was typically on the scene when his craft brothers were in trouble.

Two similar examples should suffice to show this activity of the middling man bridging the tight little circle of humbler players and the broader community, adding to himself and protecting his brethren. In 1380 Laurence Sadler, in fact a saddler, sued David Skinner, who was a skinner, for having told him a black fur was valuable when it was worthless. Skinner turned to Stephen Skinner and John Skinner, both craft brothers, to work for him and presumably to defend the craft.[68] In 1392, Skinner was called as the principal arbitrator, first-cited as the more prestigious of the pair, on behalf of the skinner Martin Skinner, who had been accused by John Pestel of poorly furring a gown. His co-arbitrator for Skinner was the glover, Thomas Piggesley.[69] A couple of conclusions emerge from these cases and many others like them. While it would be very misleading to see craft affiliation as dominant in anyone's recorded social interactions, it could play a significant role for some, both in helping them to make their enemies—competitors vying for the same journeymen or apprentices in a moment of labor shortage—and their friends. The skinners pulled together when they were under fire, choosing their strongest man Stephen Skinner to lead the way. But his power, as that of the other middling example, John Stoke, was derived from the liminal position he held, strong man in a small pod of business and social life—the craft—but also a respected figure in the wider community. On a scale manifestly humbler than the oligarchical elite, but really different in quantity rather than quality, these men linked different pools and eddies in the river system of Wells social life. Your pool helped to make you and that enabled you to hide in the protective shadow of the local big fish, who was strong enough to swim the current between the rock sheltered pools, taking messages and making reputations.

The lesser men turned to their bigger fish to secure themselves from anyone who might press into their world and damage their business, but typically their own closest relations were founded on a narrower base of politically humbler connections. We can see their social selves as less extroverted, less overtly ambitious. They interacted often but with the same people. The social networks of the humble show us that there were two kinds of relationships with the influential people mixed within the one network. There were the cherished links to a stronger man, related by craft, to whom a man was a loyal member of a precinct. I've looked at prominent craft brothers in my examples. There were also the links to the more distant and truly influential townsmen—the oligarchs—who needed activity to enlarge themselves and their prestige, *regardless of its source.*

However, most activity in the humble social network points in a different direction. They revealed the small networks of equals, whether business rivals or partners and sometimes friends, with whom the more humble citizen was more likely to compare himself, to stand on his honor, to feel the touch of independence and importance. He was also more likely to confide here and to become confident in the support of trusted friends, even when they knew the whole truth and not because of any palpable quid pro quo. In other words, this is where he found his mates. We must walk gingerly. The social world of the later Middle Ages can all too easily seem stratified and pat; the claim of the craft, the patronage of a craft leader such as John Stoke, was mild indeed. People watched each other's business, expecting the nearly inevitable decline in a rival's fortunes, and when it came, they would not hesitate to take him to court or disdain his desperate lawsuits, to contribute to the public humiliation of the shrinking man. Nevertheless, at any given moment, even in a small context such as Wells, there were varieties of men, moving shoulder to shoulder, and yet with telling differences of extent. At least until the 1380s, Stephen Skinner was in demand; Martin Skinner, was always a distant second or third fiddle—and everyone knew it, hope as he would.

Conclusion

Ever since I began work on Wells, I have been impressed by a discrepancy that sometimes turned up when I read the records of central government in Westminster. Many of the men I knew from the Wells sources as 'merchants' were called 'chapmen' in London evidence. Part of how such determinations were made was based on the company a man kept and how people kept his company. To change context was to change who you were. A large lot of merchandise in Wells was little enough in London. This happened not only when the provincial went to London but also when the skinner went to court in Wells and was faced by the chapmen—now merchants, or the merchants who styled themselves gentlemen and dined off pewter. The social self was built out of ideas but these ideas were those made in part by the people around you in friendship or in enmity. A man's meaning was fluid and variable.

This chapter shows, however, that the differences among people based on their network of interactions and friendships were very considerable. The particular community I've been focusing on had the effect of knitting people into each other's identity. There are signs of people being practically involved with each other and within each other's social networks. The social selves of all these people—unlike those who weren't members of the borough community—were defined partly in terms of each other, the community. Again, I must stress that this is a sociological point, not merely an ideological one.

This density of the overall social network gave way to significant and revealing variations. Some men, preeminently the urban leadership or oligarchy, those who were most active in arbitration, had much more extensive social selves and social networks, which allowed them to act as the blood vessels of the community. Their political influence was rooted in their social activity. Others had smaller, perhaps more intensive social selves. We analyzed more closely the commoners who tended to be defined by their trade associations and who entered the broader community with a lower profile, typically aided by the prestige of a craft patron who facilitated their interactions. This marks the thinness of some selves and the role of middling figures who were able to parley their local knowledge and skills into greater social selves, respectfully engaged with the most dominant characters.

Repeated acts of support in a small scope reinforced the identity of a man with his craft brothers. Similarly, the constant meeting of elite men in the business of arbitration and government made it possible for some of them to build durable friendships. But in both cases and many others, these people in Wells were living patterns that may well have produced a convergence of social identity. People who started as question marks, significantly empty social tablets, would find themselves made into more and more deeply chiseled patterns of interactions and identity. Social groups grow stronger as people pass lives growing *toward* each other and sometimes stagnating into predictable characters and predictable classes. If this is so, social life and small groups may feel rather like private life: an age of formation and expectation, giving way to a pattern of life and an increasingly calcified, predictable character. In a tightly woven community, governed by a few large ideas and reiterated phrases, many of these personal patterns would become increasingly similar—only a little because of hegemony and a lot because of converging experiences. What cannot go without saying, however, is that there were a great many other social connections that helped to make a person's identity. Most vividly, however, the identity pursued in chapters 3 to 5 is that of the burgess, typically the small businessman—husband and father. Records determine this focus, and a focus is anyway needed, but we must now turn to see how the imperialistic self of these burgesses spread across the broader community to subsume those who had no political standing and a wholly dependent social position.

Appendix: Social Network Analysis

This study of social networks is based on a sample of ninety-eight burgesses who flourished in the community during the period 1377–1429.[70] This represents about one-fifth of the total population of burgesses in these years.[71] By determining the political standing of the various burgesses we can thus analyze their social and political networks in terms of the political mix reflected. I have employed four political categories, as in chapter 4: first, the oligarchs or high-status burgesses. The second and third political groupings consisted of those who had held civic office but not superior office. The *middling* burgesses are the churchwardens and the rent collectors; the *petty* burgesses are the shambles-keepers and the streetwardens. The fourth group is the largest, namely, the *commoners,* those burgesses who never held any civic office in these years. The random sample turned up seven members of the judicial leadership (oligarchy), ten middling officers, twenty-one petty officers, and sixty commoners. I should stress that for the purposes of statistical simplicity, I have determined membership in these groups according to the *highest office achieved* by that individual. This is somewhat distorting, since it smoothes out the differences in status, including among the elite's numbers their activity as commoners, but it is virtually unavoidable. It is also not strictly commensurable to the analysis of arbitration in chapter 4. The reader must, moreover, bear in mind that the gaps among the political ranks would appear sharper, their kinds of social networks more disparate, if it were convenient to consider separately each individual's court interactions at different stages of his career.

Social network analysis attempts to build facts by which we can analyze some of the relations and interactions of individuals and their surrounding groups. Contacts between different individuals are the primary data of this approach. At the level at which I am employing it here, the focus is on the shape of the social network, its density and intensity, and the function of individuals within the social networks of the town. Arbitration and litigation can be characterized as the two most relevant kinds of content to the relationships I am charting. Usually someone was either involved in a case as one or the other, less frequently as a witness or third party.

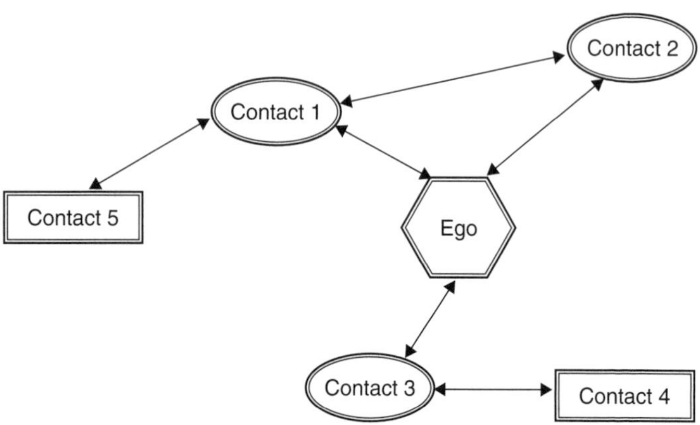

Figure 5.1   Basic network illustration

(See figure 5.1.) The theory allows one to read the relations of a case as a cluster of distinct binary interactions. Sociologists have developed many refinements and concerns over the content of social network exchanges. We should note here that our evidence simplifies or abstracts the situation. It did after all matter to an individual that a certain network contact was with someone who was your opponent's selected arbitrator rather than your own, but we can limit our analysis mainly to these two kinds of transaction (or 'content of exchange') and allow that all contacts are for our purposes equal and significant.[72]

I speak of social networks as those *demonstrable* social connections that can be viewed from the perspective of a particular individual. They are for analytic purposes alone presumed to be egocentric.[73] My conclusions, however, do say something about how the necessary mesh of the egocentric networks tells us something about Wells' broader field of social networks. Thus, a typical network is a map of the social terrain cultivated by an individual's court activity. At the center is an individual, and around him are those with whom he had official contact. First and most critically are those with whom he/she had direct contact, such as all the individuals in ellipses in figure 5.1.

This cluster of individuals—contacts 1, 2, and 3—I call the ego's *inner circle*. Those people with whom he is associated only indirectly—contacts 4 and 5—are his *outer circle*. These are connections mediated by inner circle contacts.[74] I do not try to trace social relations beyond contacts once removed, nor have I constructed the links among outer circle members.

Two features of a network's shape were explored. The first is *density*. This records the proportion (in terms of a percentage) of the members of an individual's inner circle network who had direct contact with the other members of the network (excluding ego from the calculation). Thus in figure 5.1, there was network density of one of three links actualized, or 33 percent. All individual cases necessarily have a

Table 5.2   Network density and intensity

Group	Network density (median)	Intensity (median)
Entire sample (98)	47.26	3.22
Oligarchy (7)	33.81	2.36
Middling officers (10)	39.88	2.92
Petty officers (21)	47.8	3.72
Commons (60)	47.3	3.41

density of 100 percent because in such a circumstance, everyone has contact with everyone else.

Network *intensity* is an extension of this. It asks for the number of contacts per member had by all the members of a pod, excluding ego. This has not been displayed in the diagrams. However, in figure 5.1, if Contacts 1 and 2 had two contact cases, then the intensity of ego's inner circle network would be four divided among the three inner circle members, an intensity rate of 0.667. Tables 5.1 and 5.2 summarize the findings of the analysis.

CHAPTER 6

BATTLES AT THE BOUNDARY OF THE SELF

Though the Earth and all inferior Creatures be common to all Men, yet every Man has a Property in his own Person. This no Body has any Right to but himself.

John Locke, *The Second Treatise of Government*

When a person reacts to a slight upon the honour of another, it can only be because his own is involved.

Julian Pitt-Rivers, *The Fate of Shechem*

The making of the individual through social interaction was the subject of chapters 4 and 5. We have isolated a context in which a person was fashioned amidst the needs and ideas of a group, its assumptions, and social practices. Congruently, it has become clear that the social control produced by these institutions and practices was itself limited by the individual desires that stand at the heart of all disputes. None of those disagreements began from lofty first principles. They developed from recent, irritating, and personal problems. The so-called structures include both the force of the habitus (the collected predispositions of a social world) and the consequences of everyone's individual choices and actions. As we have seen, these choices developed against the backdrop of hierarchy and differential public standing and they produced social selves of greatly varying scope and quality, inevitably made by converse with others.

This chapter looks harder at what these disputes say about the shape of the selves involved. The model of the modern self, especially the private self, is a kind of analogue to the soul: it is atomistic in the sense that every self is somehow separate, equal and of a similar quantity to all the others.[1] The social self, however, is a more fluid and varied thing. You could be more or less of a man within the public world of the medieval town. You could be more or less of a woman too, although that was judged by a different standard. The implications of status in urban society are clearer after the examination of chapters 4 and 5. Now the view from the individual's perspective needs further development if we are to see what mattered to a person, and what logic guided the variable self of social life. What I hope to suggest in this and the next chapters are the different ways that a social self marked its boundaries, like a cougar marking its territory as a challenge and a hope. I also want to indicate how a person found his or her own identity significantly intertwined, even confused, with those of others. They overlap whenever people challenged each other; but two people also ran together because of the bonds of fidelity and subordination that I examine in chapters 2 and 5. Within a particular point of history and geography, selves varied according to their dependence, their honor, and their gender.

Where selves overlap, there is room for dispute. Autonomy needed asserting. To establish their claims to recognition and power, people attacked, offended, and challenged each other in front of their community. Urban England was not a social world in which rank was cut and dried long ago: for most men it was constantly up for reappraisal. "Ultimate vindication lies in physical violence" perhaps because of the "intimate connection between honour and the physical person."[2] Theory and evidence suggest that reading some of the meaning of violence will expose the cartography of the social self. Examining petty violence will take us close to the self that existed within a hierarchy of values and individuals, whose boundaries were reflected in hard words and blows.

Petty violence is a closer relation to yelling, of cruel sarcasm, and of a snub, than of murder or rape. Putting it another way, petty violence is conversation continued by other means. This is not to demean the seriousness of the violence, but rather to take public words gravely. As Wallace Stevens said, "There's nothing, no, no, nothing sharper than the clashed edges of two words that kill." Running these two kinds of minor and endemic violence together will provide us with the kind of disputes through which social selves test their strength and their dominion.

Public discourse in the records we have is often quite negative about the disputes that involved the honor of mere individuals. Like moralists such as Langland, but for somewhat different reasons, medieval urban officialdom did not champion the individual. It saw pride and outrageous activity where we shall have to see the signs of self-affirmation and self-defense. Protecting honor matters when it is yours, but tends, like grief, to smack of the immoderate when it is someone else's: thus, sinful pride and cherished honor walk in lockstep. This suggests, however, that the stratum of value to be examined is close to the core of the autonomous self, which in the Middle Ages at least was not that autonomous or simple, but strove and struggled to be.[3]

"Words that Kill"

To understand small violence as continuous with communication is to see it as a social and emotional act, keyed to the details of status and personality, the desire to wound honor and identity as much as body. In terms of intentions, violent language is the nearest social relation to shoving, slapping, punching, and all that the puerile imagination can conjure up or recollect. A sizeable amount of the business of many courts across medieval and early modern England was in offenses of language: insults, slanders, accusations unpleasant and embarrassing, whether true or not.[4]

We must see words as actions, inevitably part of what Wittgenstein called "language games," cultural set-pieces, which follow something like rules, but are no more static than any other part of the world. Children take heavy blows mildly from the floor, but react with anger or hurt to their parents' correcting words or their friends' taunting: the pain is from the soul; the choice of appropriate response is a perfect instance of the mediation of private suffering and culturally purveyed strategies of reaction. Language understood correctly is language understood in light of a rich and changeable theory held by an interpreter of the world, a self. Slander is that act of language that asserts an interpretation of a person different from that which the individual holds. It intends to belittle you, to shrink your social self. This is the essence of much socially expressive violence.[5]

Slander and defamation are acts of violence executed by word. Neither in ancient or medieval Latin nor in modern English is violence founded on or bounded by a *physical* or *material* result. The essence of violence is the violation of personal integrity, of the self. Property, *propre,* own, refers to whatever your self drenches with its possessive identity. Besides, as R.H. Helmholz has written, "Men rarely fight in silence."[6] The outlook captured in John Locke's sentence at the head of this chapter breathes the minimal intuition that the self possessed the body and is not simply identical to it. Violence, the rubbing of selves, can reveal how people sculpted their culture.

Later medieval English people were very concerned about defending their honor and status—the trappings or code words of the social self. The impulse was nowhere stronger than among the commoners, especially the large, variegated middle classes. Kings and dukes rarely needed to defend their honor in the courts. Few were willing to challenge them. They stood more firmly in their clear hierarchical position. In the same way, the prelates of the church could act with perfect social confidence. At any rate, an attack against them was much more serious. It was a fundamental assault on the polity: for the royal family and all the magnates were individually important players in the nation in a way that no gentleman or cloth merchant was.

High treason protected the Crown; and the statute *scandalam magnatum* protected the lords.[7] To slur them was an act *across* the lines of social class rather than within a social group's internal hierarchical gradations: such a claim came close to denial of hierarchy and had therefore an almost revolutionary timbre.[8]

By contrast, for the vast majority of English people, who lived and fought mainly among their own small social groups, there was considerable uncertainty about status that was vented in insults, assaults, and defamation suits. Some have seen an increasing concern for "backbiting" over the fifteenth century, which suggests a mounting sensitivity.[9] Certainly, stretching beyond the medieval period the long-term trend was for more defamation suits.[10] Although a well-developed sense of status was a master social value, as we have seen, the location of an individual within that world was shifting and full of alternately attractive and frightening possibilities. Before 1500, slander was not for commoners an available charge at law in a royal court. It had, however, long been a large part of the business of other tribunals: ecclesiastical, local, and fraternal.[11] Church courts were especially busy with cases of defamation in the later Middle Ages, and particularly after 1450, verbal crimes increased as a proportion of those courts' activities.[12] There could be several hundred a year in London alone.[13] In the notions and procedures of the church courts, we see some of the assumptions broadly typical of defamation at this time.[14] The narrow legal meaning of defamation required that there be a claim or innuendo that a crime had been committed. There was, however, plainly some latitude in what the court could accept as sufficient to allow a suit. What was furthermore essential, however, was that there had to be ill will in the claim.[15] Plainly, here was to be the brunt of much of the evidence. Levity or ignorance might save the day.[16] In any event, you and your accuser staked your good names—what the community took you to be—in a public test.

The cultural significance of slander dawns when we consider just how rarely anyone sues to protect his or her name today.[17] Only 'celebrities' care and most of their cases are wonderfully absurd. Modern identity is determined less by rumor, reputation, and the prejudices of others in the public domain. We do not conceive of ourselves as standing in a particular order of social and political precedence with our neighbors.[18] Such considerations are less defining of who we are, but in the medieval context, these were fundamental.

It was the blending of a sense of hierarchy with the local ideology of fraternity that made the defense of honor in the towns such a pressing need for so many citizens. Although they believed in a hierarchical universe, and the importance of relative superiority within a group, there was at the same time no sure way of restraining the ambitions of other equals.

When perceived equals took contemptuous liberties of language against a person, then some legal recourse was sought. Since these were differences among people of one social group and not affronts across class boundaries, it was left to public opinion to determine where each person stood. As with arbitration, this was preeminently a social sin of equals who lived in a hierarchical universe. It could be, however, quite a violent and humiliating form of cultural negotiation.

We might say, then, that the making of the medieval urban self was given over to its social construction more than is its modern counterpart. The courts, which so few of us ever visit, even in a litigious world, are not primary organs of self-promulgation. In the small worlds of the later Middle Ages, however, the courts—at which so much business of a nonjudicial kind could pass—[19] were often the community's official voice.

It follows, then, that self and reputation were best defended in public places. The desire to honor the self in this way explains much of the heavy traffic against defamation that we find in the church courts of the fourteenth century, growing further in the fifteenth. Moreover, the social self was perhaps a more central part of the self in that period than it has become. Small communities exaggerate this tendency, just as large modern ones mitigate it. In 1400, your meaning was your name and what it conjured as a word in the mouths and ears of your companions. You were a bundle of perceptions in other people's minds.

Accusation and Aspersion

Any accusation of defamation in court was almost certainly the *second* act in a dispute over the public standing of a person. For someone to bring an accusation of slander forward was to acknowledge what the rest of the community already knew. He was already suffering dishonor because of a story making the rounds of the community's social niches: "from mouth to mouth in taverns and other places, everyone adding to the story and putting in his own bit."[20] The truth of the story may have mattered less than the need to quash it by calling your accuser into a public forum where he could be corrected, and where your reputation could be rehabilitated.

The desire to be restored to your former status was a prevalent goal. Indeed, it could be the entire reason for taking a case to court, as has been demonstrated in the context of the courts Christian.[21] A court examining an accusation against someone and finding them innocent of the claims might conclude magically by "restoring her to her pristine reputation," in a phrase meant to act as a social charm like so much of the law.[22] Wishful thinking perhaps, but it was at least official community vindication. Defending your status in the community in which you lived was therefore an explicit issue in many lawsuits, an implicit one in all. What is appealing for our examination of the social self is that the courts functioned as the voice of the community against the potent whispers of individuals, attempting publicly to amplify the truth about honor. As such, courts were clearing-houses for reputations. Of course, the courts' power could touch only the tip of the iceberg of reputation. If there was no accusation of a crime, a court's willingness to intervene was rarer, and it is not clear what someone could do about a malicious slander or false rumor that imputed no crime—the ubiquitous "backbiting" of the moralists. "Evil-speaking malebouche, because he sees only one side, pretends that he has seen the entire deed; and from having one word he immediately makes up an entire story out of his own malice."[23]

When Margery Kempe of Lynn was traveling through London, where she had not been for some time, she lamented a joke passed at the expense of her asceticism and sanctity. People were saying that Margery Kempe, sitting over a table of food, had said: "A, thu fals flesch, thu xalt ete non heryng," "and ther-wyth sche sett a-wey the reed heryng & ete the good pike." She had, they said, ostentatiously denied herself the cheap fish in order to eat the expensive one.[24] Rude and demeaning though the story was to this late-coming bride of Christ, she could only defend herself by entreating her teasers not to be so unfair, knowing that the persecution was at least penitential. Her London reputation had, however, been set in the cement of rumor long before she arrived. Nevertheless, for some kinds of claims courts could provide remedies, or at least a forum for a counterattack.

The social self is at issue here in a straightforward way. We see people taking action because they were being dishonored even where there was no direct concern for money or property. Not to act would be to settle for a debasement of your standing: and rare was the person who could act the lord and simply ignore the affair as unworthy of contradiction. The latter situation is a common one in the literature of honor, but was less likely to exist among burgesses who were all to some extent conceptual equals.[25] A beggarwoman and the mayor might have had such a relationship—rather as when Crazy Jane accosted the bishop—but it is unclear even there. If the muck stuck, it was probably worth trying to have the court scrape it off. It stuck if the public perception was that it was plausible or at least interesting. Nothing could undermine you so certainly as a good story or a clever phrase.

The means by which individuals, the church, and civic communities coped with insults of this kind when they did come to court was by recourse to an especially rich language of blame: the language of sin and subordinating relationships. A case from 1443 can illustrate this.[26] The participants were the butcher William Webbe, a burgess of at best moderate

status, who only made a handful of appearances in the town records, and
Richard Bordeaux, a blacksmith of greater stature in the town. Bordeaux
had been in the guild for sixteen years, was middle-aged, and successful. He
had already attained the political status of rent collector, the town's third
highest office. This made him socially significant although not of the civic
leadership. That was still ahead. Even now, however, it was the man of lower
political standing who was defending himself against the man with more
to lose.

The entry for the case records its end, and runs thus:

> On this day in the burgesses' hall, at the court of the master and all the
> burgesses, William Webbe, butcher, conceded that he had spoken badly and
> harmfully (*male et iniurose*) of Richard Bordeaux. For this reason, the said
> William begged (*supplicavit*) the said Richard, out of respect for God and for
> charity's sake, in view of the entire meeting, that he earnestly hoped he
> would pardon him his abusive language (*maledictum*) and the slander (*verba de
> dicto Ricardo malelocuit*) he had spoken. Then the said Richard, at the request
> of the master and burgesses, remitted and relaxed to the said William all the
> said fine and evil deed (*malefactum*) on condition that he never in the future
> publicly or openly say or proclaim defamatory words about Richard, such as
> he previously spoke so violently and harmfully, on threat of 40s. sterling to be
> paid to the current or future Master within two weeks of the relapse. And the
> said money should be applied to the restoration of St. Cuthbert's Church.[27]

We have no idea what Webbe had said to spark the dispute, but it was a slur
with public consequences.

It was not just that a court was an effective place in which to counter
false slanders and accusations. The community, the brotherhood of
burgesses, had a moral role to play by concentrating public opinion in order
to restore the 'proper' order of things.[28] It was their mediation, at least in the
rhetoric of the text, that drew Richard Bordeaux into forgiveness. From the
standpoint of public opinion, the seriousness of Webbe's guilt is such that
only the sublime force of religion could move Bordeaux to forgiveness. It is
a due regard for God, and the appropriate earthly reflection of such a
respect—charity—that is sufficient to let Webbe off the hook. It cannot
have been a deserved leniency. It is a matter of grace, and grace can be given
only by one of clearly superior standing.[29] God gives us grace. Beauty
graces our ugliness. The ability to offer grace, without it being a joke, is the
mark of the person of higher degree and superior honor. In other words,
the typical structure of a Wells slander case's conclusion underlines the superiority of Bordeaux for the good of Webbe. There was, however, another
benefit offered to the wounded Bordeaux: the community asked a favor of
him. They requested his indulgent leniency, and offered to view him all the

more favorably for that kindness, his graciousness. Ethically, it was obviously to his credit of good works to soften his heart and charitably forgive his offender. The final clause directs any future fine toward a religious purpose and so underlines the sinfulness of the deed as well as the lack of material gain for the aggrieved, and now gracious, party.[30] Formally and culturally, it was a matter of pure honor, but also a pure gain of golden social profit.

The evil nature of the offense is almost palpable in this formal extract, which hammers home the concept of evil or the bad: *male, maleficere, maledixere,* harm, injury, violence—the damage done to integrity, to the individual by vicious, deliberate words, words, words. The few of these in the text contain seven ways of indicating that the weapon of offence was language. Explicitly, too, the text tells us that language, a supremely social thing, was clearly capable of violence. Sticks and stones, indeed. It is the powerful tool of a slightly literate population and of a roughly literate fifteenth-century town clerk who were not subtle in writing. Their rhetoric was not humanistic but assertive. Writing at such moments was dominated by a rhetoric of ritual. It flamed up, circled insistently, repeating, whether in the same words or others, the same ideas.[31] Inhumanistic still, they did not write to express, or to get cozy and precise, they wrote to reveal and re-enforce the world's ways: the routines, the realities, the rights. The social perception is not left in doubt. Words could be evil, violent, and endlessly damaging. They did not even have to tell us what the words were. Their business here was the redistribution of honor and the adjustment of particular social selves in accordance with the demands of authorized order.

The Symbolic Content of the Accusations

In one of the richest cases of urban insult that has come down to us, the wardens of the London mercers' company called to account two brothers, both prominent City mercers and politicians for disobedience and their "ungoodly and inconuenyent langewage."[32] John Shelley, sheriff of London, called his elder brother Thomas a "fals harlott, knave and dryvyll [fool or kitchen servant], and said that he neuer was his trew begoten brother but as oon founde and Chaunged at the landes ende." To which Thomas had replied that John was a "horeson," and then he "japed and mokkyd his saide brother of his Shirrifhode, callyng hym boye Shirrif."[33] In his study of ecclesiastical courts, Richard Wunderli noted that "whore, thief, and bawd" were the most common slurs.[34] These were not usually directed, however, at spiritual brothers, let alone natural or changeling siblings. Sexual accusations or rumors were by far the most common in London. Their use in these situations was simple symbolic abuse rather than a comment on some people's livelihoods. Studying smalltown women, Rodney Hilton found that "women's principal form of aggression was vituperation," and sexual language was the most commonly resorted to, but usually women, not men, were called whores, even when sexual epithets flew in nonsexual circumstances.[35] Carol Clover, however, has found that one of the main kinds of insult among saga-age Icelandic men was the imputation of a femininity that suggested powerlessness. They said, in effect, that you were not really a man. In Iceland you could be outlawed for such slurs.[36]

What is so striking in this barrage of inverted fraternity is how each brother does use sexual language to debase the other. Surely they were the sons of different mothers, half-brothers, willing to challenge the lineage of each other by attacking their respective provenance from women of ill repute or fairies? The effect of these barbs is symbolically to dissolve their brotherhood, and to blacken reputation with unbridled sexual insult, and particularly with the taunt of feminity, for there was no clearly masculine language that was commonly employed for sexual sins.[37] The language for demeaning another by recourse to sexual vices was formed especially from the schedule of typically *female* vices. The lack of the continence and fidelity that were thought to be woman's special virtue was here transferred to attacks on men. Thus, they each called into doubt not only their origins in women of ill repute, but their privilege to be judged and considered as men, certainly as true and faithful men.[38] Boy sheriff, like the boy bishop of Yuletide games, was an ignoble person who acted for a joke as the opposite of what he was. Similar to innuendoes of the feminine, this slur took the masculinity of leadership and high public status away from John Shelley. This was a great tussle between near equals, brothers, but of different age. We can feel the kind of history that already existed between them, but they scandalized their community with their anger notwithstanding. Their roles as powerful men, rivals in both the company and the city, provided them with the appropriate rhetoric of attack: assimilate your opponent to the properly impotent—immoral, unrespectable women, fairies, children. Laura Gowing has argued that insults, especially perhaps "sexual insults, as public social dramas, might perhaps be seen as one of the repetitious acts or performances that. . .constitute gender."[39]

There were different ways to imply that someone's public stature was less than that person supposed it was. In most medieval towns, the most common slander for men was 'thief'.[40] This struck straight at the central 'value' behind power in small towns: honest wealth. Indeed, there are no detailed accusations of carnal or moral offences captured in Wells cases. Perhaps the Wells scribes scrupled to record worse if less actionable particulars, preferring to hide behind the ritual of outrage we have already noted. Accusations of defamation existed in part to deal with the potentially fatal charge that a man who lived and throve by commerce was a crook. In the midst of a heated dispute about the penning of oxen and who actually owned the animals, Geoffrey Bosard called John Churchstile "a lying thief."[41] Richard Spray said the same of Adam Taillour, but threw in "rascal" for good measure, thus giving us a good sense of the tone and texture that must have informed many of these uncivil exchanges.[42]

These commercial slanders attacked the basis of much urban honor and the reputation upon which a livelihood was founded. Commercial activities provided great scope for the abuse of trust, as townsmen themselves were most likely to note. A York case reminds us that usury was also an issue. It is obvious that—in a world that founded honor and power on commercial success—the claim of unfair and un-Christian business practices could be very damaging.[43] In the York case, the arbitrators who decided the suit wanted to quash any repetition of the claims that would hurt the good fame of the prosecuting party whether "publicly or secretly."[44] We see here the appreciation, not always captured in legal proceedings, that private words running "secretly" as rumor through the veins of the town's social networks could also wreak havoc on a reputation. Thievery and usury both meant reducing someone else (their wealth) by dishonorable means, and may well have been used in this sense, rather than of strict larceny.[45] It is the violation of a proper commercial and personal reciprocity in favor of the one-sided appropriation. It was a characteristic fear of the urban commoner, whose livelihood was not rooted in the soil, often not in his or her own person, and so could be carried off more easily. It was taking what you would not have gotten by honest act or right. Plainly, verbal violence could have material consequences even if it did other damage as well. Wealth and power suffered whenever reputation declined.

The blurring of verbal violence with physical violence occurred partly by the assimilation of both to the rhetoric of social sin and moral outrage. Another well-detailed case can exemplify this and point us forward toward 'real' blows. Thomas Hampton was accused in 1484 of obnoxious treatment of the Master of the town, Richard Vowell. This highlights the public and collective interest in the case—the attack on authority. He was accused of acting against his burgesses' "oath and faith," and this meant of having perjured himself, a clear and common religious crime.[46] Thus, the mundane dispute intensified and shifted into the theater of higher moral life. This moral and religious quality is apparent in the claim that he was "incited by the Devil" to yell "many very vile and shameful words to the shame and scandal of Richard Vowell, then Master of the entire community of this city. . . ."This final phrase is unusually expansive and is such just to stress the implications of his error and the object of the assault: not just Vowell but all the burgesses. Furthermore, Hampton's manner left his intentions beyond doubt, for "he spoke repeatedly, wickedly (*enormiter*), and arrogantly (*contumeliose*)." To cap it, the entire hall of burgesses was in attendance and understood his words—whatever these were.[47] Thus, we have within the public forum itself the attack on the reputation of Vowell in his role as 'superior man.' For these words and Hampton's tone were simply inappropriate directed at someone vested with high office. The context made the words an assault, nearly a battery. In many cases, the symbolic content turns out to be a function of the attack's distortion of the proper relationship between one man and another. Form becomes content.

The language is particularly overwrought here, and perhaps Hampton's was too, but probably it only extends the sort of feelings of rage and avenged humiliation that were all too common in slanderous situations. The public quality is also amplified because the guild as a whole reacted to the attack whenever the Master of the day was dishonored. At such moments, slander turned into rebellion, close kin of treason.[48] It reminds us that this was the conceptual slide that allowed verbal assaults on the king to become notionally worse than felonies and nominally as death-worthy. This was not a feature of government per se but of a society of degrees. Hampton was a man of standing in the town—a town councilor for eight years, but he too was caught by the customs of social standing. The person of the Master was superior and that meant he needed to taper his language appropriately. What might be acceptable toward one man was unacceptable spoken to another. Different social selves deserved divergent deference.

The exasperation that the community expressed in defense of its leader reflects in distorted shape the 'arrogance' of the individual. To us this arrogance is nothing less than one person's refusal to conform to the group when his sense of self, his integrity as displayed in his bearing and past words and deeds, needed vigorous defense. *Contumelia* meant outrage in classical Latin, but it had early and literally meant physical violence. In medieval Latin its meaning shifted toward arrogant outrage, but the sense of affront, egocentric aggression, in short, violence, still breathes in the Hampton dispute. In that case, the tenor of words probably moved from probing and defensive to violently offensive. When bad enough, the slander changed from a sin of wrath toward arrogance and the deadliest sin of pride. From Hampton's perspective, however, an attempt to assert, perhaps in anger, a claim for due consideration of his name and position in the town was rebuffed, indeed crushed, by the perceptions and powers around him. In frenetic form, Hampton's ambition and humiliation represent a mode of social relationship that was ongoing, and in which the meaning of a man was calibrated somewhere between his dreams and his social milieu's interpretation of his acts and his history. He struck out for his name and they struck it down.

While the various court scriveners were lured out of their collective reticence by the affronts toward the regime and its leaders, their more casual and quiet discussion of routine slanders wholly conforms to this picture. There is little reason either to imagine that they differed much from the common burgess of Wells or any late medieval Englishman. Success and self were tightly bound up with status. In the later Middle Ages, moreover, social mobility was more frequent than it had once been; a person's status was more subtly evaluated and consistently needed shoring up through alliance, reputation-building, and wealth. For the urban man, the desire to survive and perhaps grow wealthy could only be fulfilled by retaining a good reputation. You might have to yield to the forces of the collectivity, from whom you derived more of your status and support than you might have liked. They considered your standing and your character, and they slandered and defended you as was appropriate to the symbolic protocols and social relationships of this particular urban context.

Petty Violence and the Hierarchy of Selves

The link between slander and physical violence is one that I hope does not seem like a far reach after sampling the flavor of the language and apparent perceptions of defamation. This is not to equate the two kinds of affront but it is definitely to associate them. One word that does this with helpful ambiguity is insult (*insultum*). This word has shifted increasingly away from its origins in the clearly physical—jumping, possibly trampling—toward its current meaning as mainly verbal injury. In the Middle Ages, it was making its transit, but still seems usually to have meant an attack or a blow. It is on the cusp of the physical, but remains clearly violent. In 1486, we learn that Thomas Hethfelde insulted or assaulted (*insultum fecit*) Robert Grantham. The phrase "against the King's peace" suggests the spirited blow as much as anything else.[49] When, however, Richard Ferrour accused John Barstaple of a trespass during which *insultum fecit,* we must decide whether there was a physical attack (our civil assault), actual blows (battery), or simply angry words (our insult).[50] The most common usage, however, suggests there was at least the attempt to strike.[51]

The violence we are going to examine consisted mainly of slaps, punches, and shoving. Sometimes, however, it had the potential to become almost as serious as the case of the Curteys family (cited in chapter 2), and this threatened especially if weapons were involved.[52] Insult might be physical without actually involving contact—the modern common law notion of assault, without battery. The case of Fox versus Brigger of 1477 involved slanderous language, but the primary charge was that Fox had drawn a knife on Brigger. He did not strike him.[53] William Pewterer was accused of a trespass and assault (*fecit insultum*) by Thomas Vowles because he "violently struck [Vowles] with a pitchfork." This was so serious that it is surprising that it came to this court at all, especially since "Thomas was seriously injured and despaired of his life."[54] The case may have been sent on to a royal court. More typical was William Hancock's dagger attack on Robert Draper. There was no physical harm and the peace was reconstructed with a compensation gift of "two gallons of ruby red wine."[55] Suggestive of the role of personal temper in these embarrassing displays of manliness is the case three years later in which the same William Hancock was accused by John Bordeaux of having drawn possibly the very same dagger against him.[56] Indeed daggers appear to have been the urban weapon of preference,[57] simultaneously symbol of authority, proof of a fear of violence, and here in the hands of Hancock clearly a means of effectively raising your voice—if not winning your case.

For the most part burgess petty violence occurred without weapons and so without the large risk of actions getting beyond intentions and leading toward disaster. As such, the recourse to blows or slaps was not thought extraordinary, or unusually vicious. What did it mean, then? Such violence was not special or typically threatening to the broader community. Acts of violence only fit into this category when they were attached to an attack on the civic leadership or other constituted authority. Thus in the case of Thomas Hampton's nasty language cited above, he was expelled only because the object of his attack was Richard Vowell, Master of the town.[58] With the one exception of a case in 1385, the more severe sanctions commonly imposed or threatened by the court were *not* routinely used for cases of violence.[59] Other things were more egregious in the community's eyes. The sin in violence—verbal or physical—was lesser; the offence more personal, more humdrum. This reality makes me speak of beating as a form of conversation or socially charged communication that reflected deep personal concerns but few civic ones.

All accusations of physical violence that were brought to the community court shared a color of slighted honor, just as defamation cases did. Otherwise, they could differ considerably. The language used to describe violence in these cases is actually tamer, less vivid than many of the slander and defamation suits. The devil is left out of it. The words most commonly used, sometimes next to *insultum fecit,* are *percussit, verbaravit, vulneravit, male tractavit:* hit, beat, wounded, and mistreated can stand as basic translations. The legal plea was inevitably trespass,[60] although there were sometimes other issues complicating the case. We can see the offences radiating out from a person's body. The first and simplest category, which includes the weapons-offences cited above, contains those simple attempts to strike someone else's body, successful or not. Thus we learn that in 1408 Thomas Cook, a weaver, charged the somewhat more prominent weaver Richard Trote with having "struck him with a punch and shoved him." They went to arbitration and peace was reestablished.[61] Matthew Fletcher complained in 1379 that Ralph Tucker and a friend met Matthew at the nearby village of Binegar and, in some unclear context, attacked and beat him. Arbitrators were appointed.[62] A nastier accusation was made by Thomas Smart, a fractious burgess, against William Chamberlain in 1394. Smart said that Chamberlain threw a stone at him, struck him, and split his head open with inevitable loss of blood. Again, typically, arbitrators were chosen to "make peace between them."[63]

At other times, however, the violence against a person was really against his property, as much a part of a man's personal domain as his body, name, or family. In 1494, Martin Brynscombe accused a group of burgesses of having broken into his house armed with swords and daggers. There was both the threat of lethal violence and the actual violation of his own space, his home. The case sounds interesting, but we learn nothing else except that it ended in "peace."[64] Similarly, John Bowyer accused Ralph Averey of housebreaking, although no weapons were involved.[65]

To extend the field of violence further, from real property to animate, there is a case from 1396 involving the rising political star Richard Gros, who would eventually become Master of the town and was already its constable. Gros sued Adam Dodesdene for trespass, accusing him of entering his close at night and killing his dog. Arbitrators were called in to patch it up.[66] Houses, closes, and animals were defended in court as much for the affront given to a burgess as for their financial value. This was, however, only one form of proprietary association. There were other aspects of value construction by which projecting individuality into the things of your life— reputation, house, close, pets, chattels, family, and friends—enriched and *extended* the individual. It is by this process, as much as any, that a person finds him or herself saturated in social life and, eventually, caught up in disputes. The later medieval town was a fertile field for sprouting this kind of individuality. There were enough goods conspicuously consumed and flaunted, even if an unstable mound of wealth and reputation supported them all.[67]

The competitive aspect of these selves (possibly rooted in a masculine notion of honor or masculine nature) led to many of the altercations I have been discussing. Resentment at airs assumed or of small advances in local society, all could add a splash of bitters to relations that may have had many other reasons to be difficult or ambivalent. One of the best ways to antagonize or assault someone was at his extremities, that is, by striking not his own body, but those of his dependants. Examining the petty violence against women and servants can make this clear. In her survey of the culture

and ideology of later medieval violence, Philippa Maddern astutely noted
that status was crucial to the use of *licit* violence. The view prevalent in later
medieval Europe, and certainly in towns such as Wells,[68] was that violence
carried out against authority was contrary to the established, God-ordained
order of things. As Maddern argues, however, this "bore hardly, though not
invariably, on those lower on the authority scale, such as women and
servants."[69] We have already seen that in Wells verbal or physical attacks on
the town's officers were the kind to raise the bile of the court recorder and
the traditional values he embodied. It was in such cases that the guild used
its more serious sanctions and ejected the offenders. These were considered
cases of "rebellion," punished more severely than any other community
offence.[70] Similarly, the bulk of slander cases was either between equals or
was a matter of the superior man defending himself from a social and economic inferior. This suggests not that influential people spoke sweetly to
their inferiors, but "according to their degree," that is roughly, arrogantly,
but justifiably so. Furthermore, there was another kind of social differentiation at work in the guild and the town. Overlapping the grand game of
individual subordinate to Community, and individual burgess vying for
status with his brother burgesses, was the household hierarchy that included
the burgess' dependants, those bound on principles of fidelity—when
virtuous—to be part of his world and his identity, so closely bound that
for them to turn murderously against him was from 1352 legally petty
treason.[71] The world of burgess-centered households was fully suffused
with the burgess-husband's proprietary leadership. The people and goods of
his household were socially extensions of his ego. Women and servants were
plainly noncitizens. However, they were second-order members of the
Borough Community. Their actions, their words, and their wounds were
within the jurisdiction of the fraternity because of their relation to a
burgess. For burgesses' wives and widows there were also considerable privileges and responsibilities to the fraternity. They too were bound by its rules
and attendant at its court for all their disputes. Moreover, they also had to
act through the head of their household, a burgess so long as he was alive.
Widows were the only women who could act in the Borough Community
in a legal and public capacity for themselves and the burgess' household
they had come to head. It would be as wrong to see women as outside the
community as it would be to see them as full citizens of the town. In an
important sense, the members of the guild body were households, not individuals, or, more accurately, selves that extended beyond individuals to bind
people into small groups by partially common identities.

"*Another* has two senses," said Aquinas, and one is "someone who is not
completely other, for in a sense two people merge into one another."
He goes on to cite domineering identities that characterize child and father

and father and servant, but notes that husband and wife are also so bound but in a spirit of companionship rather than domination.[72] Or perhaps, following Ockham and even Hobbes, we could say that spouses had a marriage of cooperative domination over the goods and people of their households. This comes too close to arguing for their equality, for we must certainly note the hierarchy of the household, even allowing for a deep sociological and psychological identity among its members. Within this social milieu, the household constructed social identity for its inmates.[73] But not equally—there is something acute and true in the nonphilosophical outlook of the Merciless Beauty, who replies to her suitor with a sense of another reality of a wife's life, that: "Fre am I now, and fre wyll I endure;/ to be Rulyd by mannys governaunce, for erthly gode, nay! that I you ensure."[74]

The reach of social identity, the imperial stretch of the master's social self, certainly entailed his servants, although with more ambiguity than it touched his blood relations. There must have been many gradations of fidelity here, from intense—like a son, like a brother—to nearly nothing, but there was plainly a sense of responsibility. Moreover, as Rosemary Horrox said, "service could confer honour, but it was also expected to engage the honour of those involved—lord and servant alike."[75] The master who forced his two apprentices or servants to marry after a seduction in his house understood that he would be judged by the comportment even of his employees, especially those younger ones who lived in his household and under his patronage.[76] Indeed, this moralistic sense of masculine honor had much to do with the restraints and limits placed on men, even within their homes.[77] The ties between head and members were emotional and could be powerful: he was himself at stake.

William Beverley, archdeacon of Northumbria, knew this in his blood. All the witnesses agreed on the details. Beverley had killed an unfortunately placed layman. Nicholas Skelton of the bishop of Durham's household had threatened to "break the head" (*frangeret capud*)[78] of one of William's servants. Beverley overheard and interceded, saying, "It seems to me that you're talking about my servant; I don't want you to break his head because you don't have the right [*officium*] to chastise him like that."[79] Skelton met the threats that followed with a knife, and after he had been restrained, he cried out to his own servant, who must have known that the dispute had turned dangerously criminal, "Kill William, that untrue priest."[80] The servant, loyal even though the seriousness and the unacceptability of the act were by then clear, attacked the archdeacon ("Truly you're going to die, lying priest"), who in trying to defend himself killed another who tried peacefully to intercede.[81] This story is a good one for our purposes, for these were not close blood kin, but men called by their masters "ribaldus," "famulus," "serviens."[82] As critically, however, this fatal exchange shows that on both sides it was natural for a master to take offence when his servant was threatened and for a servant to reciprocate and come to the criminal aid of his master's designs. It is in this sense that I mean that people were for purposes of public life and public action bound into each other's identity.[83]

The cases of violence involving members of different burgess households are surprisingly numerous, mainly involving physical violence.[84] The use of violence points up the way that social position determined the liberties and possibilities that individuals had in their relations with others, both within and outside their own households. We can see the ease with which violence was sometimes used, as well as the passionate, resentful feelings that were vented against those of lower social standing. A man was vulnerable at the edges, among those who were under his dominion. Lowest were the servants, who typically had no rights within the borough guild. They were typically without independent social status in the city, especially those who had not yet established a home of their own. For our purposes, the key fact is that they only occur in the Borough Community's records as an extension of a burgess' business, household, and sense of self. Servants are rarely named in the fraternity's records, and this accurately reflects their impersonal standing. Your legs don't have names either, however much they do your bidding.

That could be an unpleasant role for the servants, many of whom suffered physical abuse while executing their master's business. The cook William Pynchon beat a servant of Adam Carlton, another cook.[85] Thomas Belnap attacked William Bugworth's employee;[86] Robert Webbe attacked the prominent Nicholas Cristesham's servant, apparently because he was hunting for Robert's sheep and had killed a lamb. A fuller account would probably reveal this as one of the disputes over adjacent land in which animals were getting loose on someone else's pasture or fields.[87] In this case, the damage to chattel and the attack on members of a burgess' household are well balanced. There were other cases of this sort.[88]

Sometimes the interchange was more serious and a man asked for financial compensation for the loss of his servant's labor. Therefore, in 1403, Henry Maundeware complained that John Freman broke John Colston (his employee's) arm causing him to lose his "service for the whole of Lent."[89] Like all of these cases, the court asked the men to choose arbitrators, as it tended to do whenever identity, honor, and bad feelings complicated a dispute. One thing is worth highlighting, however: the court had no interest in compensating John Colston or any servant directly. Thus, if there was a self to be redeemed directly it was that of the man of greater degree, the burgess-employer. The servant's dependent self, even though the wounded body was his, was rewarded in the guild context only by the profits of subordinate fidelity.[90]

These servants were suffering while going about their master's business but some of the alleged violence against servants is harder fully to understand. It is possible that it was physically real, but may have been only in a burgess' wishful imagination. The end of the fourteenth century and the early decades of the fifteenth were in Wells a time of scarce labor.[91] A number of cases indicate the value of servants just because opposing masters were fighting over them. In this period, the persistent attempts of employers to control employees were often frustrated.[92] The charge often amounted to kidnapping, which is a little hard to believe, but the claim was common in royal courts too.[93] Either way, however, even when a servant had a high value, they did not become the kind of person you treated with a great amount of dignity. In 1407 Richard Lichfield, a fishmonger, accused John Romesy, a weaver—whose cloth industry was particularly desperate for help—of taking a woman servant from him against her will. The kidnap was denied; the arbitrators called.[94] In an altercation that involved some violence, Hugh Baker seems to have removed a servant from Adam Baker's house, possibly as an act of reclaiming him.[95] Arbitrators fined William Janyn for his "sin" in having carried off the goods and "servant" of William Welyknowe.[96] Again, it is difficult to be sure what happened. Perhaps the usual civilities were violated or ignored, while the servant—treated here quite like a woolsack—was pulled or dragged one way or the other. The bakers John Newton and Martin Baker had disputes that involved the enticement of a worker from one employer's household to another, and even though no man-handling was implied, all such contexts were plainly susceptible to violence against servants, male or female.[97] A man had to react to the theft of his servant's labor, even if the employee consented, because it so obviously challenged a businessman's social standing. After all, he was publicly made into the cheapskate, the man who was less willing to pay, or—and rumors started here—less able. Therefore, this assault not only deprived him of part of his household and business, but potentially of part of his good name.

The status of servants is strikingly low in the urban conceptual and rhetorical framework. Of course, we know that some servants, especially apprentices, could be emotionally important to their masters, and all were contributors to the household economy.[98] At the same time, however, cases involving violence do clearly deal with these unenfranchised residents of the town as if they were nonpersons. In the eyes of the privileged burgesses, as noncitizens, that is what they were. In this limited cultural domain, they were only appendages of their master, without a separate identity worth acknowledging. I must stress, however, the obvious: assaulting them occurred more casually than striking a burgess, but it was not precisely acceptable. If it had been, it could not have been a charge in court that a servant was beaten or otherwise interfered with. The sure lesson, however, is that it was only unacceptable when the *wrong* person hit them. The conclusion is that only their master or his agents could *beat* them with ethical correctness.[99] Servants' subordinate status crystallizes with the fact that no one was ever charged in the burgesses' court with having *spoken* roughly either to or about a servant. No one, therefore, doubted their lowly status, and probably all tended to treat them as roughly as they treated their own servants. It was impossible to insult one, but to strike one was to insult a burgess who would have to stand up for himself-as-servant. Although many cases were probably dealt with privately, the fact that the burgesses' court considered this kind of case underlines the low and dependent status of servants, as well as the high position of the burgess' household as an extension of his public identity.

Servants were on the bottom of protected society; barely worth notice and treated rather like chattel, regardless of their sex. The place of burgesses' wives, however, was considerably more nuanced, perhaps confused. Nevertheless, they too, can be shown to have suffered considerable amounts of violence of a petty but possibly a frequent sort. Domestic battery was a set piece of medieval English literature, whose interpretation is famously difficult. Alison, the wife of Bath, beat and was beaten; Noah and his wife break out into two brawls in the Towneley cycle, one as the ark—and apparently, God—waits.[100] Women appear in Wells court records as often in cases involving violence as in any other. Only widows acting in defense of their rights are mentioned more frequently. Not surprisingly, wives were more central to the burgess' own identity, and protecting them—as the guild as a whole was willing to do for burgesses' widows—was a higher value than the protection of servants. Symptomatic of this, wives were more frequently mentioned by name, for their names had value in the community. Unlike servants, they could be slandered, verbally offended, and were worth defending.

In a case of 1391, William Boucher sued Walter Dyer for a complex trespass, involving the trampling of a load of woolfells and the abusing of his wife.[101] Stephen Skinner's complaint against William Pedewell was simply that he had spoken abusively to Mrs. Skinner. That was enough of a trespass. The Master told them to choose arbitrators.[102] These cases are relatively infrequent, but that the court heard any such cases established wives in their second- but not third-class ranking in the Borough Community.

The protectiveness that men showed to their own was but one side of an aggressiveness, the acceptable bounds of which are hard to determine in almost all contexts. Formed through the male-centered household, the power of the social self was, as we can see even from our infra guild evidence, a masculine power. Those working on subjects at the boundaries of masculinity, where it ended, what it was capable of, have sometimes argued that masculinity should be viewed as full of sexual predation and physical aggression.[103] Knowing that such urges and possibilities did lurk probably has much to do with the historical dynamism of the patriarchal and protective world of the burgesses, the world of couverture, the legal subordination and protection of the members of the burgess' household, preeminently its women. Sensing the elemental powers of masculinity at prey, historians have suggested that medieval masculinity made men dangerous, at least symbolically and in fantasy. In reality, however, as McSheffrey has argued, respectable men, and I would add, the men who aspired to civic honor, the men who ruled and led, were constrained to be civilized and civilizing, which generally and collectively meant to supervise the sexuality under their control: their own, their men servants', and their women's. It was not right, nor well rewarded, to run wild.[104]

Nevertheless, the vulnerability of women to assault within the acceptable ways and without was considerable, suggesting a much broader field of licit, unactionable attack. It is naturally among the harsher cases of physical assault that we get a sense of this facet of later medieval culture. Striking women was, like striking servants, a more habitual response, for men certainly, but perhaps also for women.[105] There is no prima facie reason to think women dealt with each other by other lights than men dealt with women. Both were perhaps more likely to talk longer with a man, especially one of higher social standing and to move more quickly and excitedly to their hands when they spoke to a woman, even a burgess' wife. In 1395, Walter Elys attacked Christina, John Grysel's wife, for which assault the Grysels wanted 20s. compensation. Unfortunately, the arbitration award was not recorded.[106] William Fayre complained that William Rydon had attacked him and tried to drag his wife from his hands.[107] Ominously, two years earlier Ralph Averey had accused Rydon of violating him by first entering his house, and then attacking Averey's wife while he was there.[108] Certainly where there are cases of people walking into another's house and hitting his wife *in front of* the husband, it would seem that striking a woman was common and habitual for some. Another case involved somewhat broader violence. John Thomas apparently attacked—literally "thrashed"— Mrs. Edward Forbour and her son. In this case, we do know the arbitrators' decision. Thomas was to pay 2s. to Edward Forbour, and was threatened with a 50s. fine if he acted badly in the future—a week's wages for a laborer; half a year's rent for a poor cottage, significant but not a great sum.[109] More crucially, it was Edward Forbour who brought the suit and won the damages, not his wife. She was part of his social self. " 'Sir,'. . .said [Margery Kempe], 'I am of Lynne in Norfolke, a good manys dowtyr of the same Lynne, whech hath ben meyr fyve tymes of that worsheful burwgh and aldyrman also many yerys, & I have a good man, also a burgeys of the seyd town, Lynne, to myn husbond.' "[110] Such was woman's identity.

Many of these cases give a glimpse of the very father-centered household that reflected the burgess' identity as it breathed and acted. The assaults on the servants and these on the wives seem often to have been in the line of business. For most burgesses their place of business, whether a cordwainer's shop, or even a weaver's or dyer's, was in or near the home. This naturally made the wife a crucial part of every business. When the husband was away, at market, fair, guild house meeting, or wherever, she was the ruler as certainly as a baroness ruled the castle when the baron was away.[111] Mrs. Adam Baker seems to have been defending their castle and bake-shop in 1379, when Hugh Baker, a rival, appeared to carry off one of A. Baker's servants. Mrs. Adam Baker tried to intercede on behalf of her family and was struck for her trouble. It seems only proper, of course, that the guild court protected her for acting so vigorously on behalf of a burgess. The details were presumably more complicated. Adam Baker had probably enticed Hugh's servant away with the lure of higher wages. Hugh's wife was also somehow involved, because the arbitrators declared that all four should exchange ritual kisses of peace. Future delinquent behavior by the men was to incur a fine of 6s. 8d., but if by the women, they were to pay 10d. to the altar of the virgin Mary, a fraternity popular with the women of the town.[112] Was the women's fine less because less was expected of their behavior? Possibly, but it was also so because women's violence was less disruptive of the city.

A similar house and business dispute provides us with one last illustration of violence involving burgesses' wives. Richard Ferrour, the prominent, litigious burgess, sued the much humbler William Knyght, probably a dyer, for trespass. He accused him of having placed some garbage, the leftovers from either dying or brewing, next to the door of Ferrour's house. Ferrour's servant complained and was for his trouble shown the pecking order of the town and culture, when he was beaten by Agnes Knyght, William's wife. At least, so ran the accusation.[113] This reminds us at any rate that the disciplining of children and servants within the house very likely was at least partly the wife's prerogative, and there was for a burgess' wife, something wholly natural and customary in taking a switch, a stick, or the proverbial back side of her hand to a neighbor's servant.[114] In those moments, she may well have wanted to slap the neighbor himself, but was socially and morally limited to taking it out on the servant.

Two schedules of value are clashing. On the one hand, there was an assumption that women—especially wives—and servants were eminently beatable.[115] Home truths: the male-centered family gave the right of the rod to the father and husband over his wife, children, and the other members of his *familia,* principally his servants, although the cultural and legal facts limited this use to a 'reasonable' one. Courts were harder on men who crossed the line than on women.[116] Dominance worked through language and blows that could be administered without blame. Maddern has forcefully outlined this aspect of late medieval culture, showing that from God downward there was violence that was licit and even righteous when executed by the appropriate authority. Penitence practiced on the body was another form of readily understood, impressive, disciplinary violence: the rebellious individual scourged himself just as the king or the father in his household beat his wife, his children, or his servants.[117] The key is to see that such authority was not only public, as aspect of government, but that it was about the fundamental structure of hierarchical obedience that composed family units and social interactions as well.[118] It was not that all people were quick to use their hands, but that they knew it had meaning and that it did a job of reflecting the hierarchy, order, and fidelity of the family and society. Bishop Bekyngton's statutes for the adult vicars-choral of Wells do not discipline them by violence, but those made for the child-choristers suggest their dependent and subordinate status by envisioning violence against the boys. If after repeated warnings and chastisement to attend their lessons, they continued lazy they were, "if necessity arise, to be flogged."[119] The schoolmaster, like all masters, had this authority.

Nevertheless, the family that held dependent social selves in check also defended those selves against others. For to assault the members of someone else's household was to demean and dishonor that household's head and all its members, all those positively engaged in the master's identity. The very man who was their own best disciplinarian protected the second-order members of the household. Nor did husbands have a monopoly on the right to protective violence. Wives we know beat children, and learn here that they felt quite comfortable beating neighbors, rivals, and servants, preferably someone else's.

It is at this point that the idea that petty violence and rough talk are kindred symbolic complexes looks most accurate. The appropriateness of cunning, of gossip, of violent language or words depended also on the social context, on where you were and who was watching. It mattered whether you were in the hall, in the shop, in the street, in the church, or in the convocation meeting. In any circumstance, tense speech might elide with harsh speech or violent action, but it was the particular situation that determined what effect it would have on the social selves involved.[120] Most crucially, it depended as much upon who you were and whom you sought to attack. Historians have recently showed that when it comes to sharp words, gossip, and slander, women in later medieval and early modern England played a considerable role in shaping the social self.[121] Of the sixteenth century,

Laura Gowing says, "Telling stories and judging morals made women the brokers of oral reputation."[122] It seems true of earlier times too. Even within forms of subordination, there were diverse powers open to different kinds of individuals.

We do not know how often violent acts came to the court only because they strained the definition of proper and licit violence, that is, because they crossed the boundary of how hard a person was allowed to hit someone.[123] We can say, however, that since the most common cases involved violence between burgesses, followed by violence to wives and servants, recourse to prosecution was determined by a sense of violation based on assumptions about status and identity. Within the egalitarian space of the male citizens, it was, apart from the leadership, hard to tell who was so much higher than thou that thou mightest not take a poke or swipe at them. Whoever was assaulted in this way, however, knew that he had something about which to complain. Just to think you had the right of violence over another man insinuated debasement, and was an insult. For a man to strike a woman or a servant, however, was acceptable within his household but was elsewhere a presumptuous theft of another's own rights and possessions. Barbara Hanawalt found in her examinations of felony prosecutions that the courts were generally tough on women who had dared to accuse a man, as if they usurped the standing of men by being so forward. The courts were considerably less prone to convicting women who were themselves accused because it considered them inferiors who were *naturally* less likely to rise up (and perhaps more worthy of mercy too).[124] Once again, we see the predispositions of habitus and social structure shaping different kinds of agency and the framework of interpretation through which people would read women's social identity. The rules for reading were strongly gendered, differentiated by status and the social role that a person currently held within the household that gave dependants much of their social identity.

The social self runs out across the society, protecting words, things, and people, even places by which a person defines himself. By examining the expansive social self of the burgesses, however, we have seen that the others in Wells whom we can know only dimly—servants, modest journeymen, the unemployed, women—would have had different self-understandings. The master value of fidelity and the customs of the community and its courts subsumed them. Someone else defined them: masters, parents, people whose agency and integrity were distinctly richer than theirs were.[125] Wives, children, and servants would have found this kind of subordination to be in some ways clearer than the stratification in which their husbands existed. This is only a partial insight, however, for these dependent members of the household participated in its honor and worship. Here again we see the intersection of different schedules of values. Status in the household modified gender role. The social self was a factor produced by multiplying gender by the standing within the household and then by that household's standing in the community. People acted and were evaluated according to the independence and the extent of their social selves and these selves were forged and burnished by the words and fists of their social world.

CHAPTER 7

SELF-POSSESSION

He bar a bordon ybounde with a brood liste,
In a wethewynde wyse ywrithe al aboute;
A bolle and a bagge he bar by his syde;
An hundret of ampolles on his hat sette,
Signes of Syse and shelles of Galys,
And many a crouch on his cloke, kayes of Rome,
And the vernicle bifore, for men sholde yknowe
And se by his signes wham he sought hadde. . . .

Piers Plowman C-Text, VII, 162–69

When the ladies were separating for the toilette, he said to Elizabeth,—

"Do not make yourself uneasy, my dear cousin, about your apparel. Lady Catherine is far from requiring that elegance of dress in us which becomes herself and daughter. I would advise you merely to put on whatever of your clothes is superior to the rest; there is no occasion for anything more. Lady Catherine will not think the worse of you for being simply dressed. She likes to have the distinction of rank preserved."

Jane Austen, *Pride and Prejudice*

The Outer Skin: Clothing

Chapters 5 and 6 try to show the ways in which social selves were constructed from each other, by and through other people. By contrast, this chapter is an attempt to see how the material world was appropriated to social selves and how the social expression of self took essential material forms. Every act of work, of walking, of giving, of adorning, was in part an injection of self, a marking of territory, a singing of the body that was me-in-the-world. "Oh, how much cost is bestowed nowadays on our bodies and how little upon our souls! How many suits of apparel hath the one and how little furniture hath the other!"[1] When William Harrison wrote this lament upon English customs in 1577, he was a late example of a religious and moral sentiment ignorant or disapproving of a long-lived feature of the culture.[2] When Joan of Arc put on her pants, it marked and made her destiny, her difference from the other French girls, her calling. Her judicial trials circled around her clothes and she was eventually condemned for them.[3] When Margery Kempe donned her headdress of gold pipes in early fifteenth-century Lynn, it was a projection of self, and its ethics were social rather than religious, inarticulate but deeply entrenched, albeit cast in an unfamiliar key for us and a contemptible one for the William Harrisons of the world. However, the crucial point is that the clothing mattered. It has been argued for early medieval culture that "materialism. . .utterly permeated every facet of social and personal experience."[4] The later medieval self also remained naturally expressed and understood through the things of the world.

Margery Kempe was, as she insisted, the daughter of a worshipful burgess and sometime mayor of Lynn. He had probably been a merchant. What did she say when her confessor asked her during her years of showy dress: "hast thou ben prowde of any gyse?. . .Of party hosen, of pynkede [peaked] schone, Of fytered [slashed] clothes?"[5] Certainly, she was affected. She converted her soul and changed her clothes. Working with a precise and precisely wrong and inverted sense of her social world, that mother of fourteen children moved from the ostentatious dress of a burgess wealthier than she, to the equally ostentatious dress of a symbolic virgin, pure white, that is, a woman purer than she according to the eyes of her town of Lynn. She suffered sorely, complaining to God when he ordered her to wear white: "A, der Lord, if I go arayd on other maner than other chast women don, I drede that the pepyl wyl slaw[n]dyr me. They wyl sey I am an ypocryt & wondryn up-on me."[6] This was an extreme case, but it allows us to begin to see the form of life that played around clothing, possessions that were understood to reflect you. Clothing seriously opened out onto religious choices, social claims and ambitions. Thus, it could be "socially dangerous" or, morally questionable.[7] It was not a matter of mere aesthetics. Clothing and other personal 'appurtenances', as a medieval deed have would put it, constituted a distinct domain of freedom in the medieval town where people made choices.[8] This means, nevertheless, that it was a domain in which people worked accustomed tracks of symbol-making, publicly known possibilities, through which identities were asserted, challenged, denied, and recalibrated in vigorous discussion with the surrounding social context.

What we see in the later medieval urban scene was but the sharp end of a spear of social change of which all English people were conscious. It was perhaps the paramount social fact of the period—the radical and uneasy social transformation under way even before the plague, since the growing commercialization of the economy.[9] Then the acquisition and spending of money became a common mode of personal social revolution and social expression:

> Man upon mold, whatsoever thou be,
> I warn utterly thou gettest no degree,
> Ne no worchip abid with thee,
> But thou have the penny redy to tak to.
> If thou be a yeman, a gentilman wold be,
> Into sum lordes cort than put thou thee;
> Lok thou have spending large and plenty,
> And alwey the penny redy to tak to.[10]

The England into which this perceived social upset was injected was an England whose commercial economy and towns, especially those that were growing, were heavily engaged in cloth-making. Wells was such a town, marketing thousands of cloths a year.[11]

Two things follow from this: in a poor, nonagricultural world, clothes were the quickest way to mark your pretensions; they were significant items of consumption, portable wealth, and calling card; they could project considerable wealth, but they were by no means merely a consumer item or a utilitarian one. Clothes were the special social currency of the age. They didn't depreciate as they do now. Cash on the back, they communicated with all the punch of poetry, the variety of prose. They linked pan-European fashion to the roots of the English commercial economy—wool and cloth-making. In towns such as Wells the later Middle Ages, say from 1250, were made by the success of cloth-making, and whether or not people were wearing purely local products or fancy foreign wears, they understood cloth's complex language, and spoke it to good effect. If they could, they wore lots of it, multicolored, with purpose. It was a good investment in your self.

Second, however, if the nouveau riche's pretensions made poets uncomfortable, there were many others who worried that money allowed status to be dangerously usurped by the simple expedient of *wearing* your way up. Clothing riled; it succeeded. However, its effect was almost too good. Many historians have been properly fascinated by the sumptuary legislation of the later Middle Ages. These were those strange-looking laws limiting who was allowed to wear which furs and which color cloths. Many of their details are relevant to this study, but two larger points must be made more pressingly now. The legislation was a failure. People's dress could not easily be controlled, especially away from the court. Furthermore, however, it was not about keeping the middle class down or about simple class conservatism. It may well be read as a social compromise, which acknowledged the fact that wealthy merchants as well as those rich in land and titles ought to project a strongly honorable public image through their dress. A wealthy townsman, whether merchant or artisan, could act and dress like an esquire or gentleman, according to the 1363 legislation.[12] The social scale was acknowledged by all to be shifting, now incised with money as well as blood and royal preferment.[13] In other words, it was legislation to uphold the kind of stratified society that prized ordered, but not static, hierarchy.

Clothes were assigned to roles, to estates across the culture. And eyes were well trained to read the scenes of display and procession. When worn as uniforms, clothing bolstered hierarchy by instilling the idea of conformity and order and by underlining the formal occasion and the clear-cut, ritual group. It aggrandized the self by association with a more prestigious group or individual. There were moments of detailed choreography available to anyone who lived in a medieval town, especially a cathedral city, and people were connoisseurs of public displays of the cloth. While it is unclear how many people from the local community regularly attended services in the cathedral, when they did go there was much to see. It is certainly true that there was much there upon which to look. And since a mainly illiterate culture soaked their religion up through eyes trained to color, symbol, and subtle, unlettered hierarchies, then the processions of vicars-choral pursuing the host around the great nave was an occasion for splendor and the symbolic construction of the identity of Christ as well as his servitors.[14] A regular attendant of the cathedral would watch the colored vestments of the participants shift from day to day, the complexity of clothes from service to service. Advent indigo blue for all, except that on the Ember Day the deacon and subdeacon wore white, a foretaste of Christmas itself. The choir screamed the martyrs' blood by wearing red on St. Stephen's day, Holy Innocents, and St. Thomas's day. But it was green and saffron for St. Sylvester and indigo and white for the feast of St. John the Evangelist. Meaning laced through the usual routine of life and this variety was only a part of December's lineup.[15] Trooping of the colors and interpreting attire was a regular and complex fact of urban life.

In such a formal procession the boys and men became their official roles. They capture the stereotype of the central Middle Ages, the image of clothes saying exactly who you were without saying anything about the person in particular. They were vicars or altarists or choristers, canons or bishops, pure ecclesiastical servants with their identity tempered only by the ritual calendar. Such people were supposed to be utterly precise and conforming in their dress. Their actions were governed by rule, not merely by convention, preference, or fashion. These social selves benefited so much from their class that they had to yield much of their individuality in order to conform to the group and strengthen it. But context was crucial: "The Vicars are not to go into the market-place nor to the fish and meat stalls in their choir habits, nor, on the other hand, shall they appear in church without them after the last bell has gone."[16] They nevertheless were always to be in distinctive clerical dress and haircut, to show they had a share in the "royal priesthood."[17] Eyes would be on them.

In practice, however, churchmen tried to give themselves the little touches of independent personality that came naturally given their family background and the urban context. They wanted to be the men their spiritual status had truncated. Sometimes vicars would carry swords or knives like well-heeled laymen, often enough to be warned not to.[18] In the rules crafted for the cathedral choristers—children or teenagers—in the mid-fifteenth century, Bishop Beckyngton particularly warned these boys off "the lascivious, inept or vulgar [clothes]. . .now being worn in the world, as for example pointed shoes, long stockings, narrow sleeves and cassocks scarcely long enough."[19] The laity also noticed how the clergy used fashion to cultivate secular status and values. Chaucer's ecclesiastical pilgrims cannot forget their secular status, who they might have been in the outside world. Plainly, they understand themselves in that worldly context, especially when moving among the laity. The monk rides with his cloak held by a luxurious gold pin, "ful curious"; the nun's cloak is as elegant as her table manners.[20] The church worked and hoped to drive out the previous social identities of its members, but the persistence of strong social selves, predetermined by background and attracted by an increasingly seductive secular culture often came out in the clergy's adornments and accoutrements.

It is no surprise, therefore, that citizens and burgesses across England also placed a high expressive value on clothing. Not only were they willing to go to court to recover the costs of a cloak or a gown, but they were items that were worth bequeathing, worth considering even as you tottered on the brink of the great journey. In the great litany of giving that followed the death of even a modest person, clothes found their place, along with the cloth from which they were made, the lands, the cash. Margery Churchstyle, a Wells citizen's widow, gave a friend her hood of fur-lined murrey.[21] The social climber, Richard Gros, marked his friends with his finest clothes—his "best" gown with its hood to John Pope, the second best to his brother-in-law.[22] These were not his large bequests, but they were nevertheless thoughtful and personal ones that assumed that the men who received his used clothes would wear them, perhaps parleying the cast-offs into the cast-off honor of this successful merchant and man. Another oligarch of the period, John Horewode, gave clothing to several trustworthy friends and relations and the details leave a strong impression of the colorful Horewode. Parts of a grand, social self were dissipated, dissolved into his legatees including his relation John Schephurd. However, theirs was a reflected glory. Horewode was a dandy of power: He must have strutted the muddy streets, tripped through the offal, in socially bold, power gowns. One day he was blue and green, trimmed in white fur. Other days he wore black-furred yellow or simpler blue or green gowns, followed perhaps on Saturday with a striped gown, adorned with dark fur.[23]

Ambrose Edgere, a modest burgess who died in the early sixteenth century, prized two, more subdued suits: "a gowne of sade tawney with saten of Syprys, with a doublet of tawney chamlet" and "a gowne of russet furred with fox." He may have preferred the richly subdued style that the sixteenth-century merchant was to prefer, sad, serious, in tune with a new ethics, in which merchants showed their wealth with a discretion that set them off from other classes.[24] When these men moved around town, whether in the procession that left church—oligarchs marching behind the priest while everyone else watched them—or when they walked alone or in a group in the market on their own business, you would notice them and know them. In the late fifteenth century the great master John Atwater walked the town in a favorite violet gown, which he gave to his confessor, the priest of the Trinity in the parish church. Here the ecclesiastic flourish and the mercantile linked. To be a somebody in town was to look like a somebody, even if you were a priest, even if that somebody was the dead John Horewode or great Atwater.[25]

Some of a town's set occasions enabled this social beauty pageant to intensify. Our eyes revel in the linking of identity to physicality; that is the basis for a good parade, and in the fifteenth century, it was even more obvious, as the cathedral routine suggested. Churches were a focus for the formal walk. There were corporate occasions such as the walk to and from church, in which councilors attended the master. Daily, early morning attendance was the custom for the elite, and we can imagine twilight scenes in which the pious and important emerged colorfully against the drab of the morning.[26] When the priest was done and the recession was underway, it was the master and the oligarchs (at least the town councilors) who would follow him out in their Sunday best for the gathered parish to watch.[27] Elsewhere, the potent ceremonial ridings at Midsummer, Corpus Christi, and St. Peter's allowed men to show their best and assert their place.[28]

But other routine occasions allowed a less corporate, more purely personal assertion of self. The town's courts would all have been other regular occasions, probably weekly, for the jostling of wardrobes. When the master was standing by the market cross above everyone else supervising a royal proclamation, he was dressed not only in his fancily embroidered clothes, his silk touches, and well-furred gown, he was wearing the live but faded color of monarchy, and yet it was somehow his too. And in leisure too, then as now, people probably had the most time, aside from the church service, to figure out whose clothes showed best, whose showed prosperity, whose showed wear. It was a valued privilege of the burgesses and their wives to be able to stroll the grounds of the bishop's palace, taking a turn along the pretty moat.[29] The air was pleasant, the surroundings calm and grand, but it was also an occasion for viewing. It was a low-key social spectacle. There were watchers and watched; often a person was both. These were high-end moments, and we need not multiply them to make the point. There was pure sociability possible and pure business, but in both kinds of occasions, there was the eye's assessment and this had to be met by bearing and by clothing.

This was not just a free-for-all of exploration and self-promotion—wear what you will; claim anything. There was a standard of socially accurate attire to be followed, beyond which you were likely to feel the scorn of the neighbors, as Margery Kempe did. The poor were to dress poor, and few thought it appropriate to raise the poor up briefly to look and act and be as the rich were. The principles behind the sumptuary legislation applied here. There was no doubt among respectable people that everyone should wear and spend according to his or her degree. That is why the rich burgesses typically willed their finest clothes to other richer burgesses, those of clearly respectable and substantial reputations, or close relatives. Otherwise it would have been little more than a joke or insult, a game of inversion like the cathedral's boy bishops during Pentecost, Advent and other times of the year.[30] You dressed what you were.

Looking as you should could make you socially useful and paradoxically powerful in the case of the poor, the other group regularly given clothes as charitable bequests. Such gifts were usually connected to funeral arrangements, especially the cortege, "the highly visual part of the ritual."[31] The donors were often at pains to specify that the clothes be those that were appropriate to the poor. The symbolic poor at John Horewode's 1416 funeral received russet gowns, the cheap cloth everywhere marking lack and humility, a sharp contrast to the coats of many colors that he had always worn.[32] Richard Horsford's 1405 generosity to the poor who would attend his body also specified russet clothes (as well as shoes.) This was virtually the universal uniform of subsidized poverty.[33] Dressing the poor in their proper uniforms served to underline the social order. However, the decision was more dynamic than that. Charity was only socially efficacious when it was clearly visible. The charitableness of the gift required that the poor *be* poor to receive the goods, to wear them, and to display the dead man's religious thoughts. Freshly, if cheaply dressed, paupers would be available to the public eye, placards to a dead man's piety. Furthermore, they would march in the funeral cortege and offer the deeply desired prayers of the humble that rich men needed for their purgatorial compensation. Again, the rich, even in death, get to spread their personae across the landscape of the town, and order the display of the poor person, whose very clothes are chosen by the dead man. It is a great irony—the power of the dead in life, the power of the great dead seeking the humble, and lording it over them even in their baseness, even as they needed their prayers.[34]

This amounts to appropriating the poor. The properly dressed poor became an active investment—through charity—of the richer burgess, a kind of advertisement for his soul and his self. The wearing of livery—the insignia, colors, or costume of a great lord or organization—played an ambivalent but parallel role. Within the language of clothing and identity that we have been exploring, the livery worked as the clerical pageant did but in a way that spoke of earthly power alone. A man might wear the livery of the king, of a guild, of a religious group, of the bishop, of a great lord engaged in the high and dangerous politics of this unsettled age. Whose badge was it? You were his man. For as Frédérique Lachaud has argued, "Clothing was of foremost importance in sustaining the household hierarchy."[35] Obviously, then, the meaning of the livery would vary greatly depending on your perspective. One of the bitterest testimonies the age provides is that of Richard Cely the younger, who worried: "Syr, whe ar grehytly envyd: I trwst [to] Jhesu whe schaull be abbull to wythstonde howr enmys. Syr John ys in grehyt trobull, and God knowys full whrongefully, and *parte of them that whe gawhe gownys to labors moste agayne hym.*" Clothes given to mark and retain people in an affinity were failing to the dishonor of all.[36] Plainly, however, the risks being taken by those who would shift their politics were wagers on their social selves.

In the urban context, the alliances of lords and their politics were viewed with considerable suspicion. They could undermine local values and powers, the little game of urban life overwhelmed with the serious and tougher politics of princes and their retainers. To put it in our idiom, the great social selves of the realm could undermine the locality by occupying too large a place and squeezing out the corporate community and the local leaders and burgesses. In suppressing such aggregates of social selves, the localities had an ally in the monarch,[37] who urged the towns to avoid the connection to magnates and who looked suspiciously on urban associations and guilds themselves.[38] In 1438 the burgesses of Wells had rather solemnly made clear that their obligations to each other could be imperiled by those who acted in favor of some liveried affinity rather than their group.[39]

From the individual's perspective, however, adopting the livery and badges of a lord, a guild, or the town was a physical marker of a political identity that was associative rather than independent: Not your own man, but more of a man nevertheless. It was enhancing even if it was often subordinating. The most typical urban connection was to a wholly urban association rather than any individual, which plainly added a little without yielding much. The burgesses would march in symbolic unity for entries of kings and bishops. Here the impression they made as a collective was the point. Nevertheless, within each man's own circle the competition of represented self could ensue. There were, in other words, moments when the social self sought amalgamation and gained from it, and others where the same self would be cast solely on its resources and pretensions. Even in fashion, timing turns out to be everything. Knowing which occasion was which, was of some importance to your success.[40]

Here is a story in which clothes, honor, politics, gender, and slander come together. As I have argued, it was expected that your accidents–dress, manners—fit your essence. If your social self were solidly among the poor, certain clothes would be deemed presumptuous, absurd, or somehow detrimental to your honor by misleading people about your essence. This was a grave issue for women, whose social identities might be understood purely in terms of a sociosexual honor, which might be narrowly described and more easily and decisively overthrown—recall the wryght's wife. This Cely story is only gossip, a story meant to undermine the family by besmirching the mother, recently widowed. Richard Cely the younger wrote from London to his brother in Calais, where a rumor was current, that "howr mother schowlde be maryd or in the whay of maryage. . . .[T]hay sayd howr mother schulld go on preschesyon on Corpus Kyrste Day in a cremysyn gown and hyr mayny in blake."[41] Women were more vulnerable to this kind of rumor: it insinuates that even though her husband was dead, a new marriage would be unfaithful because of her undue haste. It is telling that the occasion for the public change of the wife from chaste black to hot, harlot red, was imagined to be the public procession at the feast of Corpus Christi, the march of the sublime body of Christ, a moment when the true body, the true person was revealed. At such places and times, judgments were made, and they were adjusted by fitting realities to proprieties. The case is accentuated here because the world would see that the father's household stayed true in black mourning better than his wife, which was a kind of salting of wounded fidelity. "There's grief in the kitchen, but there's mirth in the hall" as an anxious man's folksong goes.[42] They said, Mrs. Cely's clothes were to be crimson as she pursued the body of Christ through the town. This was a symbolically rich distortion of the relicts of the elder Cely's social self, all in malicious imagination and raunchy gossip. In fact, Richard added ruefully, "at that day. . .sche whent at owr fathers monthys mynd." These were the acts and occasions for making and undoing social selves, clothes moving through their social world, announcing themselves and risking themselves.[43] Expressive social personality was everywhere, but it was nowhere free from the social gaze that determined your value in the world. In making your value, it affected that of the dead, and that of your relations, testing your judgment, your honor and your loyalty to the others with whom you were identified. Such a rumor could work its poison only because the logic of clothing was so well established.

Crafting the Self into Material

I have started with clothes and the march of identity because they are so obvious in this period, and because they were right there, first on the skin, first on the onlookers' eyes, moving with the self, and overwhelmingly social. However, while clothing had high priority, people put themselves into a lot more than their suits. People made a living out of their reputation in the town, and this meant that their handiworks, their craft, were one of the chief properties they had. We can follow the Hegelian insight here: controlling his labor because his product was identifiable, the craftsman was what he made, and his name circulated with his goods. This is still true, but the smaller scale of medieval town life requires us to intensify the connection between product, name, reputation, and wealth.

Moreover, this connection was gendered. While women were also craftspeople in the city, I don't think we can say that the dynamic between product and reputation was the same for them. They were marginal workers,[44] mainly and usually defined by their sexual role, their sexual work: virgin, wife, widow, harlot.[45] "The Wryght's Chaste Wyf" can help once again to set the scene, capturing the double scale of values that we have already seen between men and women, applied here particularly to an urban craftsman (a carpenter) and his wife. It may set the scene and show the sexual contrast. "The Wryght's Chaste Wyf" is a simple, charming tale good for teaching many lessons. This time we notice it for the way self and craft could elide. It tells of how a carpenter's work and repute gave him security and employment, and a good name. Large contracts from worthy people flowed his way soon after his marriage and, worrying, correctly as it turned out, that his beautiful wife would attract amorous interlopers, he fashioned a trap-door in a small, privy room of his house. "For hys wyfe he made that place, / That no man schuld beseke her of grace, / Nor her begyle."[46] Its clever and faultless mechanism allows her to net three importuning 'gentlemen'. She held position with her sexual honor, her husband with his crafty hands. Good hands made a good living, a good reputation, and in this case, saved two people whom social affront would have broken.[47] The model was one of crafting husband and helping wife, whatever actual work she did.

Whenever one sees a case of poor workmanship, we can easily agree that it is about money, but I hope we see that it is also more than money, and that enough has been argued so far in this book to justify the belief that concern for money is often a concern for the social self. This is why slander suits and debt suits could sometimes be interchangeable. Word of bad work was getting around, threatening ruin or decline in one's trade—and everything that depended on this. However much people were willing to cheat, no one wanted to be the fishmonger who got to sit in the stocks with the putrid haddock about his thick neck, the reek of his bad and worsening reputation in his nose. What is more, this is the humble man's self that we are tracing. Often these are men otherwise unable to make their mark on the world through fancy clothes and acquisitions or political office or land holding. Craft is all they have.

The crafted self and the enduring thing also fused in artistic and monumental work. At this point, we run up against a large medieval difference from the modern, marking a crucial limitation on the social self. The maker did not proclaim himself clearly upon the product. No one wrote a "lives of the cathedral builders," great as they were. The medieval self was submerged in social and cultural norms that differed from the explicitly self-promoting, expressivist immodesty of the renaissance, romantic, or modern ego.[48] Nevertheless, there can be little question that for contemporaries of the craftsman his mastery turned into pride, recognition, and the visible trace of a man.

One such master mason was Wells' John Stowell and throughout 1470/1 he was engaged with Jesse and his descendants. He undertook a detailed commission for the "makyng of the frounte of the Jesse atte oure lady awter at Seynt Cuthbertis Churche in Wellis." This was his own parish church, when he was not away from the city, as masons so often were, leaving their mark on a whole region's churches.[49] Often they never committed to a town for long, just to a project. Stowell was different. He had become a burgess in 1458, with impressive pledges. The year earlier he had been the stonecutter in the cathedral's quarry at Doulting, where they extracted the special stone that worked into life so well, yielding the cathedral's extensive and elaborate repertory of sculpture.[50] He must have worked those sculptures for years and by 1470 he was obviously known for his "workemanship and masonry craft." Working with the master and the wardens of the Lady Altar, he designed an intricate plan—and there must have been many discussions—surprisingly detailed even in the legal contract. He had sixteen months and £40 to fill the popular and prominent altar from the "grounding unto. . .its wol plate," making allowances so that it could be "proporcional." The plan captures everything that I am trying to argue in this book: it was conventional and yet deeply committed and unique.

There were to be "three stagis of Imagery a cordyng to the genelogy of our Lady." There were to be two wings projecting from the base and surrounding the Jesse tree, recounting Mary's lineage and decorated with "imagery such as can be thought by the maister and his brothers most accordyng to the Storye. . ." He would choose the workmen, the stones—fair and profitable free stone was specified, the lime, the sand, everything, and he was to be well paid.[51]

The results of his work are dimly beautiful still, just visible after the annihilating counterenthusiasm of later men. The job was well done. In reading the plan and considering the work, we need to stress the essential conjunction of man and world, of men with each other. The four men who apparently made up this committee were all deeply involved in making the design. The master mason was perhaps most influential from an artistic point of view, but the details are spelled out because the others also knew what they wanted, and were perhaps eager to keep the mason in line, like any contractor. By the same token, the mason was a burgess, a brother of the community, without question a contributor to the Guild of St. Mary that supported the altar. Individual and group, artist and burgess, businessman and parishioner fused in the complexity of this commission. What is more, the context for all four men was the most significant physical space and structure of the borough, for although the cathedral was larger it was not theirs. St. Cuthbert's was the place where small businessmen, barely literate, held sway and could make a difference. But in that altar, richly endowed by Thomas Tanner at the beginning of the century, by others a hundred years earlier, in the prominent south aisle, any difference they made would be noted by the passing and praying eyes of the entire town, for the meaning of the community was broadest when it gathered in its sole parish church. No wonder the wardens wanted it all spelled out: they would be there in every shilling spent, in every "profitable" stone laid; no wonder Stowell did such a job. Here was a work that he would have to wear every day, which his family would see and be seen by even when he was fixing a tower or gargoyle in East Coker. In a church-work such as this, selves brightened and bristled even as they produced a massive and spectacular collective work of worship and art. "I will not lose what I have made," says God in the Wakefield cycle, and it is the craftsman's natural word and final hope, no matter who owned the item.[52]

In the litany of giving that helped to buoy up the medieval church, the most touching acts are the small ones. The smaller-scale investment of the person into religious life could run a parallel course, allowing that the payoff to the social self was proportionately smaller, however massive the private self may have taken the acts to be and however significant the religious effect. These are smaller offerings for the social self too because they are not always products of one's own hands, although sometimes the women must have embroidered their gifts themselves. Women were in fact most likely to offer textiles, as well as jewelry.[53] Margaret Dusman invested herself into the Lady Altar with a tablecloth given in the 1440s. She made several further and similar contributions. Her cloths lay with those of Margery Tyler and Joanna Hilleman.[54] Edward Waxmaker gave similar gifts to the parish church, while Roger, Dugg, Agnes Forfall, Stephen Chapman, and John Orum gave vestments to the Altar of St. John. Official memory ranked its donors and we can imagine a subtle, not too boisterous competition. John Orum gave not only vestments but also an expensive gold cloth. Chapman may have bettered even that with his gift of a missal, a marker of a deeper devotion, maybe even of literacy.[55] Here was a collective endeavor full of personal ends: their individual salvation, their memorialization in the prayers of the guild even when they were dead, and in the historian's reading hundreds of years later, all achieved through little things.

Others thought it served the social self better to press the person through the landscape, to gain a kind of immortality through real estate. The landscape of a town tells its stories, the streets named for the tuckers or saddlers who had worked there, or the frogs that frolicked in its sodden streets. Houses got their names from people sometimes, but if you were industrious, you might even try to develop a street. You might build a house so spectacular that your name stuck to it. Hildebrand Elwell manages this, his large town house on High Street being called Elwellsplace long after his own death.[56] It was obviously not the name they were after in developing property but the profit. Yet in this posterity—seeking people, the name did matter. Peter Moniers developed a side street off of the High Street in the 1340s and his wife Margery controlled it as Monierslane until the honor and recognition went with the deed to a cathedral canon, John Aunger, when we hear of Aungerslane.[57] While its history would be brief and unsuccessful, the owner was literally part of the urban street plan. Whether people were leaving their things to the church, carving them into the church, or developing the town, there was an omnipresent problem of posterity and trying to cope with the fact that your social self might be annihilated in the end and your goods ingested into other identities, some ignorant of or uninterested in you.

Undressing/Dispossession: The Shrinking Self

That separation of social self from its accoutrements and signs, from its possessions, was often a humiliating and lingering experience. You could watch your social substance disappear and it often did so in the company of your body itself, the dying and dead body of a vibrant social self. The key is that the social self's worst moment was not death but social decay: death could be oddly triumphant for a social self as well as the religious one. But it was harder to make a good show of the decline that fortune or disease brought to most people, who needed the great luck of wealth or a very prosperous family to sustain the disaster of being unable to work for themselves. The image of poverty that Langland provides in *Piers Plowman* is one of implicit decline. It is a mother with children she must feed but without a husband, from whom so much economic gain and social status was derived. But now she and so many proud poor are "abasched for to begge." There is decline too in the comfort called for "crokede men and blynde."[58] Their physical imperfections proclaimed the piteous decline of their public person, not to speak of their inner lives. The breaking of the body and the advance of ugliness was a serious change in their social identity. Age was admirable but decrepitude was not: it was a terror to all and the gift of pity was never an adequate substitute for respect.[59]

When Wells cathedral and borough jointly developed the Hospital of the Holy Saviour in the 1430s pity led them to see that poverty meant *social* poverty and so they envisioned three categories of eligible people. They did not do a means test to see who needed it most financially. They gauged the collapse of the social self: assessing how much the person had withered from his or her prime of property-owning and how the body that was once proud and maybe even proudly attired had shrunk in power and look. If the decline was clear and the person's moral life was known to have been good, then pity and eligibility for permanent room and board followed. No doubt there were many candidates. The governors looked for people who were no longer able to support an independent household; those whose bodies had so collapsed that they could not even beg from door to door, could not even uphold the debased status of common beggar; and decrepit clergymen too weak to carry out their duties.[60] These notions of poverty were notions of social decline, of the failure of the body to sustain a shrinking social self. It was not the death of the social self, but it was certainly the death of the full member of the community, of the political self. The Middle Ages knew how much a person was his or her body and how truthfully it told their social story. When they imagined the ravages of death, they based their insight on what they knew of poverty and sickness, of what these did to a proud or rich person. Yet, this divestment of goods and of social self was almost a necessity.

Death's ambiguity was where we started this book. In the later Middle Ages no claim was more often heard than how death would transform the mores of the living, when the soul traveled to the next life and found out how much it would suffer and whether it had a right to hope. How you lived in this world, combined with God's gentleness and justice, determined the brightness or bleakness of your long future. The social self, we have seen, was largely a creature of pride. Even allowing for the fact that medieval people made distinctions between the proud well-dressed person and the foolishly overdressed Dame Purnel or the man lasciviously and pretentiously strutting in slashed clothes, the religious self would have quaked at all these displays. If it had not become a sign for hypocrisy by the last medieval centuries, the habit of the friar, the barefoot or sandaled St. Francis, was the only saving model of dress. In death, then, even in the face of death, everyone had to follow Thomas Beckyngton and manage the transition from the social self's values to those of the presently dominating religious self. The natural understanding that wealth and ostentation are an existential reply to the fact of death may have motivated much that we have seen the social self do, but at death—capital-D Death—those very things became dangerous. All the substance you had achieved needed significant conversion to aid your soul and others: on top was Bishop Thomas full of grandeur, the most expansive social self in town, builder and donor and master, below sinner Thomas's wasted corpse, worm food.

We saw traces of this process when we discussed the russet clothes of the poor, given by those richer for their funerals. I want to look now at the social self moving as the earthly body to death and to the ground, to think with the "Lyke Wake Dirge," a lyric in which the dead body is being watched with some worry. In doing so, I follow the work of many scholars who have been developing a nuanced understanding of medieval death's displays and meanings.[61] I want to develop this ground with the specific perspective of the social self in mind. The departed soul is challenged on its outward path: "If ever thou gavest hosen and shoon, / Sit thee down and put them on: / If hosen and shoon thou ne'er gavest nane, / The whins [prickle-bush] shall prick thee to the bare bane:" Whether he/she gave meat or drink is the challenge in purgatory. Sustenance, divesting oneself of the substance and stuff that gave you your earthly advantage, was the barrier to your heavenly success. How to negotiate this passage, which Dinn has suggested covered a transition period of several days, was tricky indeed. "This ae night, this ae night / fire and sleett and candle-light."[62]

The preparation for death had two parts: care of soul and of body. They were related to be sure, especially because so much of the medieval person's identity was tied up with the body and its achievements and failures. The body was the sign of the earthly, but it would also be needed for the future, for the final curtain call of the Resurrection.[63] The body was without doubt part of your chattels. "I bequeath my body. . . ." is part of the standard opening for wills, although some also bequeathed their souls to others than God alone. So, John Welshot gave his soul to "almighty God, the blessed Virgin Mary and Saints Cuthbert and Katherine myn advocates"[64]—a potent social network. However, our focus here is on the material signs of the self on its last trip and its permanent place. Even in death, some people were larger than others were, leaving a greater mark on community and on memory.

Burial was a place of social differentiation. The churchyard of the parish church was the usual burial site. People yearned to be brought to a particular place to die. One of the common purposes of many of the later medieval religious guilds or fraternities was to provide money to bring home the body of the merchant or mason who had died away from town and whose corpse needed repatriating.[65] "Lo, where have ye his body laid?" Christ asked of Lazarus' family, and it was a question whose answer the dead soul had often determined himself. They wanted to die at home and to be buried in an honorable and accustomed place where you were somebody, where friends could speak your name, and care, and remember. A central matter, it was always first or second concern in a will, before forgotten tithes, before your priest. It was your body and the priest or notary reminded you to bequeath it—little else was as important. As Margery Churchstile put it, appropriately and typically, "my body to be buried in the churchyard of St Cuthbert's, Wells," the one parish church.[66] In that churchyard were most of the people this book has been concerned with, including the ones who leave no legal traces in the records, just a will. Thomas Franckleyn, nothing else.[67] Others were there too, perhaps because of the larger fees demanded to get beyond the churchyard,[68] or perhaps, because like William Horsford they looked forward to rising in familial company. He wanted to be "next to the tomb of my father."[69] Thomas Hywode and even Richard Gros, councilors of the town, one a master even, wanted nothing more than a churchyard burial,[70] so while social prominence was an important and perhaps growing consideration in burial site, it was not nearly decisive.[71]

Without question, however, scholars have made clear that even in death more substantial people had greater options.[72] No paupers got themselves beyond the churchyard. That was the consecrated minimum for a good Christian not excommunicated.[73] Something more was an indoor place, close to the activity, nearer to the praying lips of professionals and parishioners, out of the rain too. It was also, to be fair, near to the places where your own prayers had been offered and sometimes worked, for those who sought interment within St. Cuthbert's were a blessed group on this earth.[74] They wanted to be buried in the church, and that was surely a sign of prestige, but it was not just a matter of their honor's being vindicated. They wanted special places that underlined particular aspects of their lives. True, many just requested burial in the parish church, but some were a little more particular, specifying the nave, perhaps before the high cross.[75] They were, in other words, transfixed with a sense of the continuity of self in buried body, notwithstanding their knowledge that decay would soon follow for all who were not the rosiest of saints. Walter Baker wanted to be set before the altar of St. Nicholas. He had certainly been a member of that praying guild and perhaps had felt the saint's help during his life.[76] John Atwater wanted to be buried in the north end of the Trinity Altar, the guild that operated as the establishment club in the town.[77] For Thomas Aphowell it was to be in front of the "image of St Jamys."[78] Former Master, Nicholas Trapp, wanted to lie in "a chapel there founded in the name of Jesus on the south side," for he was a devotee of that new and flourishing later medieval cult.[79] Nearby, if not next to him, was Alice Trapp, his second wife. These choices and decisions, followed by executors, show how hard it is to let go of the earthly horizon of our hope and our loves. People wanted to see the comforting images, to commune with familiar prayer companions, and to lie next to the lovers they had always had. This is all the more so if we think, hope—again and always hope—that we shall rise again and see God and family in that once-chewed, now renewed flesh. Resurrection was corporeal.[80]

In the church or out, husbands and wives often wanted to be together at the call. The Trapps perhaps, the rich and resplendent Tanners for sure, "in a tomb to be made anew there for burying my body. . .and that of my wife."[81] There was theory and poetry to support the practice: "For the body of man & woman that is wediet and knyt to theat precious soule that Crist bought so dere with his precious blood, with whyche soule iot schal tysysn ayen at the dom and lyvyn in blysse withouten ende, clereere than the cristal, bryghter than the sonne, it is of wol gret dignete, / althey it be here for a tyme in gret myschef for Adamys synne."[82] John Cokur also wanted to be inside the church "next the grave of Elizabeth."[83] Richard and Joan Burnell were also there together.[84] Places of prestige, associations of friends, of patrons, of companions. The place that the second most precious part of you laid deeply reflected your social self, for as with your honor, to lie in one place rather than another required not just a dream or a desire, but the assent of the people around you, the now dominant survivors.

They watched you as you went, to a plan of their orchestration, even if of your original devising. To be poor was to have no one around to care, no one to continue your small social self. To be a nobody was to have the minimum earthly continuity, the small farewell, no one to watch your lyke and worry about your passage to eternity. We can only see the possibilities of the dead body as emblem of the continuing social self if we look at the better recorded and wealthier folk, but there is no question of their being a cultural divide on this issue, not before 1500 at any rate. Everyone wanted the same kind of funeral and it was one in which the look of the crowd and throng would demonstrate the substance of the deceased's life and social standing. This is a tricky matter, because it is susceptible of a variety of interpretations. At least two meanings must have coexisted. The desire for a big showing was a desire for many prayers, a community chorus of support that everyone must have wanted but which the richer burgesses and clergy felt they needed, so heavy did their worldly success, their riches, hang upon them. Beyond this, however, surely some of them planned a large funerary parade to ice the cake of that worldly achievement. At his death Richard Gros knew he would lie there watched by his family and friends and the "night before his burial" was especially the time that he saw in imagination, the larger, more intense gathering. He offered money to any chaplain who would come along to help. Family and friends would have made up the watch, centering on his trustful wife Agnes, now his executrix. "This ae night, this ae night / fire and sleett and candle-light."[85] The watching time before burial was the ultimate border zone, pure liminality, dead and yet live, here and yet not. The changed body was still a man. But, the social self was thinning out, expanding beyond solidity, to be remembered only in a few starry moments and charged sites.

Throughout this book, we have seen how the strand of the personal extended all over the place. It was an entity constructed out of relationships and it was hungry for them. The collective and cooperative venture, the works of stone, the handicrafts of everyday life, the sartorial presentation of self in the streets of the town, the drama of death and divestment and deposition all were means for the social self's articulation. Whatever we might want to say about self and even soul, we would do well to stay close to Aristotle and to recognize how self properly and necessarily found its way out through the body and the world. This was so for public display, where the active social self was most engaged. But behind it all were people's own evaluation about how they were doing and how well they looked the part in the world. It is not hard to see why people might misjudge themselves and make claims in clothing that their substance could not sustain.

It may be the greatest irony of the Middle Ages that a culture so conscious of the models of selflessness should also be one so in tune with the keyboard of the body and clothing.[86] The body in the later Middle Ages was a kind of musical instrument. Tuned in the conventional mode, judged by well-established critical canons, playing it was a universal cultural achievement for social self-expression. Because it had such potent and conventional forms, however, it could also be so successfully used for a contrary message. The Christian radical could use clothing and more especially the body to undermine the world with a wonderful, frightening, but quite understandable harmonic counterpoint. Thus, mystics who played an abrasive but beautiful song of penitence on their bodies had both a confident voice and appreciative audience. To rip your flesh, allow your body to putrefy, your entire body to wither, was a comprehensible and saving response to a community of so much socially motivated and vain style.[87] God trumped community for people such as Margery Kempe. When he spoke to her the merely social self was annihilated, overwhelmed by a transvaluation of values, yet somehow included in it; even religion built itself out of the styles of social life.

CHAPTER 8

A WORLD OF INDIVIDUALS

Cecily Pontefract

It has been a common feature of medieval urban histories to conclude, typically in an appendix, with brief notes on individuals, listing the bare bones of the documentary evidence. It was not always clear what the purpose of these was, possibly help to the local antiquarians keen on family history or for future biographers or prosopographers, with large computers and high hopes. Regardless of intention, it captured the essence of the social history of previous decades, in which the individual was something of an afterthought. At any rate, this chapter, a culmination of this book in many ways, is their descendant, bred, however, to take the individuals and the notions they lived by, more seriously. Yet, here is the problem from which we started: the difficulty of scraping up the medieval individual. The meaning of individual has now changed and become a kind of dialogue of self and world as the social self, but the problem remains and we should remind ourselves with the limiting case of Cecily Pontefract.

She is immediately interesting. She interested many men in the town and especially those of the cathedral close in the 1330s. Her name tells us that she probably came from Pontefract in Yorkshire. We know of her existence because in the 1330s Bishop Ralph of Shrewsbury, a vigorous and serious clergyman, forced the cathedral to allow him to perform a visitation, that is, an on-site assessment of their ritual and personal lives. It was not a welcome advance, but after much legal bickering and posturing, the dean of the cathedral allowed the bishop in, invasion though it was. The wall between cathedral and bishop's palace was in some ways the thickest one in the town. Ralph probably succeeded because his motives were plainly reformist. He was one of the few medieval bishops of the diocese to generate a small cult after his death because some thought him a saint. At any rate, on May 1, 1336 a large meeting of canons, with extra witnesses from around the diocese and beyond in attendance, heard the bishop accuse several canons, no doubt present—but unnamed by the scribe—of being "too familiar" with Cecily of Pontefract, "a woman of evil repute."[1] Her reputation, whether based on mere rumor or certain knowledge, made the bishop move quickly but rather mildly, here. He blustered and lectured, scaring the canons "who made various excuses." However, over a year later the bishop's legal commissioner heard a case against a cathedral vicar Robert Ros. He was accused and convicted of incontinence with Cecily.[2]

While there may well be other evidence of her life somewhere, I know of none, nor of any simple or time-effective way of finding out more. Was she a prostitute? Perhaps. Was she in their sense a whore? Probably yes. The key to their definition was promiscuity, being common to all men, rather than living as a suitably subordinate extension of one man, father or husband. She was plainly not a wife; otherwise, the charge of adultery—a much graver one just because it disrupted the property and social self of a respectable man—would have been leveled. That she was not herself part of a local family, a somebody within the community, also explains why the court is less interested in her.

That she needed money was certain because who did not. That she had no other way to get it is as unclear as what she did actually receive. That she had allure beyond availability is as clear as the embarrassment of the canons, who were spared the rod that fell on the less prestigious vicar Ros. We can imagine what the canons saw in her but cannot see equally well what she was up to, what she had in mind and how that located her in the town, where she was without support. At this point, we can fall back on the stereotype of ill repute, all the innuendoes and slurs that were tossed at respectable women maliciously, fit here without the falsity if with their cruelty unaltered. To find what Cecily Pontefract thought about her life and her sexual life, about her options in making herself in medieval England, we are left at the edge of traditional history. What favors did she prefer? What aspirations did she harbor? We can fashion the social story of her type and a footnote will take you to the prostitute or loose woman in the medieval town, but I doubt that that was the whole story and our biography stops as little more than a riddle.[3] With this answer: what is someone who cannot fit into the authorized values, honorable identities, and hopeful stories of her social world?

The Sadde Man of Sufficiencee and Haultesse

We can do better in thinking through Cecily's opposite—not the also sexually odd cathedral canon—but the man of substance and extent, the influential burgess, the master of men and of the town, steward, moneyed man, propertied man, man of ambition. Take John Godwin, for instance. He was one of the most adept of citizens in medieval Wells, master of a difficult and lucrative trade that was itself the mark of a new urban prestige and of more expansive consumption. He was a glazier. Like the proliferating pewterers, for instance Godwin's prominent contemporary John Abury, glaziers were one of the first providers of luxury goods for the house-proud middle class as well as for the elite. In the fifteenth century, a business that focused on fitting windows well was a good one. Windows were now adorning middle-class townhouses, in addition to their lucrative possibilities in church work, probably even at the cathedral, in civic buildings, and the private houses of the countryside.[4] For a glazier, this was an entrée to money and to people of high honor. That was not, however, in itself the same thing as being such a person. Getting into a rich man's house isn't the same as being invited to dinner, but Godwin set out to scotch the difference. It was, nevertheless, a trajectory for all ambitious fifteenth-century burgesses and many advancing former peasants to move along toward the ranks of the privileged laity, the gentlefolk.[5]

Godwin's family background is hidden, and his emergence in the town was quiet and yet significant, suggestive of at least a modest ambition and some small family advantage. He appeared before the burgesses' convocation on April 8, 1406, a man in his early twenties, and recently married. He was probably a master glazier by then and had a small business in the town. It is possible, though pure speculation, that John Sprot, the elder glazier and a burgess of quite modest means and prestige, had been his teacher. It is even possible he married Sprot's daughter. Godwin certainly married a burgess' daughter. On that day, he was admitted to the Borough Community and brought twelve pairs of gloves, a gallon of wine, and a few pounds of wax for his admission fine. Gathered into the community, he found his networks reinforced with the potent calling card of an established family. He had begun to move up the hierarchy; his self had found a valley and began to spread in many comfortable directions.

In September 1406, just a few months after his admission he moved with his wife Matilda and their young son Stephen into a large house on the south side of the High Street. He also rented two acres of arable land in Byhyndheys furlong. For the whole, he paid two marks rent.[6] The land may have been for profit or for food, but either way he showed a taste for rural pursuits early. While his house's rent was typical for the High Street, it was well above the town's average. Godwin had by trade, by marriage, or by inheritance moved quickly into the top quarter of the town, the top half of the Borough Community. The house was well placed for trade, but it also operated as a clear social announcement to the town. Of course, he might have failed yet, ran into as many debts as profits; at this point, Godwin was only a well advantaged twenty-five-year-old, a prospect more than an achievement.

Godwin, however, did not follow the pattern of someone such as Richard Gros, prominent master of the previous generation, who had died around the time that Godwin was admitted. As we saw in chapter 5, Gros served in every office, slowly building himself up by enlarging his mercantile business and his social capital.[7] A good pig chaser, scrupulous and fair in overseeing the butchers in the shambles, careful with the money, but a slow grower, Gros scrambled, and was patient. By contrast, Godwin concentrated solely on his business–social links, probably fuelling the business as much as his skill. However, on paper he disappeared for years, leaving official politics to the side.

We can guess what he was up to: building his trade and making good on the promise. But one aspect becomes obvious upon his reemergence in 1414. He impressed people. That he made or had enough money to impress as substantial is obvious. However, he must have added the due sadness and sobriety that made people convert a confidence in him and a good reputation in all dealings into corporate trust. The result is that by 1414 powerful men considered him a man of good counsel and high worth. He shows up that year in a list of four men who were told by the burgesses at large to solve a constitutional crisis. They were bothered that some burgesses were failing to appear at court when summoned. Debts could be put off uncomfortably long. That he was perhaps a representative of men not of the elite at that time is possible, the best of the common burgesses. He had after all held no office as of yet. Furthermore, as always, the order of listing men in documents was typically the order of honor that the scribe recognized and Godwin is the last of the four men noted. He was hierarchically bottom in this list of prestige. Above him were Thomas Piggesley, a senior burgess who had been constable six times; John Cutte, who had served several times as constable or rent collector; and John Pedewell, a currently sitting constable. They were elite men, albeit of the second tier; Godwin was not of their caliber but this selection makes it clear he had caught the eye of the leadership, men such as Thomas Weye and Walter Dyer, the current and incoming masters of the time. Ambition must have been with Godwin, but that it was political in a simple sense is unclear. He had stood to the side of it all until then. Ambition seeks a person often enough. And those who needed able aides had come calling.

I have one last speculation to make about him, again using Richard Gros as a contrast. Gros was willing to work for the community at every task, every job. He grubbed his way up. Godwin, by contrast, sat prettily from the start and while he devoted himself to his business, he may very well have been of the kind of man who already had a sense of pride and self sufficiently strong that he was unwilling to chase the pigs or inspect the pork. He may have thought himself above that. There always did seem to be both kinds of ambitious men in the town. That was part of why the town never enforced a strict *cursus honorum,* such as thrived in Coventry.[8] The burgesses needed all kinds, and there were all kinds of good and useful men. The rich and snobbish were important, and they may at this particular historical juncture have been becoming more numerous and confident in their elite status, even independent of the burgesses' offices and acknowledgment, eager for those as they were.[9]

At any rate, after that auspicious triad of expansive acts: marriage to a burgess' daughter, leasing of a substantial house, selection as a politically shrewd committee man of the better common sort, he went back to business and unofficial activity. Still, he moved in the right circles. In 1419, the year of his great transition, emerging from his chrysalis of money and repute, he was selected to be Simon Bailey's arbitrator, paired with but ahead of Philip Porter—a close contemporary in the community (admitted 1404)—who had been churchwarden several times and was to be selected rent collector in 1420. Bailey would one day be a Master himself. He was an innkeeper and had only been admitted to the freedom in 1414, but he shows signs of more substance or maturity than most young burgesses do. He had been a constable in 1415–17. Bailey was, therefore, an elite figure who chose Godwin first and did so because Godwin's status was high and growing and because they were friends with parallel trajectories in town politics. Indeed, Bailey's membership in the guild may have owed something to Godwin. They were approximately the same age but Bailey was one of those men who had stayed aloof from the guild of burgesses during at least a decade of active life in the town. He was first mentioned as a property holder in 1404. He arrived later in life, but was a pretty near neighbor to John Godwin from at least that time, living in a house and inn that he kept in Wetlane, behind Godwin, who was sometimes the district's tax assessor.[10] Godwin must have supported his admission, maybe encouraged it, although Bailey needed no pledges since he had married a burgess's widow. In Bailey the innkeeper, owner of a lucrative and socially powerful business in a cathedral town, Godwin had a sure ally. When Bailey was sued in 1421 he once again called on Godwin's support.[11]

Clusters of friends working within a large and shifting group of men of like status: one could describe the political community of the town that way in the early fifteenth century. There were few overt factions, but there were fields of friendship, and by 1420 Godwin was part of one such group that was perceptibly shifting the kind of values espoused by the dominant men of the town. Wells was at the time of his ascent losing ground against the countryside in many of its economic ventures, but especially in cloth-making, its fourteenth-century strength. There was to be a long slow fifty years in the city.

There was, however, another and murkier transformation taking place, in which gentility was adopted as a model by at least some of these urban figures. Two aspects of this phenomenon need stressing here. First, it was not complete. The values of commerce and the old urban values had much life in them, indeed, are thought by some to be the more powerful cultural tendency. Nevertheless, the second aspect is decisive. The reaction against the feudal and against the overlord of the town that had dominated much of the period from the late 1330s, was dead. Thus, Godwin and others were keen to make and cultivate connections with people "of quality" and this necessarily meant stretching out to people who were not merchants or weavers, but who had achieved honorable recognition in the county. Godwin sought such men and linked his own honorable self to their manifest superiority. The difficulty of this kind of fusion of one schedule of values with another is not easy to make clear even when we know that it was going on.[12] The later medieval period witnessed the explosion of theories of stratification; it saw the slow fading of the great fact of servility, the decline of serfdom. Pristine nobility aside, ambitious people could plausibly imagine mobility, however rarely it was achieved. In the particularly urban context, however, such ambitions were more complicated because the hegemonic country model had also to coexist with a local option focused on money and the physical trappings of moveable wealth. The subtle gradations of status that we have followed in this book here meet the markedly different notions of the county. How to be the good burgess and yet strive to be the gentleman was the social problem that a self such as Godwin and his friends faced.[13]

All the signs of Godwin's advance were confirmed on September 30, 1420, when the new master Hildebrand Elwell, a grocer, named John Godwin to the post of constable. Although mentioned second behind the older Richard Peres, Godwin had unquestionably arrived among the elite. Philip Porter was also selected that day to be rent collector and their association would continue.[14] Godwin had served on the special committee and as a tax assessor for the Wet Lane district, but he would only agree to serve among the elite offices of the town, disdaining service in shambles and pigpens. He had taken sixteen years, however, to rise that high, high enough to meet his own expectation, to make as plain as his money and his house that he was the cut above, the glass window pane, transparently superior.

From that time, Godwin moved fully into the elite of the town and was a leading player. When the two men with whom he was close found themselves mired amid "diverse quarrels," he was naturally one of the neutral arbitrators selected. Hildebrand Elwell had chosen him constable and the other disputant was Simon Bailey. The other arbitrators in that case included Richard Hall, Richard Setter (both of the magisterial class) and John Cutte, who was of constabular rank like Godwin.[15] Godwin was in the politically central cluster of oligarchs now. Indeed this small group was acting as a kind of cadre, showing up elsewhere that year to solve delicate problems, virtually representing the guild of burgesses.[16] They were re-selected for office in September 1421 and that bears some comment, for it was typical for the master to be changed each year. This time we can see the desire to consolidate power as the motive. In 1422, the rest of the top burgesses moved into the three elite positions for the year (John Pedewell, Robert Elwell, and John Collys).

Pedewell selected Godwin to be Master of the Borough of Wells in September 1423. Once active in the community, Godwin's ascent was quick, but he had actually been around for twenty years. He was in his mid or early forties, not a young man but a confident and well-known one. The community selected him to be a member of parliament a month or so later. There Godwin mingled with the county and national elite, and would be able to make a new kind of connection while staying informed on matters of policy. He attended Parliament with John Rocke again in 1427.[17] In 1426, his old friend Simon Bailey became Master himself and he ended his term by choosing Godwin to succeed him. Godwin chose Robert Elwell to follow him in 1428 and this association is an important one, for Elwell was the first member of the community and the first Master who was not a businessman or a tradesman but simply a "gentilman." His acceptability within the Borough Community marks the turning of at least the elite toward the county gentry in their associations and aspirations.[18] It is probably also a sign or cause of a certain coolness of the more common tradesmen toward the Borough Community in the middle of the fifteenth century when there was a modest decline in numbers, which was possibly unrelated to population change. The cost of admission was the same, but it is possible that the meaning of membership was slightly transformed, as the dominant men were as likely to forge links away from the modest burgesses and toward the county elites. When Thomas Horewode, a future Master and son of a Master, could take the office of bishop's bailiff of the town without harm to his career, as he did in the early 1450s, then the opposition of town and bishop, of urban elite to country was gone.[19] This conjunction left the smaller burgess somewhat to the side, although we shouldn't insist that they felt there was anything inappropriate in this. Some may well have thought that it added considerably to their social selves to be linked to men higher up a social hierarchy than was possible in the old, wholly urban model, where the merchant who was master was the apex of local society.

Keeping the burgesses of high quality within the guild was Godwin's policy. He not only embraced a gentleman such as Elwell, possibly a relation to Hildebrand Elwell, the rich grocer, he also recruited other rich and socially ambitious men. Throughout his career, he was an eager sponsor of good prospects. There were butchers and craftsmen of course, but he was most eager to add merchants, traders of all kinds, and even gentlemen who like Robert Elwell saw gain in the honor and activity that the town could supply them with, in other words, quite minor gentlemen. Godwin was shaping the rulers of the guild into an elite group that could mingle well enough with the county and cathedral elites. So while he knew that there needed to be sufficient numbers of burgesses of all kinds above laborers, plainly he cherished most those who could be his friends, who reflected his own aspirations. William Vowell, perhaps the greatest merchant of the middle part of the century, was surely one of these. Godwin was one of his admission pledges in 1429.[20] Fifteen years later, the two of them admitted John Atwater, acting as his two pledges. He was to be Master six times and the greatest cloth-maker of the second half of the century, living until 1500.[21] He and Vowell were of an ilk, fully urban and equally ambitious as Godwin. Vowell's son Richard would be a Master too, but would be no merchant, but a country gentleman as much as a town one, married to a gentry woman, and even serving as king's escheator.[22] Climbing the hierarchy of society, fudging the urban–rural difference, stretching themselves into ever more exhilarating contexts, that was what these men were about. William Vowell was perhaps even more successful than Godwin was, whose son may have done well elsewhere but more probably did not outlive his parents.

Vowell was one good companion for Godwin, but perhaps even better was William Gascoigne. In 1444, he was brought into the guild by the joint pledges of Godwin and William Vowell. Even at this inaugural moment, his occupational title was described as "jentylman." He owned part of a manor at Newton Plecy and other lands around the county, some inherited from his merchant father William Sr. of Bridgewater.[23] One generation earlier than Richard Vowell, here was the merchant son turned country gentleman, who remained for all that, more comfortable with the town and its supposed honors than many of the gentry group might have been. Gascoigne was to be an important and active burgess and later a major donor to the community through his part in the founding of the almshouse, the Hospital of the Holy Saviour. In 1432, Godwin had gone one better in terms of the social hierarchy, luring John Austell into citizenship and once sponsoring him.[24] Austell was an armiger, a squire in effect, drawing the burgesses' reach, and Godwin's, toward the military and knightly class, men less ambiguously beyond their urban or peasant origins than mere yeoman, ambiguous gentleman, or landed merchants.[25]

John Godwin was touchy about his social reputation and status, but there is no sign in him of bad manners or a poor way with people. When he did sue William Crofter in 1434 for trespass it was not just because Crofter,

a brewer about the same age as Godwin, had spoken disrespectfully, although
he had. Crofter had drawn a knife on Master Godwin. But of course that is
the kind of extreme reaction that one man, one brother, will take toward
another who puts on airs of superiority and has the house, clothes, and tones
to match. Crofter was expelled from the brotherhood of citizens for over a
year, until he humbly apologized to Godwin.[26] He acknowledged the reverence that a Godwin deserved. And that was what John Godwin wanted.

In his own affairs Godwin was quiet and careful, a man who did not get
into disputes quickly, but was able at solving them. He arbitrated frequently,
was never sued by another burgess and lived a stable life. He never moved
from the house he had taken on High Street near Wet Lane. He accumulated wealth and friends across the town and country. He had some modest
amount of land near Wells and perhaps beyond. He bequeathed a house to
the Borough Community as a gift and for his soul. It was a soul he tended
to carefully. Godwin lived a long and vigorous life. When he was about
seventy-five years old, he and his second wife Joan received permission
from Bishop Beckynton, certainly an acquaintance (as was the dean of the
cathedral), to have "masses and other divine offices in the chapel or oratory"
within their house in Wells.[27] He was a religious man with the money to
succor his devotion in his declining and very old age.

However, the certainty we can have of his success may sit in a document
produced by the cathedral scribes, back in 1458, when Godwin was over
sixty. It was part of the confirmation procedures for the incoming dean of
the church, whose credentials needed proving, including his legitimate
birth and the propriety of his election. Among seven men selected in
the county was John Godwin. For him the selection may have been no surprise. He was a man of good counsel, of extraordinarily good reputation.
Even from our distance, there are no lawsuits to sully him, no signs of opposition to his rule in the town. However, when the scribe came to describe
him he did two things helpful to the historian. He gave Godwin's age and
he described him simply as "gentleman, of Wells."[28] Godwin's testimony
showed his familiarity with the gentry family from which the dean came,
but that is small stuff compared to how people saw *him*. Citizen that he still
was, venerable older man as he was then, the agenda of proud success, of
ambition to climb the social hierarchy, not only of the town but of the
county and local community, was vindicated right here. The burgess seemed
a gentleman, was known as one, lived like one. The burgess *was* a gentleman.

Honorable Paupers

From the narrower material point of view, John Godwin was a great man
because he could die at home, decline at home, to the sacred song of a
privately hired priest. John Salmon had a different end and a bit of his story

will remind us of how much the social self was shaped by the stage of life you were in. Few indeed were the people who would die as old or as apparently comfortable, respectable, and happy as had Master Godwin. His success was in keeping at bay the typical disaster that was old or even middle age decrepitude. Even people who had secure trades and made a decent living rarely had enough to live on comfortably when their power to work waned.

John Salmon is a case in point. His career as a citizen is lightly attested, but he was a burgess, which in itself is a mark of modest success or ambition and a sufficient sense of self. He had married a burgess' daughter named Joanna.[29] Furthermore, he was admired by some men enough to be chosen as a pledge by the incoming weaver John Brown in 1464.[30] That same year the borough selected him as a tax assessor for his street; and while New Street was one of the least inhabited and not among the most affluent, having a rural cast, it was still a mark of confidence and some prominence.[31] He was a man known in the town and as he had only been a burgess since 1461, he had probably built his reputation while in business earlier, laying the ground for this public responsibility. Our profile of importance is capped by his activity as a pledge at admissions.[32] He was politically active, had a sizeable cross-craft network, or made money by acting as a pledge. In any event, it adds up to a figure of minor standing. Thus, while he never held one of the regular offices and was a member of the commons of the town, far from the elite, he was an active and respected man of modest means, modest attainment, and probably of moderate ambition. He attended meetings. Did what was asked of him.

You might read ambition into his restlessness. He moved around often and this suggests a hope for better things, even if one is as often driven by troubles to change house as by successes. From New Street he moved to the High Street and then on to Chamberlain Street. This was progress. High Street was busy and valuable, but Chamberlain was the closest thing to an elegant and noncommercial street the town had outside of the cathedral precincts, although it had its rustic fringes. Furthermore, when John, Joanna, and John Jr. rented from the Borough Community in 1467 owner and tenant shared an ambition to make the house a fine, modern one. The lease was long term, for their three lives, and they were to enlarge the house, adding a fashionable new parlor to it, with a room above. The parlor was the mark of middle-class hopes, the quiet, cozy room of the domestic family and friends, purpose built for chat and ease, conveniently warmed with a fireplace and chimney, the latest thing in the latest room.[33] However, one month later his fortune or calculation changed. Perhaps it was a closer examination of the house. Perhaps a mason such as John Stowell told him how much it would all cost. At any rate, he paid 4s. to get out of the lease three weeks later.[34] It takes little imagination to sense the disappointment to himself, to Joanna. It was just a business deal, but it was a very public climb down, and it always hurt to take that step. Salmon was not a man of excessive pride. But we can read failure in this moment, perhaps physical, certainly economic. He was overextending himself and his social self never moved up again, not in the public's eyes.

Within ten years, his body, tough germ of the self, had withered. His prospects failed along with it, if not because of it. In August 1479, the community agreed that if he would pay the church fabric fund 10s. and the almshouse 40s. he would receive the next open spot in the almshouse that had become the darling of their corporate and personal charity. John Godwin had bequeathed lands to support the poor there, and at least half of them were people such as Salmon, burgesses, the so-called privileged poor, who took up a good deal of the country's better institutional places. The same alms bought his wife Joanna the subsequent opening.[35] He was the master; his responsibility to his wife was clear; his love for her probable. He took care of her, but she went subordinate to him. To be fair, of course, he may have been the one who most needed the hospital and it may have spared Joanna Salmon the suffering that Margery Kempe complained of, not to have to go on caring for her declining husband, bowel control gone in a world of rough diapers.[36]

For Salmon, this last move was one of finality but also of possibility. From the standpoint of the community, he was an official object of charity, without question. Nevertheless, he came in on rather richer terms than many. For while his property amounted to less than a laborer's income for a year, it dribbled out to the almshouse, keeping him something of a property owner, longer than the rest of the inmates. There was more, however: briefly, he became one of those dedicated to the work of God, following a routine of prayers to help others. It was a retreat and a retirement combined. Some of the paupers there were on their very last breaths, so weak or crippled they could no longer drag themselves from door to door to seek alms. Yet, the Salmons belonged to the other group, the kind favored by the burgesses when they selected paupers—the cathedral chose the other half—people whose resources were no longer sufficient to keep their house.[37] These were people like Salmon, people whom every thirty-five-year-old master craftsman understood and feared. Before the final fear of the body consumed as on Beckyngton's sarcophagus, there was the terror of the debasement of becoming unhoused, forced into the street, friendless, and saved only at the cost of all pride, all positive social self. There was a hierarchy in poverty, and security made the difference.

So Salmon had sought out the hospital to live the religious life of easy charity, certain food, help. It is hard to imagine the transition to this place where twenty-four lived and prayed together. Some, maybe half, lived there only briefly before death; the others healthy enough to continue their social lives, to canvass the town and countryside for money for the hospital stayed on much longer. Perhaps the oddest part would have been the mix of men and women, although in practice many fewer women were admitted. There the Salmons moved, not quite as a couple to our eyes, but still one for the fifteenth century, he first, she following but intrinsic. They ate certainly and pretty well, a basic diet that matched that which they had always had. Bread, ale, and meat amply provided; fish often and copiously during Lent.[38] They said their prayers in this anteroom to heaven, prayers for their dead and living benefactors: To pray for men such as John Godwin, who had left a fine property to the hospital, but also for themselves. It made things easier, even though "to asken help thee shameth in thyn herte."[39]

John Salmon lived long, however. He died in 1495 or 1496. He received a decent burial costing 20d. Furthermore, he had not parted with all his valuables upon entering the house. For the sake of security, for the sake of having some property for which he was not beholden, he had kept a few things of his own. The rules of the hospital meant that it became his heir. He had left precious things into which self and money were nicely blended: a mirror for himself and his wife to look at their selves in, and six silver spoons. The things of a life at its end, house things, encapsulating for us and possibly for him the ambitions of a life of houses that shaped the self the world knew. These things, sold off for 23s. 10d., are the last mention of the Salmons.[40] Like us perhaps, the Salmons changed the meaning of their lives every time they and their things moved. They were made by the houses that surrounded them as much as by anything they themselves thought.

The Churchwarden

If it was possible to put one's hands on the community itself, to inspect it for adequate polish, then John Rowburgh was in a position to do so, and he loved it. He served as churchwarden of the town and surrounding manor's one parish church, St. Cuthbert's, for fifteen of sixteen years between 1391 and 1406. The clear and persistent apex of his political life, the office defined his public persona during his high mature years. When he stepped down from office in 1407, he virtually disappeared from the records, worn down by age.

Rowburgh was not the only man to show an extraordinary commitment to the church. Especially in the period before 1430, but to a limited extent later too, there was a greater willingness, indeed an eagerness to serve repeatedly in this office. Furthermore, Masters of the town, who strictly speaking controlled the appointment, were willing to put into place men for whom this was the end of their political advancement, men who may not have looked at the appointment as a rung in the ladder of town office at all. Considering the fears that churchwardens might achieve excessive power or autonomy, this may have been politically expedient.[41] Certainly, being churchwarden especially marked some men. Rowburgh is the greatest example, but his friend, John Clother, was a close second, serving eleven times. John Churchstile held the post at least five times, as Richard Vykyry did in the 1430s. Edward Wylde was also an eleven-time occupant in the first decades of the fifteenth century.

A good churchwarden always needs trustworthiness and vigilance, and some tact. Before he became a warden of the goods of St. Cuthbert's for the first time in 1391, Rowburgh's whole career in the town court betrays a man to whom fidelity was important, always an issue. He made at least some of his living as a pledge, a guarantor of other's commitments, as a giver of personal credit. This probably meant loans some of the time, but certainly indicated that he was known to be true to his word. He often pledged for the baker Walter Baker, a man active about the court but only once a petty officer.[42] William Verye the tucker was also a repeat guarantee, a client of Rowburgh's.[43] These were cases in which the guarantee was called upon because the debts were outstanding, and what is as interesting is the fact that the men who called for their money were of higher social standing. Merchants Thomas Hore, a master of the town, and the middling Stephen Wyndford were typical of the caliber of men to whom money was due. We can perceive in Rowburgh's business and social relations a particular ability to manage the interface between upper and lower halves of the community, possibly of the town. The tools he used to develop this role were a modest amount of ready money and a large amount of accumulated confidence, shared across the divide of creditors and debtors.

This was his place in the town. He had joined the burgesses probably in the 1370s, possibly holding a petty office, but there is no certain evidence of office-holding until Master John Broun chose him as churchwarden in 1391. His reputable and middling status was consolidated, but unlike his simultaneously appointed companion-warden John Clother, Rowburgh fell on the bottom side of the middle. During their decade of association, he followed Clother in the official lists, strong sign of less worthiness and wealth. Furthermore, while Clother never took another position, Rowburgh had several times earlier been a rent collector. In these years, the status of the rent collectors was growing at the relative expense of the churchwardens. Concisely, the burgeoning town real estate portfolio, comprising over a quarter of the properties within the borough, bestowed its luster on the rent collectors. The churchwardens had even given up to the rent collectors their administration of real properties donated to the church.

Clother had been a rent collector when its esteem was a touch lower than a churchwarden's and he took his move as a promotion. At any rate, he was the politically more potent warden, showing up as a named witness on leases, which meant his name was worth putting down. Rowburgh, if present at such fiduciary occasions, was part of *et alia* (and others), the formulaic and inevitable last words of a charter.

Rowburgh was, I am suggesting, not just a middling man, but a middleman. It was through him that the common burgess could reach for money and modest help, without perhaps the implications or condescension of contact with the elite. At least for some commoners this was probably a useful type of man to have around. From the parish's point of view, it was an asset to have a churchwarden who was able to manage the donations and offerings of richer and poorer without snub. Every gift helped; every cup of ale consumed at the church fair was a blessing, a stone for the mason to fashion, a farthing for the windows.

Rowburgh's history is that of a man most worthy of modest trusts. Yet, when we look at what he undertook, with Clother and others, from 1391, it is easy to see that there was nothing modest about his higher motivations. And for a man used to the responsibility of supporting others, of holding goods in hock—holding them too well, the troublemaker Thomas Smart had once claimed[44] (the cloth Rowburgh brought to aulnage was perhaps someone else's!)—and thinking on their value, fingering them mentally and tactilely, the new job might have led him to an immodest but honest explosion of self—of self esteem, responsibility, vigilance, and possibility. He had become the man with the keys to the exchequer room where town executive meetings were held, to the safety cupboards and what was within. He would also have had a say in choosing the chaplains who augmented divine services in the church.

As the inventories put it, the parish and community put their goods "into the hands of John Rowburgh," (in later years his name came first, followed now by John Glasier). Into his hand a cross of gilt, "two cups of silver gilt for holding the body of Christ," quite literally; it makes him sound like a priest, to hold what holds the Body. Two silver thuribles of copper gilt with chains of silver, all "of wondrous work," into *his* hands, which otherwise sequestered Thomas Smart's cloth and sold it at wholesale. There were dozens of cloths and napkins for the altars, vestments given by bishops and others, one with "black crowns, gold and stars."[45] Then there were the banners, whose maintenance he must organize, the red banners with Mary in silver, the gold powdered ones, the nine to make the cross at Easter, another for the Lenten cross; the crowns; the books for a man who probably owned none, and the rings, which they used as an endowment fund, as well as the dozens of gloves.

What objects are more appropriate for the trustworthy man than those that surround the hand that shakes and makes the contract and deal, setting commitments under seal? Rowburgh became the custodian of rings and gloves. An interesting pair of customs sent handy goods toward the church-wardens. New citizens were admitted to the guild after bestowing an offering of a dozen pair of gloves. When they died, people would often leave the church a bequest in the form of a ring, which the churchwardens used as cash to meet special expenses, particularly to improve the fabric of the church. Rowburgh kept all these and I think of them as his special mark of authority. When the excess gloves were handed out to the burgesses, handed out from his stores, he was often among that small group of men who would choose last or, as in April 1400 and April 1403, who would forgo receiving the useful charity.[46] It was after all, as if he was the host, the bene-factor, and it was more appropriate to make the guests eat to their fill as he watched.

Yet, all of these goods that were now strangely his for eleven years, in custodianship for the parish and Borough Community, paled in comparison with the main item, even if it could not be snatched while he slept. There was the church itself. Beyond the chancel area, its maintenance and adorn-ment were the business of the parishioners. Moreover, it was also a great time to be churchwarden of St. Cuthbert's. Few other towns—no matter how large—had larger parishes and Wells and Somerset were rich at this time, the cloth trade booming, the town holding its own against larger cen-ters further afield. The money and effort, and heart, were thrown into the parish church. It was appropriate. It was already the real physical center of the civic community. The Borough Community had as an organization begun as a general parish guild; their properties had become intertwined to the point of identity. It was a happy moment too among the masons, whose success in the Perpendicular movement, were especially concentrated in the West Country.[47] However, the money still needed getting, and that always was a tough job that needed a dogged personality.

Rowburgh was there, as the good churchwardens always were. They could be tough on those who didn't keep faith with their word and with the community. Local custom regarded the pledge seriously. The politics could get heavy and grumbling could undermine the collective good work. When, therefore, in 1396, Rowburgh and Clother heard that William Webber was urging "many people" not to contribute to the spectacular new window underway; they took him to court. Webber denied it but was commanded to refrain from such uncivil talk.[48] Rowburgh was almost inevitably the community defender in its parochial guise, perhaps a small man in some ways, made larger by the cosseting of his reputation and the investment of so much self in the grandest part of the world around him.

The Omnispresent Property Man: Richard Ferrour

Rowburgh was a genius loci of the community's spiritual center, but Richard Ferrour somehow blended with the whole town itself. He was everything that the town contained. He saw almost everything of significance that happened for forty years, his eyes on everyone, an ear as filled as the priest's with other people's problems and the awkward details of their past. He could be a kind of emblem of the medieval townsman. For Richard Ferrour was a success. He was a long-standing member of the judicial leadership, but could not quite keep his eager and anxious self from upsetting other people and from upsetting himself. He could get angry and even violent. Age did not mellow him even if wealth insulated him from its most grotesque social forms. Yet, he was the greatest of friends and had the whole world as his familiar acquaintance, probably bringing some to the point of love and certainly leading others, for a time at least, beyond the boundary of hatred.

No person is mentioned more often in the later medieval town. From 1369 till 1403, Ferrour shows up perhaps 300 times in the records, in a dizzying 200 legal entries. He was the greatest arbitrator of the period, sure sign of the respect given him and of skills of negotiation and persuasion in this pre-lawyer court at the edges of the lawyerly world. However, he was also one of the greatest litigants in the period. Ferrour was taken to the local court twice; but he aggressively brought suit against others no fewer than thirty-six times from 1377 to 1402, and was still at it as the life went out of him. There were others who were aggressively litigious, protecting themselves, their rights, their family, their things, but Ferrour stands out for the scope and one-sidedness of his activity, and because he was an oligarch. The peaceful type of oligarch is the most common one. However, Ferrour was his own type. The dominant men tended to show up in court as arbitrators but rather infrequently as litigants. Contemporaries such as Thomas Tanner or John Broun were involved as litigants in only one and nine suits respectively. Ferrour did share with other elite men, however, the one-sidedness of his suits. These men were rarely sued by each other or by lesser men in the local court.

Such litigiousness was most often a mark of the lower-status burgess, someone whose abrasiveness was considered "unsadde" and unlikely to be worthy of too much trust. Such a man did modest arbitration. Here again, Ferrour made his own mould by being a frequent arbitrator. The meaning of this is respect, authority, the ability to work with people. It is easy proof that he was a man who was literally among the most knowing of the community. In a certain sense, his social self had fused with that of the body politic of the city. This was a different kind of identity than that which a paragon of the community might have achieved. For Ferrour possessed the community's faults too. He was never selected to be Master, which seems an oddity or an oversight considering some of his other credentials and achievements. In part, his elite brethren had judged against him. It meant that the other dominant men would keep him by them—what important deed or action does not mention his presence in these years?—but there was sufficient resistance to his magistracy to contain his political achievement and put a cap on his respectability, reflecting the slightly bitter flavor of his massive social self.

Who knows where he was born or when, possibly in the Devon vill of Berry Pomeroy?[49] He owned property far beyond Wells and its vicinity but how much or where we don't know. It could have been ancestral land, inherited from his father. He was also known as Richard Thorny and that name must have brought a few smirks and remarks, but he was always known in the local records as Ferrour-Smith—and that was probably the trade in which he had been apprenticed in Wells, coming from the countryside or another small town. Names still spoke. Born in Pomerey, Thorny by nature, Ferrour by design. Perhaps the family prickliness was honed in the ancestral village in Devon where the line was first established. At any rate, he is one of those people whose family life and marriages are unknown. He was probably in Wells by the early 1350s and mentioned as a witness in 1356.[50] He may have been born as early as the 1320s but he was at any rate an important man by around 1370, nestled in the upper middle or lower elite part of the town.[51] His path to wealth and influence is obscure.

While we cannot speculate about how much of an advantage family inheritance gave him, we can say that Ferrour achieved a particularly successful mix of business activities. He was a smith, but there's good reason to believe that he had withdrawn from day-to-day work in this line himself, although he may have kept journeymen employed. One of his properties as late as the fifteenth century was equipped with an oven and possibly a forge. It was definitely a workshop, although dyers may have taken over the workshop where once he had swung the anvil.[52] Forging had become combined with real estate ventures that went far beyond his own shop's premises on prime High Street property.

Unless you were a merchant or a dyer, you had to mix up your businesses to do well. Ferrour invested in loans, in land, in agriculture, and in cloth. This helped to bolster his standing as an arbitrator too, for he had interests and experience in a wide range of activities. Knowing again comes to mind as a key adjective of his social self. The business mix is typical, but he went much more heavily into agriculture, actively managing some land around town and the adjoining manors. For all his businesses and interests, it was land that mattered most to Ferrour. It was not that he made most of his money from it. This would be hard to determine and would make him quite exceptional for someone so often about town. There were burgesses who were also countryman. John Forest, a contemporary, was described as "yoman"; we've seen that later burgesses show up who were plainly minor country gentlemen with small town presences and modest interests.[53] Among burgesses, some such as Richard Vowell and John Godwin shifted resources to the country, buying small manors, parts of greater estates that were being farmed out in the fifteenth century.[54] But Ferrour had no mark of the gentleman, of the armiger, dreaming of a crest or coat of arms. He was active nearby, collecting bits of land within the borough and just beyond. These were mainly lands to which you could walk. There is reason to think he lived in New Street ward, and that was one of the least urban ones in the town, most of the holdings beyond a few good houses were little more than pockets of field or grass. He had probably added lands along New Street, the odd close picked up here or there, good for a bit of grass for sheep. He had land at Burcott that he rented from the bishop and that he put crops on, possibly wheat or the equally essential barley for malt.[55]

The medieval model of success, even in the towns, was a model of land, and land meant arable and pasture, preferably worked by others, fields "full of folk." The lucre of the towns, its hoard of portables was always thought unstable, and therefore a little bit immoral. In any event, the stability of land was something that Richard Ferrour sought. Nostalgia may have come into it: townsmen were usually displaced country folk. Profit certainly was an undertone of the aroma of manure and tall two-row barley stalks. But with whatever nuances, this man had invested more of himself in his land than was probably good for his soul. For all his activities in the town, diverse and long-standing as they were, Ferrour had most of his fights over his land and people's infringement of it.

In chapter 5 we saw some of this from the side of John Benet, who had formed a reputation as a good arbitrator in land disputes. Bearing those disputes in mind, let us look at it from Richard Ferrour's side and the context of his life, a most physically formed social self. Good fences make good neighbors: but in the Frost poem and in life it takes good neighbors to make good fences (which weren't so much "good" as agreed on anyway). Thorny was not a good neighbor, but an avid owner, a marker of fence posts, probably a provocateur. Perhaps the clearest evidence of this is that he didn't care how small the offense was, and with an attitude like that, feelings hardened and disputes lingered. William Knyght was called to court to answer Ferrour's complaints in March 1379 because he had placed some industrial dregs, perhaps from dyeing, perhaps from brewing, by the door of Ferrour's house. Ferrour's servant must have acted with the confidence of an influential and irritable master, and so was struck by Agnes Knyght for his impertinence. "Stay off my stoop" was the Ferrour welcoming mat.[56] In 1396 he accused his neighbor, John Pestel, of obstructing his gutter with more noxious substances, the flotsam of woad dye—the essential blue.[57] To Laurence Iforde he complained of a pig trespassing on his property.[58] Ralph Tucker couldn't keep gates closed conscientiously and Ferrour's barley suffered as a result.[59] Eight years later, in 1390, William Wynd also couldn't keep the close sealed off, to Richard's damage and continuing irritation. These land skirmishes escalated into the wars fought with John Benet, Thomas Smart, and Robert Horn (discussed in chapter 5). As we observed in chapter 6, the apparently trivial trespass was the most telling proof of an especially full investment of the social self in the dispute.

An oppressive neighbor is usually a bad landlord too. Perhaps John Worin, the master dyer, was careless of his craft, but Ferrour was at least careful of his property and told Worin and the court that he had "ruined" the woad furnace in the workshop he had rented from Ferrour because of his "slipshod operation."[60] In 1398, he and his tenant John Barstaple exchanged rough and insulting words over the state of repair in which Barnstaple was keeping Ferrour's house.[61] Badgering his tenants, his neighbors, he must have seemed omnipresent, even at seventy years old, and fearless too. Yet, we shouldn't conclude that anyone saw anything unethical in all this. It was merely exaggerated; too quick to press to law even when in the right. Ferrour must have felt the care of his self in the integrity of his lands, the cleanliness and polish and prosperity of his properties, with a neurotic regard.

The difficult part is finding the man of peace and compromise in all this. While he sued and sallied against his enemies, he was helping to fix social fences all over town. But one senses that when a man such as Ferrour was involved, the battles and conflicts were subtly transformed and the language of reconciliation arrived only after hard and subtle bargaining. Ferrour *was* the most active arbitrator on record, playing the role no fewer than 139 times from 1377 to 1402. But he was also best friend of the aggressor, serving as the plaintiff's arbitrator about 60 percent of the time.[62]

It was perhaps enough for him to be involved in everything, a part of the entire town's affairs. I am not sure. People could have many faces, and shifting these may have been part of the success of a man of Ferrour's social reaches. He wanted so much to be the man on the scene, involved, protective, even helpful. He fully barged into the town's business. Sometimes he crossed a line and paid for his aggressiveness by watching himself chosen constable often, considered to be the perfect man for the courts, charging and arbitrating, arguing, arguing, arguing. However, he had to watch others move past him into the Master's stool.

There is an odd quality to research Richard Ferrour that symbolizes so much of this study's difficulty for me. It is easy to understand my failure to know the social self of a woman so lightly attested like Cecily Pontefract, and then only through the aggressive, conflicted eyes of the clergy, but to find Richard Ferrour still out of focus, riddled with black spots, is a problem of a different order. He is fuzzy, notwithstanding the hundreds of pieces of evidence of his activities in the town. Moments, small conflicts, certain relationships can be made clearer, but the whole story remains vague because the whole story is not there before us. The fight with narrative here, and with the social self so often best exemplified by its own narrative, is the great historical fight written small. We know so much and have such rich debates about those historical ages that provided us with a primary chronicle. Thucydides' war, the time of David and Solomon, the Roman empire in the first century, but without such texts, masses of facts leave one feeling quite like an archaeologist, so many bits requiring so much cleverness to make still speculative points that leave the social self somewhat in shadow. Richard Ferrour, alias Thorny, alias Pomerey, which man was he? When he died in 1402, he had a will and we know it was proved and by whom, but perhaps typically the will itself didn't survive.

The Corporate Director

Every city had its official leaders and rulers. It's hard to be certain that Ferrour was one of these, but certainly the Master of the Borough Community, the bishop or his steward, and the cathedral dean each may have felt justified to call themselves the town's chief man, at least when one of the others was not present. However, it was possible to gather great importance in unique ways, working the church and lay social systems idiosyncratically and to end up with a rich social identity, even power. To start with, we must remember that the lay people of Wells were constantly rubbing shoulders, doing work for, drinking with, and talking to the numerous clergy of the town. Sometimes nearly 10 percent of the town's population were clergy in the broad sense. This included the bishop and much of his staff, the canons of the cathedral, the vicars-choral who sang in the cathedral and undertook the bulk of its liturgical life, their many servants and aides, the priests who sang endowed masses and served the altars, as well as the schoolboys who were choristers in the church.[63] These men often lived in the cathedral precincts, but their presence within the town was substantial—commerce alone saw to that, and legal and social concerns made interaction rich and enriching.

The church in Wells was a complex structure of institutions and privileges. The cathedral administration was rich and large, including its own area of special jurisdiction, the liberty. The bishop's palace was similarly autonomous and the episcopal officers loomed large there, moving into both cathedral and town affairs. The bishop was the lord of the town and the nominal lord of the cathedral too, but was usually away. There was a small monastic hospital, dedicated to St. John the Baptist in the western part of the town, which had been there since the early thirteenth century.[64] Modest, it still was a prize, an institution of local importance. The cathedral establishment had also spawned several corporations, holding property and some clout and dedicated to the different groups of functionaries: vicars-choral, altarists, choristers, school children, and the like. The single parish church was a large and rich one, whose incumbent was chosen by the cathedral canons, but which employed other priests, hired by the borough and disciplined by them. Lastly, there was the almshouse of the Holy Saviour, established by clergy and laity in 1436 and overseen by both the Borough Community and the cathedral canons.[65] Institutions spawn offices and committees; offices and committees cultivate power; power attracts ambitious selves; and some selves work intensely to extend themselves. If the dedicated churchwarden John Ronburgh wanted little else than to serve and care for the parish church, another man, Thomas Cornish—Master Cornish, Fellow Cornish, Vicar Cornish, Holy Father Cornish, Brother Thomas, Precentor Thomas, Canon Cornish, Bishop Thomas, the Lord Bishop of Tine—wanted his hand in every institutional pot and by the first years of the sixteenth century he had virtually achieved this.

Thomas Cornish was a fixture of the local ecclesiastical hierarchy for about three decades from the 1480s until he died in 1513. He was a suffragan bishop and the master of the hospital of St. John for over a decade before he became the vicar of the parish church. That he liked Wells' world of church and town, that he had set his barren roots in the area, is certain, for as he gathered preferment and property, he never moved elsewhere. He ordered his tomb early, as Bishop Beckynton had decades earlier. His name makes his Cornish origins clear, but perhaps it was his father or grandfather who had migrated from that most foreign of counties to Somerset. It was the family locale, his sisters and their children settled not only in Wells but also in Bristol and Taunton, apparently all turned townsfolk, but West Country folk even if Cornwall was behind them.

Thomas knew what it was like elsewhere; as a messenger, a representative, and a mediator, he had often enough ridden around southern England in service. But he had probably first gone East in his mid-teens, probably in the late 1460s when he had gone to Oxford, where his love of books and good friends was satisfied for some time. He received an M.A. and by 1475, he had already made his first deep institutional affiliation at Oriel College, where he was elected a fellow. He learned administration, working impressively in small groups and became trusted with money. He became very good at accumulating it too. At Oriel, he served as rent collector and treasurer before being elected provost in 1493. Far beyond the urban oligarchy of a small town, Cornish acted as the best Wells burgesses did, building power by dominating social networks. As head of an Oxford house, he was in touch with an extensive group of other men linked to government, to the church hierarchies, and to the county elites.

While at Oriel the hankering for the West Country became evident and he plainly sought economic and ecclesiastical advancement in that home quarter. Like Beckyngton before him, he shows how the call of region was strong, even among the moderately ambitious. Local preferment came in 1483 when he was appointed master of the Hospital of St. John the Baptist in Wells. Whether he had long been a member of the order of St. John of Jerusalem is unknown, but he was to spend the next fifteen or so years at the head of the little house. It was modest indeed and even what religious role it served in these years is unclear. He had a lot of time for other things and the appointment can be seen as the successful cultivation of Bishop Stillington of Bath and Wells, who had the advowson and soon gave Cornish some work to do as the suffragan bishop of the diocese. He was invested as the Bishop of Tine in the Archbishop of Jerusalem's diocese in September of 1485.[66] There is no question that a suffragan bishop had work to do. Depending on who your bishop was you might have a greater or lesser amount of work filling in where only a bishop would do, at ordinations and the like. There was prestige to it also. A suffragan was not the kind of man who would become a powerful diocesan bishop, but he had precedence and honor nevertheless and much of Cornish's later career looks like an attempt to be more of a bishop and ecclesiastical power than suffragans typically were. In 1487, Bishop Richard Fox of Exeter made him suffragan for that West Country diocese too. For income, he was given the rectorship of Backwell, soon swapping it for a similar position in St. Peter's near Calais (1484). He probably never visited the place. He became an impressive pluralist, gaining rectorships, wardenships and vicarages and swapping them for advantage, sometimes quickly.[67] He lived in the hospital of St. John in Wells but he rode far and by the early 1490s had built a powerful network of supporters in the West Country to link with that which he had in Oxford. For some years thereafter his ambitions focused on Wells, its hinterland, and its institutions. He became a big man in this world and he relished it and the way its institutions buoyed him up, kept him high in the water and with unusually good visibility and vision.

His investment in networks, his hard work, and intelligence started paying off in 1493 when his good efforts at administering funds for the "House of St Mary and the King's College called Orialle"[68] and diocesan activity in the West led to his appointment as Provost of the College. He continued as suffragan bishop and as master of St. John the Baptist, Wells, but the residency requirement would have kept him more often in Oxford and probably in London too. Subsequently, the College was somewhat concerned by his absences and eager to make sure he only collected a daily allowance when he was "actually resident in the college."[69] Still, it had returned him to England's intellectual center, albeit in a modest administrative role.

It is very possible that as Cornish was receiving his Oxford position he was already conscious of another possibility for advancement in the West Country. It came in late October 1494 when he was made canon of Cudworth and was two weeks later admitted as a canon residentiary of Wells Cathedral. This meant he was to be one of the active minority of canons who spent much of their time in the city and were most active in the cathedral administration. Because men had often shirked this responsibility, drawing "commons" while in residence but actually avoiding the city, all canons now had to pay caution money and Thomas Cornish was able to hand over the tidy sum of 100 marks, well over £60.[70] The compensations were extensive. There was more money for on-site service, access to higher ecclesiastical office through the same service, and all the perquisites of working for a great corporation. He had the prebend and its income, but he also received a fine house between the Dean's and Archdeacon of Wells' house and oversaw its renovation, winning leave to continue living in St. John's Hospital while the renovations were underway. As impressively, he continued to operate as Prior of the house until 1497, keeping at that moment a triple residency as well as his work as suffragan and the responsibility of his rectorships.[71] Plainly, he was sensitive to hierarchy and had moved up the ecclesiastical ladder toward the upper echelons. He had advanced from the top rank of the irregular clergymen, the men who made their living at the edges of the wealth of the church, to the affluent center. Eventually, he did resign as the head of the hospital but continued his episcopal work and no doubt used that prestige to raise his standing within the cathedral chapter too. He was a grand pluralist, fulfilling the residence requirements of both institutions and using his need to travel between them as an advantage. He was often enough in the home counties to be able to serve the cathedral chapter there and perhaps he executed Oriel's west country business in a similar way when living in Wells.[72]

Leaving the Hospital of St. John allowed him to take up another position in 1497. He was appointed vicar of St. Cuthbert's parish church in Wells.[73] The rector was the dean and chapter of the cathedral, so he was in effect appointed rector by himself and his friends. However, it was not a position that many of the canons would have sought. It was a large and rich parish to be sure and we know Cornish was elsewhere eager to acquire tithes, but he most probably sought it to provide an outlet for his abiding desire to preach and to lead a lay religious community. Cornish enjoyed conducting religious services. After the death of Bishop Robert Stillington in 1491, he had begged permission to perform the requiem service even though it was against the cathedral's customs and he was not yet a canon or at all affiliated with them. The chapter granted it: he must have been known to do a good job and he plainly knew how to make a good case.[74] He would later be closely involved with serving and endowing prayers for Bishop Oliver King.[75]

Nevertheless, a parish gave you moral force in a different kind of community. As the vicar of St. Cuthbert's he had to deal with the leadership of the town, cooperatively planning the improvements to the church, the raising of money, the selection of other chaplains, and even the education of children, such as that was. Having lived in the city for so long he was well acquainted with the people and his nephew the mercer John Welshot was one of the rising stars of the merchant community. The two men were close. They acquired land together in 1511.[76] In 1502, Cornish interceded in a political dispute with the Master of the town on Welshot's advice, going so far as to threaten the Master, a lawyer and sometime agent of the cathedral, Nicholas Trapp, with the royal council's intervention.[77] A rich piece of evidence it is that shows how the Bishop of Tine's ecclesiastical networks, stretching across the country, could entail through family and residency the little political world of Wells. What Cornish had done in committing to Wells even as he rode to Oxford and London, to Exeter and Bath, was to cling to his real family and a virtual family in the parish of Wells. John Welshot was one of his executors when he died and he passed the gifts that Cornish gave him on to his children at his own death.[78]

Cornish was a pluralist but one who actually served with skill and eagerness in many of his roles. He was not in it just for the power or the money. Education and the love of the things of education mark his career not only in Oxford but also in Wells. While it is speculation that this was part of his role as vicar of the parish church, it was part of his duties at the cathedral. Almost as soon as he joined the chapter, he turned up as librarian and was chosen chancellor for three years from 1499.[79] He was now a cathedral executive, and as chancellor he examined and selected the new headmaster of the cathedral school and administered the education and preaching program of the church.[80] He valued books himself and may have transmitted their prestige to his family. To a young relative John Welshot, son of his nephew, he bequeathed "six or eight of his best books." No one else in the will was favored with a direct grant of books. His tastes in books were serious. The one title we're sure of is *Lincoln College MS 70,* a book of philosophical theology, displaying the Christian response to the errors lurking in pagan philosophy.[81] If Cornish represents an abuse of later medieval

Catholicism in his pluralism, he also represents its success in his pastoral commitment and learnedness. He possessed these qualities above the ordinary for churchmen and in rewarding him, they recognized the ecclesiastical virtues he had. All the responsibility given to him over learning and administration in Wells came from cathedral canons who were themselves mainly university graduates of all kinds, including doctors of civil and canon law and bachelors of theology. He inspired their confidence.[82]

They repaid him further by allowing him to become the precentor in 1502. This meant leaving the chancellorship for a richer and more prestigious office, in many ways second only to the cathedral's dean.[83] It was his last official promotion; but in practice he had reached a kind of pinnacle, since the bishop of Bath and Wells from 1504 till the end of Cornish's life was the papally appointed absentee cardinal Hadrian de Costello. For many purposes, Cornish was the only bishop in the diocese. He enjoyed high prestige, but perhaps in the end he had too much to do. Pluralists were not supposed to execute many of the offices they held. However, in 1505 he was acting as provost in Oxford, precentor at the cathedral, vicar of a large parish church, and suffragan bishop in two dioceses, one of which had no bishop in the country at all. If nothing else, it gave him the leeway to stick to his principles: he no longer needed more money; he cannot have doubted his success and stature. Furthermore, he had already made the decision to stay near Wells and to be buried there in a lavish tomb appropriate to bishops, in the north transept of the cathedral. Thus when in 1507 a dispute emerged at Oriel between himself and the dean of the college John Goodrych, each supported by the usual factions, he was stubborn. The college rules limited the number of fellows from each county to two and the dean wanted a third from Gloucestershire, at least that is how Cornish interpreted it. He did not receive the support that he had hoped for at Oriel and, resigning in absentia on October 26, 1507, he retired to the West.[84]

In the early spring of 1513, Cornish felt unwell and drew up his will, styling himself bishop of Tine and precentor of the cathedral church. These were the titles that said the most, but his commitment to St. Cuthbert's parish and its community was strongly reflected in his bequests; nor did he forget the cathedral servitors or the Hospital of St. John the Baptist. However, Oriel was snubbed; only a friend, William Canynges, a fellow who must have supported him in the collegiate feuds and a member of the great Bristol family, was remembered with a gift of two marks. Cornish's nieces Ellen and Margaret were given masers, perhaps in memory of hospitality and the feeling of home they provided when he often visited their towns on his episcopal business. Ellen was in Bristol; Margaret in Taunton. Perhaps this made the job of perpetual traveling easier, little homes spotted around the diocese, where he could go, where he might help and advise, be respected, not be lonely or too sinful. At Wells itself, the Welshots provided the family hearth, although his own house was fine enough to play the role of host for them. He remembered family and many friends that March. He was generous. Beyond his corporate communities and families and servants, there were national networks of divines and clergy such as the Bishop of Meath Dr. Yng, another suffragan, and Dr. Peter Carslegh, a Devonshire native and Exeter College fellow who had turned up at Wells as a canon. He would later become a royal chaplain and advisor on Henry VIII's divorce.[85] This reminds us Cornish worked regionally, nationally even, and simultaneously locally, a bridge of disparate and far-flung groups of people.

It was certainly not the first time he had considered his afterlife. In 1500, he had reserved his place in the cathedral and had the tomb erected near the chapter house door where the canons would have seen it as a perpetual reminder of him. In 1504, he had established and officiated at an anniversary obituary service "on the morrow of St Jerome's day for 99 years," funded with the rents from the Antelope Inn, which he had refurbished.[86] It was in special honor of his recently dead friends Bishop Oliver King and fellow canon John Lugwardine and was to include him in its obsequies after his death. He saw and lived and spoke his death in these acts of early commemoration. In his will, he had further arranged a variety of prayers to be offered for his soul, encouragement to the cathedral staff to attend his requiem services. That spring as he was dying, he considered what more he had to give to reward his best friends, to encourage them, to help them. He had never doubted that he was a bishop in earnest and the canon law agreed. He gave what only a bishop could: pardon. In the usual language of indulgences, he granted to each person lending a hand to his will's execution forty days off their temporal penance.[87] This was a rare gift indeed. Cornish the typical, contradictory, late medieval churchman died in early July. Forty-two cathedral dignitaries attended the final service.[88] At his obit in 1515, £1 in donations were received. In 1518–19, one penny came in at his anniversary. Someone in the cathedral still cared enough to come.

Cornish's life comes out as a career, an easy if superficial marker of a social self, and it would have been an odd if complex man who would not have compensated internal sorrows or difficulties with such public success. His achievement was based on skills that the burgesses themselves would have admired: temperate nature, willingness to negotiate, sufficient wealth and business sense. Strange that it is so much harder to judge his curial skills. But, there was learning and pastoral care in this career and these clerical virtues as well as his celibacy gave his unworldly worldliness, his social self, a more complex character than some pluralists. However, since he was a reader rather than a writer, an administrator and preacher rather than a monk or philosopher, his worldliness left a heavier mark on the records, and probably on his life.

Dame Tanner

The nature of the medieval social self, especially that of the towns, makes it more difficult to write the life of many women. The objectified, somewhat diabolical void of Cecily Pontefract can barely be contradicted from Wells material. The life of wives is especially difficult to recover. Furthermore, as the reader knows, the material I have been working with is especially masculine in its origins and uses. The men felt that the women were theirs, key elements of their selves and the records reflect this. A woman emerges in little ways in widowhood, a state from which she continues her husband's persona and can act more freely and even publicly. A transaction of 1387 illustrates the documentary states possible for respectable women. It was a charter of Margery Moniers "in her pure and liege widowhood and full power," a widowhood she had worn well for thirty years and more, conveying a valuable property in Wells High Street to "Thomas Tanner and Isabel his wife."[89] That Margery was prominent followed from the lucky wealth of her retained widowhood. She was wealthy enough to remain single. (And, as Judith Bennett has showed, where resources were available perpetual widowhood flourished.)[90] She was a highly trusted figure in the town, the only woman on record to be selected to execute the will of a man who wasn't her husband, and one of the richest men in the town to boot.[91] The chance identification here is Isabel Tanner. In an enrolment of a deed in a register book, she might just have been called "his wife" or, as in many other grants of land that Thomas Tanner took up, there might be no mention of a wife at all, no property rights explicitly given to her. For Isabel Tanner to show up, therefore, was for her to be of a class wealthy enough and to have a husband willing enough to vest the land in her. In this world, in this book, women cannot be known separately from their husbands, even when the men are dead.

Isabel Tanner is a little better known to us in great part because of the closeness that existed between husband and wife in necessary conjunction, notwithstanding the far-flung business of a merchant in cloth and wine, the town's greatest merchant of the second half of the fourteenth century.[92] He was often in Bristol, often enough in France and perhaps in Ireland, sometimes in London or at parliamentary sessions at Westminster. She may well have accompanied him some time. It is very hard to guess how much a respectable, rich woman could have traveled. Margery Kempe did so with her husband, once pilgrimage became the reason and the wife of Bath traveled too, but neither did so without some taint to their honor and Margery's confessor was very angry when she chose to leave against his advice and to travel without a group or a protecting man.[93] But we know nothing particular of Isabel's scope of life beyond Somerset. She heard the stories from her husband, of fashion and trade in France and Ireland; of the death of their friend and servant Robert Ashby while with the armies in France. However, during the years of married life, her documentary appearance is thin.

That she knew the Mendip Hills and Wells Forum Hundred is easier for us to say. She was an immigrant of the most common kind, coming from within ten miles, from the village of Woky in the lordship of the Bishop of Bath and Wells, a vill under the hill, near caves but in Wells' hinterland. She was probably born in the early 1350s, a child of plague survivors who had probably made good from the extra land that became available after the debacle. At any rate, when Thomas Tanner first knew her she was Isabella Lode, the daughter of Walter and Christina. They were peasants, perhaps the grander kind who had accumulated land, animals and rights, teetering on the edge of even better things but still serfs. Isabel married Thomas by 1371, for that is when she is first mentioned as feofee of a house and butcher stalls on the High Street of Wells, as well as of five acres of land.[94] She moved to the town; ceased to be a peasant's daughter, and became a merchant's wife.

This was a rise in status, to be sure. But to be Thomas Tanner's wife was something further already. He was master of the town by 1374 and repeated the honor in 1379, 1386, 1392, and 1395. During the 1380s and 1390s he was thrice a member of parliament for the town, agitating there over the vagaries of the wine trade. For his wife, this all meant prominence locally, growing with every office, every ship safely returned to Bristol, and every graceful social gesture. As the Master's wife she led the elite women of the town in church and in social life, presiding at the annual wives' feast as her husband entertained the men. She participated in his honor and developed it further by her good and appropriate deportment. She must have worried about her reputation. Who wouldn't, but more precisely, as she rose in grandeur she worried about her origins.

Isabella loved and honored her parents, never forgetting to name them for special prayers in the intercessory endowments of her later life. She must have understood too that they would have wanted her to rise as far as possible, to attain a large and impeccable social self. Proper chastity she could take care of; due sadness and care in public affairs and diligence in private business, but at some point the mark of serfdom bothered her. Perhaps some backbiter reminded people that she was after all a serf, not a great lady. To be a lady did mean leaving servility behind. The Tanners waited till Isabella's father was dead—perhaps it would have reflected negatively on him—but as she entered middle age, they entered the negotiations with the bishop of Wells' officers to have her manumitted, freed from bondage.

Later medieval hierarchies are difficult to keep clear. What was irrelevant to your advancement at one moment could become significant later on, when you found your children's advance into the clergy was complicated by bastardy or serfdom. Within a few decades of the great risings of 1381, serfdom was in permanent decline in England. It did not carry much weight in these years aside from an emotional charge and the pack of dues and rents that tended to go with the status in the countryside. For instance, most probably someone had had to pay for Isabella's marrying Thomas, a freeman not of her manor. However, in towns these things counted for almost nothing until you had a certain kind of ambition for your children or yourself. Even then, if Isabella had moved further afield, if she and Thomas had settled in London or Coventry, she might have buried the issue. As probably, however, honesty and the urges of the ambitious self would have pushed them to the decision. Whatever the precise springs, she wanted freedom from the taint. She might well have been pleased to hear in 1381, in the midst of the alarming uproar, the letter of emancipation that Richard II had issued, one of which seems actually to have made its way to Somerset, before they were all canceled. It would have saved time, money and the ambiguous publicity of manumission.[95]

At any rate, to become legally free required money and only those with money would have bothered to pay for the legal status. Poorer folk grubbed their way to freedom in a generation or two of moving or town life. In 1393, Thomas had used one of his magistracies to lobby Bishop Ralph Erghum. That September the bishop issued the manumissions of his bondswoman Isabella, daughter of Walter Lode of Woky "with all her goods." It was not enough to have the act done. Reputation and the needs for proving it meant more money and time had to be spent getting other authorities to know it. The dean and chapter of Wells and the prior and convent of Bath Abbey Cathedral inspected and registered the bishop's charter.[96] Even this didn't satisfy the Tanners' desire to secure her reputation against evil words or the future. In addition, the motivation was personal, wholly so, for Thomas and Isabella had no surviving children. Six years later they paid £2 to the exchequer to have a royal registration of the bishop's acts and their ratification by the cathedral officials. It was a good thing too. For only this last enrolment has come down to us to save Isabella's status for posterity. The woman was not ambitious for power but for perfection and a kind of purity of honor.

Both she and Thomas were committed to the perfect Virgin Mary. Thomas bequeathed his soul to her specifically and the two of them had planned to be buried in the chapel of St. Mary in St. Cuthbert's church, a plan that it was left to Isabel to undertake when Thomas died in late 1401. Thomas left her lands and houses in particular, the residue of his estate generally, and he charged her first among a group of friends to be the executor of his will. There was much to do; dozens of bequests to transmit to individuals and institutions. Those that appealed to them included the Carthusian houses of Witham and Henton, islands of pure religion—the monastic order that boasts of never having needed reform—both dedicated to the Virgin. Thomas's will gave 40s. to Henton to pray for his soul, but Isabel six years later paid 100s. for the right to give a permanent grant of land to the monastery. In return, she asked that they keep a quiet lamp burning eternally in the priory church.[97] Two years later Witham was given three messuages and the bulk of Isabel's landed holdings—sixty acres of arable and eighteen of meadow—in her home manor of Woky and in Yardley.[98] Thomas had been dead for eight years and she was deciding with the counsel of the other executors, especially John Wykyng, what would be most helpful to purify Thomas's soul and expedite the painful purgatorial cleansing. In this latter case, she did not ask for any elaborate memorial for Thomas or herself. The money was simply to help a monastery with which she and Thomas sympathized, whose work they admired. It was generous; it cost all of 12 marks just to receive the royal license to make the gift.[99]

Devotion to godly beauty, the silent perfections of Mary and the Carthusians, guided Isabel Tanner's long liege widowhood. She did not neglect her lands and income, but she kept her eye on the help that her husband could receive in purgatory. Her greatest work here was the nearest, the construction of the chantry devoted to the Virgin in St. Cuthbert's church. By the time she had turned to divesting herself of land and endowing the Carthusians, she had already discharged the great religious works in aid of the souls she loved most—her own, her parents', and her husband's. In a way, she presided over his death by executing their ideas. In 1404, she turned lands, buildings, and leases over to the Borough Community of Wells, who were to undertake the supervision of Tanner's new chantry. Isabel had arranged for this robust perpetual service, led daily by a priest dedicated to that work "forever." Thomas had wanted to be buried in the Mary chapel in front of a stupendous new south window, all colorful light, but it was just a dream. He assigned £20 for it, his largest bequest, but the planning and work were left to Isabel and others. She and the other executors worked over the next three years to make St. Catherine's Day, his death day, into a principle feast of the Wells civic calendar. Money was offered to the vicar and the chaplains to make sure they were there and to the poor who could best work against the wealth that Thomas and Isabel had so enjoyed. Sixty shillings of bread was distributed annually, enough for a crowd of poor more numerous than the population of the town.[100] Moreover, anyone who entered that chapel saw the wall tablet reminding them: "The anniversary service of Thomas Tanner is on St Katherine's Day."[101]

The physical work of shaping the chapel was already underway. The great new window was being carved, the plan for the glazing executed.

In July 1403, the town council granted an unusual request Isabel had sent them. They said that the "entire old window" from the chapel where Thomas was could be transferred to Isabel's private house.[102] The connection to the Virgin's chapel to which she was devoted and in which her beloved husband's body waited was physically manifested in this transfer. She built the new window and received the old one, a part of the church, an objective correlative of her husband back into her house. On the one hand she directed building in the parish church, while on the other she remodeled her home for an oratory. The blended identity of wife and husband is well represented here. It was a kind of clinging, a stubborn social and religious self, which wouldn't give up on the other self. That wasn't all.

Isabel furnished the new chaplaincy and chantry. She kept control over the initial furnishings, even though the town and parish would have to take care of the future maintenance and replacement. The foundation charter specified this and later inventories at least partly reflect what she provided to St. Mary's furnishings. Her own testament directed even more to the chapel, and her executor Thomas Atwood knew that it was her favorite.[103] These gifts give us a last sense of a woman who worked toward high goals for herself and her world and admired the silence of Wytham as much as she recognized and acknowledged that regular worldly meaning spoke best through ornament, charter, ritual, and show.

Within the church, the competing chantry was that of the Trinity. It was a corporate place for the whole Borough Community. But what might have struck you most had you regularly frequented both altars or that of St. James nearby, was that in contrast to the barrage of colors and stripes and leopard-emblazoned curtains found elsewhere, was the consistency of Isabel's taste. The priest appeared in either a white chasuble or the ruby color she apparently preferred. There were two of these, one in velvet set off with green, one in ruby damask with a green cross in the middle of the back. Rich reds and green were her colors. For the sacrament, she shunned pewter as too cheap and went for a chalice and paten set of silver, ornamentally gilt, and added two silver cruets. It all has an elegant, unfussy quality to it, the force of one mind seeking a perfect resolution rather than the succession of selves that gave isolated gifts to the Trinity or St. James altars. But even if Isabel designed it herself, she did not do it herself and it could not be hers only. She took the window home but the community and particular individuals would seize a share of her action for themselves. Churchwardens like John Ronburgh would count the things and inventory them, adding a touch of themselves, altar priests would act their social identity through the vestments they wore and the chalice they made God in, and a community of communicants and beseechers made St. Mary's altar their own by joining the related guild, appropriating the place with their friends, even as their prayers remembered Isabella Tanner and the husband she spent three decades commemorating, naming, waiting for.[104]

Conclusion

How far do these biographical moments, focused on individuals in their community context, succeed in conveying the social meaning of life in the medieval town? This is a key criterion we should use to judge this kind of chapter. It has tried to turn the interpretations of the previous chapters onto known individuals and the known, albeit quite limited, facts of their lives. Here what is added is not exactly an argument, but a context that has to be convincing for the entire interpretation of this book to be compelling. Only after examining these lives lived through the prism of the social self can we be sure that the path I've described is the right one, a fully plausible one. It is not that the biographical perspective is a privileged one, but that it is a necessary one and can be accounted for within the same structure of concepts and relationships as the rest of later medieval social life. It does more of course: it redeems the humanity that motivates history, but in the context of the social self it does so as part of a global interpretation of social life, focusing on the later medieval urban possibilities of status, hierarchy, and the cleaving of individual to individual. In the conclusion, I try to sum up that interpretation and speculate about the shape of the social self beyond the later medieval urban world.

CHAPTER 9

CONCLUSION: THE SHAPE OF
THE SOCIAL SELF

The Later Medieval Social Self

To understand the significance of the life narratives in chapter 8 is to see that
agency exists even when nothing of "importance" happens. It is really an
effect of a mind. It is the place of meaning, not only of action. It belongs to
the politically and the economically insignificant person as surely at to the
powerful. Action itself, the great business that needs explanation, is intelligible
only in the boundaries of meaning, in the domain of petty intentions and
failures. Part of the job of history is to render embodied meaning in all its
manifestations; it is to understand the human situation—all its probable
potential—in a historical moment. The social self is a cultural complex, a category that enables our understanding by drawing social history and agency
together. It is a powerful aide to seeing the "structuration"—in Giddens'
sense—of the world, of self and society, body and idea, person and person.

The ideas and concepts that cloaked and shaped the action and understanding of later medieval people, men preeminently, had myriad sources
but the embedded master values of honor, fidelity and hierarchy constituted
the operating system of this social world. I have tried to outline this in
chapter 2 and believe that subsequent chapters, including the biographies,
work to effect a global historical demonstration. The later medieval person
was no atom to be understood fundamentally as an expression of his class or
country. Honor thrives only in a socially intense and public system, for
honor is the self preying on other selves. It captures best the perspective of
the agent, of the "individual."

The role of fidelity, however, is to regulate affairs between two "competing"
selves. It compels them to assess their respective honor, to negotiate their
positions, and to bring each other under social obligations and expectations.
They can then "come through" for each other or let each other down.

Although argued here through lawsuits and the business of arbitration, it was in fact a constant of this social life. Social selves worked upon each other to get beyond and above each other. Social networks function on this axis. Consequently, however, even quite modest social selves were authentic actors. They drew on their honor and upon others for their ends. Those ends included the desire to grow in status (including wealth) and to become more of an *event* in their social milieux. Because the local institution—the Burgesses Court—enhanced the scope of honor-building activity for its members, we can conclude that Wells's burgesses had social selves that were especially robust in the public forums of the community. To some extent, it was an open community, cultivating the agency of its members by judiciously advancing, protecting, and limiting them. Community remains a social actor, setting the ground rules and transcending the small groups and individuals it regulates and encloses, as well as excluding others to enhance its own.[1] This kind of community is not all encompassing, but is a large club with sometimes-vague boundaries.

There is, however, a larger conclusion. Access to participation in a self-governing court engenders more robust social selves, whose political standing is more considerable than those who lack such an outlet. On such a reading, the possibilities would be significant for the burgesses of all towns and even to people in the villages, whose courts and system of jurors provide many parallels to the urban fraternities of my focus. Greater distance from access to such a court would measure the decline of the social selves of common people. Without such a venue for their selves, they increasingly became people who reacted rather than acted. One can perhaps glimpse here how the modern social self in a metropolitan environment could become very thin, compensated perhaps by the massive advance of the private self.

Increased exclusionary pressure by an elite or by demographic change might tend to concentrate elite social selves, encouraging them to form social links beyond the community and limiting the identity-enrichening features of the local scene. Some may believe this study too insular, and while we should be cautious in assuming that even the small town merchant's links ranged strongly abroad,[2] big men made contacts beyond their communities, which could weaken lesser selves' ambitions. Sherri Olson has in effect argued that such a transformation was taking place in village life after the plague and deep into the fifteenth century.[3] Others have argued for the urban concentration of power from the mid-fifteenth century, decisively in the sixteenth century, which we might correlate with the decline of the possibilities of social-self development.[4] It must be said, however, that it is not a foregone conclusion that the transformation of the urban governmental system away from a "democratic" element toward a more purely "aristocratic" one could not be achieved without the development of compensations for more modest social selves, including the fruits of social and economic patronage.[5] Similarly, it is unclear what role greater social regulation and control would have had on the quantity of the social self: it might have reshaped it, reduced its autonomy, without actually reducing it. This is, I suppose, an argument Michel Foucault would have admired: to say that power may produce more self through its regulatory gaze rather than less.[6]

Wells' regime in the mid-fifteenth century, however, still allowed for many of its members to be arbitrators and thereby aggrandize their honor and construct larger networks of fidelity than are visible elsewhere. This makes very clear that fraternity does not sidestep the question of power or of hierarchy, although it does tend to transform it. Medieval fraternity worked its own way toward delivering the differentiated social world required by its century and milieu. The extraordinary fact that in Wells power was constructed for the elite from a process that also enriched the agency of the common run of men is a lesson in the subtlety of institutions that historians have too often overlooked in favor of simple explanations. Power is not a zero sum game. It is also, however, a reason not to scorn the study of the locality in favor of the purely grand account, where simplicities can reign. Social power was manufactured in Wells, distributed unevenly among the populace, and constantly calibrated and exchanged.

There is another feature to this: those excluded from access to the honors this system cultivated were positively disadvantaged. It helps to explain what was at stake. Cut off from the resources of power meant being cut off from the personal possibilities for honor and advancement. This mattered greatly in a world without notions to sustain the self on its own. Religion, the blessedness of the poor, and a kind of contempt for society and power were perhaps all that those in the social basement could fall back on. Such people lived with distinct social limitations and small social selves.

All but the saddest and most hopeless self played at the game of honor. The social selves of the later Middle Ages were part of a regime of life characterized by ambition and hope, but plagued by anxiety of failure. Association could help protect and advance you. Social networks represent only one kind of group connection. These small, evanescent groups allowed people to harness others for their benefit, knowing that they might have to reciprocate later. Networks could be of friends of similar social status, but at certain moments their effectiveness required the presence of more influential people, mediators between oligarchs and commoners, for instance. However, the people who moved into the most social networks were inevitably the most influential men. Networks reveal graphically the differences among social selves, some imperial and expansive, some exploited colonisers, and some enabling colonials. Without forgetting that the "group" did function to set rules to its game, the players made the choices, coped with the system, and succeeded very unevenly. Some had advantages in terms of resources—wealth, family connections, charm, wit; some simply had good luck.

Plainly, the exploitation of institutional and community power resources varied greatly, even in an open space such as Wells'. Nevertheless, this large, porous space for the competition of social selves was a mainly male arena. It was simultaneously an institution to uphold a certain model of the relation of the sexes. Women's social selves were seriously dependent on particular men, to whom they were bound—husbands and fathers. Women's selves were subordinated and partially merged into that of their protecting man's identity. This was true even of widows, and it was an advantage over being without such protection. Women were ranked according to their husbands' statuses; even in widowhood, they played roles and covered social space as allotted by their husbands' social selves, little more, little less so long as they remained pure in their sociocultural character of virtuous female— either virgin daughter or chaste wife or widow. They were not, however, without influence even though they lacked all public authority.

A merit of the concept of the social self is that it enrichens the political perspective because it forces the simultaneous recognition of the place of women within their households and as junior partners in a small group endeavour—building the family's wealth and honor. By their fidelity— recall *The Wryght's Chaste Wyf*—they were to uphold the standing of the husband and to receive praise for doing so. Like Isabel Tanner, this duty was carried through even after the husband's death and might live on love and on hope and honorable pride in what husband and wife had been. All depended, of course, on their worldly success. Women deployed social power within this well circumscribed context. They worked through the social rankings that they had, extensions and abettors of a man. In this role, the wife was in fact a larger self than were the other dependants of a man's household and identity: in the urban context, children, apprentices, and servants. The give and take of harsh words and petty violence revealed the nuances of this hierarchy of selves. The appropriation and control of the physical trappings of the social self further sustained the wife's preeminence, little though that would mean in an impoverished family, little as it must have meant to Mrs. Payn in her "next available" almoner's spot.

Comparisons and Speculations

The social selves that emerged from all these institutions and practices were variable. They waxed and waned over the course of a life; some were massive, stretching beyond the social horizon of the town, whereas others clung to a small circle of friends or craft brothers, flinching before the world. But as a small town, Wells had certain social structures in place that delivered the contours of possibility for social selves who lived there. We can see that the shape of selves elsewhere in England, even among those relatively low down the social scale, may have been quite different. Obviously, the ability to make money and buy goods affects the range of expressive possibilities available; it may not remove the desire to parade status, but it may force people to have subtler eyes for seeing it. Class mattered little in most Wells transactions, but wherever it did come into play, the marking of social identity must have been quite different. I suggest that people would have different identities to wear when they mingled outside their little social world and those who jostled with nobility, even their own feudal lord, would have been reminded of the significance of that difference in ways usually foreign to the local urban scene. The aristocratic viewer may well have lacked the subtle eyes to see the differences among burgesses: we lump what we don't understand and don't need to understand to thrive. A challenge for those studying the social self of peasants is to determine how much class mattered there; how much class identity and class "conflict" formed the social self. For some, the social self would no doubt be an epiphenomenon of class, but even for them the challenge is to demonstrate the necessity and character of this relationship. By contrast, in a village imagined under the model of the Toronto school of social history, with its active, rather liberated peasants and its absentee landlords, the question of class might never come up. To some extent, the role of making room for hierarchy is to say that even the social world that lives without lordship may still *think* under its shadow and be constrained by it. The broader culture, the master values, cannot be forgotten and may not be revealed by some classes of local records. Among the peasantry—people like Isabella Tanner's parents—this may have been a crucial background assumption of their social lives and identity. Its residue helps to explain her manumission, the proud social self she possessed. Thus, in every social circumstance, the goal must be to see what general *and* particular conditions determine the girth of a social self. This is to go beyond the case study to start understanding better the general shape of people as we cut the cloth of sociocultural history. The differences town and country make; the differences wealth makes; the differences that peculiar institutions make can all be judged that way only if a general enabling concept like the social self is employed. Yet, for the later medieval period, I suspect that the master values of honour, fidelity, and hierarchy may have a nearly universal relevance.

As in all centuries, it would seem that gender difference and gender interaction were mastering variables of the later Middle Ages. Across the culture respectable women were socially shadows of some man, lacking the chance for valued or honorable independence. The "good" woman was the dependent woman and the virtues available to her in the social world were those that would keep her out of the public world except as a discreet servant of her husband, and "a word to the wise" among other women. Like Isabel Tanner, she should disappear as an independent legal presence during her husband's life, act though she did.

We shouldn't, however, flinch from recognizing that in the Middle Ages the reverse side of this coin of women's subordination is not the go-it-alone man, simple proprietor of family and goods—the independent agent. On the contrary, the "singleman" was an anomaly. For his own sense of completion required marriage and household as extension and improvement of his self. Again, *the Wryght's Chaste Wyf* develops from this assumption. The wife was the chief aide of his potential status; the servants, apprentices, and goods were added to this moral core. The more there were the greater he was, but this *he* was really a small corporation.[7] The records mislead us a little in identifying a man by name like a mere thing. Each person is a bit like "France" in Shakespeare; it represents a king, a community, a country, a swarm of society, simply personified in a word and an individual, its titular head. This kind of family surely entails subordination but also union, the fusing of selves more than bodies, and in the world we've examined it was a highly durable relationship too. To look to other communities and historical moments and to assess the social self there is to look for how things might be different. Uncoupling the essential couple may open the road to a different conception of the social self, appropriate or central, depending on the different historical circumstances.

I conceived this inquiry into the medieval social self partly from the realization that a history of the typical medieval private self was most unlikely to be successful. It could only thrive by giving priority to one of the great mystical souls or philosophers and their typicality has always seemed to me a thing to show, not to assume. The hope was to do something different anyway, to speak for social history's ability to recover the common self and its social world. Now, we can see the way people worked and thought among other people, even about themselves. More crucially, however, we understand how individuals can be meaningfully integrated with a broader social analysis. However, it is no longer clear that the medieval social self we have interpreted is an analytical leftover, the proverbial tip of the more interesting but invisible iceberg of the secret self.

The "individual" is less a social entity than a cultural one. It is a mode of literature, a cluster of tropes discovered and developed, elegantly elaborated with uneven but increasing intensity since the late eleventh century. The meditative and literary power of the inward turn to the well of consciousness is undeniable. But the question remains as to whether it has great historical significance and if so, when. Heathcliff's, "I cannot live without my life" captures the self-reflective quality—and inanity—of the romantic individual, but does that paradigm—receding in some ways now—have any relevance for medieval social history? It seems, in other words, fitting that Karl Weintraub's *The Value of the Individual*[8] is a tale of lonely and autobiographical ruminations, the moments when people, often worried and disturbed people, reflected. Nevertheless, it seems to me that unless the facts of culture and power have opened a large space around the ego, this reflective self doesn't underlie and enable the social self in ways we might have assumed. It is not the noumenon, the real self; rather it's the secular Sunday afternoon self, the self the medieval convert drops once he's done talking about it and probably boring his interlocutor.

Obviously, the development of such a self as ubiquitous and as achieving a hierarchical control over the conceptualization of who we are is one of the great stories of modernity. Others can take up that story, although I note that I don't think anyone has yet done justice to the fact that the actual hegemony of that private self over the social one is uncertain. Too often, it emerges when we change subjects, when we go mystic and literary. Again, we need stories that better integrate mind and world to be sure of the relationship of different kinds of selves and identities. Working only within the world of ideas, Charles Taylor has gone a long way in this direction because he recognized the diverse elements that have a grip on contemporary western people, but the socially rooted demonstration is partial at best.[9] We need perhaps to raise the question for other historians and to ask where in the medieval world, in the medieval town particularly, could the more atomistic and private self begin to develop? Where to look for an empowered self separate from the social networks and the family hierarchy? Caroline Bynum showed that even among the contemplative population of monasteries the community perspective was rhetorically strong.[10] Perhaps it really did take an oddity, a touch of paranoia to see the world as an individualist would. That may be what unites Margery Kempe and Abelard across the centuries and against their many glaring differences. In their cases, however, it would seem that the feeling of isolation and loneliness, elements of social and psychological difficulty and failure, worked to develop the inner self, which mulled over its errors and the sleights it had received. While everyone usually acted from an egocentric posture, few wallowed in their expressivism or pain—they got even! To react this way was still an anomaly, a sign of a social self gone wrong like a backed up drain, a self out of sorts with the world that nurtured it. Too many children; too little honor; Margery Kempe's ale went bad; people laughed; the world was too much with her; she went mad, went mystic.

Still, she was not alone in finding a sanctioned outlet for her emotions in the narrow, difficult way of mysticism. A crucial access to the inner self was conscience and this "faculty" developed in the confessional and its accessory and preparatory sermons. Contrition cleaned the conscience and allowed the scrupulous and nervous soul to open itself up, guided by the questions of the confessor. Those who wanted it found that their ghostly father might help them to develop the special language of private guilt and morality that brought Abelard's insight into the intentions together with sin. Still, if the private self were to be stimulated, this was the most likely late medieval avenue.

What this produced was a double schedule of values. An act of social life was seen as on the one side supportive of the social self—its honor, status, and loyalty—but on the other, a risk for the other self. It could be sin—our master values were stalked by sins of greed, sloth, and pride at every turn. The man in the confessional was not a secret sharer alone. He was a nuncio to the other world, that society of eternity where everybody knew all your secrets. This other self was not truly private, however. It was eternal and would *come out* and be evaluated in that otherworldly—not nonworldly—context. This double aspect of life—not my values and society's values—but values shared by two societies, two cities, and me, is the meaning of Beckyngton's tomb once more. One social self for here and now, one religious self for then, both usually articulated in closely related languages and gestures. To read Dante is to read stories, confessions of lives lived, but always with a sense of certainty. In the afterlife, stories find their closure; people are known in their essence.

In the medieval world, then, the counterpart to the social self is a kind of religious self, tuned to the perfect society and the godly values. In later medieval structures of thought and practice, there was no room for the purely "personal" self. It was channeled and cajoled and caressed out of this posture toward religious and social ends. Practical survival required the preeminence of the social self for most people. It fed you best. Furthermore, church life and language were so well interwoven with social life that there was little chance for someone to go it alone and become happier. Why pursue a path that was really a companion to unhappiness, to poverty, that self alone? There was no permanent place for the simple private self. The turn in that direction was, however, a feature of religious practice and reflection; it had a slim tradition from Augustine; a rich one in mysticism. But the latter's goal was union with another, God, ending in the near annihilation of self. It also included *self-less* service to the others around you, even in their ignorance of the truer values. Mysticism and charity made you special, but left you with less self rather than more. You faded into a socioreligious role, a certain stereotype.

Even the turn to death didn't bolster the self. Anxiety aside, death involved confession, judgment at the hands of a hierarch. It then handed you over to that new society, either of the damned or the saved. In Dante as in *The Dance of Death,* death is all socializing: dancing, holding hands, sneering, chatting, going about in groups, telling your tale. For the private self to flourish there had to be other cultural patterns developed, and if they were no more than the pleasures of renaissance chat their scope could hardly be revolutionizing throughout the social world.

This was especially so for most townspeople and peasants. The lack of comfortable leisure must have kept this kind of self alien for a very long time. For the social self to yield some ground to its private, self-assessing sister, it would help if the close world of social networks that could cut as well as kiss, receded. Versions of the state, of benign or at least beneficial government, could be expected to play a role providing and mandating other forms of support, centralizing the trough, weakening the lords. The social self would certainly change in such a moment, although it would be rash and wrong to equate state growth with more private self and less social self. It may lead, however, to a homogenizing and trivializing of some of the older ways of the social self. Nation and monarchy might stitch you nominally to others in a way that weakened the vitality of small groups and communities. A man was left with social skills of little importance because the people just above him on the ladder of power no longer needed his help. They looked above and received authority from more centralized power. Some such process of decline possibly took place as the greater integration of royal power in the English and British kingdoms ensued over the early Modern period. Furthermore, this may aid the development of class, as people feel their agency alienated from the chains of power and influence bearing increasingly upon them. But then again, it may not. Speculations and hypotheses grow quickly enough but need proving within this paradigm.

It has, nevertheless, been argued that modern religion dealt a radical and debilitating blow to traditional community all across Europe. It was not a question of Protestant versus Catholic as was once thought, but a wholesale transformation of the nature of religion.[11] Such changes certainly had a large impact on the possible kinds of social selves developed. In England, a good case has been made to see how structures of communal action and identity formation were swept away.[12] It may be that fewer people could now develop their social selves through common structures, or it may be that the gap between religious and social selves was narrowed in some milieux. Part of what Luther started was a displacement of authority from structure to conscience, a boiling and steaming that has been difficult to keep under control ever since. Conscience may compensate for community. The sixteenth century may have transformed the social self. The seminal work of Stephen Greenblatt over twenty years ago began from the notion that the sixteenth-century self was different. Powerfully expressive, this self sought to fashion itself uniquely. While not socially valid, the renaissance model does suggest a link between conforming medieval social self and modern self-fashioning self.[13]

The trouble with all these speculations, however, is to prove them rather than to enjoy them and their unruly kind. These come perilously close to losing sight of the social self as rooted in social structures and embedded social notions and marching off on the path of speculative history of ideas: the rise of the individual, the impact of the Reformation, the fruits of the Renaissance.[14] If what I have done in this book is at all meritorious or even promising, we should be shy of insisting only on the big picture, but will want to test it with the social self at the analytic center. We need to look for this social self and its transformations rather than to set up too many dichotomies. There are social networks, affiliations, and institutions that structure agency and make up social groupings, and we need in each historical context to find them, linking them both to embedded ideas, practical theories, and the lay of the local land. Within cultures and in comparative contexts over time, the historical complex of the social self is analytically rich and subtle enough to let us see more coherently the pattern and meaning of social history. The difference now is that we mean a social history that is not a history of society but of a place where actors—that means people—make history together from the stuffs they find lying inevitably around them.

NOTES

Chapter 1   Introduction: The Self in Social History

1. *Official Correspondence of Thomas Bekynton, Secretary to King Henry VI, and Bishop of Bath and Wells,* ed. George Williams, Rolls Series 56.1 (London: Longman & Co., 1872), appendix to introduction no. 7, "Dr Boyd's Account of the Exhumation of Bekynton, March 1850," p. cxxv. On Beckygnton, see also A. Judd, *The Life of Thomas Bekynton* (Chichester: Marc Fitch Fund, 1961); and Guy Fitch Lytle, " 'Wykehamist Culture' in Pre-Reformation England," in *Winchester College: Sixth-Centenary Essays,* ed. Roger Custance (Oxford: Oxford University Press, 1982), pp. 143–48.

2. Bekynton in Oxford, Bodleian Library, Oxford MS New College C.288, fol. 4r.; it is reproduced in *Illustrated History of Oxford University* ed. John Prest (Oxford: Oxford University Press, 1993), p. 43; see also frontispiece image in Judd, *Life of Thomas Bekynton.*

3. *Middle English Lyrics,* ed. Richard L. Hoffman and Maxwell Luria (New York: Norton, 1974), #240. For a discussion of this tomb form, see Kathleen Cohen, *Metamorphosis of a Death Symbol. The Transi Tomb in the Late Middle Ages and Renaissance* (Berkeley: University of California Press, 1973), pp. 8–10; Christopher Daniell, *Death and Burial in Medieval England 1066–1550* (London: Routledge, 1997), pp. 69–70 and 184–86; Margaret Aston, "Death," in *Fifteenth-Century Attitudes,* ed. Rosemary Horrox (Cambridge, Eng.: Cambridge University Press, 1994), pp. 225–27.

4. *The Oxford Book of Medieval Latin Verse,* ed. Stephen Gaselee (Oxford: Clarendon Press, 1928), p. 150. "*Mors stupebit et natura/ cum resurget creatura/ judicanti responsura.*"

5. Hoffman and Luria, *Middle English Lyrics,* #232.

6. William Worcestre, *Itineraries,* ed. John Harvey (Oxford: Clarendon Press, 1969), p. 294.

7. This line appears in dozens of vernacular poems in its Latin form, and is from the office for the dead. See, for example, William Dunbar, *Selected Poems,* ed. Priscilla Bawcutt (London: Longman, 1996), pp. 105–110.

8. Taunton, Somerset Records Office DD/B Reg. 6, fol. 137.

9. Wells City Ch. #20.

10. The bishop's water still runs through the streets of the town.

11. For his interesting political work, see *Official Correspondence of Thomas Bekynton,* ed. George Williams, 2 vols., Rolls Series 56 (London: Longman & Co., 1872), passim.

12. Here's a point of unoriginality. I reinvented this phrase, and then stumbled over the work of George H. Mead, who actually originated the term, and whose ideas were quite congenial. I learned of the relevance of them from Ronald F.E. Weissman's article, "Reconstructing Renaissance Sociology: The 'Chicago School' and the Study of Renaissance Society," in *Persons in Groups. Social Behavior as Identity Formation in Medieval and Renaissance Europe,* ed. Richard C. Trexler (Binghamton: Medieval & Renaissance Texts & Studies, 1985), pp. 39–46; Mead also inspired Richard D. Logan, "A Conception of the Self in the Later Middle Ages," *Journal of Medieval History* 12 (1986): 253–68. See Mead, *Mind, Self and Society,* ed. Charles Morris (Chicago: University of Chicago Press, 1934), pp. 178–86, 200–209; *The Individual and the Social Self,* ed. David L. Miller (Chicago: University of Chicago Press, 1982). My approach gives more stress to the individual's action and interpretive power.

13. *Creation of a Community.*

14. See, for instance, Miri Rubin, "Small Groups: Identity and Solidarity in the Late Middle Ages," in *Enterprise and Individuals in Fifteenth-Century England,* ed. Jennifer Kermode (Stroud: Alan Sutton Publishing, 1991), pp. 132–50; Gervase Rosser, "Essence of Medieval Urban Communities," in *The English Medieval Town. A Reader in English Urban History 1200–1540,* ed. Richard Holt and Gervase Rosser (London: Longman, 1990), pp. 216–37; Sheila Lindenbaum, "Ceremony and Oligarchy: The London Midsummer Watch," in *City and Spectacle in Medieval Europe* ed. Barbara A. Hanawalt and Kathryn L. Reyerson (Minneapolis: University of Minnesota Press, 1994), pp. 171–88; and Heather Swanson, *Medieval British Towns* (Houndmills, Basingstoke: St. Martin's Press, 1999), pp. 90–96.

15. The significant exception in medieval England is Margery Kempe; for instance, see Karma Lochrie, *Margery Kempe and the Translations of the Flesh* (Philadelphia: University of Pennsylvania Press, 1991); Hope Weissman, "Margery Kempe in Jerusalem: *Hysteria Compassio* in the Late Middle Ages," in *Acts of Interpretation: The Text in the Contexts 700–1600,* ed. Mary J. Carruthers and Elizabeth D. Kirk (Norman, OK: Pilgrim Books, 1982), pp. 201–217; Clarissa Atkinson, *Mystic and Pilgrim: The Book and World of Margery Kempe* (Ithaca: Cornell University Press, 1983). There has, however, been a long tradition of biographical and prosopographical work, beyond the biographical appendixes to urban histories, for example, Jennifer Kermode, *Medieval Merchants: York, Beverly, and Hull in the Later Middle Ages* (Cambridge, UK: Cambridge University Press, 1998); Caroline Barron, "Richard Whittingdon: The Man Behind the Myth," in *Studies in London History Presented to Philip Edmund Jones,* ed. A.E.J. Hollaender and W.J. Kellaway (London: Hodder and Stoughton, 1969), pp. 197–248; Sylvia Thrupp, *The Merchant Class of Medieval London* (Ann Arbor: University of Michigan Press, 1948), pp. 191–377; Robert Gottfried, *Bury St. Edmunds and the Urban*

Crisis of the Later Middle Ages, 1290–1530 (Princeton: Princeton University Press, 1982), p. 131–32 and Appendix F, 288–90. Owing to methodological, evidentiary and conceptual limitations all these works appear tentative or seriously limited for pursuing the social self.

16. Natalie Zemon Davis, "Boundaries and the Sense of Self in Sixteenth-Century France," in *Reconstructing Individualism. Autonomy, Individuality and the Self in Western Thought,* ed. Thomas C. Heller, Morton Sosna, and David E. Wellerby (Stanford: Stanford University Press, 1986), p. 53.

17. Emmanuel Le Roy Ladurie, *Montaillou. Cathars and Catholics in a French Village, 1294–1324,* trans. Barbara Bray (London: Penguin, 1978); cf. Carlo Ginzburg, *The Cheese and the Worms. The Cosmos of a Sixteenth-Century Miller,* trans. John and Anne Tedeschi (Harmondsworth: Penguin Books, 1980). The same came be seen in Nancy Partner, "Reading the Book of Margery Kempe," *Exemplaria* 3 (1991): 29–66, who uses a psychoanalytic close reading to achieve complex results.

18. Such as communities, classes or their interests, or "society."

19. *Renaissance Self-Fashioning. From More to Shakespeare* (Chicago: University of Chicago Press, 1980).

20. Pierre Bourdieu, *Outline of a Theory of Practice,* trans. Richard Nice (Cambridge, UK: Cambridge University Press, 1977), p. 86.

21. On atomism in political theory, see Charles Taylor, *Philosophy and the Human Sciences* (Cambridge, UK: Cambridge University Press, 1985), pp. 187–210, a critique of the kind of assumptions in Hobbes and Locke, but see also Richard Tuck, "Rights and Pluralism," in *Philosophy in an Age of Pluralism,* ed. James Tully (Cambridge, UK: Cambridge University Press, 1994), pp. 159–70.

22. For instance, Richard Southern, *St. Anselm. A Portrait in a Landscape* (Cambridge, MA: Blackwell, 1990); Michael Prestwich, *Edward I* (Berkeley: University of California Press, 1988); Michael Clanchy, *Abelard. A Medieval Life* (Oxford: Blackwell, 1999); C.E. Moreton, *The Townshends and their World* (Oxford: Oxford University Press, 1992), pp. 5–49; Nigel Saul, *Scenes from Provincial Life. Knightly Families in Sussex. 1280–1400* (Oxford: Oxford University Press, 1986); Colin Richmond, *John Hopton. A Fifteenth-Century Suffolk Gentleman* (Cambridge, UK: Cambridge University Press, 1981). See also the excellent collection, *Medieval London Widows, 1300–1500,* ed. Caroline Barron and Anne F. Sutton (London: Hambledon Press, 1994).

23. This is not meant as criticism of what *is* said. The chapters by Gervase Rosser and Stephen Rigby on urban culture and power respectively, are certainly excellent, as is the summary chapter by R.B. Dobson, but the question of the self or social agency had plainly no place as of yet.

24. Swanson, *Medieval British Towns.*

25. Judith M. Bennett, *A Medieval Life: Cecilia Penifader of Brigstock, c. 1295–1344* (Boston: McGraw-Hill College, 1998).

26. *Townspeople and Nation. English Urban Experiences 1540–1640* (Stanford: Stanford University Press, 2001).

27. See Alison Hanham, *The Celys and their World* (Cambridge, UK: Cambridge University Press, 1985). Colin Richmond, *The Paston Family in the*

Fifteenth Century, 2 vols. (Cambridge UK: Cambridge University Press, 1990, 1996). This is true of other biographical successes, for instance, Southern, *St. Anselm;* Michael Prestwich, *Edward I* (Berkeley: University of California Press, 1988); Clanchy, *Abelard.*

28. See, for example, "Craft Guilds, The Corpus Christi Play, and Civic Government," in *The Government of York in the Middle Ages,* ed. Sarah Rees Jones (York: Borthwick Institute of Historical Research, 1997), pp. 141–63; " 'For Better, For Worse': Marriage and Economic Opportunity for Women in Town and Country," in *"Woman is a Worthy Wight." Women in English Society, 1200–1500,* ed. P.J.P. Goldberg (Gloucester: Sutton Pub., 1992), pp. 108–125.

29. Sherri Olson, *A Chronicle of All that Happens. Voices from the Village Court in Medieval England* (Toronto: Pontifical Institute of Mediaeval Studies, 1996); Zvi Razi, "Intrafamilial ties and relationships in the medieval village: a quantitative approach employing manor court rolls," in *Medieval Society and the Manor Court,* ed. Zvi Razi and Richard Smith (Oxford: Oxford University Press, 1996), pp. 369–91.

30. Olson, *Chronicle of All that Happens,* p. 4.

31. Olson, *Chronicle of All that Happens,* p. 233.

32. Marjorie Keniston McIntosh, *Controlling Misbehavior in England, 1370–1600* (Cambridge, UK: Cambridge University Press, 1999), p. 23.

33. (New York and Oxford, 1993); see also her *The Ties that Bound* (New York and Oxford, 1986).

34. Kermode, *Medieval Merchants,* p. 68. Kermode discusses the use of biography and prosopography in medieval social history: see p. 5.

35. *Discovery of the Individual, 1050–1200* (New York: Harper & Row, 1973); John F. Benton, ed., *Self and Society in Medieval France. The Memoirs of Abbot Guibert de Nogent* (Toronto: University of Toronto Press, 1984; orig. ed. 1970); Walter Ullmann, *The Individual and Society in the Middle Ages* (Baltimore: Johns Hopkins Press, 1966); Robert Hanning, *The Individual in Twelfth-Century Romance* (New Haven, Conn.: Yale University Press, 1977); Richard W. Southern, *Medieval Humanism and other Studies* (Oxford: B. Blackwell, 1970); Southern *Medieval Humanism, St. Anselm and his Biographer* (Cambridge, UK: Cambridge University Press, 1963), revised as *St. Anselm.* See Aron Gurevich, *The Origins of European Individualism,* trans. Katherine Judelson (Oxford: Blackwell, 1995), which productively reopens the individualism discussion. Alan Macfarlane's questions were somewhat different, closer in many ways to social historical notions. See *The Origins of English Individualism* (Oxford: Blackwell, 1978); and *The Culture of Capitalism* (Oxford: Blackwell, 1987); and for response, Stephen D. White and Richard T. Vann, "The Invention of English Individualism: Alan Macfarlane and the Modernization of pre-Modern England," *Social History* 8 (1983): 345–63.

36. Caroline Walker Bynum, "Did the Twelfth Century Discover the Individual?" in *Jesus as Mother. Studies in the Spirituality of the High Middle Ages* (Berkeley: University of California Press, 1982), pp. 82–109. In a similar vein is Natalie Zemon Davis, "Boundaries and the Sense of Self in Sixteenth-Century France," in *Reconstructing Individualism. Autonomy, Individuality and*

the Self in Western Thought, ed. Thomas C. Heller, Morton Sosna, and David E. Wellbrey (Stanford: Stanford University Press, 1986), pp. 53–63.

37. Binary, that is. Her subsequent work has continued this approach of self and world, especially *Holy Feast, Holy Fast* (Berkeley: University of California Press, 1987).

38. Weissman, "Reconstructing Renaissance Historiography," and "The Importance of Being Ambiguous: Social Relations, Individualism, and Identity in Renaissance Florence," in *Urban Life in the Renaissance,* ed. Susan Zimmerman and Ronald F.E. Weissman (Newark: Associated University Presses, 1989), pp. 269–80; Giddens, *Constitution of Society.*

39. Logan "Conception of the Self," 262. His view remains too egocentric to capture the *social* quality adequately, but is a useful reflection on the issues surrounding the nature of the ego in this period.

40. See her "No Sex, No Gender," *Speculum* 68 (1993): 419–43; and "Reading the Book of Margery Kempe," 29–66. Her line of work independently advances the critique of Jean-Claude Schmitt, "La découverte de l'individu, une fiction historiographique?" in *La fabrique, la figure, la feinte: Fictions et Statut des Fictions en Psychologie,* ed. P. Mingal and F. Parot (Paris: Vrin, 1989), pp. 213–36, who argued that personality not individualism was the key issue.

41. A relevant example of this approach is Rubin, "Small Groups."

42. Gurevich, *Origins of European Individualism,* 14.

43. See Joan Scott, "The Evidence of Experience," *Critical Inquiry* 17 (1991): 773–97; and Jay Smith, "Between *Discourse* and *Experience:* Agency and Ideas in the French Pre-Revolution," *History and Theory* 40 (2002): 116–42.

44. Partner, "Reading *The Book of Margery Kempe,*" 62. I obviously agree with Partner, but I should point out that the imputation that may rile some is the particularly psychoanalytic one. The difficulty with this is an extreme form of the general concern. But in the psychoanalytic form a person's situation is interpreted in a lexicon that is radically distant from their own, suggesting that the imputation of feeling leads to the subversion of the individual's particular life for the sake of understanding it rather than a wholly sympathetic attempt to understand them on their own terms. Obviously, Freudians do not think or understand their interpretations in this light, and the real problem is at the level of the acceptability of their theory. Those outside see it as a heavyhanded import; *they* see it as a sympathetic key to reading difficult and obscured messages. Compare the remarks of Lee Patterson, "Chaucer's Pardoner on the Couch: Psyche and Clio in Medieval Literary Studies," *Speculum* 76 (2001): 638–80.

45. R.G. Collingwood, *The Idea of History,* revised edition, ed. Jan van der Dussen (Oxford: Oxford University Press, 1993), pp. 282–302.

46. Example, David Hume, *History of England* (Indianapolis: Liberty Classics, 1985), almost any page will show this.

47. See, for instance, Peter Gay, *Freud for Historians* (New York: Oxford University Press, 1985), pp. 78–115.

48. *Ecstasies. Deciphering the Witches' Sabbath,* trans. Raymond Rosenthal (New York: Pantheon Books, 1991), p. 22.

49. Ginzburg uses it to associate diverse past cultures more than to eliminate the gap between inquirer and object of inquiry.

50. This is part of the problem in the fascinating narrative of time-travelers in the pay of the historian, provided by Keith Hopkins, *A World Full of Gods. The Strange Triumph of Christianity* (New York: Free Press, 1999).

51. See from a hermeneutic perspective, Hans-Georg Gadamer, *Truth and Method* (New York: Seabury Press, 1984; orig. 1960); Paul Ricoeur, *Oneself as Another*, trans. Kathleen Blamey (Chicago: University of Chicago Press, 1994); Charles Taylor, *Sources of the Self* (Cambridge, Mass.: Harvard University Press, 1989); on reader response criticism, a good introduction is Susan Suleiman and Inge Crosman, ed., *The Reader in the Text* (Princeton: Princeton University Press, 1980), especially Susan R. Suleiman, "Introduction: Varieties of Audience-Oriented Criticism," pp. 3–45; a medieval case study is Madeline H. Caviness, "Patron or Matron? A Capetian Bride and a *Vade Mecum* for Her Marriage Bed," *Speculum* 68 (1993):333–62.

52. Rosemary Horrox, ed. (Cambridge, UK: Cambridge University Press, 1994).

53. Perhaps the most comprehensive example is Richard Firth Green, *A Crisis of Truth* (Philadelphia: University of Pennsylvania Press, 1999).

54. While not putting the issues this way, Rigby, *English Society in the Later Middle Ages* (New York: St. Martin's Press, 1995) does provide much for understanding the constitution of social groupings.

55. Rigby, *English Society*, p. ix.

56. Michael Fitzhugh and William Leckie, "Agency, Postmodernism, and The Causes of Change," *History and Theory* 40 (2001): 59–81.

57. Rigby, *English Society*, p. 12 indicates that the concept of systacts is borrowed from W.G. Runciman's theories.

58. I might say that for the purpose of this point, awareness, consciousness, and understanding are synonymous. Understanding is perhaps a stretch, for it seems to be a somewhat fuller state. The point is that a self is a place where meaning exists.

59. Bonaventure, as quoted in Caroline Walker Bynum, *The Resurrection of the Body in Western Christianity, 200–1336* (New York: Columbia University Press, 1995), pp. 243–44. One of the things that most perplexes Dante is the question of how bodies and souls interact and how the semblance of bodies he encounters in the otherworlds are explained. See, for instance, *The Divine Comedy*, ed. C.S. Singleton, *Purgatorio XXV* (Princeton: Princeton University Press, 1970, paperback edition), pp. 269–75.

60. See below, chapters 6 and 7.

61. David Hume, *A Treatise of Human Nature* (Harmondsworth: Penguin, 1969), p. 300 (bk. I, sect. 6).

62. Initially I was thinking of the kind of full articulation or narrative that is developed in Richard Wollheim, *The Thread of Life* (Cambridge, Mass.: Harvard University Press, 1984), which is familiar from many other recent works, but I have come to think that this model, like the psychoanalytic work to which it is allied, is altogether too rich, too full a story to cover

most cases; narrative models *did* help to construct the medieval self, as I argue in chapter 2 and later, but these were not typically the full and developing stories *of my* life, but virtue tales that could apply to acts or propensities *in* my life. The full lifestory *was* a possibility for later medieval townspeople. Margery Kempe tells us her story, and she told it to all her confessors, but this was not anything like the usual condition of selfhood— nor do I think it is today, notwithstanding the powerful models, that we possess, to encourage it. The life story is a little too much to be normative. In the event, I have preferred a formulation of Charles Taylor, "The Dialogical Self," in *The Interpretive Turn. Philosophy, Science, Culture,* ed. David R. Hiley, James F. Bohman, and Richard Shusterman (Ithaca: Cornell University Press, 1991), pp. 304–314, which develops a hermeneutical perspective.

63. This theme is found in Martin Heidegger, *Being and Time,* trans. John Macquarrie and Edward Robinson (New York: Harper, 1962), pp. 85–87, and *passim*; it is a principal theme in Gadamer, *Truth and Method,* pp. 235–341.

64. "Inescapable framework" is a phrase from Charles Taylor's *Sources of the Self,* p. 3.

65. Heidegger, *Being and Time;* Wittgenstein, *Philosophical Investigations;* Giddens, *The Constitution of Society* (Berkeley: University of California Press, 1984); Pierre Bourdieu, *Logic of Practice,* trans. Richard Nice (Cambridge, UK: Cambridge University Press 1990); Bourdieu, *Outline of a Theory of Practice.*

66. Taylor, "Dialogic Self," pp. 311–14 explains well why the model of Mead's interactionism is limited by its failure to give sufficient scope to the agent in whom meanings coalesce. See also the critique of Giddens, *Constitution of Society,* p. 43, focused on the problematic notion of the "I" in Mead.

67. For an explication of this very useful term see, Bourdieu, *Logic of Practice,* pp. 52–65.

68. Jakob Burckhardt, *The Civilisation of the Renaissance in Italy,* trans. S.G.C. Middlemore (London, 1944), p. 81.

69. *The Book of Margery Kempe,* ed. Sanford Brown Meech and Hope Emily Allen, EETS, O.S. 212 (London: Oxford University Press, 1940), Book I, chapter 62.

70. Burke "Thoughts on the Present Discontents," in *The Writings and Speeches of Edmund Burke,* vol. II, ed. Paul Langford and William B. Todd (Oxford: George Allen and Unwin, 1981), p. 320. I thank Russell Murphy for bringing this to my attention.

71. Gadamer, *Truth and Method,* pp. 235–53.

72. Nelson Goodman, *Ways of Worldmaking* (Indianapolis: Hackett Pub. Co., 1978), p. 6.

73. This critique comes from a variety of positions: the skepticism of Hume is carried on by Derek Parfit, *Reasons and Persons* (Oxford: Oxford University Press, 1984); but it is also an issue of concern for others, perhaps most resonantly in the French post-structuralism of Foucault, for example, in *Discipline and Punish,* trans. Alan Sheridan (New York: Vintage Books, 1979); or any of the volumes of *The History of Sexuality,* 3 vols., trans. Robert Hurley

(New York: Pantheon Books, 1978–88); see also Taylor, *Sources of the Self,* pp. 480–82 and David Gary Shaw, ed., *Agency after Postmodernism,* theme issue of *History and Theory* 40 (2001).

74. This is strongly, if typically obscurely, argued, for instance, in *The Logic of Practice,* pp. 98–111.

75. For instance, see Giddens, *Constitution of Society, passim* and pp. 288–93 for a modern case study.

76. According to Joan Scott one of the key criteria for analyzing the power relationship that is gender is to analyze how the structures and symbols get into subjective identities and thus can affect them: see *Gender and the Politics of History* (New York: Columbia University Press, 1988), p. 44.

77. It is not clear how much Bourdieu, for instance, is in line with this perception, for he perhaps overrates the independent standing of "objective indicators," namely wealth. These, it seems to me, are factored in via social perception, but this may again be a matter of emphasis: see Bourdieu, *The Logic of Practice,* pp. 139–40: he quotes two of my intellectual ancestors on this point: Proust: "Our social personality is created by the thoughts of other people," and Erving Goffman, "The individual must rely on others to realize his self-image."

78. I am certainly not sure this is so. The phrase is the evocative title of Robert J. Lifton's book *The Protean Self: Human Resilience in an Age of Fragmentation* (New York: Basic Books, 1993).

79. Kermode, *Medieval Merchants,* p. 13.

80. See chapter 3. See her *Controlling Misbehavior.*

81. See chapters 3 and 4 in this book.

82. See chapter 5 in this book.

83. See chapter 6 in this book.

84. See chapter 7 in this book.

85. See chapters 5 and 8 in this book.

86. Cf. R.H. Britnell, *Growth and Decline in Colchester, 1300–1525* (Cambridge, UK: Cambridge University Press, 1986), p. 4. Cf. Partner, "No Sex, No Gender," 429–31, inspired by George Devereux, *Ethnopsychoanalysis: Psychoanalysis and Anthropology as Complementary Frames of Reference* (Berkeley: University of California Press, 1978).

Chapter 2   Master Values of Town Life

1. Sylvia Thrupp, *The Merchant Class of Medieval London* (Ann Arbor: University of Michigan Press, 1948); Rodney Hilton, *Class Conflict and the Crisis of Feudalism;* Philippa Maddern, *Violence and Social Order: East Anglia, 1422–42* (Oxford: Oxford University Press, 1992); Rosemary Horrox, ed., *Fifteenth-Century Attitudes* (Cambridge, UK: Cambridge University Press, 1994); Marjorie McIntosh, *Controlling Misbehavior in England* (Cambridge, UK: Cambridge University Press, 1998); this is also true of recent related works on early modern England, for example, Elizabeth Foyster, *Manhood in Early*

Modern England. Honour, Sex and Marriage (London: Longman, 1999). This is in addition to the work of literary scholars.

2. In other words, radical commentators are probably right to assert, for instance, that advice literature "is in fact the values and outlook of those with a stake in the smooth-running of local society and the respectability of the working household" but this doesn't even address the important question of who had such a stake. It is a common problem of certain critical lines that they assume only the police have an interest in keeping the peace, and interest aside, the power of ideas is such that often, almost everyone already has a prejudice in favor of the dominant interest. This may be a measure of the success of some ancient power but often this is pure conjecture. Felicity Riddy, "Mother Knows Best. Reading Social Change in a Courtesy Text," *Speculum* 71 (1996): 66. See also Jonathan Nicholls, *The Matter of Courtesy. Medieval Courtesy Books and the Gawain Poet* (Woodbridge: Brewer, 1985), pp. 57–74 for context.

3. Popular means directed at or with an interest in the "populo," the broader society.

4. On literacy and the dissemination of ideas, see Jo Ann Hoeppner, *The Growth of English Schooling, 1340–1548: Learning, Literacy and Laicisation in pre-Reformation York Diocese* (Princeton: Princeton University Press, 1985); Anne Hudson, *The Premature Reformation* (Oxford: Oxford University Press, 1988), pp. 174–211, esp. 205 on plebeian access to literate materials; compare Margaret Aston, "Lollards and Literacy," *History* 62 (1977): 193–218; on access to sermons, see H. Leith Spencer, *English Preaching in the Late Middle Ages* (Oxford: Oxford University Press, 1993), pp. 70–76, 95–108; more generally, Roger Chartier, "Leisure and Sociability: Reading Aloud in Early Modern Europe," in *Urban Life in the Renaissance,* ed. Susan Zimmerman and Ronald F.E. Weissman (Newark: University of Delaware Press, 1989), pp. 103–120. On the association of lay and clergy, see Wells Reg. I-III, passim; Ann J. Kettle, "City and Close: Lichfield in the Century Before the Reformation" in *The Church in Pre-Reformation Society,* ed. Caroline M. Barron and Charles Harper-Bill (Woodbridge: Boydell Press, 1988), pp. 158–65; R.B. Dobson, "Cathedral Chapters and Cathedral Cities: York, Durham, and Carlisle in the Fifteenth Century," *Northern History* 19 (1983): 15–44.

5. See, for a concrete example, Riddy, "Mother Knows Best," 70–73.

6. *The Book of Margery Kempe,* ed. Sanford Brown Meech (EETS 212, 1940), p. 37; and Barry Windeatt, "Introduction," *Book of Margery Kempe,* ed. Windeatt (London: Longman, 1985), pp. 15–18. There is a dispute about the level of literacy in England. Moreover, it has been argued that women's rate of literacy and its growth were very low. See Shannon McSheffrey, "Literacy and the Gender Gap in the Late Middle Ages: Women and Reading in Lollard Communities," in *Women,* the *Book and the Godly,* ed. Lesley Smith and Jane H.M. Taylor (Cambridge, Eng.: Brewer, 1995), pp. 157–70; and L.R. Poos, *A Rural Society after the Black Death* (Cambridge, UK: Cambridge University Press, 1991), pp. 280–87; cf. Moran, *Growth of English Schooling,* pp. 152–62. The rise in urban rates, especially among the merchants, seems agreed.

7. Marjorie McIntosh, "Finding Language for Misconduct. Jurors in Fifteenth-Century Local Courts," in *Bodies and Disciplines. Intersections of Literature and History in Fifteenth-Century England,* ed. Barbara A. Hanawalt and David Wallace (Woodbridge: Brewer, 1996), p. 102.

8. *Book of Margery Kempe,* p. 37.

9. For more on how agents, remaining free, work with discourse and pre-given structures, see chapter 1 and David Gary Shaw, "Happy in Our Chains: Agency and Language in the Postmodern Age," *History and Theory* 40 (2001): 1–9.

10. She is not easy to evaluate in these terms, as she was a realist, working with the constraints of her world. For an introduction, see *Selected Writings of Christine de Pisan,* ed. Renate Blumenfeld-Kosinski (New York: W. W. Norton & Co., 1997).

11. Two good and concrete discussions of these questions in urban context are Shannon McSheffrey, "Men and Masculinity in Late Medieval London Civic Culture, Governance, Patriarchy, and Reputation," in *Conflicted Identities and Multiple Masculinities. Men in the Medieval West,* ed. Jacqueline Murray (New York: Garland, 1999), pp. 243–78; and Derek Neal, "Suits Make the Man: Masculinity in Two English Law Courts, *c.* 1500," *Canadian Journal of History* (2002): 1–21.

12. *Middle English Lyrics,* ed. Richard L. Hoffman and Maxwell Luria (New York: Norton, 1974), #125 (anon.).

13. That is, when they weren't the straightforward prejudice against outsiders.

14. Especially in chapter 6, "Taking Possession."

15. See chapters 5 and 8.

16. *A Crisis of Truth. Literature and Law in Ricardian England* (Philadelphia: University of Pennsylvania Press, 1999). This is a complex book, a sterling example of literary history doing "real" history by its shrewd deployment of legal and social texts and evidence. My belief is that many of the values that once were covered by truth (see Green's catalogue, p. 9) found other ways out, through different words. Fidelity goes on and on, but narrows over time as the circle of true friendship itself narrowed. Green is exciting for his assertion that *c.*1400 is the time of the crisis and the role that he assigns the growth of literacy in the change.

17. Rosemary Horrox, "Service," in Horrox, ed., *Fifteenth-Century Attitudes,* p. 61. Her article is the most apposite for my discussions in this chapter, although it is mainly concerned with another context of these master values, namely, that of country society.

18. Other examples of this were central to ecclesiastical rhetoric, see the 86 sermons of Bernard de Clairvaux, *Sermones super Canticorum,* ed. J. Leclercq, C.H. Talbot, and H.M. Rochais (Rome: Editiones Cistercienses, 1957–58); and Caroline Walker Bynum, "Jesus as Mother and Abbot as Mother," in *Jesus as Mother. Studies in the Spirituality of the High Middle Ages* (Berkeley: University of California Press, 1982), pp. 110–69.

19. *Middle English Lyrics,* #103 (anon.). The editors gloss this as heaven, but I like the idea that trone might here refer to a different word, the public scales.

Thus God's scales are true, not deceitful, the mercantile and majestic blending.

20. *Compendium of Theology,* trans. Cyril Vollert (St. Louis: B. Herder Book Co., 1947), p. 5.

21. *Middle English Lyrics,* #128 (anon.).

22. In addition to the Towneley Plays cited in n. 23, see and compare, *Ludus Coventriae, or, the Plaie Called Corpus Christi,* ed. K.S. Block (EETS 120, 1922), pp. 43–51; and *Chester Plays,* ed. Hans Deimling, (EETS 62, 1893), pp. 63–83.

23. *The Towneley Plays,* ed. George England and Alfred W. Pollard (EETS 71, 1897), p. 43.

24. *Towneley Plays,* pp. 41–42.

25. *Towneley Plays,* p. 47.

26. *Book of Margery Kempe,* p.111.

27. For the fascinating link between faithfulness, social life, and the law of contract underlying so much business dealing, see F. Pollock and F.W. Maitland, *The History of English Law Before the Time of Edward I,* 2nd edition (Cambridge, Eng.: Cambridge University Press, 1967), pp. 188–203.

28. On oath and faith breaking as a church crime see Pollock and Maitland, *History of English Law,* p. 198; and Richard Wunderli, *London Church Courts* (Cambridge, Mass.: Medieval Academy of America, 1981), p. 104. See also, Green, *A Crisis of Truth,* pp. 78–120; for the effects on his status and masculinity, see Neal, "Suits Make the Man."

29. Craig Muldrew, "Interpreting the Market: the ethics of credit and community relations in early modern England," *Social History* 18 (1993): 177 and generally, 163–83.

30. Gervase Rosser, with E. Patricia Dennison, "Urban Culture and the Church," *Cambridge Urban History of Britain,* ed. David Palliser (Cambridge, UK: Cambridge University Press, 2000), p. 368.

31. *The Book of Vices and Virtues,* ed. W. Nelson Francis (EETS 217, 1942), pp. 40–41.

32. *Cal. Pat. R.,* 37 Edward III, p. 391 (9–29–1363); the pardon itself is dated 10–12–1363; the story, as narrated, would be more plausible to us if Henry willfully but justifiably stabbed his brother with the knife his brother had, or indeed another. But justice taught juries and others to frame narratives to the law's means and language, so it was better to have Richard do himself in. For juries' manipulation of cases, see Maddern, *Violence and Social Order,* pp. 123–29.

33. *Commentary on the Nicomachaean Ethics,* trans. C.I. Litzinger (Chicago: Regnery, 1964), II, p. 576.

34. *Book of Vices and Virtues,* p. 98.

35. *Cely Letters, 1472–1488,* ed. Alison Hanham (EETS 273, 1975), *passim.*

36. *Cely Letters,* pp. 60 and 62 show the father's worry when his son was sick.

37. John Mirk, *Mirk's Festial. A Collection of Homilies,* ed. Theodor Erbe (EETS 96, 1905), p. 1.

38. *Cely Letters,* e.g. pp. 143, 155.

39. *Cely Letters,* p. 59.

40. *Chaucer, The Canterbury Tales*, p. 654.

41. Barbara Hanawalt, "Keepers of the Lights: Later Medieval Parish Guilds," *Journal of Medieval and Renaissance Studies* 14 (1984): 21–37; A.G. Rosser, "Communities of Parish and Guild in the Late Middle Ages," in *Parish, Church, and People,* ed. S.J. Wright (London: Hutchinson, 1988), pp. 29–55; Katherine L. French, "Maiden's Lights and Wives' Stores: Women's Parish Guilds in Late Medieval England," *Sixteenth-Century Journal* 29 (1998): 399–425; Ben R. McRee, "Charity and Gild Solidarity in Late Medieval England," *Journal of British Studies* 32 (1993): 195–225; *English Gilds,* ed. Joshua Toulmin Smith and Lucy Toulmin Smith (EETS 40, 1870), passim.

42. Julian Pitt-Rivers, *The Fate of Shechem, or the Politics of Sex* (Cambridge: Cambridge University Press, 1977), pp. 94–112; A. G. Rosser, "Going to The Fraternity Feast: Commensality and Social Relations in Late Medieval England," *Journal of British Studies* 33 (1994): 430–46.

43. *Acts of the Court of the Mercers' Company,* ed. Laetitia Lyell (Cambridge: Cambridge University Press, 1936), pp. 148–51.

44. On other familial aspects of fidelity, see on the master–apprentice relationship, Barbara Hanawalt, *Growing up in Medieval London* (New York: Oxford University Press, 1993), pp. 129–72; on the marital allegiance, Jennifer Ward, "Townswomen and their Households," in *Daily Life in the Late Middle Ages,* ed. Richard Britnell (Stroud: Sutton Publishing, 1998), pp. 27–42; Ralph A. Houlbrooke, *The English Family 1450–1700* (London: Longman, 1984), pp. 96–105.

45. See J.A. Sharpe, *Defamation and Sexual Slander in Early Modern England: the Church Courts at York* (York: Borthwick Institute of Historical Research, 1980), pp. 19–20.

46. See, for example, Mervyn James, "English Politics and the Concept of Honour, 1485–1645," in *Society, Politics, and Culture: Studies in Early Modern England* (Cambridge: Cambridge University Press, 1986), pp. 308–415; Foyster, *Manhood in Early Modern England;* and *Transactions of the Royal Historical Society* Sixth Series 6 (1996), which contained a collection of essays on early modern honor.

47. Thomas Hobbes, *Leviathan,* ed. Richard Tuck (Cambridge: Cambridge University Press, 1991, orig. 1651), p. 248.

48. Pitt-Rivers, *The Fate of Shechem,* p. 1.

49. For honor as a right, see Frank Stewart Henderson, *Honor* (Chicago: University of Chicago Press, 1994).

50. Hobbes, *Leviathan,* p. 63.

51. Pierre Bourdieu, "The Sentiment of Honour in Kabyle Society," in *Honour and Shame. The Values of Mediterranean Society,* ed. J.G. Peristiany and Julian Pitt-Rivers (Chicago: University of Chicago Press, 1965), p. 208. 'Cost what it may' may be considered the Mediterranean effect, rarer in England than in the southern ideal.

52. See James, "English Politics and the Court of Honour"; and Philippa Maddern, "Honour among the Pastons," *Journal of Medieval History* 14 (1988): 357–71.

53. " 'To pluck bright honour from the pale-faced Moon': Gender and Honour in the Castlehaven Story," *Transactions of the Royal Historical Society,* Sixth Series 6 (1996): 137.

54. This postmodernist view seems represented by, for instance, Laura Gowing, *Domestic Dangers. Women, Words, and Sex in Early Modern London* (Oxford: Oxford University Press, 1996), p. 113.

55. Maddern, "Honour among the Pastons," 370.

56. Christine de Pisan, *The Treasure of the City of Ladies,* trans. Sarah Lawson (Harmondsworth: Penguin, 1985), p. 55, to risk a cross-channel proof.

57. *The Dance of Death,* ed. Florence Warren (EETS 181, 1931), p. 21, slightly amended to conform to my sentence's grammar.

58. Bourdieu, "Sentiment of Honour," p. 228.

59. Its existence in all social milieux was argued by Sharpe, *Defamation and Slander,* pp. 2–3.

60. *Dives and Pauper,* ed. Patricia Heath Barnum (EETS 275, 1976), p. 104.

61. See Richard C. Trexler, *The Journey of the Magi. Meanings in History of a Christian Story* (Princeton: Princeton University Press, 1997), esp. pp. 69–71.

62. Jean-Claude Bibolet, "Les gestes d'adoration, de prière, d'offrande et de violence dans 'Le mystère de la passion de Troyes'," in *Le geste et les gestes au moyen âge* (Aix-en-Provence: Université de Provence, Centre d'Aix, 1998), p. 94.

63. Barnum, *Dives and Pauper,* p. 105.

64. "If ony man biddith the worshcip, and wolde wedde thee. . ." ll. 32 "How the Good Wijf taught hir Doughtir," in *The Babees Book,* ed. James Frederick Furnivall (EETS 32, 1923), p. 37.

65. "How the Good Wijf taught hir Doughtir," p. 37.

66. "The Young Children's Book" in Furnivall *The Babees Book,* p. 25. (c. 1500).

67. "Of the manners to bring one to Honour and Welfare" in *Babees Book,* p. 34.

68. *A Relation, or Rather a True Account, of the Island of England,* trans. Charlotte Augusta Sneyd (London: Camden Society 37, 1847), p. 22.

69. For example, *Towneley Plays, passim.*

70. *Coventry Leet Book, or Mayor's Register,* ed. Mary Dormer Harris (EETS 134, 135, 138 and 146, 1907–13), passim.

71. Russell Hope Robbins, ed., *Secular Lyrics of the Fourteenth and Fifteenth Centuries* (Oxford: Clarendon Press, 1952), #197, p. 198.

72. *Political, Religious and Love Poems,* ed. Frederick J. Furnivall (EETS 15, 1866, reedited 1903), p. 97.

73. See, for instance, Faramerz Dabhoiwala, "The Construction of Honour, Reputation, and Status in Late Seventeenth- and early Eighteenth-Century England," *Transactions of the Royal Historical Society,* 6th Series (1996): 201–13; more generally and chronologically closer to our concerns, Gowing, *Domestic Dangers,* chapter 4.

74. Whether or not his sexual life factored into his honor at all is a different question, for which, see Foyster, *Manhood in Early Modern England;* Neal, "Suits Make the Man," p. 8.

75. Gowing, *Domestic Dangers,* p. 110.

76. *Le Menagier de Paris,* ed. Georgine E. Brereton and Janet M. Ferrier (Oxford: Oxford University Press, 1981), p. 55.
77. *English Lyrics* #129, p. 121.
78. Furnivall, *Babees Book,* p. 34.
79. Gowing, *Domestic Dangers,* p. 106; whether men's honor was significantly sexual is a matter of debate, but the stakes were certainly lower for them. Cf. Neal, "Suits make the Man," 6–7 and n. 22; Foyster, *Manhood in Early Modern England;,* Susan D. Amussen, *An Ordered Society: Gender and Class in Early Modern England* (Oxford: B. Blackwell, 1988), pp. 98–104.
80. *Book of Margery Kempe,* p. 15. I've modernized the spelling.
81. See also Lee Patterson, *Chaucer and the Subject of History* (Madison: University of Wisconsin Press, 1991), pp. 183–85.
82. For example, Meech, *Book of Margery Kempe,* p. 37. Her father was at the top of the urban elite, her husband at best in the middle and probably sinking: see David Gary Shaw, "The Worshipful Ferrour and Kempe. Social Selves in a Medieval Town," in *Studying Medieval People,* ed. Nancy F. Partner (London: Edward Arnold, 2005), pp. 3–21.
83. Mirk's *Festial,* p. 290.
84. Keith Wrightson, " 'Sorts of People' in Tudor or Stuart England," in *The Middling Sort of People. Culture, Society and Politics in England, 1550–1800,* ed. Jonathan Barry and Christopher Brooks (London: St. Martin's Press, 1994), pp. 28–51.
85. For the cosmic background, see the classic discussion by A.O. Lovejoy, *The Great Chain of Being* (Cambridge, Mass.: Harvard University Press, 1936), esp. chapter three. Aquinas, Dante, and Nicholas of Cusa are all important medieval sources.
86. See K.L. Kurtz, *The Dance of Death and the Macabre Spirit in European Literature* (New York: Columbia University, 1934); Paul Binski, *Medieval Death. Ritual and Representation* (Ithaca: Cornell University Press, 1996), pp. 153–59; and Edelgard E. DuBruck, "Death, Poetic Perception and Imagination (Continental Europe)," in *Death and Dying in the Middle Ages,* ed. Edelgard E. DuBruck and Barbara I. Gusich (New York: Peter Lang, 1999), pp. 296–314.
87. From the "Verba transaltoris" of the Ellesmere ms. "The Daunce of Death," in *The Dance of Death,* (EETS 181, 1931), p. 2.
88. *The Dance of Death,* p. 6.
89. Plainly Thrupp, *Merchant Class of Medieval London,* pp. 288–99 even in assuming its relevance, realized how inadequate it was.
90. This was also the case with Chaucer. The Ellesmere manuscript has a "lady of gret astate," an "Abbesse" and a "Gentilwoman amerous," while the Landsdowne manuscript substitutes an empress for the great lady.
91. Cordelia Beattie, "The Problem of Women's Work Identities in Post-Black Death England," in *The Problem of Labour in Fourteenth-Century England,* ed. J. Bothwell, P.J.P. Goldberg, and W.M. Ormrod (York: York Medieval Press, 2000), pp. 1–19; see also Patterson, *Chaucer and the Subject of History,* p. 282–85. On the women's dances, see *The Danse Macabre of Women,*

ed. Ann Tukey Harrison and Sandra L. Hindman (Kent, Ohio: Kent State University Press, 1994); and Suzanne F. Wemple and Denise A. Kaiser, "Death's Dance of Women," *Journal of Medieval History* 12 (1986): 333–43.

92. *The Dance of Death,* p. 40.

93. *The Dance of Death,* p. 27.

94. *The Dance of Death,* p. 47.

95. *The Dance of Death,* p. 66.

96. Maurice Keen, *English Society in the Later Middle Ages, 1348–1500* (Harmondsworth: Penguin, 1990), pp. 1–24; Rodney Hilton, "Ideology and Social Order in Late Medieval England," in *Class Conflict and the Crisis of Feudalism,* 2nd ed. (London:Verso, 1990), pp. 173–79.

97. *Chaucer,* ll. 37–40, p. 24.

98. *English Society in the Later Middle Ages,* p. 154.

99. To some extent, this jostling for position must represent the substratum of the development of the kind of social changes, both of exclusion and "usurpationary struggles" that Stephen Rigby has discussed. See *English Society in the Later Middle Ages* (New York: St. Martin's Press, 1995), chapter 4, but see chapter 9 on the role of ideology.

100. "Estate, Nobility, and the Exhibition of Estate in the Later Middle Ages," *Speculum* 68 (1993): 684–709. The language of performance is widespread now, partly deriving from postmodernist theoretical work. For a medieval application, see Kathleen Biddick, "Genders, Bodies, Borders:Technologies of theVisible" *Speculum* 68 (1993): 389–418; but there are other traditions, see Giddens, *Constitution of Society,* pp. 83–6.

101. Thomas Hoccleve, *Hoccleve's Works, I, The Minor Poems,* ed. Frederick H. Furnivall (EETS 61, 1892), p. 135.

102. *Caxton's Mirrour of the World,* ed. Oliver H. Prior (EETS 90, 1913), pp. 90, 145.

103. *Statutes of the Realm,* volume I (London: Eyre and Strahan, 1819), 380 and II, pp. 468–70. For discussion of the sumptuary laws in Europe, see Francis E. Baldwin, *Sumptuary Legislation and Personal Regulation in England* (Baltimore: The Johns Hopkins Press, 1926); Diane Owen Hughes, "Sumptuary Law and Social Relations in Renaissance Italy," in *Disputes and Settlements: Law and Human Relations in the West,* ed. John Bossy (Cambridge: Cambridge University Press, 1983), pp. 69–99; and Catherine Koves Killerby, *Sumptuary Law in Italy, 1200–1500* (Oxford: Oxford University Press, 2002); and John Scattergood, "Fashion and Morality in the Late Middle Ages," in *England in the Fifteenth Century. Proceedings of the Harlaxton Symposium,* ed. Daniel Williams (Woodbridge: Boydell Press, 1987), pp. 257–59. The efficacy of these laws is beside the point here.

104. *Chaucer, The Canterbury Tales,* I. A. 716.

105. "Urbanitatis," *Babees Book,* p. 15.

106. *Coventry Leet Book,* p. 220; see the important articles of M.R. James, "Ritual Drama and the Social Body in the Later Medieval Town," *Past and Present* 98 (1983): 1–29; and Sheila Lindenbaum, "Ceremony and Oligarchy: The London Midsummer Watch," in *City and Spectacle in Medieval Europe,*

ed. Barbara A. Hanawalt and Kathryn L. Reyerson (Minneapolis: University of Minnesota Press, 1994), pp. 171–88.

107. *York Memorandum Book,* vol. 2, ed. Maud Sellars (Surtees Society 125, 1915), p. 156.

108. Serel, p. 40.

109. "Urbanitatis," *Babees Book,* p. 14.

110. "John Russell's Book of Nurture," *The Babees Book,* p. 187.

111. For example, *The Dance of Death* or Christine de Pisan, *The Treasury of the City of Ladies,* trans. Sarah Lawson (Harmondsworth: Penguin, 1985), pp. 171–80, who spends a page on laborers, three on the poor and three on prostitutes.

112. "John Russell's Book of Nurture," *The Babees Book,* pp. 188–89.

113. See Bridget Ann Henisch, *Fast and Feast* (University Park, Pa: Pennslyvania State University Press, 1976), p. 158.

114. SRO, DD/B Reg 6, fo. 208.

115. "John Russell's Book of Nurture," p. 194.

116. On hierarchy, degree and class in general see, Georges Duby, *The Three Orders: Feudal Society Imagined,* trans. Arthur Goldhammer (Chicago: University of Chicago Press, 1980); Alexander Murray, *Reason and Society in the Middle Ages* (Oxford: Oxford University Press, 1978); Jill Mann, *Chaucer and Medieval Estates Satire: the Literature of Social Classes in the General Prologue to the Canterbury Tales* (Cambridge: Cambridge University Press, 1973); Rigby, *English Society in the Later Middle Ages,* passim.

117. Dante, *Inferno,* V.

118. Thomas Walsingham, *Historia Anglicana,* II, ed. Henry T. Riley (London: RS 28, 1864), p. 32.

Chapter 3   *E Pluribus Unum:* Peer Pressures

1. See Marjorie McIntosh, *Controlling Misbehavior in England, 1370–1600* (Cambridge, UK.: Cambridge University Press, 1998), p.39, who discusses the context and development of community control of individual behavior. She suggests that public negative discipline was rising in urban contexts in the fifteenth century. See also Margaret Spufford, "Puritanism and Social Control," in *Order and Disorder in Early Modern England,* ed. Anthony Fletcher and John Stevenson (Cambridge, UK.: Cambridge University Press, 1985), pp. 41–57.

2. Gervase Rosser and E. Patricia Dennison, "Urban Culture and the Church," in *Cambridge Urban History of Britain, 600–1540,* vol. I, ed. D.M. Palliser (Cambridge, UK.: Cambridge University Press, 2000), p. 340. Cf. D.M. Palliser, "Urban Society," in *Fifteenth-Century Attitudes,* ed. Rosemary Horrox (Cambridge, UK.: Cambridge University Press, 1994), p. 146.

3. McIntosh, *Controlling Misbehavior.*

4. This would seem to be the view for the later Middle Ages of Sherri Olson, *A Chronicle of All that Happens* (Toronto: Pontifical Institute of Mediaeval Studies, 1996), pp. 231–33 and passim.

5. Lorraine Attreed, *The King's Towns. Identity and Survival in Late Medieval English Boroughs* (New York: Peter Lang, 2001).

6. On such towns, see Norman M. Trenholme, *The English Monastic Boroughs* (Columbia, Missouri: University of Missouri Press, 1927); Rodney Hilton, *English and French Towns in Feudal Society. A Comparative Study* (Cambridge, UK.; Cambridge University Press, 1992), pp. 25–52; Margaret Bonney, *Lordship and the Urban Community. Durham and its Overlords* (Cambridge, UK.: Cambridge University Press, 1992), chapter 4; Christopher Dyer, "Small Towns, 1270–1540," in *Cambridge Urban History,* I; and Dyer, "Small Town Conflict in the Later Middle Ages: Events at Shipston-on-Stour," *Urban History* 19 (1992): 184–210; but also Jennifer Kermode, "The Larger Towns: 1300–1540," in *Cambridge Urban History,* I, p. 456, who notes how often the weakly franchised towns managed to evince a good deal of self-government comparable to the more richly enfranchised.

7. For details of this story, Shaw, *Creation of a Community,* pp. 114–38.

8. See Rigby, *English Society in the Later Middle Ages,* chapter 4 generally, esp. pp. 158–59 and 170–76. In his language, this chapter also shows the parameters of a "systact," a group that was the product of interests and the success of exclusionary mechanisms. The hard part is being sure that a club that wants members has some prestige, but still can't attract as many members as it wants, can properly be said to be employing exclusionary methods. Yet, this was the situation with borough communities and the franchise across England. There were certainly important transitions toward de facto exclusion in the later fifteenth century, for which see Rigby and Ewan, "Government, Power and Authority," pp. 309–12; Stephen Rigby, *Medieval Grimsby. Growth and Decline* (Hull: University of Hull Press, 1993), pp. 108–12.

9. D.M. Owen, *The Making of King's Lynn. A Documentary Survey* (London: Oxford University Press, 1984), p. 63.

10. It is worth noting that the pleas the court supervised were pretty much identical with other borough courts: cf. Rigby, *Medieval Grimsby,* p. 80.

11. Pierre Bourdieu, *Outline of a Theory of Practice,* trans. Richard Nice (Cambridge, UK.: Cambridge University Press, 1977), p. 40: "Strategies aimed at producing regular practices are one category, among others, of officializing strategies, the object of which is to transmute 'egoistic', private, particular interests (notions definable only within the relationship between a social unit and encompassing social unit at a higher level) into disinterested, collective, publicly avowable, legitimate interests."

12. Much importance was attached to these symbols of masculine power: see *York Memorandum Book,* vol. 3, ed. Joyce M. Percy (Surtees Society 186, 1973), p. 123; *The Great White Book of Bristol,* ed. Elizabeth Ralph (Bristol Record Society 32, 1979), p. 73; and *Coventry Leet Book, or Mayor's Register,* ed. Mary Dormer Harris (London: EETS 134, 135, 138, and 146, 1907–13), p. 425.

13. For such benefits, see Maryanne Kowaleski, "The Commercial Dominance of a Medieval Provincial Oligarchy: Exeter in the Fourteenth Century," in *The Medieval English Town. A Reader in English Urban History,* ed. R. Holt and A.G. Rosser (London: Longman, 1990), pp. 184–215; and the outline of such links in Kermode, *Medieval Merchants. York, Beverley and Hull in the Later Middle Ages* (Cambridge: Cambridge University Press, 1998), pp. 90–115.

14. The phrase is Pierre Bourdieu's adaptation of the anthropological concept of rite of passage: see Bourdieu, "Rites as Acts of Institution," in *Honor and Grace in Anthropology,* trans. Roger Just, ed. John. G. Peristiany and Julian Pitt-Rivers (Cambridge: Cambridge University Press, 1992), pp. 78–89.

15. The admission oath is recorded in CBII: 1.

16. See Shaw, *Creation of a Community,* pp. 197–99 on initiation, 142–52 on the meaning of membership.

17. For the extreme view, Sheila Lindenbaum, "Ceremony and Oligarchy: The London Midsummer Watch," in *City and Spectacle in Medieval Europe,* ed. Barbara A. Hanawalt and Kathryn L. Reyerson (Minneapolis: University of Minnesota Press, 1994), pp. 184–215. I am content to use the term ritual in the light, easygoing manner I have here, notwithstanding the pitfalls of the term outlined in Philippe Buc, *The Dangers of Ritual* (Princeton: Princeton University Press, 2001); or Catherine Bell, *Ritual Theory, Ritual Practice* (Oxford: Oxford University Press, 1992). Similarly, the functionalism latent in my interpretation here is offset by the later egocentric assumptions I develop throughout the book below.

18. *York Memorandum Book,* vol. 2, pp. 200–201.

19. *York Memorandum Book,* vol. 2, pp. 201–202.

20. These were the cases involving more than 40s. *Statutes of the Realm,* I (London: Eyre and Strahan, 1810), p. 48.

21. This oath-supported jurisdiction was also a feature of other guilds: see for example, *English Gilds,* ed. Joshua Toulmin Smith and Lucy Toulmin Smith (London: EETS 40, 1870), pp. 450–51 for the St. George Guild of Norwich, but compare the more ambiguous rule of the St. Katherine's Guild, Norwich, p. 21. The St. George's Guild appears to have many similarities to the Wells Community fraternity, see pp. 443–60; and Ben R. McRee, "Religious Gilds and Civic Order: the Case of Norwich in the Late Middle Ages," *Speculum* 67 (1992): 69–97.

22. There were 66 debt cases, 10 trespass, 3 bailment, 9 withholding chattel, and 26 unidentified.

23. See chapter 4 in this book.

24. For example, see Rigby, *Medieval Grimsby;* or R.H. Britnell, *Growth and Decline in Colchester, 1300–1525* (Cambridge, UK: Cambridge University Press, 1986).

25. *The Black Book of Southampton,* ed. A.B. Wallis Chapman (Southampton Record Society 13, 1912), pp. 6–9: probably dated 1482, possibly 1349.

26. CBI:158–59 (March 27–May 15, 1404).

27. Failure to answer summonses between 1377 and 1429 was as follows: broken contract (9.5%); broken guarantee (20.5%); debt (28.1%); trespass (11.5%); withholding chattels (9.4%).

28. The percentage of suitors failing to reply to summons varied by kind of offence. It is clear, however, that those cases in which cash was at issue—debt and guarantee—were much more likely to have absent defendants than the more personal affronts of trespass, broken contract, or the most material charge of detaining chattel. See n. 29.

29. In the event, even after 1404, the traditional practices continued, apparently unless the plaintiff brought pressure against dilatory defendants.

30. CBI: 231.

31. CBI: 101: they were Stephen Windford and John Ronburgh.

32. Only nine cases failed after arbitrators were appointed.

33. CBI: 44.

34. For example, CBI: 251 *Leste vs. Stokes;* CBI: 220 *Tapener vs. Tucker;* CBI: 196 *Romesy vs. Sholer.*

35. CBI: 191.

36. *York Memorandum Book,* II, p. 201.

37. Barbara Hanawalt, *Of Good and Ill Repute. Gender and Social Control in Medieval England* (New York: Oxford University Press, 1998), pp. 23–24 shows that assault on the mayor was also, in London, the most heinous civic crime.

38. Elsa Gyllyng was the only woman admitted *qua* burgess. She was apparently a widow but possibly not a burgess'; why the admission was necessary is unknown, and probably speaks more to a moment of conceptual confusion on the part of the burgesses as a whole, or to particular circumstances. Perhaps her husband had previously been ejected from the fraternity. She doesn't appear to have had any privileges superior to the other widows CBI: 72 (1387). On the status of women in the fraternity, see Shaw, *Creation of a Community,* pp. 146–48.

39. Shaw, *Creation of a Community,* pp. 213–214.

40. *York Memorandum Book,* II, p. 261.

41. *Contumelia* was a favorite word of the fifteenth-century town clerk John Beynton.

42. This from a 1516 ordinance: *Coventry Leet Book,* pp. 647–48.

43. For example, CBI: 31 *Shorthose vs. Galon.*

44. Cutte vs. Chynnok, CBI: 295–96.

45. *Coventry Leet Book,* pp. 647–48.

46. CBI: 186 (1410).

47. CBI: 156, 174, 281 (1403, 1408, 1433).

48. CBII: 2.

49. CBI: 79.

50. CBI: 60 (11–9–1385).

51. Shaw, *Creation of a Community,* pp. 213–14.

52. See Ruth M. Karras, *Common Women. Prostitution and Sexuality in Medieval England* (New York: Oxford University Press, 1996), pp. 15–19.

53. There are many specific cases in the *York Memorandum Book,* II, principally of Scots in the time of war.

54. *Acts of the Court of the Mercers' Company,* pp. 148–51. Cf. Hanawalt, *Of Good and Ill Repute,* 29–31; see chapter 2 in this book, p. 28.

55. The locus classicus on reciprocity is Marcel Mauss, *The Gift,* trans. I.G. Cannison (Glencoe, Ill.: Free Press, 1954); see also Peter Blau, *Exchange and Power in Social Life* (New York: J. Wiley, 1964), for a different direction; a useful overview is Hans van Wees, "The Law of Gratitude: Reciprocity in Anthropological Theory," in *Reciprocity in Ancient Greece,* ed. Christopher Gill, Norman Postelthwaite, and Richard Seaford (Oxford: Oxford University Press, 1998), pp. 13–49. See also J.K. Chadwick-Jones, *Social Exchange Theory. Its Structure and Influence in Social Psychology* (London: Academic Press 1976).

56. *York Memorandum Book,* II, p. 60; courts of criminal law always made a clear determination in sharp contrast to the old system in which compositions would be negotiated between families or individuals in the hope of avoiding blood. For a taste of the old, see William Ian Miller, *Bloodtaking and Peacemaking. Feud, Law, and Society in Saga Iceland* (Chicago: University of Chicago Press, 1990), chapters 6 and 8. Generally, a sense for the ending of law cases can be found from Alan Harding, *The Law Courts of Medieval England* (London: Allen and Unwin, 1973); this was the case even in local courts of limited jurisdiction, such as Wells's own Hundred and Frankpledge courts: see, for example, London, Lambeth Palace Library ED 1176–89.

57. CBI: 53.

58. CBI: 66.

59. CBI: 73.

60. CBI: 101.

61. CBI: 133.

62. See Clanchy, M.T., "Law and Love in the Middle Ages," in *Disputes and Settlements: Law and Human Relations in the West,* ed. John Bossy (Cambridge, UK: Cambridge University Press, 1983), p. 59 explicitly establishes the connection of kisses of peace and the custom of love and love-days.

63. CBI: 36.

64. Similar transactions occurred in other urban communities of course: see, for example, Hanawalt, *Of Good and Ill Repute,* p. 48.

65. CBI: 137.

66. See Julian Pitt-Rivers, "The Place of Grace in Anthropology," in *Honor and Grace,* pp. 215–46.

67. CBI: 207.

68. Richard M. Wunderli, *London Church Courts and Society on the Eve of the Reformation* (Cambridge, Mass.: Medieval Academy of America, 1981), p. 51 notes that practice and theory (Lyndwood's) in the ecclesiastic courts also required that the financial "penance" be made to a charity rather than the court *per se;* civic and parish guilds such as Wells' were close kin to the church.

69. The Borough Community's economic resources were based on real estate, donated by the membership over the years. See *Creation of a Community*, pp. 48–54; and A.J. Scrase and Joan Hasler, *Wells Corporation Properties* (Somerset Record Society, 87, 2002), pp. 29–41 for some of the extensive evidence of rentals, etc.

70. Hanawalt, *Of Good and Ill Repute*, p. 24.

71. The significance of the crimes is the concern of chapter 6.

72. *Munimenta Gildhallae Londoniensis*, ed. Henry T. Riley, II (Rolls Series, 1859), p. 600; see Hanawalt, *Of Good and Ill Repute*, pp. 24–26.

73. See McIntosh, *Controlling Misbehavior*, pp. 63–65, 69, and 87–88 and 115.

74. *An English Chronicle of the Reigns of Richard II, Henry IV, Henry V and Henry VI*, ed. John Silvester Davies (CS 64, 1856), p. 59. See Ralph Griffiths, "The Trial of Eleanor Cobham," *Bulletin of the John Rylands Library* 51 (1968–69): 381–99.

75. *Lincoln Diocese Documents: 1450–1544*, ed. Andrew Clark (EETS 149, 1914), pp. 126–28.

76. "The Spectacle of Suffering in Spanish Streets," in *City and Spectacle in Medieval Europe*, p. 158.

77. See McIntosh, *Controlling Misbehavior*; and Robert Tittler, *The Reformation and the Towns in England* (Oxford: Oxford University Press, 1998), part IV.

78. For the collective notions, see Shaw, *Creation of a Community*, pp. 183–97.

79. This speculation might be part of an answer that links the McIntosh views with those of Olson, *Chronicle of All that Happens*, pp. 231–33, who reads the decline of community as the rise of individualism, but it may mean the rise of a subgroup of a formerly more coherent community.

Chapter 4 The Marriage of Self and Structure

1. *Towneley Plays*, ed. George England and Alfred W. Pollard (EETS 71, 1897), pp. 114–15.

2. *Towneley Plays*, p. 115.

3. *Towneley Plays*, p. 100.

4. *Towneley Plays*, p. 101.

5. *English Society in the Later Middle Ages* (New York: St Martin's Press, 1995), p. 323. Master values, I should add, are not an ideology but at most an ideology's talking points, closer to the terms that make conversation possible.

6. "Honour and Social Status," in *Honour and Shame. The Values of Mediterranean Society*, ed. J.G. Peristiany (Chicago: University of Chicago Press, 1966), p. 39, as well as the other papers in that same seminal collection; see also, the reflections of Pitt-Rivers and Peristiany in their introduction to *Honour and Grace in Anthropology*, ed. J.G. Peristiany and Julian Pitt-Rivers (Cambridge, UK: Cambridge University Press, 1992).

7. To some extent, this is the underlying justification for chapter 2. Note especially again, Craig Muldrew, "Interpreting the Market: The Ethics of Credit

and Community Relations in Early Modern England," *Social History* 18 (1993): 163–83.

8. Other works whose approach to the meaning of arbitration are especially important for me are Fredric Cheyette, "*Suum Cuique Tribuere*," *French Historical Studies* 6 (1970): 287–99; Stephen D. White, "'*Pactum . . . Legem Vincit et Amor Judicium.*' The Settlement of Disputes by Compromise in Eleventh-Century Western France," *American Journal of Legal History* 22 (1978): 281–308.

9. The history of urban arbitration remains incomplete partly because of its frequent informality. Most suggestive is Ben R. McRee, "Peacemaking and Its Limits in Later Medieval Norwich," *English Historical Review* 109 (1994): 831–66, who nicely reveals how an institution that fosters community exists within a world of tension and disharmony; Barbara Hanawalt, *Of Good and Ill Repute. Gender and Social Control in Medieval London* (New York: Oxford University Press, 1996), esp. pp. 36, 38–41; see also Lorraine Attreed, "Arbitration and the Growth of Urban Liberties in Late Medieval England," *Journal of British Studies* 31 (1992): 205–35, although this is really about corporate arbitration; and ibid., *The King's Towns. Identity and Survival in Late Medieval English Boroughs* (New York: P. Lang, 2001), pp. 244–46. See also *Select Cases Concerning the Law Merchant, II–III,* ed. Hubert Hall (Selden Society 44, 49, 1930, and 1932). It is notable, however, that arbitration is both infrequent *and* mainly involves foreign merchants. The local court records in *Select Cases Concerning the Law Merchant, I,* ed. Charles Gross (Selden Society 23, 1908) contain many more indications of love-days and licenses to compromise outside court, although few actual cases of arbitration. For the limited discussion in the common and royal law context, see S.F.C. Milsom, *Historical Foundations of the Common Law* (London: Butterworths, 1969); more helpful is E.W. Ives, *The Common Lawyers of Pre-Reformation England* (Cambridge, UK: Cambridge University Press, 1983), pp. 126–30, although the place of the practice still seems small. For its development and the role of equity, see J.B. Post, "Equitable Resorts before 1450," in *Law, Litigants and the Legal Profession,* ed. E.W. Ives and A.H. Manchester (London: Royal Historical Society, 1983), pp. 68–79; arbitration may have been involved in thirteenth-century compromises such as those noted in Sue Sheridan Walker, "The Action of Waste in the Early Common Law," in *Legal Records and the Historian,* ed. J.H. Baker (London: Royal Historical Society, 1978), p. 189. For the violent possibilities from which arbitration may have emerged, see William I. Miller, "Avoiding Legal Judgment: The Submission of Disputes to Arbitration in Medieval Iceland," *American Journal of Legal History* 28 (1984): 107–11.

10. Edward Powell, "Arbitration and the Law in England in the Later Middle Ages," *Transactions of the Royal Historical Society,* 5th ser., 33 (1983): 49–67; ibid., "Settlement of Disputes by Arbitration in Fifteenth-Century England," *Law and History Review* 2 (1984): 21–43; McRee, "Peacemaking and Its Limits." Llinos Beverley Smith, "Disputes and Settlements in Medieval Wales: The Role of Arbitration" *English Historical Review* 106 (1991): 835–60; Ian Rowney, "Arbitration in Gentry Disputes of the Later Middle Ages," *History*

67 (1982): 367–76; William Palmer, "Scenes from Provincial Life: History, Honor, and Meaning in the Tudor North," *Renaissance Quarterly* 53:2 (2000): 425–48; Carole Rawcliffe, "The Great Lord as Peacekeeper: Arbitration by English Noblemen and their Councils in the Later Middle Ages," in *Law and Social Change in British History,* ed. J.A. Guy and H.G. Beale (London: Royal Historical Society, 1984), pp. 34–54; ibid., " 'That Kindliness Should Be Cherished More, and Discord Driven Out': The Settlement of Commercial Disputes by Arbitration in Later Medieval England," in *Enterprise and Individuals in Fifteenth-Century England,* ed. Jennifer Kermode (Stroud, Glos.: Alan Sutton, 1991), pp. 99–117; Simon Payling, "The Ampthill Dispute: A Study in Aristocratic Lawlessness and the Breakdown of Lancastrian Government," *English Historical Review* 104 (1989): 881–907; Cheyette, "*Suum Cuique Tribuere*"; H. Janeau, "L'arbitrage en Dauphiné au Moyen Âge," *Revue historique de droit français et etranger* 24–25 (1946–47): 229–71; Jenny Wormald, "An Early Modern Postcript: The Sandlaw Dispute, 1546," in *Disputes and Settlements: Law and Human Relations in the West,* ed. John Bossy (Cambridge, UK: Cambridge University Press, 1983), pp. 191–205. An interesting discussion of the approaches of historians and their anthropological sources is Thomas Kuehn, *Law, Family and Women* (Chicago: University of Chicago Press, 1991), pp. 20–24.

11. The selection of an even number of arbitrators was the norm in medieval Europe. Remarkably, the Romans had preferred an odd number, and the difference is culturally pregnant. Consensus was the medieval way, especially because the ability of an individual to flout the system was greater than in the Roman imperial context. See Janeau, "L'arbitrage en Dauphiné," p. 247; and Jan Rogozinski, *Power, Caste, and Law. Social Conflict in Fourteenth-Century Montpellier* (Cambridge, Mass.: Medieval Academy of America, 1982), pp. 101–102 and n. 60; and Marc Bouchat, "La justice privée par arbitrage dans le diocèse de Liège au XIIIe siècle: Les arbitres," *Móyen Age* 95 (1989): 450–51.

12. CBI: 54.

13. CBI: 33.

14. And 41.6 percent of all cases.

15. On love-days, see M.T. Clanchy, "Law and Love in the Middle Ages," in *Disputes and Settlements: Law and Human Relations in the West,* ed. John Bossy (Cambridge, UK: Cambridge University Press, 1983), pp. 47–67; and Josephine Waters Bennett, "The Mediæval Loveday," *Speculum* 33 (1958): 351–70.

16. Cf. Christopher Dyer, "The Small Towns, 1270–1540," *Cambridge History of Urban Britain, 600–1540* (Cambridge, UK: Cambridge University Press, 2000), p. 528. On similarity to guild tribunals, see Sarah Rees Jones, "Household, Work and the Problem of Mobile Labour: The Regulation of Labour in Medieval English Towns," in *The Problem of Labour in Fourteenth-Century England,* ed. James Bothwell, P.J.P. Goldberg, and W.M. Ormrod (York: York Medieval Press, 2000), p. 150; and Ben R. McRee, "Religious Guilds and the Regulation of Behavior in Late Medieval Towns," in *People, Politics and Community in the Later Middle*

230   NOTES

Ages, ed. Joel T. Rosenthal and Colin Richmond (Gloucester: A. Sutton, 1987), pp. 108–122. See evidence in *English Gilds,* ed. Joshua Toulmin Smith and Lucy Toulmin Smith (EETS 40, 1870), pp. 55, 76, 84, passim.

17. John S. Beckerman, "Adding Insult to *Iniuria:* Affronts to Honor and the Origins of Trespass," in *On the Laws and Customs of England,* ed. Morris S. Arnold, Thomas A. Green, Sally A. Scully, and Stephen D. White (Chapel Hill: University of North Carolina Press, 1981), pp. 159–81; Morris S. Arnold, ed., *Select Cases of Trespass from the Royal Courts, 1307–99,* vol. I (Selden Society 100, 1985), p. ix. More generally, Julian Pitt-Rivers, "Honour and Social Status," in *Honour and Shame. The Values of a Mediterranean Society,* ed. J.G. Peristiany (Chicago: University of Chicago Press, 1966), pp. 21–77.

18. *Middle English Sermons,* ed. Woodburn O. Ross (EETS 209, 1940 for 1938), p. 50. See the relevant discussion on the linkages among trespass, defamation and honor, R.H. Helmholz, ed., *Select Cases of Defamation,* Selden Society 101 (London: Selden Society, 1985), p. li.

19. See Helmholz, *Select Cases of Defamation* for its complex history in a wide variety of courts; and Milsom, *Historical Foundations,* pp. 332–33.

20. *Middle English Sermons,* p. 177.

21. CBI: 12.

22. CBI: 24.

23. There is a substantial literature on the meaning of practices such as arbitration and non-adjudicated dispute resolution. A good overview of the interpretive issues is Simon Roberts, "The Study of Dispute: Anthropological Perspectives," in Bossy, *Disputes and Settlements,* pp. 1–24; see also thoughtful comments by White, " '*Pactum. . .Legem Vincit et Amor*"; Cheyette, "*Suum Cuique Tribuere*"; Clanchy, "*Law and Love.*"

24. Richard Firth Green, *A Crisis of Truth. Literature and Law in Ricardian England* (Philadelphia: University of Pennsylvania Press, 1999), pp. 39–40 and passim. Cf. Barbara Hanawalt's view of arbitration as a traditional or folk mode that coexisted with "normative law" in *Of Good and Ill Repute,* p. 36.

25. Delays were involved in approximately 35 percent of debt cases, but only 18 percent of trespass cases. Failed guarantees and broken contracts—also involving written, financial arrangements—saw delay rates of about 30 percent. The role of time-techniques of dispute resolution was discussed in chapter 3 in this book, pp. 62–63.

26. Interestingly, Barbara Hanawalt, *Of Good and Ill Repute,* p. 41 argued that in London arbitration was less effective in these cases and that mediation was preferred.

27. Such a tendency was also bolstered by the practices of other urban and common law courts, which tended to solve debt cases by wager of law, the assembling of supportive oath-helpers. It should be noted, however, that nowhere in local and urban courts was there an easy and simple division of pleas and settlement techniques. Law merchant practices were various, flexible, and case-specific, while the customs of London long preferred wager of law for all kinds of cases—criminal, debt, and trespass. See *Select Cases in the Law Merchant, I, II, III;* and "Liber Albus" in *Munimenta Gildhallae*

Londoniensis, ed. H.T. Riley (Rolls Series 12.1, 1859), pp. 203–204; see Robert L. Henry, *Contracts in the Local Courts of Medieval England* (London: Longmans, Green and Co., 1926), pp. 48–90; Frederick Pollock and F.W. Maitland, *The History of English Law,* ed. S.F.C. Milsom (Cambridge, UK: Cambridge University Press, 1968; orig. ed. 1895), pp. 634–36.

28. It is certainly possible that arbitration functioned differently elsewhere. In some places it was apparently used as a mode of avoiding the ignorant, slow, or arbitrary determination of the courts. Rawcliffe has shown—and some Wells evidence agrees—that the arbitrators were sometimes particularly skilled in the business in which the dispute arose "That Kindliness Should Be Cherished More," pp. 100–102, and passim.

29. This was a universal term for arbitrators, sometimes used in Wells, and capturing well the culture of arbitration. See Karl S. Bader, "Arbiter, Arbitrator seu amicabilis compositor," *Zeitschrift der Savigny-Stiftung für Rechtsgeschichte. Kanonistische Abteilung* 77 (1960): 239–76 illustrates the term's prevalence.

30. The power of the leadership was the great political issue of the first part of the fifteenth century: see *Creation of a Community,* pp. 167–76, 188–89 for a discussion of oligarchy and the mentality connected to it. The quotations are from a sort of constitution that was transcribed in Thomas Serel, *Historical Notes on the Church of St Cuthbert in Wells, etc.* (Wells: J.M. Atkins, 1875), pp. 37 and 40; the original is apparently lost.

31. *Middle English Lyrics,* #121.

32. Cf. Jennifer Kermode, *Medieval Merchants:York, Beverly, and Hull in the Later Middle Ages* (Cambridge, UK: Cambridge University Press, 1998), p. 47; S.H. Rigby and Elizabeth Ewan, "Government, Power and Authority, 1300–1540," in *The Cambridge Urban History of Britain, volume 1, 600–1540,* ed. David M. Palliser (Cambridge, UK: Cambridge University Press, 2000), p. 302. Problems of office avoidance were not systematic or endemic in Wells in this period.

33. Wells had only one parish, and this was particularly in the control of the Borough Community who directed the lay business of the church and selected churchwardens annually, and audited their accounts: see *Creation of a Community,* pp. 258–61.

34. It should be stressed that this is not a biographical summary. That is, I have not followed individuals through their entire careers and then declared them elite or commoner. Rather, one individual counts as a commoner until he is elected to an office and his cases from then on are classed in the new status. The pre-promotion cases remain as evidence of activity at that lower level. Needless to say, this is an imperfect system but for present purposes superior to treating, for instance, a given burgess as always having been of magisterial standing because he would one day, sometimes decades later, attain it. The fluid basis of this analysis makes it difficult to say how many commoners there were in the period. Everyone was a commoner for some amount of time. But I can report the numbers of individuals who held the various offices in the period under examination. There were twenty-two different masters and thirty-seven constables, constituting the elite group. There were thirty-six rent collectors and twenty-nine different churchwardens combined

into the middling category in my analysis. The petty offices were filled by 50 different shambleskeepers and 101 streetwardens. Everyone was for at least a few minutes a commoner. But the analytic group includes about 400 men who never attained any civic office. By contrast, a total of 182 different people did hold office in the years under examination. The few women who appear in the court record—generally widows—have been set aside, their complex status often hidden and their legal standing hybrid or confused.

35. For examples, see CBI: 3, 83, 91 (2), 96, 98, 111, and 190 (2).

36. For more on the status of women in the guild and in Wells, see *Creation of a Community,* pp. 145–48, 242–43, 248–53.

37. Women's status in towns could vary considerably. They could be fuller citizens in some places in some ways. See Martha C. Howell, "Citizenship and Gender: Women's Political Status in Northern Medieval Cities," in *Women and Power in the Middle Ages,* ed. Mary Erler and Maryanne Kowaleski (Athens, Ga.: University of Georgia Press, 1988), pp. 37–60.

38. Maddern, *Violence and Social Order. East Anglia, 1422–1442* (Oxford: Oxford University Press, 1992), pp. 98–104, detailing the vulnerability of women and servants especially.

39. CBI: 221.

40. For example, William Ian Miller, "Choosing the Avenger: Some Aspects of the Blood-Feud in Medieval Iceland and England," *Law and History Review 1* (1983): 159–204.

41. This idea, developed by Marcel Mauss, *The Gift. Forms and Functions of Exchange in Archaic Societies,* trans. Ian Cunnison (Glencoe, Illinois: Free Press, 1954).

42. Pitt-Rivers, "Honour and Social Status," p. 31.

43. Rawcliffe, "The Great Lord as Peacekeeper"; Smith, "Disputes and Settlements," pp. 853–56, who notes also the place of kin and experts, mainly of fairly high status themselves; Cheyette, "*Suum Cuique Tribuere,*" pp. 291–93.

44. In what follows, I have limited all my counting and numerical analyses to arbitration in trespass and debt cases. This was done for pure convenience, but is easily justified as such cases comprised about 93 percent of all arbitration cases. It should also be kept in mind that I have for the most part been counting the individual shares of arbitration rather than the cases that were arbitrated. Thus, a typical case includes four such shares or acts of arbitration, one per arbitrator.

45. Other fifteenth-century towns banned arbitration by their principal officers: see Bennett, "The Mediaeval Loveday," p. 363. By the sixteenth century, the masters formed a kind of official inner cabinet of the Community reflected in the Elizabethan charter, Wells City Ch. 29.

46. *Medieval English Lyrics,* #112.

47. *Medieval English Lyrics,* #112.

48. See *Creation of a Community,* pp. 211–212.

49. See *Creation of a Community,* pp. 178–79, 190–97, 201, 205; M.K. James, "Ritual Drama and the Social Body in the Later Medieval Town," *Past and Present* 98 (1983): 1–29; Charles Phythian-Adams, *Desolation of a City.*

Coventry and the Urban Crisis of the Late Middle Ages (Cambridge, UK: Cambridge University Press, 1979), pp. 128–41; Sylvia L. Thrupp, *The Merchant Class of Medieval London* (Ann Arbor: University of Michigan Press, 1948), pp. 13–41, 164–66, 288–311; Heather Swanson, *Medieval Artisans* (Oxford: B. Blackwell, 1989), pp. 150–71; and of course the reflected images in Chaucer's *Canterbury Tales*.

50. This was commonly the story in Wells, *Creation of a Community*, pp. 173–75 and n.117 for bibliography; but see also Maurice Keen, *English Society in the Later Middle Ages* (Harmondsworth: Penguin, 1990), pp. 1–24; Thrupp, *Merchant Class of Medieval London,* pp. 199–206; Robert S. Gottfried, *Bury St Edmunds and the Urban Crisis of the Later Middle Ages* (Princeton: Princeton University Press, 1982), pp. 60–61; see Payling, "The Ampthill Dispute": pp. 881–907 to watch men of lordly status look very unsure and unstable; Maddern, *Violence and Social Order,* pp. 75–110 is particularly rich in material linking status and anxiety, although with a greater assumption of hierarchical stability than might actually have been the case.

51. For a variety of views on oligarchy, see Sheila Lindenbaum, "Ceremony and Oligarchy: The London Midsummer Watch," in *City and Spectacle in Medieval Europe,* ed. Barbara A. Hanawalt and Kathryn L. Reyerson (Minneapolis: University of Minnesota Press, 1994), pp. 171–88; Heather Swanson, *Medieval British Towns* (Basingstoke: St. Martin's Press, 1999), pp. 89–96; Susan Reynolds, "Medieval Urban History and the History of Political Thought," *Urban History Yearbook* (1986): 14–23; Stephen Rigby, "Urban 'Oligarchy' in Late Medieval England," in *Towns and Townspeople in the Fifteenth Century,* ed. John A.F. Thomson (Gloucester: Alan Sutton, 1988), pp. 62–86; Jennifer Kermode, "Obvious Observations on the Formation of Oligarchies in Late Medieval English Towns," in *Towns and Townspeople,* pp. 87–106. See also Maryanne Kowaleski, "The Commercial Dominance of a Medieval Provincial Oligarchy: Exeter in the Late Fourteenth Century," *Mediaeval Studies* 46 (1984): 355–84. See Robert Tittler, *The Reformation and the Towns in England: Politics and Political Culture, c. 1540–1640* (Oxford: Oxford University Press, 1998), pp. 182–244 for subsequent crucial developments.

Chapter 5   Friends, Enemies, Patrons

1. Indeed, some might assume that the prima facie concern should be that our court records only tell us of enmity and tensions.

2. Josephine Waters Bennett, "The Mediaeval Loveday," *Speculum* 33 (1958): 363–65. More balanced worries are represented in *Middle English Sermons,* ed. Woodburn O. Ross (EETS 209, 1940 for 1938), p. 132, which warned that "ye that have mad lovedayes, be-ware that it be not iudas loveday, that spake fayre to Crist, and yitt he be-trayed him."

3. Serel, 37 and 40 original lost.

4. *English Gilds,* ed. Joshua Toulmin Smith and Lucy Toulmin Smith (EETS 40, 1870), p. 38.

5. Depending on the social and legal circumstances, pledging could be of considerable importance, sometimes connected to money, sometimes to security. See Martin Pimsler, "Solidarity in the Medieval Village? The Evidence of Personal Pledging at Elton, Huntingdonshire," *Journal of British Studies* 17 (1977): 1–11; Sherri Olson, *A Chronicle of All that Happens* (Toronto: Pontifical Institute of Mediaeval Studies, 1996), pp. 44–103 and passim.

6. See below, p. 113.

7. CBI: 58.

8. CBI: 44.

9. CBI: 49.

10. CBI: 29.

11. CBI: 40.

12. CBI: 58–60.

13. CBI: 60

14. CBI: 65.

15. CBI: 68.

16. CBI: 73.

17. CBI: 77.

18. I take the phrase "imperial self" from Christopher Lasch, *The Minimal Self* (New York: W. W. Norton, 1984), pp. 15–17.

19. Burgesses were usually first admitted to the freedom in their mid-twenties. See *Creation of a Community,* pp. 143–45; Phythian-Adams, *Desolation of a City. Coventry and the Urban Crisis of the Late Middle Ages* (Cambridge, UK: Cambridge University Press, 1979), pp. 124–28; Jennifer Kermode, *Medieval Merchants: York, Beverly, and Hull in the Later Middle Ages* (Cambridge, UK: Cambridge University Press, 1998), p. 86 finds her merchants surviving into their fifties.

20. While all kinds of burgesses did arbitration, there were sharp disparities. As a group, commoners did 26.4 percent of the arbitration. It was the oligarchs, however, who were the impressively recurrent figures on a per capita basis. They did the largest share of arbitration notwithstanding the smallness of their group (37.9% of all arbitration was done by men who currently held that status). See chapter 4, table 4.3. Masters and constables arbitrated at a rate of about ten times that of commoners.

21. See table 4.3. The median for the commoners in the sample was 0. The commoners had a group average of .8, but certain individuals contributed much of this.

22. The pioneering use of this technique in medieval history is Richard Smith, "Kin and Neighbours in a Thirteenth-Century Suffolk Community," *Journal of Family History* 4 (1979): 219–56; an important, more recent application is Christine Carpenter, "Gentry and Community in Medieval England," *Journal of British Studies* 33 (1994): 340–80, esp. 365–74. The notion of "social network," in distinction to the technique, is now quite common. A recent modern contribution is Charles Wetherall, Andrejs Plakans, and Barry Wellman,

"Social Networks, Kinship, and Community in Eastern Europe," *Journal of Interdisciplinary History* 34 (1994): 639–63. There are other micro-relational approaches being pursued in European history, for instance, Claire Dolan, "The Artisans of Aix-en-Provence in the Sixteenth Century: A Micro-Analysis of Social Relationships," in *Cities and Social Change in Early Modern France,* ed. Philip Benedict (London: Unwin Hyman, 1989), pp. 174–93. There is, however, growing interest and use of the general idea if not the methodology of networks within history. See, for instance, Geneviève Xhayet, "Autour des solidarités privées au moyen âge: partis et réseaux de pouvoir à Liège du xiiie au xve siècle," *Le Moyen Age* 100 (1994): 205–219, although her model relies rather more on a concept of patronage, one kind of substantial network, and related structures. An interesting connection exists in work on financial networks and the social facts underlying them in several articles in *Annales. Economies, Sociétés, Civilizations* 49 (Nov.–Dec. 1994), "Les Réseaux de crédit en Europe, xvie au xviiie siècles:" esp. 1359–409. An example of the construction, with subtlety and an excellent source, of a very late medieval network is Barbara A. Hanawalt, "Lady Honor Lisle's Networks of Influence," in *Women and Power in the Middle Ages,* ed. Mary Erler and Maryanne Kowaleski (Athens, Ga.: University of Georgia Press, 1988), pp. 188–212. For details on methodology, the sample group, etc., please see the appendix.

23. I reiterate that those with whom an individual had direct, recorded links constitute his inner circle.

24. The correlation was .942 across the sample.

25. C.J. Calhoun, "Community: Toward a Variable Conceptualization for Comparative Research," *Social History* 5 (1982): 105–29 uses the term "diffuse obligations" to capture this kind of relation.

26. This also shows the intergenerational element in civic social relations: not all contacts were contemporaries with each other.

27. This concern is weakened by the fact that the size of the outer circles exceeded the entire live community in most cases, indicating that they are reflecting vicissitudes, the diachronic element of soured relationships and a changing population.

28. Mark Granovetter, "The Strength of Weak Ties," in *Social Networks,* ed. Samuel Leinhardt (New York: Academic Press, 1977), pp. 347–67; Carpenter, "Gentry and Community," 370–71 did not corroborate the importance of these in her study of Philip Chetwynd. But there is some support from Kermode, *Medieval Merchants,* pp. 15–17.

29. I discuss the community-building consequences of the guild elsewhere: *Creation of a Community,* ch. 6 passim; see also, Gervase Rosser, "Essence of Medieval Urban Communities," in *The English Medieval Town: A Reader in English Urban History 1200–1540,* ed. Richard Holt and Gervase Rosser (London: Longman, 1990), pp. 216–37; ibid., "Going to The Fraternity Feast: Commensality and Social Relations in Late Medieval England," *Journal of British Studies* 33 (1994): 430–46; Phythian-Adams, *Desolation of a City,* pp. 118–22, 170–79; and his "Ceremony and the Citizen: The Communal

Year at Coventry 1450–1550," in Holt and Rosser, *English Medieval Town,* pp. 238–64; McRee, "Religious Gilds and Civic Order: The Case of Norwich in the Late Middle Ages," *Speculum* 67 (1992): 69–97.

30. In fact, Pope appears strongly and positively attached to Ralph Averey and strongly, but perhaps somewhat ambiguously or negatively related to John Bowyer.

31. Of course the problem for Arnold was more metaphysical than social and thus less easily solved. Cf. to the concept of brokerage in Roger V. Gould, "Power and Social Structure in Community Elites," *Social Forces* 68 (1989): pp. 531–52.

32. WcaCh 629 (1447).

33. CBI: 43 and 21.

34. CBI: 64.

35. AH 94, 96 (Broun witnessing a transaction of Tanner's), 100, 101.

36. CBI: 95, 103, 115, and 122.

37. *SMW I,* pp. 6–8.

38. *Selected Poems of William Dunbar,* ed. Priscilla Bawcutt (London: Longman, 1996), p. 175.

39. Taunton, Somerset Record Office, DD/WM/1/5.

40. Cf. Hanawalt, "Lady Honor Lisle," pp. 188–212.

41. Martha C. Howell, "Citizenship and Gender: Women's Political Status in Northern Medieval Cities," in *Women and Power in the Middle Ages,* ed. Mary Erler and Maryanne Kowaleski (Athens, GA: University of Georgia Press, 1988), pp. 37–60; Cf. Phythian-Adams, *Desolation of a City,* pp. 90–91; see also chapter 6, pp. 132–43.

42. Note that they both go with their collections of supporters to make their complaint at court, but the women come, as it were, as a consequence of the men's previous discussion, although the women are noted first as the actors: as crucial, the citizen acted so that he "wold of that despit be venged" but vengeance works here in a wholly civil and sociable manner, the high emotion in the quotidian action.

43. See Caroline M. Barron, "The 'Golden Age' of Women in Medieval London," *Reading Medieval Studies* 15 (1989): 35–58.

44. *Creation of a Community,* p. 278.

45. *Calendar of the Manuscripts of the Dean and Chapter of Wells, I* (London: H.M. Stationery office, 1907–1914), p. 254 for the year 1298. The document captures the ongoing interaction, but repeats old complaints that may no longer reflect the situation in the fourteenth century. Interaction with the cathedral as opposed to the bishop conforms to the basically positive view of R.B. Dobson, "Cathedral Chapters and Cathedral Cities: York, Durham, and Carlisle in the Fifteenth Century," *Northern History* 19 (1983): 15–44. But see Kermode, "The Greater Towns, 1300–1540," in *Cambridge Urban History,* I, p. 457 who is less optimistic. See also Ann J. Kettle, "City and Close: Lichfield in the Century Before Reformation," in *The Church in Pre-Reformation Society,* ed. Caroline Barron and Christopher Harper-Bill (Woodbridge: Boydell Press, 1985), pp. 158–65; Michael Franklin, "The

Cathedral as Parish Church: The Case of Southern England," in *Church and City, 1000–1500,* ed. David Abulafia (Cambridge: Cambridge University Press, 1992), pp. 173–98 dealing with the central Middle Ages.

46. I suspect this was just a matter of record-keeping rather than of changing levels of interaction or ethical standards.

47. Wells Reg. II, fo. 61.

48. Wells Reg. II, fos. 61d.–3. See Ruth M. Karras, *Common Women. Prostitution and Sexuality in Medieval England* (New York: Oxford University Press, 1996), p. 77 on clergy–prostitute relations; and R.N. Swanson, "Angels Incarnate: The Clergy and Masculinity from the Gregorian Reform to the Reformation," in *Masculinity in Medieval Europe,* ed. Dawn Hadley (London: Longman, 1999), pp. 160–77 on the clergy and masculinity.

49. Karras, *Common Women,* pp. 95–101 on their marginality.

50. CBII: 220.

51. William Worcestre, *Itineraries,* ed. John H. Harvey (Oxford: Clarendon Press, 1969), pp. 78–79. See Rosemary Horrox, "The Urban Gentry in the Fifteenth Century," in *Towns and Townspeople in the Fifteenth Century,* ed. J.A.F. Thomson (Gloucester: Alan Sutton, 1983), pp. 22–44; and Stephen O'Connor, "Adam Fraunceys and John Pyel: Perceptions of Status among Merchants in Fourteenth-Century London," in *Trade, Devotion, and Governance,* ed. Dorothy J. Clayton, Richard G. Davies, and Peter McNiven (Stroud: A. Sutton, 1994), pp. 17–35.

52. AH 172.

53. John Henry Parker, *The Architectural Antiquities of the City of Wells* (Oxford: J. Parker, 1866), p. 45.

54. See Stephen O'Connor, "Adam Fraunceys and John Pyel," pp. 17–35, especially the analysis of Adam Fraunceys.

55. See, for instance, *The Book of Margery Kempe,* ed. Sanford Brown Meech and Hope Emily Allen (EETS 212, 1940), pp. 225–26.

56. CBII: 220, 224.

57. "Putting Thieving Millers and Bakers to the Pillory" in *Political, Religious and Love Poems,* ed. Frederick J. Furnivall (EETS 15, 1866), p. 56.

58. Kermode, *Medieval Merchants,* p. 136 notes how smaller groups such as guilds and fraternities "signaled group identities on a scale smaller than the entire town." Cf. Stephen Rigby, *English Society in the Later Middle Ages* (New York: St. Martin's Press, 1995), pp. 158–59; see Phythian-Adams, *Desolation of a City,* pp. 104–117 for an account of craft guild coherence, in which, however, little attention is paid to the distinctly interpersonal features of the association, as opposed to the corporate quality possible. The relative importance of craft guilds in Europe was wide and their importance remains contentious. See David Nicholas, *The Later Medieval City, 1300–1500* (Harlow, Essex: Longman, 1997), pp. 217–27; Heather Swanson, "The Illusion of Economic Structure: Craft Guilds in Late Medieval English Towns," *Past & Present* 121 (1988): 29–48; M.P. Davies, "Artisans, Guilds and Government in Medieval London," in *Daily Life in the Late Middle Ages,* ed. R.H. Britnell (Stroud: Sutton Publishing, 1998), pp. 125–50; A.G. Rosser, "Crafts, Guilds, and the

Negotiation of Work in Medieval Towns," *Past & Present* 154 (1997): 3–31; and Sarah Rees Jones, "Household, Work and the Problem of Mobile Labour: The Regulation of Labour in Medieval English Towns," in *The Problem of Labour in Fourteenth-Century England,* ed. James Bothwell, P.J.P. Goldberg, and W.M. Ormrod (York: York Medieval Press, 2000), pp. 133–53.

59. Heather Swanson, *Medieval Artisans* (Oxford: B. Blackwell, 1989), pp. 10–14; see also *English Gilds,* pp. 336–37 and 381 for bakers regulation suggesting their importance and limitations.

60. LPL, Estate Document 1181; five or so does seem plausible given numbers recorded elsewhere, for example, Swanson, *Medieval Artisans,* p. 14; Richard H. Britnell, *Growth and Decline in Colchester, 1300–1525* (Cambridge: Cambridge University Press, 1986), p. 274.

61. CBI: 68.

62. A.H. Nelson, *The Medieval English Stage: Corpus Christi Pageants and Plays* (Chicago: University of Chicago Press, 1974); and P.J.P. Goldberg, "Craft Guilds, The Corpus Christi Play, and Civic Government," in *The Government of Medieval York,* ed. Sarah Rees Jones (York: Borthwick Institute of Historical Research, 1997), pp. 141–63.

63. See, for example, *Coventry Leet Book,* ed. Mary Dormer Harris (EETS 134, 1907), p. 220. Less cozy conclusions about such occasions are drawn by Sheila Lindenbaum, "Community and Oligarchy: The London Midsummer Watch," in *City and Spectacle in Medieval Europe,* ed. Barbara A. Hanawalt and Kathryn L. Reyerson (Minneapolis: University of Minnesota Press, 1994), pp. 171–88.

64. For example, John Skinner (CBI: 57), Richard White (CBI: 66), and Thomas Baker (CBI: 70).

65. He only served once (1388) and held no other offices; CBI: 76.

66. On the role of master to his apprentices see Barbara Hanawalt, *Growing up in Medieval London* (New York: Oxford University Press, 1993), pp. 155–72.

67. Rawcliffe, "That Kindliness Should Be Cherished More," pp. 100–102.

68. CBI: 33.

69. CBI: 98.

70. I began with a sample of 125 burgesses and a few of their wives. But for statistical reasons, I have eliminated all men and women who had only one or two court appearances, reducing the core sample group to ninety-eight men and no women. Women disappear because very few of them had a lively independent court presence. There were women, however, who did not turn up in the random sample, who would have made the cut. The links that I have analyzed are limited to those recorded in the Convocation Books' legal disputes; I have not attempted to integrate material from property transactions, witness lists, wills, or the pledges recorded in the admission to the freedom of the city. This is partly for practical convenience, but also to present a level political playing field for all burgesses. These additional sources all tend to focus even more on the economic elite rather than their cross-group interactions.

71. *Creation of a Community,* pp. 54–58, 142–43 provides some context for the estimate of total population and total burgess population.

72. Such aspects are introduced clearly in J. Clyde Mitchell, "The Concept and Use of Social Networks," in *Social Networks in Urban Situations,* ed. J. Clyde Mitchell (Manchester: Manchester University Press, 1969), pp. 20–24. There is much variation in the social scientists' formulations on this and other points, and I believe historians can for the most part remain indifferent to the contradictory theoretical approaches and issues that Mitchell discusses and that have developed since; however, there are important additional discussions and help that can be recommended: J.A. Barnes, "Networks and Political Process," in Mitchell, ed., *Social Networks in Urban Situations,* pp. 51–76; J. Scott, *Social Network Analysis: A Handbook* (London: Sage Publications, 1991); *Social Networks,* ed. Samuel Leinhardt (New York: Academic Press, 1977), a key anthology: note especially parts II and III, and preeminently, J.A. Barnes, "Class and Committees in a Norwegian Island Parish," pp. 233–52; Elizabeth Bott, "Urban Families: Conjugal Roles and Social Networks," pp. 253–92; Adrian C. Mayer, "The Significance of Quasi-Groups in the Study of Complex Societies," pp. 293–315; and Granovetter, "The Strength of Weak Ties," pp. 347–67; Claude S. Fischer et al., *Networks and Places. Social Relations in the Urban Setting* (New York: Free Press, 1977); Barry Wellman and S.D. Berkowitz, "Introduction: Studying Social Structures," in *Social Structures: A Network Approach,* ed. Wellman and Berkowitz (Cambridge: Cambridge University Press, 1988), pp. 1–14, but many of the articles are suggestive: see especially, Barry Wellman, Peter J. Carrington, and Alan Hall, "Networks as Personal Communities," pp. 130–84; see also Barry Wellman and Barry Leighton, "Networks, Neighbourhoods, and Communities," in *New Perspectives on the American Community,* ed. Ronald L. Warren and Larry Lyon (Belmont, CA.: Wadsworth Publishing Co., 1988), pp. 57–72; Karen S. Cook, "Linking Actors and Structures: An Exchange Network Perspective," in *Structures of Power and Constraint,* ed. Craig Calhoun, Marshall C. Meyer, and W. Richard Scott (Cambridge: Cambridge University Press, 1990), pp. 113–28. For medieval work taking this literature into account and practicing the technique in a preliminary way, see Carpenter, "Gentry and Community," pp. 365–74.

73. Many who have promoted social network theory have been especially attracted to its nonindividualistic possibilities, its capturing dynamic structure, see for example, Wellman and Berkowitz, "Introduction."

74. Carpenter, "Gentry and Community," p. 373 uses the terms first-order and second-order for these relations. My formulation is more suggestive and in this respect begins to capture the kind of potential implicit in the Granovetter, "Strength of Weak Ties" idea of weak and strong ties. Carpenter does make considerable use of strong and weak ties in a way that I don't here.

Chapter 6   Battles at the Boundary of the Self

1. Charles Taylor, *Sources of the Self. The Making of the Modern Identity* (Cambridge, Mass.: Harvard University Press, 1989), pp. 195–97.

2. Julian Pitt-Rivers, *Fate of Shechem, or The Politics of Sex* (Cambridge, UK: Cambridge University Press, 1977), pp. 4 and 8. See also Pierre Bourdieu,

Outline of a Theory of Practice, trans. Richard Nice (Cambridge, UK: Cambridge University Press, 1977), p. 11; and George Herbert Mead, *Mind, Self, and Society* (Chicago: University of Chicago Press, 1962), pp. 42–43.

3. Autonomy here does not mean complete independence but something closer to mastery, the status of the superior, who typically has a large number of dependents, upon whom he reciprocally depends.

4. Speech as violence, mainly against authority, is discussed briefly by Guido Ruggiero, *Violence in Early Renaissance Venice* (New Brunswick: Rutgers University Press, 1980), pp. 125–27.

5. Authority could also employ violent language in a licit way. The pronouncement of solemn excommunication was partly this kind of act in the later Middle Ages, as was the formulaic curse: see Elizabeth Vodola, *Excommunication in the Middle Ages* (Berkeley: University of California Press, 1986), esp. pp. 44–69, on its community impact; and Lester K. Little, *Benedictine Maledictions* (Ithaca: Cornell University Press, 1993).

6. R.H. Helmholz, ed., *Select Cases of Defamation* (Selden Society 101, 1985), p. l.

7. *Statutes of the Realm,* volume 2 (London: Dawsons, 1816), p. 9.

8. Similarly, some anticlerical assaults such as those that the Lollards made were taken as more serious cross-class attacks, and were treated as fundamentally more dangerous.

9. Marjorie McIntosh, *Controlling Misbehavior in England, 1370–1600* (Cambridge, UK: Cambridge University Press, 1998), p. 200.

10. Laura Gowing, *Domestic Dangers: Women, Words, and Sex in Early Modern London* (Oxford: Clarendon Press; Oxford University Press, 1996), p. 33. This needs, however, careful collation with the medieval evidence. See Helmholz, *Select Cases of Defamation,* p. xliii, on the trajectory of business in church courts.

11. Helmholz, *Select Cases of Defamation,* introduction; Richard M. Wunderli, *London Church Courts and Society on the Eve of the Reformation* (Cambridge, Mass.: Medieval Academy of America, 1981), pp. 63–80; R.H. Helmholz, "Canonical Defamation in Medieval England," *American Journal of Legal History* 15 (1971): 255–68; S.F.C. Milsom, *The Historical Foundations of the Common Law* (London: Butterworths, 1969), pp. 332–34, which mainly indicates its nonexistence in the common law; my examples below indicate sources for the local and guild cases.

12. Wunderli, *London Church Courts,* p. 72; and Brian L. Woodcock, *Medieval Ecclesiastical Courts in the Diocese of Canterbury* (London: Oxford University Press, 1952), pp. 87–89.

13. Wunderli, *London Church Courts,* p. 63.

14. See Helmholz, *Select Cases of Defamation,* pp. xiv–xli.

15. The key idea was articulated in the fifth canon of the Council of Oxford of 1222: "*maliciose crimen imponunt alicui.*" See *Councils and Synods II, part I: 1205–65,* ed. F.M. Powicke and C.R. Cheney (Oxford: Oxford University Press, 1964), p. 107.

16. The cases were decided generally by compurgation, the mustering of a number of helpers who could swear in favor of your claim. This further

indicates that the assessment of reputation rather than the narrow and technical finding of fact was at issue. But from around 1500, at least in some jurisdictions, there was an increasing use of witnesses: see Wunderli, *London Church Courts,* pp. 68–72.

17. Wunderli, *London Church Courts,* p. 63 makes this point.

18. Virgil, *Aeneid,* lines 101–102 for the mysterious way rumor stalked the city like a bird; for recent historical considerations, see Steve Hindle, "The Shaming of Margaret Knowsley: Gossip, Gender and the Experience of Authority in Early Modern England," *Continuity and Change* 9 (1994): 391–419; Phillipp R. Schofield, "Peasants and the Manor Court: Gossip and Litigation at the Close of the Thirteenth Century," *Past and Present* 159 (1998): 3–43; and Chris Wickham, "Gossip and Resistance Among the Medieval Peasantry," *Past and Present* 160 (Oxford: Oxford University Press, 1998), pp. 3–24.

19. Perhaps the quickest clear study of such a court's omnibus character is J.A. Raftis, *Tenure and Mobility* (Toronto: Pontifical Institute of Mediaeval Studies, 1964); or, Zvi Razi and Richard Smith, eds., *Medieval Society and the Manor Court* (Oxford: Clarendon Press, 1996).

20. Christine de Pisan, *The Treasure of the City of Ladies, or the Book of the Three Virtues,* trans. Sarah Lawson (London: Penguin, 1985), p. 116.

21. Helmholz, "Canonical Defamation," p. 266.

22. For example, in *Depositions and Other Ecclesiastical Proceedings from the Court of Durham* (Surtees Society 21, 1845), p. 29: "restituta est pristinae famae," and on p. 27 "restituta ad famam."

23. John Gower, *Mirour de l'Homme / The Mirror of Mankind,* trans. William Burton Wilson and Nancy Wilson Van Baak (East Lansing: Colleagues Press, 1992), p. 41. See also "Yit is ther on, and that is he / Which cleped in Detraccioun. / And to conferme his accioun, / He hath witholde Malebouche, / Whos tunge neither pyl ne crouchem [plunder nor coin] / Mai hyre, so that he pronounce / A plein good word withoute frounce / Awher behinde a mannes bak." John Gower, *The English Works of John Gower,* ed. G.C. Macauley, vol. 2 (London: EETS 81, 1900), p. 141.

24. *Book of Margery Kempe,* p. 244.

25. Cf. Bourdieu, "Sentiment of Honour in Kabyle Society," in *Honour and Shame: The Values of Mediterranean Society,* ed. J.G. Peristiany and Julian Pitt-Rivers (Chicago: University of Chicago, 1966), p. 199.

26. It should be noted that the Wells Borough Community Court continued to see defamation cases, even though they apparently died out mysteriously in other borough courts around 1400. See Helmholz, "Select Cases of Defamation," pp. viii–lxi; L.R. Poos, "Sex, Lies and the Church Courts in Pre-Reformation England," *Journal of Interdisciplinary History* 25 (1995): 587.

27. CBI: 309 (7/19/1443).

28. This is in line with the meaning of their interventions that we describe in chapters 3 and 4. Gowing, *Domestic Dangers,* p. 113 has said rightly that there was "an overall system of beliefs and ideals in which a definition of morality was used to judge reputation."

29. Julian Pitt-Rivers, "The Place of Grace in Anthropology," in *Honor and Grace in Anthropology,* ed. John G. Peristiany and Julian Pitt-Rivers (Cambridge, UK: Cambridge University Press, 1992), pp. 217–218.

30. Wunderli, *London Church Courts,* p. 64, notes that fines were not to be paid as damages to the accuser.

31. Cf. Peter Fleming, "Conflict and Urban Government in later Medieval England: St Augustine's Abbey and Bristol," *Urban History* 27 (2000): 321–43 for a comparable official posturing after an important dispute.

32. *Acts of the Court of the Mercers' Company,* ed. Laetitia Lyell (Cambridge: Cambridge University Press, 1936), p. 85. Another case of brothers and slandering is recorded by Daniel R. Lesnick, "Insults and Threats in Medieval Todi," *Journal of Medieval History* 17 (1991): 71–72.

33. *Acts of the Mercers' Company,* pp. 85–86. Poos, "Sex, Lies, and the Church Courts," p. 591 notes that 'harlot' was only at this time becoming predominantly a sexual term.

34. These were all crimes, either lay or spiritual or both: see Wunderli, *London Church Courts,* p. 76. Cf. also the high prominence of money concerns in Lesnick, "Insults and Threats," p. 75; and Mary Beth Norton, "Gender and Defamation in Seventeenth-Century Maryland," *William and Mary Quarterly* 44 (1987): 9.

35. Rodney Hilton, "Small Town Society in England before the Black Death," in *The English Medieval Town. A Reader in English Urban History 1200–1540,* ed. Richard Holt and Gervase Rosser (London: Longman, 1990), pp. 89–90; this is developed by Poos, "Sex, Lies, and the Church Courts," p. 592; and in later context, in considerable detail, by Gowing, *Domestic Dangers,* esp. p. 62: "There was no way of calling a man a whore. . . ."

36. Carol Clover, "Regardless of Sex: Men, Women, and Power in Early Northern Europe," *Speculum* 68 (1993): 363–87; she interprets this in light of the "one-sex model" discussed as a principal premodern option by Thomas Laqueur, *Making Sex: Body and Gender from the Greeks to Freud* (Cambridge, Mass.: Harvard University Press, 1990).

37. Whether men's sexuality was an important part of their proper public identity, a different question, is debated, especially in early modern Britain: see Elizabeth Foyster, *Manhood in Early Modern England. Honor, Sex and Marriage* (London: Longman, 1999); Susan D. Amussen, *An Ordered Society: Gender and Class in Early Modern England* (Oxford: B. Blackwell, 1988), pp. 98–104; Gowing, *Domestic Dangers,* ch. 3. For medieval material, see Clover, "Regardless of Sex"; and most relevant, Derek Neal, "Suits Make the Man: Masculinity in Two English Law Courts, c. 1500," *Canadian Journal of History* 37 (2002): 1–22.

38. Neal, "Suits Make the Man," pp. 13–15 develops a dichotomy of a moralistic masculinity, not associated merely with strength and weakness. Truth is a central part. See also Richard Firth Green, *A Crisis of Truth. Literature and Law in Ricardian England* (Philadelphia: University of Pennsylvania Press, 1999).

39. Gowing, *Domestic Dangers,* p. 4.

40. Cf. Neal, "Suits Make the Man," pp. 7–8; Poos, "Sex, Lies, and the Church Courts," p. 595.

41. CBI: 18 (10/15/1383).
42. CBI: 24 (6/30/1384).
43. Here again secular value and church value were probably divergent: confessors asked "Hast thow I-land any thynge / To have the more wynnynge," and the manual commanded: "Usure and okere that beht al on/ Teche hem that they use non," which represents a high standard for usury that was probably not fully replicated in urban courts or assumptions. John Myrc, *Instructions for Parish Priests,* ed. Frederick James Furnivall (EETS 31, 1868 and 1902), pp. 36 and 12.
44. *York Memorandum Book,* vol. 2, ed. Maud Sellars (Surtees Society 125, 1915), p. 67. John Besyngby sr. vs. Henry Appilby (1418), *"publice vel occulte."*
45. See Green, *A Crisis of Truth,* pp. 1–40 who sets out this understanding of truth.
46. CBII: 142 (Thursday after St Matthew 1484). Ruggiero, *Violence in Early Renaissance Venice,* 125–37 focuses on this kind of verbal violence. On oaths, see Green, *Crisis of Truth,* pp. 78–120.
47. CBII: 142.
48. See, *The Creation of a Community,* pp. 191–97. Cf. Barbara Hanawalt, *Of Good and Ill Repute: Gender and Social Control in Medieval England* (New York: Oxford University Press, 1998), pp. 16–31, 48.
49. CBII: 150.
50. CBI: 158.
51. One of the helpful qualities of the Wells court material is that we can be sure that all the violence we find was indeed minor. The right and requirement to preserve the peace and apprehend violent criminals and judge their crimes was firmly within the royal prerogative. This power was of course considerably devolved when it came to enforcement. Minor disturbances of the peace—perhaps some quite like our cases—would have been brought by those on watch and ward or others to the attention of the town constables of the peace. They reported to both the Master and the Bishop of Bath and Wells, who had jurisdiction over the city. But any act or affray that smacked of felony, of serious or bloody wrongdoing should have ended up in a royal court, with the exception of thieves caught in the act or with the goods, whom the bishop had the authority—whether or not used—to execute summarily. See *Placita de Quo Warranto Edward I–Edward II,* ed. W. Illingworth, vol. ii (London: G. Eyre and A. Strahan, 1818), p. 703; "Statute of Winchester," *Statutes of the Realm,* vol. I (London: Dawsons, 1810), pp. 96–98 for the role of petty policemen such as the constables, required in all communities.
52. On the mundane, accidental quality of medieval violence, see A.J. Finch, "The Nature of Violence in the Middle Ages: An Alternative Perspective," *Historical Research* 70 (1997): 249–68.
53. CBII: 112.
54. CBII: 122.
55. CBII: 152.
56. CBII: 162.

57. See also CBII: 186. This was the case elsewhere: *The Bailiff's Minute Book of Dunwich,* ed. Mark Bailey (Suffolk Record Society 34, 1992), p. 28; Barbara A. Hanawalt, *Crime and Conflicts in English Communities 1300–48* (Cambridge, Mass.: Harvard University Press, 1979), p. 100.

58. CBII: 142.

59. CBI: 57 Philip Don insulted John Noreys, for which he was fined and expelled, an unusually harsh treatment. But Don was readmitted and forgiven because he returned to active participation in the guild the year following (CBI: 63/64).

60. See chapter 4 in this book, for an interpretation of the honor- and self-centered nature of trespass pleas.

61. CBI: 175.

62. CBI: 44.

63. CBI: 112.

64. CBII: 186.

65. CBI: 165.

66. CBI: 117.

67. This is the theme of chapter 7, in this book.

68. *Creation of a Community,* pp. 178–80.

69. Philippa Maddern, *Violence and Social Order. East Anglia 1422–42* (Oxford: Oxford University Press, 1992), p. 98. Pages 98–104 examine women as perpetrators and victims of violence.

70. *Creation of a Community,* pp. 190–97, 213–215.

71. Barbara Hanawalt, "Violence in the Domestic Milieu of Late Medieval England," in *Violence in Medieval Society,* ed. Richard W. Kaeuper (Woodbridge: Boydell, 2000), pp. 197–99.

72. *Summa Theologiae* (Ottawa: University of Ottawa Press, 1941), 2a–2ae, lvii, art. 4; I've favored the strong translation of *St Thomas Aquinas. Philosophical Texts,* ed. and trans. Thomas Gilby (London: Oxford University Press, 1951), p. 375.

73. See William of Ockham, *A Short Discourse on Tyrannical Government,* ed. and trans. Arthur Stephen McGrade and John Kilcullen (Cambridge, UK: Cambridge University Press, 1992), pp. 101–102; Thomas Hobbes, *Leviathan,* ed. Richard Tuck (Cambridge, UK: Cambridge University Press, 1991), pp. 139–40.

74. "La Belle dame sans merci," in *Political, Religious and Love Poems,* ed. Frederick J. Furnivall (EETS 15, 1866 and 1903, reedited), p. 92. It should be noted that this is overtly a play of rhetoric, as the lover counters that love makes women the masters and men the servants.

75. Rosemary Horrox, "Service," in *Fifteenth-Century Attitudes,* ed. Rosemary Horrox (Cambridge: Cambridge University Press, 1994), p. 68.

76. This case from cause paper evidence is recounted in P.J.P. Goldberg, " 'For Better, For Worse': Marriage and Economic Opportunity for Women in Town and Country," in *'Woman is a Worthy Wight'. Women in English Society, 1200–1500,* ed. P.J.P. Goldberg (Stroud: A. Sutton, 1992), p. 118.

77. See Hanawalt, "Violence in the Domestic Milieu," pp. 200–207; Shannon McSheffrey, "Men and Masculinity in Late Medieval London Civic Culture. Governance, Patriarchy, and Reputation," in *Conflicted Identities and Multiple Masculinities. Men in the Medieval West,* ed. Jacqueline Murray (New York: Garland, 1999), pp. 243–78.

78. *Depositions and Other Ecclesiastical Proceedings from the Courts of Durham,* ed. James Raine (Surtees Society 21, 1845), pp. 14–20, which records all the witnesses using the same terms. This case took place in 1370.

79. *Depositions and Ecclesiastical Proceedings,* p. 18.

80. Depositions and Ecclesiastical Proceedings, pp. 15, 17, and 18 provide three slightly different direct quotations; I translate: "Vade tu et interficias ipsum Willelmum, falsum presbiterum."

81. *Depositions and Ecclesiastical Proceedings,* p. 18.

82. Nor is it unique. See Hanawalt, *Growing up in Medieval London. The Experience of Childhood in History* (New York: Oxford University Press, 1993), p. 190, although the following pages show servant-on-master violence. On the tenor and context of master–servant relations, see P.J.P. Goldberg, "Masters and Men in Later Medieval England," in *Masculinity in Medieval Europe,* ed. Dawn Hadley (London: Longman, 1999), pp. 56–70.

83. Cf. Hanawalt, "Violence in the Domestic Milieu," pp. 212–213.

84. Discussions of serious violence are as numerous as small violence is unstudied: see, for instance, Maddern, *Violence and Social Order;* C.I. Hammer, "Patterns of Homicide in a Medieval University Town: Fourteenth-Century Oxford," *Past and Present* 78 (1978): 3–23; J.G. Bellamy, *Criminal Law and Society in Late Medieval and Tudor England* (Gloucester: A. Sutton, 1984); Barbara Hanawalt, *Crime and Conflict in English Communities, 1300–1348* (Cambridge, Mass.: Harvard University Press, 1979); and Hanawalt, "Violence in the Domestic Milieu."

85. CBI: 49.

86. CBI: 97.

87. CBI: 113.

88. For example, CBI: 128 Stephen Skynner vs. Richard Gros. Cf. Hanawalt, *Growing up in Medieval London,* p. 184.

89. CBI: 153.

90. Servants must have had recourse to other courts, the royal or the manorial, but it is an open question how often they would have used them or whether their concerns would have been considered legitimate. See, however, Goldberg, "Masters and Men," pp. 57–64.

91. *Creation of Community,* pp. 98–101.

92. See Chris Given-Wilson, "The Problem of Labour in the Context of English Government, c. 1350–1450," in *The Problem of Labour in Fourteenth-Century England,* ed. J. Bothwell, P.J.P. Goldberg, and W.M. Ormrod (York: York Medieval Press, 2000), pp. 85–100.

93. See *Select Cases of Trespass from the Royal Courts,* vol. 1, ed. Morris S. Arnold (Selden Society 100, 1985), pp. 99–106.

94. CBI: 173.
95. CBI: 43.
96. CBI: 64.
97. CBI: 68.
98. See Barbara Hanawalt, *Growing up in Medieval London,* pp. 170–72, 190ff.
99. On this, see Maddern, *Violence and Social Order,* pp. 99–100.
100. Chaucer, *Canterbury Tales,* "The Wife of Bath's Prologue," pp. 115–16; *Towneley Plays,* ed. George England and Alfred W. Pollard (EETS 71, 1897), pp. 29–30, 34–35.
101. CBI: 97.
102. CBI: 85.
103. See R.N. Swanson, "Angels Incarnate: The Clergy and Masculinity from the Gregorian Reform to the Reformation," in Hadley, *Masculinity in Medieval Europe,* pp. 160–77; and P.H. Cullum, Clergy, "Masculinity and Trangression in Later Medieval Europe," in Hadley, *Masculinity in Medieval Europe,* pp. 178–92.
104. McSheffrey, "Men and Masculinity in Late Medieval London."
105. Hilton, "Small Town Society," p. 84 found relatively little female-initiated violence, ranging in the first part of the fourteenth century in the small town of Halesowen from 15–35 percent of the attackers in cases of presentment, but he notes: "Women were frequently the victims of men; men rarely the victims of women." Courts were tough on women who sued, but indulgent of those who were being prosecuted, even for felonies—see Hanawalt, *Crime and Communities,* p. 54.
106. CBI: 114.
107. This confusing entry could mean that the assailant was trying to take his *own* wife from Rydon, for whom she may have worked or been otherwise involved. Some violence, although of different timbre, is implied either way. CBI: 160.
108. CBI: 147.
109. CBI: 33. Literally, the 2s. was to guarantee his future behavior, but it appears to have been given to Forbour, a *de facto* fine.
110. *Book of Margery Kempe,* p. 111.
111. See Christine de Pisan, *Treasury of the City of Ladies;* and Rowena Archer, " 'How Ladies. . .Who Live on their Manors ought to Manage their Households and Estates': Women as Landholders and Administrators in the Later Middle Ages," in *Woman is a Worthy Wight,* pp. 149–81.
112. CBI: 43. *Creation of a Community,* p. 264.
113. CBI: 42.
114. Some of this is evident in Nicholas Orme, *Medieval Children* (New Haven: Yale University Press, 2001), pp. 84–85.
115. Maddern, *Violence and Social Order,* 99 quotes from the *Paston Letters,* ii, p. 85: "[he] asked hym if a man myth not betyn hes owyn wyfe."
116. Hanawalt, "Violence in the Domestic Milieu," p. 206.
117. See for penitential practices of an extreme sort, Caroline Walker Bynum, *Holy Feast, Holy Fast* (Berkeley: University of California Press, 1987), passim.

118. Maddern, *Violence and Social Order,* pp. 75–110.

119. "Ordinances and Statutes of the Cathedral Church of Wells," in *Dean Cosyn and Wells Cathedral Miscellanea,* ed. Aelred Watkin (SRS 56, 1941), p. 103; the vicars-choral rules are at pp. 139–49.

120. Cf. the situation in Florence, D. Kent and F.W. Kent, *Neighbourhood and Neighbours in Renaissance Florence. The District of the Red Lion* (Locust Valley, NY: J.J. Augustin, 1982), p. 53.

121. For example, Poos, "Sex, Lies and Church Courts"; Gowing, *Domestic Dangers.*

122. Gowing, *Domestic Dangers,* p. 123.

123. Again, Maddern, *Violence and Social Order,* p. 99, provides some evidence; see also, Barbara Hanawalt, *The Ties that Bound* (New York: Oxford University Press, 1986), pp. 208–210.

124. Hanawalt, *Crime and Conflict,* p. 25; Maryanne Kowaleski, "Women's Work in a Market Town: Exeter in the Late Fourteenth Century," in *Women and Work in Preindustrial Europe,* ed. Barbara Hanawalt (Bloomington: Indiana University Press, 1986), pp. 150–51.

125. Pierre Bourdieu, "Rites as Acts of Institution," in *Honor and Grace in Anthropology,* p. 88, suggests that facts of social life do provide people with a greater or lesser amount of identity or being.

Chapter 7   Self-Possession

1. William Harrison, *Description of England* (Washington and New York: Dover Publications, 1994), p. 146.

2. See John Scattergood, "Fashion and Morality in the Late Middle Ages," in *England in the Fifteenth Century. Proceedings of the Harlaxton Symposium,* ed. Daniel Williams (Woodbridge: Boydell Press, 1987), pp. 255–72.

3. See Susan Crane, "Clothing and Gender Definition: Joan of Arc," *Journal of Medieval and Early Modern Studies* 28 (1996): 297–320; see also, Katherine French, "The Legend of Lady Godiva and the Image of the Female Body," *The Journal of Medieval History,* 18 (1992): 3–19.

4. Thomas Patterson, "Self-worth and Property: Equipage and Early Medieval Personhood," in *Social Identity in Early Medieval Britain,* ed. William D. Frazer and Andrew Tyrell (London: Leicester University Press, 2000), p. 66.

5. John Myrc, *Instructions for Parish Priests,* ed. Frederick James Furnivall (EETS 31, 1868 and 1902), p. 32.

6. *The Book of Margery Kempe,* ed. Sanford Brown Meech and Hope Emily Allen, EETS, O.S. 212 (London: Oxford University Press, 1940), p. 32.

7. Scattergood, "Fashion and Morality," p. 269. Cf. P.J.P. Goldberg, "Women," in *Fifteenth-Century Attitudes,* ed. Rosemary Horrox (Cambridge: Cambridge University Press, 1994), p. 124.

8. Dyan Elliott, "Dress as Mediator Between Inner and Outer Self: The Pious Matron of the High and Later Middle Ages," *Mediaeval Studies* 53 (1991): 290 speaks of a wife's "paraphernalia" as part of her identity.

9. On the question of commercialization's ambiguous later medieval advance, see R.H. Britnell, *The Commercialisation of English Society* (Cambridge: Cambridge University Press, 1996); on the question of mobility, see J. Ambrose Raftis, *Peasant Economic Development,* passim (Montreal: McGill-Queen's University Press, 1996), passim; and R.H. Hilton, "Social Concepts in the English Rising of 1381," *Class Conflict and the Crisis of Feudalism* (London: Hambledon Press, 1985), pp. 216–26; and "Ideology and Social Order in Late Medieval England," in *Class Conflict,* pp. 246–52, where the argument between group mobility and frustration and individual mobility is discussed.

10. *Middle English Lyrics,* ed. Richard L. Hoffman and Maxwell Luria (New York: Norton, 1974), p. 120.

11. *Creation of a Community,* pp. 70–85. See A.R. Bridbury, *Medieval Clothmaking* (London: Heinemann, 1982).

12. *Statutes of the Realm,* I (London: Dawson, 1810), p. 380. Similarly, the second poll tax (1379) assimilated civic worthies to country ones. Wells' Master was probably taxed like a knight: see *Anonimalle Chronicle, 1333–1381,* ed. V.L. Galbraith (Manchester and London: Longman, Green & Co., 1927), pp. 127–28.

13. Hilton, "Some Concepts," doubts there was significant real mobility, although he perhaps underestimates the importance of mobility *within* a social group.

14. Who controlled such meanings throughout the culture is now much debated. See, for example, Sarah Beckwith, "Making the World in York and the York Cycle," in *Framing Medieval Bodies,* ed. Sarah Kay and Miri Rubin (Manchester: St. Martin's Press, 1994), pp. 254–76.

15. *Dean Cosyn and Wells Cathedral Miscellanea,* ed. Aelred Watkin (SRS 56, 1941), p. 130; cf. Johan Huizinga, *The Autumn of the Middle Ages,* trans. Rodney J. Paton and Ulrich Mammitzsch (Chicago: University of Chicago Press, 1996), pp. 325–28 surveying secular rituals finds another and inconsistent level of color-meaning.

16. *Wells Cathedral Miscellanea,* p. 12.

17. *Wells Cathedral Miscellanea,* p. 22.

18. This was in the 1330s. *Wells Cathedral Miscellanea,* p. 23.

19. *Wells Cathedral Miscellanea,* p. 104.

20. *Chaucer, Canterbury Tales,* I, A 195–97, p. 157.

21. AH 17.

22. *SMW,* I, p. 27.

23. *SMW,* I, p. 75.

24. *SMW,* II, p. 169. See Harrison, *Description of England,* p. 146.

25. *SMW,* II, pp. 389–90.

26. CBII: 251 and 266.

27. CBII: 567.

28. Cf., *The Coventry Leet Book: or Mayor's Register,* ed. Mary Dormer Harris (EETS 134, 135, 138, 146 combined, 1907–13), pp. 220 and 230.

29. CBIII: 40, a mid-sixteenth-century document. For examples of processions, *English Gilds,* ed. Joshua Toulmin Smith and Lucy Toulmin Smith (EETS 40, 1870), p. 55; *York Memorandum Book,* vol. 2, ed. Maud Sellars (Surtees Society 125, 1915), p. 118; Miri Rubin, *Corpus Christi* (Cambridge, UK: Cambridge University Press, 1991), pp. 243–71.

30. *Wells Cathedral Miscellanea,* p. xxvii; See Ronald Hutton, *The Rise and Fall of Merry England* (Oxford: Oxford University Press, 1996), pp. 10–12. On the role of such dressing and acting as social criticism, reinforcing the order see Natalie Z. Davis, "Women on Top," in *Society and Culture in Early Modern France* (Stanford: Stanford University Press, 1975), pp. 124–51.

31. Robert Dinn, "Death and Rebirth in Late Medieval Bury St Edmunds," in *Death in Towns. Urban Responses to the Dying and Dead,* ed. Steven Bassett (Leicester: Leicester University Press, 1992), p. 155.

32. *SMW,* I, p. 74. Dinn, "Death and Rebirth," p. 155 found that funeral colors were still settling toward black.

33. R.H. Britnell, *Growth and Decline in Colchester, 1300–1525* (Cambridge, UK: Cambridge University Press, 1986), pp. 55–56 on russet cloth, which was typically a gray or russet color, never at any rate bold or bright.

34. On the entire process of managing the end of life and its immediately following actions, see Dinn, "Death and Burial," pp. 151–69.

35. "Liveries and Robes in England, c. 1200–1339," *English Historical Review* 111 (1996): 289.

36. *Cely Letters, 1472–1488,* ed. Alison Hanham (EETS 273, 1975), #175, lines 12–13, p. 162. This is a double association: Celys to Sir John Weston; and Sir John to his liveried "friends."

37. See, for example, *York Memorandum Book,* II, pp. 200–202 (1456) and *Coventry Leet Book,* p. 374 (1472).

38. Richard II's 1389 guild inquiries were motivated by such political suspicions: see *English Gilds,* pp. 127–31.

39. Serel, p. 39.

40. Barbara Hanawalt, "At the Margin of Women's Space in Medieval Europe," in *Matrons and Marginal Women in Medieval Society,* ed. Robert R. Edwards and Vickie Ziegler (Woodbridge: Boydell Press, 1995), p. 17 makes this point in the context of women's space, that is, of where certain kinds of clothes were required.

41. *Cely Letters,* #175, p. 161.

42. From the "Baron O'Brackley," *Folk Songs and Ballads of Scotland,* ed. Ewan MacCull (Music Sales Corp.: New York, 1965), Child #203.

43. Cely Letters, #175, p. 161.

44. See, for instance, the nuanced discussion of women, work and society in Judith Bennett, *Ale, Beer, and Brewsters in England: Women's Work in a Changing Society, 1300–1600* (New York: Oxford University Press, 1996), esp. the conclusion pp. 145–57.

45. In reality, women sometimes did achieve recognition based on the economic roles they played although these were less certain than men's similar

work identities: see Cordelia Beattie, "The Problem of Women's Work Identities in Post-Black Death England," in *The Problem of Labour in Fourteenth-Century England,* ed. J. Bothwell, P.J.P. Goldberg, and W.M. Ormrod (York: York Medieval Press, 2000), pp. 1–19.

46. Adam of Cobsam, *The Wright's Chaste Wyf,* ed. Frederick J. Furnivall (EETS 12, 1865), pp. 3–4.

47. The commitment to work and a work ethic may be related, but Christopher Dyer, "Work Ethics in the Fourteenth Century," in *Problem of Labour,* pp. 21–41 is unfortunately too little interested in the master craftsmen to consider them as workers rather than mere employers of labor. A sense for the full seriousness of craftperson and his product can be gleaned from John Harvey, *Mediaeval Craftsmen* (London: Batsford, 1975); see too Heather Swanson, *Medieval Artisans* (Oxford: B. Blackwell, 1989).

48. Charles Taylor, *Sources of the Self* (Cambridge, Mass.: Harvard University Press, 1989), pp. 368–90 for very un-medieval manners.

49. CBII: 89. Stowell had a typical mason's pattern of no official office-holding, few lawsuits, and sometimes missed appearances at those. On his career, see John H. Harvey with Arthur Oswald, *English Mediaeval Architects: a Biographical Dictionary down to 1500* (Gloucester: Sutton, 1987), p. 286.

50. Wells, Wells Cathedral, Fabric Account, 1457–58.

51. CBII: 89.

52. "I will not tyne that I have wroght." *Towneley Plays,* ed. George England and Alfred W. Pollard (EETS 71, 1897), "The Annunciation," p. 86.

53. Katherine French, *The People of the Parish* (Philadelphia: University of Pennsylvania Press, 1999), pp. 102–105; Julia Carnwath, "The Churchwardens' Accounts of Thame, Oxfordshire, c. 1443–1524," in *Trade, Devotion, and Governance,* ed. Dorothy J. Clayton, Richard G. Davie, and Peter McNiven (Stroud: A. Sutton, 1994), p. 191 where the evidence of making with one's hands for the church is clear.

54. Mr. Goodall's Book, p. 33.

55. Mr. Goodall's Book, p. 34.

56. AH 226k.

57. See A.J. Scrase, "Development and Change in Burghage Plots: The Example of Wells," *Journal of Historical Geography* 15 (1989): 49–65, which provides some background.

58. William Langland, *Piers Plowman: The C Version,* ed. George Russell and George Kane (Berkeley: University of California Press, 1997), p. 373.

59. Useful on old age, with some attention to decrepitude are Nicholas Orme, "Sufferings of the Clergy: Illness and Old Age in Exeter Diocese, 1300–1540," in *Life, Death and the Elderly. Historical Perspectives,* ed. Margaret Pelling (London: Routledge, 1994), pp. 62–73; Richard M. Smith, "Manorial Court and the Elderly Tenant in Late Medieval England," in Pelling, *Life, Death and the Elderly,* pp. 39–61; Barbara Harvey, *Living and Dying in England,* pp. 72–145 provides a global account of dealing with sickness and mortality.

60. AH 172.

61. See, for instance, Christopher Daniell, *Death and Burial in Medieval England 1066–1550* (London: Routledge, 1998); Margaret Aston, "Death," in Horrox, *Fifteenth-Century Attitudes,* pp. 202–28; Dinn, "Death and Rebirth" and "Monuments Answerable to Man's Worth. Burial Patterns, Social Status and Gender in Late Medieval Bury St Edmunds," *Journal of Ecclesiastical History* 46 (1995): 237–55; Clare Gittings, "Urban Funerals in Late Medieval and Reformation England," in *Death in Towns,* pp. 170–83.

62. "A Lyke Wake Dirge" in *Norton Anthology of Poetry,* ed. Alexander W. Allision, 3rd Edition (New York: Norton, 1983), p. 61; Dinn, "Death and Rebirth," pp. 159–60.

63. See Caroline W. Bynum, *The Resurrection of the Body* (New York: Columbia University Press, 1995), esp. part 3 for the theological and spiritual discussion of the problem.

64. *SMW,* II, p. 199; Margery Churchstile "commends her soul to God, and St Mary and all the saints of heaven" (AH 17); and Thomas Tanner left his "to God Almighty my redeemer, the Blessed Mary and all the saints" (*SMW,* I, p. 6.)

65. For example, *English Gilds,* pp. 7, 10 from among many.

66. AH 17 (1313).

67. *SMW,* I, pp. 160–61.

68. Vanessa Harding, "Burial Choice and Buried Location in later Medieval London," *Death in Towns,* p. 130 shows that in some places variable sums were charged according to desirability.

69. AH 116 (1405).

70. *SMW,* I, pp. 230–31; *SMW,* I, pp. 25–27.

71. This is perhaps the difference of thinking with the social self and represents a difference of emphasis to the comprehensive results of Dinn, "Monuments Answerable to Men's Worth," esp. pp. 244–45.

72. See especially Dinn, "Monuments Answerable to Men's Worth"; and Harding, "Burial Choice and Burial Location." Cf. Kermode, *Medieval Merchants,* p. 141; and Margaret Aston, "Death," in Horrox, *Fifteenth-Century Attitudes,* pp. 216–19.

73. For the citizens it was akin to the cloister churchyard in the cathedral at the other end of town, to which all vicar and canons could expect burial, if their wealth and social selves did not validate something more.

74. Not everyone would be permitted to be buried inside the church. A Chichester council may have been typical in admitting only church benefactors from among the common laity. See *Councils and Synods,* ed. F.M. Powicke and C.R. Cheney (Oxford: Clarendon Press, 1964), II, p. 1117.

75. For example, oligarchs Richard Vowell (*SMW,* I, p. 368), John Horewode (SMW, I, p. 74), Edward Curteys requested burial before the altar of the High Cross in the nave (*SMW,* I, p. 64). This was much sought after: Harding, "Burial Choice and Burial Location," p. 131.

76. *SMW,* I, p. 237.

77. *SMW,* I, p. 195.

78. *SMW,* I, p. 77.

79. *SMW,* II, p. 107.
80. Bynum, *Resurrection of the Body.*
81. *SMW* I, p. 6.
82. *Dives and Pauper,* ed. Patricia Heath Barnum, vol. I (EETS 275, 1976), pp. 214–15.
83. *SMW,* II, p. 17.
84. *SMW,* II, p. 114.
85. *Norton Anthology,* p. 61.
86. Elliott, "Dress as Mediator Between Inner and Outer Self," 279–308 has argued, however, that the regimented focus on conformity and the "exterior" self could lead to the development of the inner self typical of later medieval spiritual religion, especially among women.
87. Caroline Bynum, *Holy Feast and Holy Fast: The Religious Significance of Food to Medieval Women* (Berkeley: University of California Press, 1987) for this kind of argument. It is all the more striking that this mode was less performed in England.

Chapter 8   A World of Individuals

1. Wells Reg. II, fo. 63.
2. Wells Reg. II, fo. 67.
3. On prostitution in England generally, see Rose Mazo Karras, *Common Women* (New York: Oxford University Press, 1996), esp. pp. 48–64 and 95–101; see also, Ann J. Kettle, "Ruined Maids: Prostitution and Servant Girls in Later Medieval England," in *Matrons and Marginal Women in Medieval Society,* ed. Robert E. Edwards and Vickie Ziegler (Woodbridge: Boydell Press, 1995), pp. 19–31; and Goldberg, *Women, Work, and Life Cycle,* pp. 149–55; and Leah Otis, *Prostitution in Medieval Society: The History of an Institution in Langued'oc* (Chicago: University of Chicago Press, 1985), who notes (p. 63) the difficulty of learning details about the individual women involved.
4. See, for instance, John Schofield, *Medieval London Houses* (New Haven: Yale University Press, 1994), pp. 106–108.
5. Stephen O'Connor, "Adam Fraunceys and John Pyel: Perceptions of Status among Merchants in Fourteenth-Century London," in *Trade, Devotion, and Governance,* ed. Dorothy J. Clayton, Richard G. Davies, and Peter McNiven (Stroud: A. Sutton, 1994), pp. 17–35 shows that this doesn't necessarily mean giving up the urban focus of their identity or aspirations.
6. CBI: 169.
7. Chapter 5 in this volume.
8. Charles Phythian-Adams, *Desolation of a City: Coventry and the Urban Crisis of the Late Middle Ages* (Cambridge, UK: Cambridge University Press, 1979), pp. 124–28.
9. Even a seigneurial borough such as Wells may well have been on a trajectory to arrive at the "triumph of oligarchy" discussed for the later sixteenth century by Robert Tittler, *The Reformation and the English Towns* (Oxford: Clarendon

Press, 1998), part III; and by S.H. Rigby and Elizabeth Ewan, "Government, Power and Authority, 1300–1540," in *The Cambridge Urban History of Britain, Volume 1, 600–1540,* ed. David M. Palliser (Cambridge: Cambridge University Press, 2000), pp. 309–12.

10. CBI: 160; CBI: 222.

11. CBI: 226.

12. For the dynamics of group formation, particularly of 'systacts', with common interests, see Stephen Rigby, *English Society in the Later Middle Ages. Class, Status and Gender* (New York: St. Martin's Press, 1995).

13. Rosemary Horrox, "The Urban Gentry in the Fifteenth Century," in *Towns and Townspeople in the Fifteenth Century,* ed. J.A.F. Thomson (Gloucester: Alan Sutton, 1983), pp. 22–44; O'Connor, "Adam Fraunceys and John Pyel," pp. 17–35 has effectively argued for the complexity of the gentleman-citizen nexus, which was not inevitably about land; Sylvia L. Thrupp, *The Merchant Class of Medieval London* (Ann Arbor: University of Michigan Press, 1948), pp. 256–87 charts the complexities of citizen-gentlemen intersection, as well as the mentality of social climbing, pp. 300–11.

14. CBI: 225.

15. CBI: 226.

16. See, for example, CBI: 227; CBI: 231; CBI: 233 (2); CBI: 240.

17. CBI: 257.

18. Christine Carpenter, "Town and 'Country': The Stratford Guild and Political Networks of Fifteenth-Century Warwickshire," in *The History of an English Borough. Stratford-upon-Avon,* ed. R. Bearman (Stroud: Sutton, 1997), pp. 62–79 mainly considers the countryside of the equation and in considering the town (p. 77) focuses on the collective rather than the individual relevance of such networks and links.

19. Wells Cath. R. III, fo. 259. See also *Creation of a Community,* pp. 129–38 for the political context of this transition.

20. CBI: 269.

21. CBI: 312.

22. *List of Escheators for England and Wales,* List and Index Society 72 (London: Swift, 1971), *anno* 1474.

23. *Bridgwater Borough Archives, 1400–1445,* ed. T.B. Dilks (SRS 54, 1938), *sub* Gascoigne; see also WCaCh 669, which outlines some of his extensive lands, including church advowsons and parts of manors.

24. CBI: 279.

25. On the whole question of urban gentry, see Horrox, "The Urban Gentry in the Fifteenth Century," pp. 22–44.

26. CBI: 290.

27. SRO D/D/B Reg. 6 (Beckyngton), fo. 231.

28. SRO D/D/B Reg. 6 (Beckyngton), fos. 432–33.

29. CBII: 36 and 67.

30. CBII: 47.

31. CBII: 48.

32. For example, CBII: 96; CBII: 75.

33. CBII: 67. See Schofield, *Medieval London Houses,* pp. 66–67.

34. CBII: 68.

35. CBII: 123. Miri Rubin, "The Poor," in *Fifteenth-Century Attitudes,* ed. Rosemary Horrox (Cambridge: Cambridge University Press, 1994), p. 171; on the question of hospital and almshouse admissions and the life within, see, for instance, Miri Rubin, *Charity and Community in Medieval Cambridge* (Cambridge: Cambridge University Press, 1987), pp. 148–72; and Patricia H. Cullum, " 'For Pore Popele Haberles': What was the Function of the Maisondieu?" in *Trade, Devotion and Governance,* pp. 36–54, which focuses on almshouses more modest than Wells'.

36. *The Book of Margery Kempe,* ed. Sanford Brown Meech and Hope Emily Allen (EETS 212, 1940), book I, chapter 76.

37. See AH 172, the almshouse foundation charter of 1436; and see *Creation of a Community,* pp. 241–48.

38. AH 275–78, 289, 302–303, 305.

39. *Chaucer,* Fragment II, Group B, line 101, p. 88.

40. AH 275.

41. This is the argument of Katherine French, *People of the Parish: Community Life in a Late Medieval English Diocese* (Philadelphia: University of Pennsylvania Press, 2001) pp. 68–98, the best look at the role of this newly important later medieval lay officer; *Creation of a Community,* p. 166.

42. CBI: 84, 100, and 101.

43. CBI: 58, 102, and 117.

44. CBI: 93 for a loan of 5s. 6d. Rowburgh had taken cloth from Smart.

45. Serel p. 102; cf. "Mr Goodall's Book," pp. 32–38.

46. CBI: 137 and 153.

47. See N. Pevsner, *North Somerset and Bristol* (Harmondsworth: Penguin Books, 1958).

48. CBI: 117.

49. He is sometimes, rarely, called Pomerey.

50. WCC 133, where he appeared as a witness, listed last and perhaps not a regular.

51. See, for example, Wells City Ch. 143, 152, and 155–57.

52. WCaCh 504–506. He held the property till 1402. It was in the High Street opposite La Pool lane, and it was worth 20s. along with a nearby house of Agnes or Joan Riche.

53. "Yeoman of Wells" in *Calendar of the Patent Rolls, 6 Henry V,* p. 166.

54. On these men, farming out and the transition of rural life in these years, J.A. Raftis, *Peasant Economic Development within the English Manorial System* (Montreal: McGill-Queen's University Press, 1997), esp. pp. 75–8.

55. London, Lambeth Palace Library ED 1184/6 (1390).

56. CBI: 42.

57. CBI: 121.

58. CBI: 33.

59. CBI: 12.

60. CBI: 31.

61. CBI: 130.

62. On 81 of 139 occasions.

63. *Creation of a Community*, pp. 44, 277–81.

64. See *Victoria County History Somerset*, vol II, W. Page (London: Constable, 1911), pp. 158–60.

65. *Creation of a Community*, pp. 241–43 and AH 172.

66. Tarsus according to *Le Neve's Fasti Ecclesiae Anglicanae, Bath and Wells Diocese, 1300–1541*, vol. 8, ed. B. Jones (London: Athlone Press, 1964), p. 7.

67. *Le Neve's Fasti Ecclesiae, sub nomine*; A.B. Emden, *Biographical Register of Oxford University to 1500*, vol. I (Oxford: Oxford University Press, 1957), pp. 491–92.

68. The common fifteenth-century term for Oriel, for example, *Oriel College Records*, ed. Shadwell and Salter (Oxford Historical Society 85, 1926), p. 141.

69. *The Dean's Register of Oriel, 1446–61*, ed. Richards and H.O. Salter (Oxford Historical Society 84, 1926), p. 6; this was in 1504.

70. Wells Cath. Reg. IV, fo. 52.

71. SRO D/D/B Reg. 7 (Stillington), f. 113.

72. For example, Wells Cath. Reg. IV, fos. 59 and 92.

73. Wells Cath. Reg. IV, fos. 59 and 92.

74. Wells Cath. Reg. IV, fo. 34d: May 15, 1491 "In the great parlour within the dean's house, Thomas, Bishop of Tine, prayed leave to perform the office at the burial of Robert, late bishop of Bath and Wells; which leave was granted, without prejudice to the statutes and customs of the cathedral."

75. In 1503/04: Wells Cath. Reg. IV, fo. 100.

76. WCaCh. 736. Very possibly, this was in anticipation of Cornish's death and a kind of trust agreement.

77. CBII: 220 and see *Creation of a Community*, 196.

78. *SMW*, II, 169, 199.

79. Wells Cath. Reg. IV, fos. 55d., 61 (1495–97), and 72d.

80. See Kathleen Edwards, *The English Secular Cathedrals in the Middle Ages* (Manchester: Manchester University Press, 1967), pp. 195–208.

81. *Biographical Register of the University of Oxford*, I, 492.

82. Oliver King, former bishop of Bath and Wells had appointed him an executor: *SMW, 1501–30*, pp. 45; *Calendar of the Manuscripts of the Dean and Chapter of Wells*, II, ed. William H. Bird and W. Paley Baildon (Historical Manuscript Commission, 1914), p. 175.

83. Wells Cath. Reg. IV, fo. 90; on precentors, see Edwards, *Secular Cathedrals*, pp. 159–67.

84. *The Dean's Register of Oriel College, 1446–1661*, 15.

85. Emden, *Biographical Register*, 363–64.

86. He rented this from the cathedral for 4s. p.a. and then fixed it up and was receiving 40s. from its tenants. *SMW II*, 168.

87. *SMW II*, 169.

88. *Wells Cathedral*, II, 238.

89. Wells City ch. 178.

90. Judith Bennett, *Women in the Medieval English Countryside* (New York: Oxford University Press, 1987), 142–76.

91. *Creation of a Community,* 252; I discuss Isabel Tanner in one paragraph on pp. 251–52.
92. Cf. Jennifer Ward, "Townswomen and their Households," in *Daily Life in the Late Middle Ages,* ed. Richard Britnell (Stroud: Sutton Publishing, 1998), pp. 30–31. See also Ralph A. Houlbrooke, *The English Family 1450–1700* (London: Longman, 1984), pp. 96–105; and Barbara Hanawalt, *The Ties that Bound* (New York: Oxford University Press, 1986).
93. *Book of Margery Kempe,* pp. 225–26, 247.
94. Wells City ch. 151, 153, 154, 156.
95. See B.F. Harvey, "Draft Letters Patent of Manumission and Pardon for the Men of Somerset in 1381," *English Historical Review* 80 (1965): 89–91; Raftis, *Peasant Economic Development,* p. 116 categorizes some manumissions as "prestige," which probably fits this case. See also Raftis, *Tenure and Mobility* (Toronto: Pontifical Institute of Mediaeval Studies, 1964), pp. 83–89.
96. *Calendar of Patent Rolls, 1 Henry IV,* pp. 53–54.
97. *Calendar of Patent Rolls, 9 Henry IV,* p. 370.
98. *The Register of Nicholas Bubwith, Bishop of Bath and Wells,* ed. T. Scott Holmes (SRS 29, 1914), p. 86.
99. *Calendar of Patent Rolls, 10 Henry IV,* p. 48.
100. Wells City ch. 16.
101. This tablet can still be seen at St. Cuthbert's.
102. CBI: 154.
103. Mr Goodall's Book, p. 35, identifies Atwood as her executor. His role is hard to know for sure as her will has not survived. The inventory of bequests is at Mr Goodall's Book, pp. 34–35 and is dateable to 1446.
104. While there is a possibility that Isabel lived till 1437, she was certainly alive into the 1420s.

Chapter 9   Conclusion: The Shape of the Social Self

1. Again, this is stressed by Stephen Rigby, *English Society in the Later Middle Ages* (New York: St. Martin's Press, 1995).
2. See Christopher Dyer, "Small Town Conflict in the Later Middle Ages. Events at Shipston-on-Stour," *Urban History* 19 (Cambridge: Cambridge University Press, 1992), 190.
3. *Chronicle of All that Happens,* ch. 4 and pp. 231–33. Obviously, I can't believe the community–individual polarity she uses is the best way to work through this problem.
4. Tittler, *Reformation and the Towns,* who discusses this in terms of the political and cultural transformation that followed the Reformation; Rigby and Ewan, "Government, Power and Authority, 1300–1540," pp. 309–12; Stephen Rigby, *Medieval Grimsby,* pp. 108–112, although the evidence is ambiguous, much of which remains is susceptible of the kind of interpretation provided by Carl I. Hammer, "Anatomy of an Oligarchy: The Oxford Town Council in the Fifteenth and Sixteenth Centuries,"

Journal of British Studies 18 (1978–79): 1–27; and Stephen Rappoport, *Worlds Within Worlds. Structures of Life in Sixteenth-Century London* (Cambridge: Cambridge University Press, 1989).

5. This was always important to many towns' power systems: see Maryanne Kowaleski, "The Commercial Dominance of a Medieval Provincial Oligarchy: Exeter in the Late Fourteenth Century," *Mediaeval Studies* 46 (1984): 355–84.

6. Any of Foucault's works would do, for example, *Discipline and Punish,* trans. Alan Sheridan (New York: Vintage Books, 1979).

7. Or, in John Demos' phrase "A Little Commonwealth," from the book of the same (Oxford: Oxford University Press, 1970).

8. *The Value of the Individual. Self and Circumstance in Autobiography* (Chicago: University of Chicago Press, 1978).

9. Charles Taylor, *Sources of the Self* (Cambridge: Cambridge University Press, 1989).

10. *Jesus as Mother* (Berkeley: University of California Press, 1982).

11. Most powerfully argued by John Bossy, *Christianity in the West, 1400–1700* (Oxford: Oxford University Press, 1985).

12. Phythian-Adams, *Desolation of a City;* Tittler, *The Reformation and the Towns;* Eamon Duffy, *The Stripping of the Altars: Traditional Religion in England, c.1400-c.1580* (New Haven: Yale University Press, 1992).

13. Stephen Greenblatt, *Renaissance Self-Fashioning* (Chicago: University of Chicago Press, 1980).

14. It is a virtue of Alan Macfarlane's work to have tried to capture the social feature, but unfortunately without the social self. See his *Origins of English Individualism* (Oxford: Blackwell, 1978) and *Culture of Capitalism* (Oxford: Blackwell, 1987).

BIBLIOGRAPHY

Primary Sources

Manuscript

Wells, Wells Town Hall. Convocation Book I.
———. Convocation Book II.
———. Convocation Book III.
———. "Mr Goodall's Book."
———. Wells City Charters 1–30.
———. Wells Title Deeds 1–247.
Wells, Wells Cathedral Library. Wells Cathedral Register I (Liber Albus I).
———. Wells Cathedral Register II (Liber Ruber I).
———. Wells Cathedral Register III (Liber Albus II).
———. Wells Cathedral Register IV (Liber Ruber II).
———. Wells Almshouse Charters.
———. Wells Cathedral Charters.
———. Wells Cathedral Fabric Accounts, 1390–1501.
———. Wells Cathedral Communar's Accounts, 1327–1505.
Taunton, Somerset Records Office. DD/WM/1/5–7 wills.
———. DD/B Register 1 Register of Bishop John Droxford.
———. DD/B Register 2 Register of Bishop Ralph of Shrewsbury.
———. DD/B Register 4 Register of Bishop Nicholas Bubwith.
———. DD/B Register 6 Register of Bishop Thomas Beckyngton.
London, Lambeth Palace Library. Estate Documents 1181–89.
London, Public Records Office. E179/4 and 169.

Printed

Acts of the Court of the Mercers' Company. Ed. Laetitia Lyell. Cambridge: Cambridge University Press, 1936.

Adam of Cobsam. *The Wright's Chaste Wyf.* Ed. Frederick J. Furnivall. London: EETS 12, 1865.

Alighieri, Dante. *The Divine Comedy.* Ed. C.S. Singleton. Princeton: Princeton University Press, 1970.

Anonimalle Chronicle, 1333–1381. Ed. V.H. Galbraith. Manchester and London: Longman, Green & Co., 1927.

Aquinas, Thomas. *Commentary on the Nicomachaean Ethics.* Trans. C.I. Litzinger. Chicago: Regnery, 1964.

———. *Compendium of Theology.* Trans. Cyril Vollert. St. Louis: B. Herder Book Co., 1947.

———. *On the Truth of the Catholic Faith. Summa Contra Gentes.* Ed. Vernon J. Bourke. Garden City, NY: Image Books, 1956.

———. *Philosophical Texts.* Ed. and trans. Thomas Gilby. London: Oxford University Press, 1951.

———. *Summa Theologiae.* Ed. Institute of Medieval Studies. 5 volumes. Ottawa: University of Ottawa Press, 1941–45.

The Babees Book. Ed. Frederick J. Furnivall. London: EETS 32, 1868.

The Bailiffs' Minute Book of Dunwich, 1404–1430. Ed. Mark Bailey. Suffolk Records Society, vol. 34, 1992.

The Black Book of Southampton. Ed. A.B. Wallis Chapman. Southampton Record Society vols. 13–14, 1912–15.

The Book of Margery Kempe. Ed. Sanford Brown Meech and Hope Emily Allen. London: EETS vol. 212, 1940.

The Book of Vices and Virtues. Ed. W. Nelson Francis, London: EETS vol. 217, 1942.

Bridgwater Borough Archives, 1400–1445. Ed. T.B. Dilks, Somerset Record Society vol. 54, 1938.

Calendar of Patent Rolls. Henry III–Henry VIII. 45 vols. HMSO, 1891–1916.

Caxton's Mirrour of the World. Ed. Oliver H. Prior. London: EETS extra series 110, 1912.

Cely Letters, 1472–1488. Ed. Alison Hanham. London: EETS 273, 1975.

Chaucer, Geoffrey. *Riverside Chaucer.* Ed. Larry Dean Benson. Boston: Houghton Mifflin, Co., 1987.

Chester Plays. Ed. Hans Deimling. London: EETS 62, 1893.

Clairvaux, Bernard de. *Sancti Bernardi Opera,* vols. 1 and 2: *Sermones super Canticorum.* Ed. J. Leclercq, C.H. Talbot, and H.M. Rochais. Rome: Editiones Cistercienses, Rome, 1957–58.

Christine de Pisan. *Selected Writings of Christine de Pisan.* Ed. Renate Blumenfeld-Kosinski. New York: W.W. Norton, 1997.

———. *The Treasury of the City of Ladies, or the Book of the Three Virtues.* Trans. Sarah Lawson. London: Penguin, 1985.

Chronicles of Calais. Ed. John G. Nichols. Camden Society vol. 35, 1846.

Councils and Synods. Volume II, part I: 1205–65. Ed. F.M. Powicke and C.R. Cheney. Oxford: Oxford University Press, 1964.

The Coventry Leet Book, or Mayor's Register. Ed. Mary Dormer Harris. London: EETS 134, 135, 138, and 146, 1907–13.

The Dance of Death. Ed. Florence Warren and Beatrice White. London: EETS 181, 1931.

The Danse Macabre of Women. Ed. Ann Tukey Harrison and Sandra L. Hindman. Kent, Ohio: The Kent State University Press, 1994.

Dean Cosyn Manuscripts and Wells Cathedral Miscellany. Ed. Aelred Watkin. SRS vol. 56, 1941.

The Dean's Register of Oriel, 1446–61. Ed. G.C. Richards and H.O. Salter. Oxford Historical Society vol. 84, 1926.

Depositions and Other Ecclesiastical Proceedings from the Courts of Durham. Ed. James Raine. Surtees Society vol. 21, 1845.

Dives and Pauper. Ed. Patricia Heath Barnum. London: EETS vol. 275, 1976.

Dunbar, William. *Selected Poems*. Ed. Priscilla Bawcutt. London: Longman, 1996.

Emden, Alfred Brotherston. *Biographical Register of Oxford University to 1500*. Oxford: Oxford University Press, 1974.

An English Chronicle of the Reigns of Richard II, Henry IV, Henry V and Henry VI. Ed. John Silvester Davies. Camden Society vol. 64, 1856.

English Gilds. Ed. Joshua Toulmin Smith and Lucy Toulmin Smith. London: EETS vol. 40, 1870.

Gower, John. *Confessio Amantis*. Ed. Russell A. Peck. Toronto: University of Toronto Press, 1980.

———. *The English Works of John Gower*. Ed. G.C. Macauley. Vol. 2. London: EETS 81, 1900.

———. *Mirour de l'Homme / The Mirror of Mankind*. Trans. William Burton Wilson and Nancy Wilson Van Baak. East Lansing: Colleagues Press, 1992.

The Great White Book of Bristol. Ed. Elizabeth Ralph. Bristol Record Society vol. 32, 1979.

Harrison, William. *Description of England*. Washington and New York: Dover Publication, 1994.

Hobbes, Thomas. *Leviathan*. Ed. Richard Tuck. Cambridge, UK: Cambridge University Press, 1991.

Hoccleve, Thomas. *Hoccleve's Works, I: The Minor Poems*. Ed. Frederick J. Furnivall. London: EETS, Extra Series 61 1892.

Langland, William. *Piers Plowman: The C Version*. Ed. George Russell and George Kane. Berkeley: University of California Press, 1997.

Le Neve's Fasti Ecclesiae Anglicanae: Bath and Wells Diocese, 1300–1541. Ed. B. Jones. Vol. 8. London: Athlone Press, 1964.

Lincoln Diocese Documents: 1450–1544. Ed. Andrew Clark. London: EETS 149, 1914.

List of Escheators for England and Wales. List and Index Society vol. 72, 1971.

Ludus Coventriae, or, the Plaie Called Corpus Christi. Ed. Katherine S. Block. London: EETS, Extra Series 120, 1922.

Le Ménagier de Paris. Ed. Georgine E. Brereton and Janet Ferrier. Oxford: Oxford University Press, 1981.

Middle English Lyrics. Ed. Richard L. Hoffman and Maxwell Luria. New York: Norton, 1974.

Middle English Sermons. Ed. Woodburn O. Ross. EETS 209, 1940 for 1938.

Mirk, John. *Mirk's Festial. A Collection of Homilies*. Ed. Theodor Erbe. London: EETS 96, 1905.

Mirk {Myrc}, John. *Instructions for Parish Priests*. Ed. Frederick J. Furnivall. London: EETS 31, 1868 and 1902.

Munimenta Civitatis Oxonie. Ed. H.E. Salter. Oxford Historical Society vol. 71, 1917.

Munimenta Gildhallae Londoniensis. Liber Albus, Liber Custumarum et Liber Horn. Ed. H.T. Riley. Rolls Series 12, 1859–62.

Official Correspondence of Thomas Bekynton. Ed. George Williams. 2 vols. Rolls Series vol. 56, 1872.

Oriel College Records. Ed. Charles L. Shadwell and H.E. Salter. Oxford Historical Society vol. 85, 1926.

The Oxford Book of Medieval Latin Verse. Ed. Stephen Gaselee. Oxford: Clarendon Press, 1928.

Paston Letters. Ed. Norman Davis. Oxford: Clarendon Press, 1971.

Placita de Quo Warranto temporibus Edward I–Edward II. Ed. William Illingworth. Vol. 2. London: Eyre and Strahan, 1818.

Political, Religious and Love Poems. Ed. Frederick J. Furnivall. London: EETS 15, 1866, reedited 1903.

A relation, or rather a true account, of the island of England, with sundry particulars of the customs of these people, and the royal revenues under King Henry the Seventh, about the year 1500. Trans. Charlotte Augusta Sneyd. Camden Society vol. 37, 1847.

Sarum Missal. Ed. J. Wickham. Oxford: Clarendon Press, 1916.

Secular Lyrics of the Fourteenth and Fifteenth Centuries. Ed. Russell Hope Robbins. Oxford: Clarendon Press, 1955.

Select Cases Concerning the Law Merchant. Vol. II–III, Ed. Hubert Hall. Selden Society vols. 46 and 49, 1930 and 1932.

Select Cases Concerning the Law Merchant, I. Ed. Charles Gross. Selden Society vol. 23, 1908.

Select Cases of Trespass from the Royal Courts, 1307–99, vol. 1. Ed. Morris S. Arnold. Selden Society vol. 100, 1985.

Self and Society in Medieval France. The Memoirs of Abbot Guibert de Nogent. Ed. John F. Benton. Toronto: University of Toronto Press, 1984.

Somerset Medieval Wills 1383–1500. 3 vols. Ed. F.W. Weaver. Somerset Record Society 16, 19, 21, 1901–05.

Statutes of the Realm. Vol. 1. London: Eyre and Strahan, 1810.

Thomas Walsingham. *Historia Anglicana*. 2 vols. Ed. Henry T. Riley. Rolls Series vol. 28, 1863–64.

Towneley Plays. Ed. George England and Alfred W. Pollard. London: EETS 71, 1897.

William of Ockham. *A Short Discourse on Tyrannical Government*. Ed. and trans. Arthur Stephen McGrade and John Kilcullen. Cambridge, UK.: Cambridge University Press, 1992.

Worcester, William. *Itineraries*. Ed. John Harvey. Oxford: Clarendon Press, 1969.

York Memorandum Book. 3 vols. Ed. Maud Sellars and Joyce W. Percy. Surtees Society vols. 120, 125, 186, 1912–73.

Secondary Sources

Amussen Dwyer, Susan. *An Ordered Society: Gender and Class in Early Modern England*. Oxford: B. Blackwell, 1988.

Archer, Rowena." 'How Ladies . . .Who Live on their Manors ought to Manage their Households and Estates': Women as Landholders and Administrators in the Later Middle Ages." In *Woman is a Worthy Wight. Women in English Society c. 1200–1500.* Ed. P.J.P. Goldberg, 149–81.Wolfeboro Falls, NH: Alan Sutton, 1992.

Aston, Margaret. "Death." In *Fifteenth-Century Attitudes.* Ed. Rosemary Horrox, 202–28. Cambridge, UK: Cambridge University Press, 1994.

Aston, Margaret. "Lollards and Literacy." *History* 62 (1977): 193–218.

Atkinson, Clarissa. *Mystic and Pilgrim: The Book and World of Margery Kempe.* Ithaca: Cornell University Press, 1983.

Attreed, Lorraine. "Arbitration and the Growth of Urban Liberties in Late Medieval England." *Journal of British Studies* 31 (1992): 205–35.

Attreed, Lorraine. *The King's Towns. Identity and Survival in Late Medieval English Boroughs.* New York: Peter Lang, 2001.

Baldwin, Francis E. *Sumptuary Legislation and Personal Regulation in England.* Baltimore: The Johns Hopkins Press, 1926.

Barnes, J.A. "Class and Committees in a Norwegian Island Parish." In *Social Networks.* Ed. Samuel Leinhardt, 233–52. New York: Academic Press, 1977.

———. "Networks and Political Process." In *Social Networks in Urban Situations.* Ed. J. Clyde Mitchell, 51–76. Manchester: Manchester University Press, 1969.

Barron, Caroline M. "The 'Golden Age' of Women in Medieval London." *Reading Medieval Studies* 15, 35–58. Reading, UK: Parker and Son Ltd.,1989.

———. "Richard Whittingdon: The Man Behind the Myth." In *Studies in London History Presented to Philip Edmund Jones.* Ed. A.E.J. Hollaender and W.J. Kellaway, 197–248. London: Hodder, 1969.

Barron, Caroline and Anne F. Sutton. *Medieval London Widows, 1300–1500.* London: Hambledon Press, 1994.

Bader, Karl S. "Arbiter, Arbitrator seu amicabilis compositor." *Zeitschrift der Savigny-Stiftung für Rechtsgeschichtekanonistische Abteilung* 77 (1960): 239–276.

Beattie, Cordelia. "The Problem of Women's Work Identities in Post-Black Death England." In *The Problem of Labour in Fourteenth-Century England.* Ed. J. Bothwell, P.J.P. Goldberg, and W.M. Ormrod, 1–19. York: York Medieval Press, 2000.

Beckerman, John S. "Adding Insult to *Iniuria*: Affronts to Honor and the Origins of Trespass." In *On the Laws and Customs of England.* Ed. Morris S. Arnold, Thomas A. Green, Sally A. Scully, and Stephen D. White, 159–81. Chapel Hill: University of North Carolina Press, 1981.

Beckwith, Sarah. "Making the World in York and the York Cycle." In *Framing Medieval Bodies.* Ed. Sarah Kay and Miri Rubin, 254–76. Manchester: Manchester University Press, 1994.

Bell, Catherine. *Ritual Theory, Ritual Practice.* Oxford: Oxford University Press, 1992.

Bellamy, J.G. *Criminal Law and Society in Late Medieval and Tudor England.* Gloucester: Sutton, 1984.

Bennett, Josephine Waters. "The Mediæval Loveday." *Speculum* 33 (1958): 351–70.

Bennett, Judith M. *Ale, Beer, and Brewsters in England: Women's Work in a Changing Society, 1300–1600.* New York: Oxford University Press, 1996.

———. *A Medieval Life: Cecilia Penifader of Brigstock, c. 1295–1344.* Boston: McGraw-Hill, 1999.

Bennett, Judith M. *Women in the Medieval English Countryside*. New York: Oxford University Press, 1987.

Benton, John F. "Consciousness of Self and Perception of Individuality." In *Renaissance and Renewal in the Twelfth Century*. Ed. Robert L. Benson and Giles Constable, 263–95. Cambridge, Mass.: Harvard University Press, 1982.

Bibolet, Jean-Claude. "Les gestes d'adoration, de prière, d'offrande et de violence dans Le mystère de la passion de Troyes." In *Le geste et les gestes au moyen âge*, 93–107. Aix-en-Provence: CUER MA, Université de Provence (Centre d'Aix), 1998.

Biddick, Kathleen. "Genders, Bodies, Borders: Technologies of the Visible." *Speculum* 68 (1993): 389–418.

Binski, Paul. *Medieval Death. Ritual and Representation*. Ithaca, NY: Cornell University Press, 1996.

Blau, Peter. *Exchange and Power in Social Life*. New York: J. Wiley, 1964.

Bonney, Margaret. *Lordship and the Urban Community. Durham and its Overlords*. Cambridge, UK: Cambridge University Press, 1992.

Bossy, John. *Christianity in the West*. Oxford: Oxford University Press, 1985.

Bott, Elizabeth. "Urban Families: Conjugal Roles and Social Networks." In *Social Networks*. Ed. Samuel Leinhardt, 253–92. New York: Academic Press, 1977.

Bouchat, Marc. "La justice privée par arbitrage dans le diocèse de Liège au XIIIe siècle: Les arbitres." *Môyen Age* 95 (1989): 439–74.

Bourdieu, Pierre. *Outline of a Theory of Practice*. Trans. Richard Nice. Cambridge, UK: Cambridge University Press, 1977.

———. *Logic of Practice*. Trans. Richard Nice. Stanford: Stanford University Press, 1990.

———. "Rites as Acts of Institution." In *Honor and Grace in Anthropology*. Ed. John G. Peristiany and Julian Pitt-Rivers, 78–89. Trans. Roger Just. Cambridge, UK: Cambridge University Press, 1992.

———. "The Sentiment of Honour in Kabyle Society." In *Honour and Shame: The Values of Mediterranean Society*. Ed. J.G. Peristiany and Julian Pitt-Rivers, 193–237. Chicago: University of Chicago, 1966.

Bridbury, A.R. *Medieval English Clothmaking*. London: Heinemann Educational, 1982.

Britnell, R.H. *The Commercialisation of English Society*. Cambridge, UK: Cambridge University Press, 1993.

———. *Growth and Decline in Colchester, 1300–1525*. Cambridge, UK: Cambridge University Press, 1986.

Buc, Philippe. *The Dangers of Ritual*. Princeton: Princeton University Press, 2001.

Burckhardt, Jakob. *The Civilisation of the Renaissance in Italy*. Trans. S.G.C. Middlemore. London: George Allen and Unwin, 1944.

Bynum, Caroline Walker. *Holy Feast and Holy Fast: The Religious Significance of Food to Medieval Women*. Berkeley: University of California Press, 1987.

———. *Jesus as Mother. Studies in the Spirituality of the High Middle Ages*. Berkeley: University of California Press, 1982.

———. *The Resurrection of the Body in Western Christianity, 200–1336*. New York: Columbia University Press, 1995.

Calhoun, C.J. "Community: Toward a Variable Conceptualization for Comparative Research." *Social History* 5 (1982): 105–29.

Carnwath, Julia. "The Churchwardens' Accounts of Thame, Oxfordshire, *c.* 1443–1524." In *Trade, Devotion, and Governance.* Ed. Dorothy J. Clayton, Richard G. Davie, and Peter McNiven, 177–97. Stroud: A. Sutton, 1994.

Carpenter, Christine. "The 'Town' and 'Country'. The Stratford Guild and Political Networks in Fifteenth-Century Warwickshire." in *The History of an English Borough,* Ed. R. Bearman, 62–79. Stroud: Sutton, 1997.

———. "Gentry and Community in Medieval England." *Journal of British Studies* 33 (1994): 340–80.

Caviness, Madeline H. "Patron or Matron? A Capetian Bride and a Vade Mecum for Her Marriage Bed." *Speculum* 68 (1993): 333–62.

Chadwick-Jones, J.K. *Social Exchange Theory. Its Structure and Influence in Social Psychology.* London: Academic Press, 1976.

Chartier, Roger. "Leisure and Sociability: Reading Aloud in Early Modern Europe." In *Urban Life in the Renaissance.* Ed. Susan Zimmerman and Ronald F.E. Weissman, 103–20. Newark: University of Delaware Press, 1989.

Cheyette, Fredric. "*Suum Cuique Tribuere.*" *French Historical Studies* 6 (1970): 287–99.

Clanchy, Michael. *Abelard: A Medieval Life.* Oxford: Blackwell Publishers, 1999.

———. "Law and Love in the Middle Ages." In *Disputes and Settlements: Law and Human Relations in the West.* Ed. John Bossy, 47–67. Cambridge, UK: Cambridge University Press, 1983.

Clover, Carol. "Regardless of Sex: Men, Women, and Power in Early Northern Europe." *Speculum* 68 (1993): 363–87.

Cohen, Kathleen. *Metamorphosis of a Death Symbol. The Transi Tomb in the Late Middle Ages and Renaissance.* Berkeley: University of California Press, 1973.

Collingwood R.G. *The Idea of History.* Ed. Jan van der Dussen. Oxford: Oxford University Press, 1993.

Cook, Karen S. "Linking Actors and Structures: An Exchange Network Perspective." In *Structures of Power and Constraint.* Ed. Craig Calhoun, Marshall C. Meyer, and W. Richard Scott, 113–28. Cambridge, UK: Cambridge University Press, 1990.

Crane, Susan. "Clothing and Gender Definition: Joan of Arc." *Journal of Medieval and Early Modern Studies* 28 (1996): 297–320.

Cullum, Patricia H. " 'For Pore Popele Haberles': What was the Function of the Maisondieu?" In *Trade, Devotion and Governance.* Ed. Dorothy J. Clayton, Richard G. Davies, and Peter McNiven, 36–54. Stroud: A. Sutton, 1994.

———. "Masculinity and Trangression in Later Medieval Europe." In *Masculinity in Medieval Europe.* Ed. Dawn Hadley, 178–92. London: Longman, 1999.

Dabhoiwala, Faramerz. "The Construction of Honour, Reputation, and Status in Late Seventeenth- and Early Eighteenth-Century England." *Transactions of the Royal Historical Society,* 6th Series (1996): 201–13.

Daniell, Christopher. *Death and Burial in Medieval England 1066–1550.* London: Routledge, 1998.

Davies, M.P. "Artisans, Guilds and Government in Medieval London." In *Daily Life in the Late Middle Ages.* Ed. R.H. Britnell, 125–50. Stroud: Sutton, 1998.

Davis, Natalie Z. "Women on Top." In *Society and Culture in Early Modern France,* 124–151. Stanford: Stanford University Press, 1975.

———. "Boundaries and the Sense of Self in Sixteenth-Century France." In *Reconstructing Individualism: Autonomy, Individuality and the Self in Western Thought.* Ed. Thomas C. Heller, Morton Sosna, and David E. Wellerby, 53–63, 332–36. Stanford: Stanford University Press, 1986.

Demos, John. *A Little Commonwealth.* Oxford: Oxford University Press, 1970.

Devereux, George. *Ethnopsychoanalysis: Psychoanalysis and Anthropology as Complementary Frames of Reference.* Berkeley: University of California Press, 1978.

Dinn, Robert. " 'Monuments Answerable to Men's Worth': Burial Patterns, Social Status and Gender in Late Medieval Bury St Edmunds." *Journal of Ecclesiastical History* 46 (1995): 237–55.

———. "Death and Rebirth in Late Medieval Bury St Edmunds." In *Death in Towns: Urban Responses to the Dying and Dead.* Ed. Steven Bassett, 151–69. Leicester: Leicester University Press, 1992.

Dobson, R.B. "Cathedral Chapters and Cathedral Cities: York, Durham, and Carlisle in the Fifteenth Century." *Northern History* 19 (1983): 5–44.

Dolan, Claire. "The Artisans of Aix-en-Provence in the Sixteenth Century: A Micro-analysis of Social Relationships." In *Cities and Social Change in Early Modern France.* Ed. Philip Benedict, 174–93. London: Unwin Hyman, 1989.

Dronke, Peter. *Poetic Individuality in the Middle Ages.* Oxford: Clarendon Press, 1970.

DuBruck, Edelgard E. "Death, Poetic Perception and Imagination (Continental Europe)." In *Death and Dying in the Middle Ages.* Ed. Edelgard E. DuBruck and Barbara I. Gusich, 296–314. New York: Peter Lang, 1999.

Duby, Georges. *The Three Orders: Feudal Society Imagined.* Trans. Arthur Goldhammer. Chicago: University of Chicago Press, 1980.

Dyer, Christopher. "Small Town Conflict in the Later Middle Ages: Events at Shipston-on-Stour." *Urban History* 19 (1992): 184–210.

———. "The Small Towns, 1270–1540." In *Cambridge History of Urban Britain, 600–1540.* Ed. David M. Palliser, 505–40. Cambridge, UK: Cambridge University Press, 2000.

———. "Work Ethics in the Fourteenth Century." In *The Problem of Labour in Fourteenth-Century England.* Ed. James Bothwell, P.J.P. Goldberg and W.M. Ormrod, 21–41. York: York Medieval Press, 2000.

Edwards, Kathleen. *The English Secular Cathedrals in the Middle Ages: A Constitutional Study with Special Reference to the Fourteenth Century.* Manchester: Manchester University Press, 1967.

Elliott, Dyan. "Dress as Mediator Between Inner and Outer Self: The Pious Matron of the High and Later Middle Ages." *Mediaeval Studies* 53 (1991): 279–308.

Finch A.J. "The Nature of Violence in the Middle Ages: An Alternative Perspective." *Historical Research* 70 (1997): 249–68.

Fischer, Claude S. *To Dwell Among Friends: Personal Networks in Town and City.* Chicago: University of Chicago Press, 1982.

Fitzhugh, Michael and William Leckie. "Agency, Postmodernism, and The Causes of Change." *History and Theory* 40 (2001): 59–81.

Fleming, Peter. "Conflict and Urban Government in later Medieval England: St Augustine's Abbey and Bristol." *Urban History* 27 (2000): 321–43.

Flynn, Maureen. "The Spectacle of Suffering in Spanish Streets." In *City and Spectacle in Medieval Europe*. Ed. Barbara Hanawalt and Kathryn L. Reyerson, 153–68. Minneapolis: University of Minnesota Press, 1984.

Foucault, Michel. *Discipline and Punish: The Birth of the Prison*. Trans. Alan Sheridan. New York: Vintage Books, 1979.

———. *The History of Sexuality*, 3 vols. Trans. Robert Hurley. New York: Pantheon Books, 1978–88.

Foyster, Elizabeth. *Manhood in Early Modern England. Honour, Sex and Marriage*. London: Longman, 1999.

Franklin, Michael. "The Cathedral as Parish Church: The Case of Southern England." In *Church and City, 1000–1500*. Ed. David Abulafia, 173–98. Cambridge: Cambridge University Press, 1992.

Frazer, William D. "Identities in Early Medieval Britain." In *Social Identity in Early Medieval Britain*. Ed. William D. Frazer and Andrew Tyrell, 1–22. London: Leicester University Press, 2000.

French, Katherine L. "The Legend of Lady Godiva and the Image of the Female Body." *Journal of Medieval History* 18 (1992): 3–19.

———. "Maiden's Lights and Wives' Stores: Women's Parish Guilds in Late Medieval England." *Sixteenth-Century Journal* 29 (1998): 399–425.

———. *The People of the Parish. Community Life in a Late Medieval English Diocese*. Philadelphia: University of Pennsylvania Press, 2001.

———. " 'To Free Them from Binding': Women in the Late Medieval English Parish." *Journal of Interdisciplinary History* 27 (1997): 387–412.

Gadamer, Hans-Georg. *Truth and Method*. New York: Seabury Press, 1984, orig. 1960.

Gay, Peter. *Freud for Historians*. New York: Oxford University Press, 1985.

Giddens, Anthony. *The Constitution of Society*. Berkeley: University of California Press, 1984.

Ginzburg, Carlo. *The Cheese and the Worms: The Cosmos of a Sixteenth-Century Miller*. Trans. John and Anne Tedeschi. Harmondsworth: Penguin Books, 1980.

———. *Ecstasies: Deciphering the Witches' Sabbath*. Trans. Raymond Rosenthal. New York: Panthenon Books, 1991.

Given-Wilson, Chris. "The Problem of Labour in the Context of English Government, c. 1350–1450." In *The Problem of Labour in Fourteenth-Century England*. Ed. J. Bothwell, P.J.P. Goldberg, and W.M. Ormrod, 85–100. York: York Medieval Press, 2000.

Goldberg, P.J.P. "Craft Guilds, the Corpus Christi Play, and Civic Government." In *The Government of York in the Middle Ages*. Ed. Sarah Rees Jones, 141–63. York: York Medieval Press, 1997.

———. " 'For Better, For Worse': Marriage and Economic Opportunity for Women in Town and Country." In *"Woman is a Worthy Wight": Women in English Society, 1200–1500*. Ed. P.J.P. Goldberg, 108–25. Stroud: Sutton, 1992.

———. "Masters and Men in Later Medieval England." In *Masculinity in Medieval Europe*. Ed. Dawn Hadley, 56–70. London: Longman, 1999.

Goldberg, P.J.P "Women." In *Fifteenth-Century Attitudes. Perceptions of Society in Late Medieval England*. Ed. Rosemary Horrox, 112–31. Cambridge, UK: Cambridge University Press, 1994.

Goodman, Nelson. *Ways of Worldmaking*. Indianapolis: Hackett, 1978.

Gottfried, Robert. *Bury St Edmunds and the Urban Crisis of the Later Middle Ages, 1290–1530*. Princeton: Princeton University Press, 1982.

Gould, Roger V. "Power and Social Structure in Community Elites." *Social Forces* 68 (1989): 531–52.

Gowing, Laura. *Domestic Dangers: Women, Words, and Sex in Early Modern London*. Oxford: Oxford University Press, 1996.

Granovetter, Mark. "The Strength of Weak Ties." In *Social Networks*. Ed. Samuel Leinhardt, 347–67. New York: Academic Press, 1977.

Green, Richard Firth. *A Crisis of Truth*. Philadelphia: University of Pennsylvania Press, 1999.

Greenblatt, Stephen. *Renaissance Self-Fashioning. From More to Shakespeare*. Chicago: University of Chicago Press, 1980.

Griffiths, Ralph. "The Trial of Eleanor Cobham." *Bulletin of the John Rylands Library* 51 (1968–69): 381–99.

Gurevich, Aron. *The Origins of European Individualism*. Trans. Katherine Judelson. Oxford: Blackwell, 1995.

Hammer, Carl I., Jr. "Anatomy of an Oligarchy: The Oxford Town Council in the Fifteenth and Sixteenth Centuries." *Journal of British Studies* 18 (1978–79): 1–27.

———. "Patterns of Homicide in a Medieval University Town: Fourteenth-Century Oxford." *Past and Present* 78 (1978): 3–23.

Hanawalt, Barbara. "At the Margin of Women's Space in Medieval Europe." In *Matrons and Marginal Women in Medieval Society*. Ed. Robert R. Edwards and Vickie Ziegler, 1–19. Woodbridge, UK: Boydell Press, 1995.

———. *Crime and Conflict in English Communities 1300–48*. Cambridge, Mass.: Harvard University Press, 1979.

———. *Growing up in Medieval London*. New York: Oxford University Press, 1993.

———. "Keepers of the Lights: Later Medieval Parish Guilds." *Journal of Medieval and Renaissance Studies* 14 (1984): 21–37.

———. "Lady Honor Lisle's Networks of Influence." In *Women and Power in the Middle Ages*. Ed. Mary Erler and Maryanne Kowaleski, 188–212. Athens, GA: University of Georgia Press, 1988.

———. *Of Good and Ill Repute. Gender and Social Control in Medieval England*. New York: Oxford University Press, 1998.

———. *The Ties That Bound*. New York: Oxford University Press, 1986.

———. "Violence in the Domestic Milieu of Late Medieval England." In *Violence in Medieval Society*. Ed. Richard W. Kaeuper, 197–215. Woodbridge, UK: Boydell Press, 2000.

Hanning, Robert. *The Individual in Twelfth-Century Romance*. New Haven, Conn.: Yale University Press, 1977.

Harding, Alan. *The Law Courts of Medieval England*. London: Allen & Unwin, 1973.

Harvey, B.F. "Draft Letters Patent of Manumission and Pardon for the Men of Somerset in 1381." *English Historical Review* 80 (1965): 89–91.

Harvey, John H. with Arthur Oswald. *English Mediaeval Architects: A Biographical Dictionary Down to 1500*. Gloucester: Sutton, 1987.

———. *Mediaeval Craftsmen*. London: Batsford, 1975.

Heidegger, Martin. *Being and Time*. Trans. John Macquarrie and Edward Robinson. New York: Harper, 1962.

Helmholz, R.H. "Canonical Defamation in Medieval England." *American Journal of Legal History* 15 (1971): 255–68.

Henry, Robert L. *Contracts in the Local Courts of Medieval England*. London: Longmans, Green and Co., 1926.

Henisch, Bridget Ann. *Fast and Feast*. University Park, Pa.: Pennsylvania State University Press, 1976.

Hilton, Rodney. *Class Conflict and the Crisis of Feudalism*, 2nd ed. London: Verso, 1990.

———. *English and French Towns in Feudal Society: A Comparative Study*. Cambridge, UK: Cambridge University Press, 1992.

———. "Small Town Society in England Before the Black Death." *Past & Present*, 105 (1984): 53–78.

Hindle, Steve. "The Shaming of Margaret Knowsley: Gossip, Gender and the Experience of Authority in Early Modern England." *Continuity and Change* 9 (1994): 391–419.

Holt, Richard and Gervase Rosser. *The English Medieval Town. A Reader in English Urban History 1200–1540*. London: Longman, 1990.

Hopkins, Keith. *A World Full of Gods. The Strange Triumph of Christianity*. New York: Free Press, 1999.

Horrox, Rosemary, ed. *Fifteenth-Century Attitudes*. Cambridge, UK: Cambridge University Press, 1994.

———. "The Urban Gentry in the Fifteenth Century." In *Towns and Townspeople in the Fifteenth Century*. Ed. J.A.F. Thomson, 22–44. Gloucester: Sutton, 1988.

Houlbrooke, Ralph A. *The English Family 1450–1700*. London: Longman, 1984.

Howell, Martha C. "Citizenship and Gender: Women's Political Status in Northern Medieval Cities." In *Women and Power in the Middle Ages*. Ed. Mary Erler and Maryanne Kowaleski, 37–60. Athens, GA: University of Georgia Press, 1988.

Hudson, Anne. *The Premature Reformation*. Oxford: Oxford University Press, 1988.

Hughes, Diane Owen. "Sumptuary Law and Social Relations in Renaissance Italy." In *Disputes and Settlements: Law and Human Relations in the West*. Ed. John Bossy, 69–100. Cambridge, UK: Cambridge University Press, 1983.

Huizinga, Johan. *The Autumn of the Middle Ages*. Trans. Rodney J. Paton and Ulrich Mammitzsch. Chicago: University of Chicago Press, 1996.

Hume, David. *History of England*. Indianapolis: Liberty Classics, 1983.

———. *A Treatise of Human Nature*. Harmondsworth: Penguin, 1969.

Hutton, Ronald. *The Rise and Fall of Merry England*. Oxford: Oxford University Press, 1996.

Ives, E.W. *The Common Lawyers of Pre-Reformation England*. Cambridge, UK: Cambridge University Press, 1983.

James, Mervyn. "Ritual Drama and the Social Body in the Later Medieval Town." *Past and Present* 98 (1983): 1–29.

James, Mervyn. *Society, Politics, and Culture: Studies in Early Modern England*. Cambridge: Cambridge University Press, 1986.

Janeau, H. "L'arbitrage en Dauphiné au Moyen Âge." *Revue historique de droit français et etranger* 24–25 (1946–47): 229–71.

Jones, Sarah Rees. "Household, Work and the Problem of Mobile Labour: The Regulation of Labour in Medieval English Towns." In *The Problem of Labour in Fourteenth-Century England*. Ed. James Bothwell, P.J.P. Goldberg and W.M. Ormrod, 133–53. York: York Medieval Press, 2000.

Judd, A. *The Life of Thomas Bekynton*. Chichester: Marc Fitch Fund, 1961.

Kaminsky, Howard. "Estate, Nobility, and the Exhibition of Estate in the Later Middle Ages." *Speculum* 68 (1993): 684–709.

Karras, Ruth M. *Common Women: Prostitution and Sexuality in Medieval England*. New York: Oxford University Press, 1996.

Keen, Maurice. *England in the Later Middle Ages: A Political History*. London: Methuen, 1973.

———. *English Society in the Later Middle Ages, 1348–1500*. Harmondsworth: Penguin, 1990.

Kent, D. and F.W. Kent. *Neighbourhood and Neighbours in Renaissance Florence: The District of the Red Lion in the Fifteenth Century*. Locust Valley, NY: J.J. Augustin, 1982.

Kermode, Jennifer I. "The Greater Towns 1300–1540." In *The Cambridge Urban History of Britain, vol. 1: 600–1540*. Ed. David M. Palliser, 441–66. Cambridge: Cambridge University Press, 2000.

———. *Medieval Merchants: York, Beverly, and Hull in the Later Middle Ages*. Cambridge, UK: Cambridge University Press, 1998.

———. "Obvious Observations on the Formation of Oligarchies in Late Medieval English Towns." In *Towns and Townspeople in the Fifteenth Century*. Ed. John A.F. Thomson, 87–106. Gloucester: Sutton, 1988.

Kettle, Ann J. "City and Close: Lichfield in the Century Before the Reformation." In *The Church in Pre-Reformation Society*. Ed. Caroline M. Barron and Christopher Harper-Bill, 158–65. Woodbridge, UK: Boydell Press, 1985.

———. "Ruined Maids: Prostitution and Servant Girls in Later Medieval England." In *Matrons and Marginal Women in Medieval Society*. Ed. Robert E. Edwards and Vickie Ziegler, 19–31. Woodbridge, UK: Boydell Press, 1995.

Killerby, Catherine Koves. *Sumptuary Law in Italy, 1200–1500*. Oxford: Oxford University Press, 2002.

Kowaleski, Maryanne. "The Commercial Dominance of a Medieval Provincial Oligarchy: Exeter in the Late Fourteenth Century." *Mediaeval Studies* 46 (1984): 355–84.

———. *The Local Customs Accounts of the Port of Exeter, 1266–1321*. Devon and Cornwall Record Society 36, 1993.

———. "Women's Work in a Market Town: Exeter in the Late Fourteenth Century." In *Women and Work in Preindustrial Europe*. Ed. Barbara Hanawalt, 145–64. Bloomington, IN: Indiana University Press, 1986.

Kuehn, Thomas. *Law, Family and Women*. Chicago: University of Chicago Press, 1991.

Kurtz K.L. *The Dance of Death and the Macabre Spirit in European Literature*. New York: Gordon Press, 1934.

Lachaud, Frédérique. "Liveries of Robes in England, *c.* 1200–1339." *English Historical Review* 111 (1996): 279–98.

Laqueur, Thomas. *Making Sex: Body and Gender from the Greeks to Freud*. Cambridge, Mass.: Harvard University Press, 1990.

Lasch, Christopher. *The Minimal Self*. New York: W.W. Norton, 1984.

Le Roy, Ladurie Emmanuel. *Montaillou: Cathars and Catholics in a French Village, 1294–1324*. Trans. Barbara Bray. Harmondsworth: Penguin, 1978.

Lesnick, Daniel R. "Insults and Threats in Medieval Todi." *Journal of Medieval History* 17 (1991): 71–90.

Lifton, Robert J. *The Protean Self: Human Resilience in an Age of Fragmentation*. New York: Basic Books, 1993.

Lindenbaum, Sheila. "Ceremony and Oligarchy: The London Midsummer Watch." In *City and Spectacle in Medieval Europe*. Ed. Barbara A. Hanawalt and Kathryn L. Reyerson, 171–88. Minneapolis: University of Minnesota Press, 1994.

Little, Lester K. *Benedictine Maledictions*. Ithaca: Cornell University Press, 1993.

Lochrie, Karma. *Margery Kempe and the Translations of the Flesh*. Philadelphia: University of Pennsylvania Press, 1991.

Logan, Richard D. "A Conception of the Self in the Later Middle Ages." *Journal of Medieval History* 12 (1986): 253–68.

Lovejoy, A.O. *The Great Chain of Being*. Cambridge, Mass.: Harvard University Press, 1936.

Lytle, Guy Fitch. " 'Wykehamist Culture' in Pre-Reformation England." In *Winchester College: Sixth-centenary Essays*. Ed. Roger Custance, 129–66. Oxford: Oxford University Press, 1982.

Macfarlane, Alan. *The Culture of Capitalism*. Oxford: Blackwell, 1987.

———. *The Origins of English Individualism*. Oxford: Blackwell, 1978.

Maddern, Phillipa. "Honour among the Pastons. Gender and Integrity in Fifteenth-Century English Society." *Journal of Medieval History* 14 (1988): 357–71.

———. *Violence and Social Order: East Anglia 1422–42*, 123–29. Oxford: Oxford University Press, 1992.

Mann, Jill. *Chaucer and Medieval Estates Satire: The Literature of Social Classes in the General Prologue to the Canterbury Tales*. Cambridge, UK: Cambridge University Press, 1973.

Masschaele, James. "The Trial of Partnership in Medieval England: A Case History, 1304." In *The Salt of Common Life*. Ed. Edwin Brezette DeWindt, 57–143. Kalamazoo, MI: Western Michigan University, 1995.

Mauss, Marcel. *The Gift: Forms and Functions of Exchange in Archaic Societies*. Trans. I.G. Cannison. Glencoe, Ill.: Free Press, 1954.

Mayer, Adrian C. "The Significance of Quasi-Groups in the Study of Complex Societies." In *Social Networks*. Ed. Samuel Leinhardt, 293–315. New York: Academic Press, 1977.

McIntosh, Marjorie Keniston. *Controlling Misbehavior in England, 1370–1600*. Cambridge, UK: Cambridge University Press, 1998.

McIntosh, Marjorie Keniston. "Finding Language for Misconduct. Jurors in Fifteenth-Century Local Courts." In *Bodies and Disciplines: Intersections of Literature and History in Fifteenth-Century England*. Ed. Barbara A. Hanawalt and David Wallace, 87–122. Minneapolis: University of Minnesota Press, 1996.

McRee, Ben R. "Charity and Gild Solidarity in Late Medieval England." *Journal of British Studies* 32 (1993): 195–225.

———. "Religious Gilds and Civic Order: The Case of Norwich in the Late Middle Ages." *Speculum* 67 (1992): 69–97.

———. "Religious Guilds and the Regulation of Behavior in Late Medieval Towns." In *People, Politics and Community in the Later Middle Ages*. Ed. Joel T. Rosenthal and Colin Richmond, 108–22. Gloucester: Sutton, 1987.

McSheffrey, Shannon. "Literacy and the Gender Gap in the Late Middle Ages: Women and Reading in Lollard London." In *Women, the Book and The Godly*. Ed. Lesley Smith and Jane Taylor, 157–70. Woodbridge, UK: Brewer, 1995.

———. "Men and Masculinity in Late Medieval London Civic Culture, Governance, Patriarchy, and Reputation." In *Conflicted Identities and Multiple Masculinities: Men in the Medieval West*. Ed. Jacqueline Murray, 243–78. New York: Garland, 1999.

Mead, George Herbert. *Mind, Self and Society*. Ed. Charles Morris. Chicago: University of Chicago Press, 1934.

———. *The Individual and the Social Self*. Ed. David L. Miller. Chicago: University of Chicago Press, 1982.

Milsom, S.F.C. *Historical Foundations of the Common Law*. London: Butterworths, 1969.

Miller, William I. "Avoiding Legal Judgment: The Submission of Disputes to Arbitration in Medieval Iceland." *American Journal of Legal History* 28 (1984): 95–134.

———. *Bloodtaking and Peacemaking. Feud, Laws and Society in Viking Iceland*. Chicago: University of Chicago Press, 1990.

———. "Choosing the Avenger: Some Aspects of the Blood-Feud in Medieval Iceland and England." *Law and History Review* 1 (1983): 159–204.

Mitchell, J. Clyde. "The Concept and Use of Social Networks." In *Social Networks in Urban Situations*. Ed. J. Clyde Mitchell, 12–29. Manchester: Manchester University Press, 1969.

Moran, Jo Ann Hoeppner. *The Growth of English Schooling, 1340–1548: Learning, Literacy and Laicisation in pre-Reformation York Diocese*. Princeton: Princeton University Press, 1985.

Moreton, C.E. *The Townshends and Their World: Gentry, Law, and Land in Norfolk c. 1450–1551*. Oxford: Oxford University Press, 1992.

Morris, Colin. *The Discovery of the Individual, 1050–1200*. Toronto: University of Toronto Press, 1987, orig. 1972.

Muldrew, Craig. "Interpreting the Market: The Ethics of Credit and Community Relations in Early Modern England." *Social History* 18 (1993): 163–83.

Murray, Alexander. *Reason and Society in the Middle Ages*. Oxford: Oxford University Press, 1978.

Murray, Jacqueline, ed. *Conflicted Identities and Multiple Masculinities: Men in the Medieval West*. New York: Garland, 1999.

Neal, Derek. "Suits Make the Man: Masculinity in Two English Law Courts, c. 1500." *Canadian Journal of History* (2002): 1–22.

Nelson, A.H. *The Medieval English Stage: Corpus Christi Pageants and Plays*. Chicago: University of Chicago Press, 1974.

Nicholas, David. *The Later Medieval City, 1300–1500*. Harlow, Essex: Longman, 1997.

Nicholls, Jonathan. *The Matter of Courtesy: Medieval Courtesy Books and the Gawain Poet*. Woodbridge, UK: Brewer, 1985.

Norton, Mary Beth. "Gender and Defamation in Seventeenth-Century Maryland." *William and Mary Quarterly* 44 (1987): 3–39.

O'Connor, Stephen. "Adam Fraunceys and John Pyel: Perceptions of Status among Merchants in Fourteenth-Century London." In *Trade, Devotion, and Governance*. Ed. Dorothy J. Clayton, Richard G. Davies, and Peter McNiven, 17–35. Stroud: Sutton, 1994.

Olson, Sherri. *A Chronicle of All that Happens*. Toronto: Pontifical Institute of Mediaeval Studies, 1996.

Orme, Nicholas. "Sufferings of the Clergy: Illness and Old Age in Exeter Diocese, 1300–1540." In *Life, Death and the Elderly. Historical Perspectives*. Ed. Margaret Pelling, 62–73. London: Routledge, 1994.

Otis, Leah. *Prostitution in Medieval Society: The History of an Institution in Langued'oc*. Chicago: University of Chicago Press, 1985.

Owen, D.M. *The Making of King's Lynn*. London: Oxford University Press, 1984.

Palliser, D.M. "Urban Society," in *Fifteenth-Century Attitudes*. Ed. Rosemary Horrox, 132–49. Cambridge, UK: Cambridge University Press, 1994.

Palmer, William. "Scenes from Provincial Life: History, Honor, and Meaning in the Tudor North." *Renaissance Quarterly* 53 (2000): 425–48.

Parfit, Derek. *Reasons and Persons*. Oxford: Clarendon Press, 1984.

Parker, J.H. *The Architectural Antiquities of the City of Wells*. Oxford: J. Parker, 1866.

Partner, Nancy F. "Reading the Book of Margery Kempe." *Exemplaria* 3 (1991): 29–66.

———. "No Sex, No Gender." *Speculum* 68 (1993): 419–43.

Patterson, Lee. *Chaucer and the Subject of History*. Madison, WI: University of Wisconsin Press, 1991.

———. "Chaucer's Pardoner on the Couch: Psyche and Clio in Medieval Literary Studies." *Speculum* 76 (2001): 638–80.

Patterson, Thomas. "Self-worth and Property: Equipage and Early Medieval Personhood." In *Social Identity in Early Medieval Britain*. Ed. William D. Frazer and Andrew Tyrell, 53–67. London: Leicester University Press, 2000.

Payling, Simon. "The Ampthill Dispute: A Study in Aristocratic Lawlessness and the Breakdown of Lancastrian Government." *English Historical Review* 104 (1989): 881–907.

Pevsner, N. *North Somerset and Bristol*. Harmondsworth, Eng: Penguin Books, 1958.

Phythian-Adams, Charles. *Desolation of a City: Coventry and the Urban Crisis of the Late Middle Ages*. Cambridge, UK: Cambridge University Press, 1979.

Phythian-Adams, Charles. "Ceremony and the Citizen: The Communal Year at Coventry 1450–1550." In *The English Medieval Town*. Ed. Richard Holt and Gervase Rosser, 238–64. London: Longman, 1990.

Pimsler, Martin. "Solidarity in the Medieval Village? The Evidence of Personal Pledging at Elton, Huntingdonshire." *Journal of British Studies* 17 (1977): 1–11.

Pitt-Rivers, Julian. *The Fate of Shechem, or the Politics of Sex*. Cambridge, UK: Cambridge University Press, 1977.

———. "Honour and Social Status." In *Honour and Shame. The Values of a Mediterranean Society*. Ed. J.G. Peristiany, 21–77. Chicago: University of Chicago Press, 1966.

———. "The Place of Grace in Anthropology." In *Honor and Grace in Anthropology*. Ed. John G. Peristiany and Julian Pitt-Rivers, 215–46. Cambridge, UK: Cambridge University Press, 1992.

Platt, Colin. *King Death. The Black Death and its Aftermath in Late Medieval England*. London: UCL Press, 1996.

Pollock, F. and F.W. Maitland. *The History of English Law Before the Time of Edward I*, 2nd edition. London: Cambridge University Press, 1968.

Poos, L.R. *A Rural Society after the Black Death*. Cambridge, UK: Cambridge University Press, 1991.

———. "Sex, Lies and the Church Courts of Pre-Reformation England." *Journal of Interdisciplinary History* 25 (1995): 585–607.

Post, J.B. "Equitable Resorts before 1450." In *Law, Litigants and the Legal Profession*. Ed. E.W. Ives and A.H. Manchester, 68–79. London: Royal Historical Society, 1983.

Powell, Edward. "Arbitration and the Law in England in the Later Middle Ages." *Transactions of the Royal Historical Society*, 5th ser., 33 (1983): 49–67.

———. "Settlement of Disputes by Arbitration in Fifteenth Century England." *Law and History Review* 2 (1984): 21–43.

Prest, John, ed. *Illustrated History of Oxford University*. Oxford: Oxford University Press, 1993.

Prestwich, Michael. *Edward I*. Berkeley: University of California Press, 1988.

Raftis, J.A. *Peasant Economic Development Within the English Manorial System*. Montreal: McGill-Queen's University Press, 1996.

———. *Tenure and Mobility*. Toronto: Pontifical Institute of Mediaeval Studies, 1964.

Rappoport, Steven. *Worlds Within Worlds: Structures of Life in Sixteenth-Century London*. Cambridge, UK: Cambridge University Press, 1989.

Rawcliffe, Carole. "The Great Lord as Peacekeeper: Arbitration by English Noblemen and their Councils in the Later Middle Ages." In *Law and Social Change in British History*. Ed. J.A. Guy and H.G. Beale, 34–54. London: Royal Historical Society, 1984.

———. " 'That Kindliness Should Be Cherished More, and Discord Driven Out': The Settlement of Commercial Disputes by Arbitration in Later Medieval England." In *Enterprise and Individuals in Fifteenth-Century England*. Ed. Jennifer Kermode, 99–117. Stroud, UK: Alan Sutton, 1991.

Razi, Zvi. "Intrafamilial Ties and Relationships in the Medieval Village: a Quantitative Approach Employing Manor Court Rolls." In *Medieval Society and the Manor Court*. Ed. Zvi Razi and Richard Smith, 369–91. Oxford: Clarendon Press, 1996.

Reynolds, Susan. "Medieval Urban History and the History of Political Thought." *Urban History Yearbook* (1982): 14–23.

Richmond, Colin. *John Hopton: A Fifteenth-Century Suffolk Gentleman*. Cambridge, UK: Cambridge University Press, 1981.

———. *The Paston Family in the Fifteenth Century*. 2 vols. Cambridge UK: Cambridge University Press, 1990, 1996.

Ricoeur, Paul. *Oneself as Another*. Trans. Kathleen Blamey. Chicago: University of Chicago, 1994.

Riddy, Felicity. "Mother Knows Best. Reading Social Change in a Courtesy Text." *Speculum* 71 (1996): 66–86.

Rigby, Stephen. *Chaucer in Context*. Manchester: Manchester University Press, 1996.

———. *English Society in the Later Middle Ages*. New York: St. Martin's Press, 1995.

———, and Elizabeth Ewan. "Government, Power and Authority, 1300–1540." In *The Cambridge Urban History of Britain, volume 1, 600–1540*. Ed. David M. Palliser, 291–312. Cambridge: Cambridge University Press, 2000.

———. *Medieval Grimsby. Growth and Decline*. Hull: University of Hull Press, 1993.

———. "Urban 'Oligarchy' in Late Medieval England." In *Towns and Townspeople in the Fifteenth Century*. Ed. John A.F. Thomson, 62–86. Gloucester: Sutton, 1988.

Roberts, Simon. "The Study of Dispute: Anthropological Perspectives." In *Disputes and Settlements: Law and Human Relations in the West*. Ed. John Bossy, 1–24. Cambridge, UK: Cambridge University Press, 1983.

Rogozinski, Jan. *Power, Caste, and Law: Social Conflict in Fourteenth-Century Montpellier*. Cambridge, Mass.: Medieval Academy of America, 1982.

Rosser, Gervase. "Communities of Parish and Guild in the Late Middle Ages." In *Parish, Church, and People. Local Studies in Lay Religion, 1350–1750*. Ed. S.J. Wright, 29–55. London: Hutchinson, 1988.

———. "Crafts, Guilds, and the Negotiation of Work in Medieval Towns." *Past & Present* 154 (1997): 3–31.

———. "Essence of Medieval Urban Communities." In *The English Medieval Town. A Reader*. Ed. Richard Holt and Gervase Rosser, 216–37. London: Longman, 1990.

———. "Going to the Fraternity Feast: Commensality and Social Relations in Late Medieval England." *Journal of British Studies* 33 (1994): 430–46.

Rosser, Gervase with E. Patricia Dennison. "Urban Culture and the Church." In *Cambridge Urban History of Britain, 600–1540*, volume I. Ed. D.M. Palliser, 335–370. Cambridge, UK: Cambridge University Press, 2000.

Rowney, Ian. "Arbitration in Gentry Disputes of the Later Middle Ages." *History* 67 (1982): 367–76.

Rubin, Miri. *Corpus Christi*. Cambridge, UK: Cambridge University Press, 1991.

———. "The Poor." In *Fifteenth-Century Attitudes. Perceptions of Society in Late Medieval England*. Ed. Rosemary Horrox, 169–82. Cambridge: Cambridge University Press, 1994.

———. "Small Groups: Identity and Solidarity in the Late Middle Ages." In *Enterprise and Individuals in Fifteenth-Century England*. Ed. Jennifer Kermode, 132–50. Stroud: Alan Sutton Publishing, 1991.

Ruggiero, Guido. *Violence in Early Renaissance Venice*. New Brunswick, NJ: Rutgers University Press, 1980.

Saul, Nigel. *Scenes from Provincial Life: Knightly Families in Sussex, 1280–1400*. Oxford: Oxford University Press, 1986.

Scattergood, John. "Fashion and Morality in the Late Middle Ages." In *England in the Fifteenth Century: Proceedings of the 1986 Harlaxton Symposium*. Ed. Daniel Williams, 255–72. Woodbridge, UK: Boydell Press, 1987.

Schmitt, Jean-Claude. "La découverte de l'individu, une fiction historiographique?" In *La fabrique, la figure, la feinte: Fictions et Statut des Fictions en Psychologie*. Ed. P. Mingal and F. Parot, 213–36. Paris: Vrin, 1989.

Schofield, John. *Medieval London Houses*. New Haven: Yale University Press, 1994.

Schofield, Phillipp R. "Peasants and the Manor Court: Gossip and Litigation at the Close of the Thirteenth Century." *Past and Present* 159 (1998): 3–43.

Scott, Joan. "The Evidence of Experience." *Critical Inquiry* 17 (1991): 773–97.

———. *Gender and the Politics of History*. New York: Columbia University Press, 1988.

Scott, J. *Social Network Analysis: A Handbook*. London: SAGE Publications, 1991.

Scrase, A.J. "Development and Change in Burghage Plots: the Example of Wells." *Journal of Historical Geography* 15 (1989): 49–65.

———. and Joan Hasler. *Wells Corporation Properties*. Somerset Record Society 87, 2002.

Serel, Thomas. *Historical Notes on the Church of St Cuthbert in Wells, etc*. Wells: J.M. Atkins, 1875.

Sharpe, J.A. *Defamation and Sexual Slander in Early Modern England: the Church Courts at York*. York: Borthwick Institute of Historical Research, 1980.

Shaw, David Gary. "Happy in Our Chains: Agency and Language in the Postmodern Age." *History and Theory* 40 (2001): 1–9.

———. *The Creation of a Community: The City of Wells in the Middle Ages*. Oxford: Oxford University Press, 1993.

———. "The Worshipful Ferrour and Kempe. Social Selves in a Medieval Town." In *Studying Medieval People*. Ed. Nancy F. Partner, 3–19. London: Arnold, 2005.

Shephard, Alexandra. "Manhood, Credit and Patriarchy in Early Modern England." *Past and Present* 167 (2000): 75–106.

Smith, Jay. "Between *Discourse* and *Experience*: Agency and Ideas in the French Pre-Revolution." *History and Theory* 40 (2002): 116–42.

Smith, Llinos Beverley. "Disputes and Settlements in Medieval Wales: The Role of Arbitration." *English Historical Review* 106 (1991): 835–60.

Smith, Richard. "Neighbours in a Thirteenth-Century Suffolk Community." *Journal of Family History* 4 (1979): 219–56.

Southern, Richard W. *Medieval Humanism and Other Studies*. Oxford: B. Blackwell, 1970.

———. *St Anselm and his Biographer*. Cambridge, UK: Cambridge University Press, 1963.

———. *St Anselm. A Portrait in a Landscape*. Cambridge, MA: Blackwell, 1990.

———. *Robert Grosseteste: The Growth of an English Mind in Medieval Europe*. Oxford: Oxford University Press, 1986.

Spencer, H. Leith. *English Preaching in the Late Middle Ages*. Oxford: Oxford University Press, 1993.

Spufford, Margaret. "Puritanism and Social Control." In *Order and Disorder in Early Modern England*. Ed. Anthony Fletcher and John Stevenson, 41–57. Cambridge, UK: Cambridge University Press, 1985.

Stewart, Frank Henderson. *Honor*. Chicago: University of Chicago Press, 1994.

Stock, Brian. *The Implications of Literacy*. Princeton: Princeton University Press, 1983.

Strocchia, Sharon. "Gender and the Rites of Honour in Italian Renaissance Cities." In *Gender and Society in Renaissance Italy*. Ed. Judith C. Brown and Robert C. Davis, 39–60. London: Longman, 1998.

Suleiman, Susan R. "Introduction: Varieties of Audience-Oriented Criticism." In *The Reader in the Text*. Ed. Susan Suleiman and Inge Crosman, 3–45. Princeton: Princeton University Press, 1980.

Swanson, Heather. "The Illusion of Economic Structure: Craft Guilds in late Medieval English Towns". *Past & Present* 121 (1988): 29–48.

———. *Medieval Artisans*. Oxford: B. Blackwell, 1989.

———. *Medieval British Towns*. Basingstoke: St. Martin's Press, 1999.

Swanson, R.N. "Angels Incarnate: the Clergy and Masculinity from the Gregorian Reform to the Reformation." In *Masculinity in Medieval Europe*. Ed. Dawn Hadley, 160–77. London: Longman, 1999.

Taylor, Charles. "The Dialogical Self." In *The Interpretive Turn: Philosophy, Science, Culture*. Ed. David R. Hiley, James F. Bohman, and Richard Shusterman, 304–14. Ithaca: Cornell University Press, 1991.

———. *Philosophy and the Human Sciences*. Cambridge, UK: Cambridge University Press, 1985.

———. *Sources of the Self*. Cambridge, Mass.: Harvard University Press, 1989.

Thrupp, Sylvia. *The Merchant Class of Medieval London*. Ann Arbor, MI: University of Michigan Press, 1948.

Tittler, Robert. *Townspeople and Nation: English Urban Experiences 1540–1640*. Stanford: Stanford University Press, 2001.

———. *The Reformation and the Towns in England: Politics and Political Culture, c. 1540–1640*. Oxford: Clarendon Press, 1998.

Trenholme, Norman M. *The English Monastic Boroughs*. Columbia, Missouri: University of Missouri Press, 1927.

Trexler, Richard C. *The Journey of the Magi. Meanings in History of a Christian Story*. Princeton: Princeton University Press, 1997.

Tuck, Richard. "Rights and Pluralism." In *Philosophy in an Age of Pluralism*. Ed. James Tully, 159–70. Cambridge, UK: Cambridge University Press, 1994.

Ullmann, Walter. *The Individual and Society in the Middle Ages*. Baltimore: Johns Hopkins Press, 1966.

Victoria County History of Somerset. Ed. William Page, 2 vols. London: Constable, 1906–11.

Vodola, Elizabeth. *Excommunication in the Middle Ages*. Berkeley: University of California Press, 1986.

Walker, Sue Sheridan. "The Action of Waste in the Early Common Law." In *Legal Records and the Historian*. Ed. J.H. Baker, 185–206. London: Royal Historical Society, 1978.

Ward, Jennifer. "Townswomen and their Households." In *Daily Life in the Late Middle Age*. Ed. Richard Britnell, 27–42. Stroud: Sutton, 1998.

Wees, Hans van. "The Law of Gratitude: Reciprocity in Anthropological Theory." In *Reciprocity in Ancient Greece*. Ed. Christopher Gill, Norman Postelthwaite, and Richard Seaford, 13–49. Oxford: Oxford University Press, 1998.

Weintraub, Karl J. *The Value of the Individual: Self and Circumstance in Autobiography*. Chicago: University of Chicago Press, 1978.

Weissman, Hope. "Margery Kempe in Jerusalem: *Hysteria Compassio* in the Late Middle Ages." In *Acts of Interpretation: The Text in the Contexts 700–1600*. Ed. Mary J. Carruthers and Elizabeth D. Kirk, 201–17. Norman, OK: Pilgrim Books, 1982.

Weissman, Ronald F.E. "The Importance of Being Ambiguous: Social Relations, Individualism, and Identity in Renaissance Florence." In *Urban Life in the Renaissance*. Ed. Susan Zimmerman and Ronald F.E. Weissman, 269–80. Newark: Associated University Presses, 1989.

———. "Reconstructing Renaissance Sociology: The 'Chicago School' and the Study of Renaissance Society." In *Persons in Groups: Social Behavior as Identity Formation in Medieval and Renaissance Europe*. Ed. Richard C. Trexler, 39–46. Binghamton, NY: Medieval & Renaissance Texts & Studies, 1985.

Wellman, Barry and S.D. Berkowitz. "Introduction: Studying Social Structures." In *Social Structures: A Network Approach*. Ed. Wellman and Berkowitz, 1–14. Cambridge, UK: Cambridge University Press, 1988.

Wellman, Barry, Peter J. Carrington, and Alan Hall. "Networks as Personal Communities." In *Social Structures: A Network Approach*. Ed. Barry Wellman and S.D. Berkowitz, 130–84. Cambridge, UK: Cambridge University Press, 1988.

Wemple, Suzanne F. and Denise A. Kaiser. "Death's Dance of Women." *Journal of Medieval History* 12 (1986): 333–43.

Wetherall, Charles, Andrejs Plakans, and Barry Wellman. "Social Networks, Kinship, and Community in Eastern Europe." *Journal of Interdisciplinary History* 34 (1994): 639–63.

White, Stephen D. "*Pactum. . .Legem Vincit et Amor Judicium*": The Settlement of Disputes by Compromise in Eleventh-Century Western France." *American Journal of Legal History* 22 (1978): 281–308.

White, Stephen D. and Richard T. Vann. "The Invention of English Individualism: Alan Macfarlane and the Modernization of pre-Modern England." *Social History* 8 (1983): 345–63.

Wickham, Chris. "Gossip and Resistance Among the Medieval Peasantry." *Past and Present* 160 (1998): 3–24.

Wollheim, Richard. *The Thread of Life*. Cambridge, Mass.: Harvard University Press, 1984.

Woodcock, Brian L. *Medieval Ecclesiastical Courts in the Diocese of Canterbury*. London: Oxford University Press, 1952.

Wormald, Jenny. "An Early Modern Postcript: The Sandlaw Dispute, 1546." *Disputes and Settlements: Law and Human Relations in the West*. Ed. John Bossy, 191–205. Cambridge, UK: Cambridge University Press, 1983.

Wrightson, Keith. " 'Sorts of People' in Tudor or Stuart England." In *The Middling Sort of People. Culture, Society and Politics in England, 1550–1800*. Ed. Jonathan Barry and Christopher Brooks, 28–51. London: St. Martin's Press, 1994.

Wunderli, Richard. *London Church Courts*. Cambridge, Mass.: Medieval Academy of America, 1981.

Xhayet, Geneviève. "Autour des solidarités privées au moyen âge: partis et réseaux de pouvoir à Liège du xiiie au xve siècle." *Le Moyen Age* 100 (1994): 205–19.

INDEX

Abraham, 25–6
admission to citizenry, 56, 96–7, 113,
    167, 169, 171–2
adultery, 36, 109, 166
affinity, 96, 152
agency, 21, 23, 68
    early modern, 206
    and group, 197–9, 205
    of the self, 13–15
    social history and, 3–8
    social networks and, 94–5, 99
    women's, 36, 82, 143
aliens, 61, 205
alliances, 86, 91, 152
almshouse, see Hospital of the Holy
    Saviour, Wells
animals, 97, 130, 134, 137, 192
anthropology, 19, 31
apprentices and apprenticeship,
    52, 97, 114, 136, 138,
    200, 202
Aquinas, St. Thomas, 25, 28, 135
arbitration, 71–90, 125
    arbitrators and factions, 94–5,
        98–106
    failed, 55–6,
    reciprocity and, 62, 67
    and social networks, 112–14,
        116–17
    as time-technique, 62–3
aristocrats, 30, 70
armigers, 172, 182
Arnold, Matthew, 104
arrogance, 131

art, 2–3, 11, 98, 107, 155–6
    see also craftspeople
Attreed, Lorraine, 49
Atwater, John, citizen, 150, 161, 172
Aunger, John, citizen, 59, 157
Austell, John, citizen, 110–11, 172
autonomous self, 122
avarice, 26–7, 39
    see also usury
Averey, Ralph, citizen, 103, 134, 140

backbiting, see verbal abuse
Bailey, Simon, citizen, 169, 171
Baker, Adam, citizen, 138, 141
Baker, Hugh, citizen, 138, 141
Baker, Martin, citizen, 113, 138
Baker, Walter, citizen, 161, 177
bakers, 113–14, 138, 141, 161, 177
Barstaple, John, citizen, 132, 183
bastard feudalism, 96
Beattie, Cordelia, 38
Beckerman, John, 74
Beckyngton, Thomas, Bishop of Bath
    and Wells, 43
    disciplines choristers and vicars, 149
    Thomas Cornish compared to,
        175, 186
    tomb and funeral of, 1–5, 14, 17,
        19–20, 37, 159, 204
beggars and begging, 66, 70, 158
    see also charity; poverty
Benet, John, citizen, 97–100, 182–3
Bennett, Judith, 7, 191
biography, 7, 19, 166, 197

bishops, 23, 192–3
boy bishop, 129, 151
in *Dance of Death*, 40, 43
of Durham, 136
suffragan, 111, 185–7, 189
Bishops of Bath and Wells, 14, 20, 37,
43, 65, 175, 186, 204
bailiff of, 171
courts of, 50, 55, 58–9, 75, 85, 106
as lord of Wells, 49–50, 97, 108,
182, 185
palace, 151, 165, 185
visitation of cathedral, 109,
165–6
see also under individual bishops
body
Corpus Christi, 153, 178
death and burial of, 2, 151, 157,
159–62, 175
decrepitude and old age, 158, 175
expressive, 145
gestures of subordination, 33, 66
as instrument, 162
penance, 142, 162
politic, 49, 56, 113, 180
relationship to self, 12, 197
servants' dependant, 137
trespass and violence to, 74, 123,
133–5
Book of Vices and Virtues, The, 26
books, 157, 178, 185, 188
Borough Community, 49–50, 55, 83,
86, 98, 100
membership and admission, 52, 96,
116, 137, 167, 171
and parish church, 179, 184–5,
194–5
property of, 173–4, 194
as regulatory community, 31, 47–9,
51, 64–7
as social network, 102
women in, 57, 135, 139
see also admission; arbitration; Master
of Wells; *for officers see under
individual offices*

borough court, 16–18, 67–8,
180–4, 198
arbitration, 72–91
broken agreement, 26
church courts, 124–5
cultivating social networks, 97–101,
104–6
described, 49–50
as disciplinary structure, 49–65
failures to appear in, 168
reciprocity in, 62–4
and social network analysis, 117–18
time-techniques of resolution, 62–3
unenfranchised in, 137–9
violence in, 132–5, 143
see also Bishops of Bath and Wells;
Borough Community;
expulsion; licenses to prosecute;
royal courts; violence
Bourdieu, Pierre, 6, 13–14, 32–3, 52
bowing, 33
brewers, 173
Bristol, 50–1, 53, 60, 106, 185, 189,
191–2
broken contracts, suit of, 73–4
broken guarantee, suit of, 27, 50, 63,
73–4, 177
brothers and burgess brotherhood, 25,
47–68, 96, 127, 153, 173
craft, 114–16, 156, 201
disputes and peacemaking, 60–4,
80–1, 90
fictional, 27–30, 57–8
sibling rivalry, 30, 128–9
as social network, 102–5, 127, 129
Broun, John, citizen, 96–7, 106–7,
177, 180
Bubwith, Nicholas, Bishop of Bath and
Wells, 110
Burckhardt, Jakob, 6
burgess-centered households, 135
burgesses and citizens, 4, 198, 201
arbitration among, 72–90
biographies of, 166–84, 198, 201
exposure to clerical culture, 22

and hierarchy, 38–9, 41–3
honor of, 35, 124
importance of fraternity to, 47–9,
      50 62, 67–8
networks of modest, 113–15
relations with clergy, 108–11
as 'systact', 12
see admission; Borough Community;
      expulsion
Bynum, Caroline, 8, 203

Calais, 29, 153, 186
Cambridge, 2, 6
canons
   in *Dance of Death*, 38
canons of Wells, 106, 185–90
   dean and chapter, 165, 193
   discipline of, 108–9, 165–6,
      187–8, 190
   socializing in town, 108–11
   see also Wells Cathedral
Canterbury Tales, The, 36, 40
carpenters, 112, 153–4, 200, 202
Carthusians, 194
Cely Family, 29, 35, 152–3
chapels, 1–2, 17, 112, 161
   private, 173, 193–5
chaplain, 162, 190
chapmen, 116
character
   and contingency, 9, 18, 60, 71,
      81, 105
   reputation and, 84–5, 87, 132, 190
charitable bequests, 151
charity, 64, 67, 127, 151–2, 175
chastity, 35, 192
Chaucer, Geoffrey, 40–1, 149
Chepman, Roger, citizen, 103–4, 106
child-choristers, 142
children, 67, 149, 158, 188
   disciplining, 141–3
   fidelity and, 25–8, 67
Christine de Pisan, 23
Churchstile, John, citizen,
      130, 177

churchwardens, 50, 77, 80, 112, 117,
      169, 176–9, 185, 195
   see also St. Cuthbert's Church
churchyard, 66, 107, 160
Chynnok, Thomas, citizen, 55, 58
citizens, see burgesses and citizens
citizenship, 52, 172
civic elites, 48–9
   arbitration and, 77–90
   associated fraternities, 30
   biographies of, 166–73, 180–96
   church attendance by, 150
   factional, 97–8, 105
   and group discipline, 55
   limited power of, 70, 76
   networks, 104–8, 112–14,
      116–17, 169
   as oligarchy, 149, 180
   relation to county elites, 40, 86
   women, 107, 190–6
civic officers, 18
class difference, 69, 111
clergy, 22, 149, 184–5
   clergy–citizen social relations, 108–11
   higher, 106
   and social imaginary, 38
   see also bishops; *individual clergymen*
clothes, 24, 114, 145
   exhibiting status and identity, 41, 66,
      145–55
   sinful, 145–6, 149, 159
   vestments, 148, 157, 178, 195
Clover, Carol, 129
collective interests, see Borough
      Community
Collingwood, R.G., 9
commerce, 129, 170, 184
   borough court and, 55, 62, 76
   commercialization, 147
   and networks, 51
   social ethics, 25, 27, 30, 33
commoners (citizens), 55, 174, 178, 199
   arbitration and, 77–80, 84, 86–8, 100
   social networks, 100–3, 111–14,
      116–17

284 INDEX

commoners (non-nobles), 123–4, 130
community, 3, 59, 116–17
  almshouse, 158
  arbitration and, 89–91
  decline of, 48
  ecclesiastical, 3, 38, 51, 108–11,
    148–9, 185–90
  hierarchy in the, 42
  historiographical discussion of, 5,
    7–8, 16–18
  honor and the, 31–2
  individual and, 8, 18, 200–5
  parochial, 4
  as social actor, 198
  see also Borough Community;
    St. Cuthbert's Church
conceptual frameworks, 16
confession, 59, 204
Confessio Amantis, 108
constables, 43, 50, 77, 83–5, 87
consumption, 18–19, 147, 167
contempt of Community, 41, 56,
    59–60, 199
contingency, 14, 64, 71
cooks, 133, 137
Cornish, Thomas, Bishop of Tine,
    110–11, 184–90
courts, see Bishops of Bath and Wells,
    sub court; borough court
couverture, see women
Coventry, 35, 42, 48, 51, 58, 169, 193
craft leader, 115
craftspeople
  in Dance of Death, 38–9, 111
  networks of, 113–16
  sociocultural identity of, 26, 154–6
crime, 66, 136–7
Cristesham, Nicholas, citizen, 97, 137
Crofter, William, citizen, 80, 172
cuckstool, 65
cultural divide between clergy and lay,
    108, 161
cultural exchanges (gifts, gift-giving)
  bequests, 189–90
  community, 156–7, 173, 178–9, 194

  funerary, 151
  reciprocity of, 62–3, 81, 89
  symbolic, 52, 56, 141
  of time, 62
cultural history, 19
cultural values, 13–15
  changing elite, 169–70
  community and, 47–8, 52–3,
    61–8, 152
  conservative, 14, 135
  hierarchical, 141–4
  religious, 159, 162–3, 204
  schedules of, 141–3, 154, 170, 204
  theory of, 19–24
  see also community; fidelity; gender;
    hierarchy; honor; master values
Curteys Family, 28–9, 132
customs, 10, 13, 59, 72
Cutte, John, citizen, 80, 168, 171

Dante, 37–8, 204–5
Davis, Natalie, 5
dean, see Wells Cathedral
death
  Beckyngton's, 1–3, 14
  burial near friends, 107
  clothing after death, 149, 152
  funerals and burial, 158–62, 176, 188
  post mortem prayers, 190
  and the private self, 204–5
  and social hierarchy, 37–41
  see also tombs and burials
debt, 98, 177
  dispute resolution, 59, 62–3, 71
  failure to appear in cases of,
    54–5, 168
  lawsuits for, 54–5, 74, 76, 89
  and recourse to arbitration, 73–6,
    78–9, 89, 98, 107
  relation to slander suits, 155
defamation, see verbal abuse
degree, 37–44, 58, 147, 151
  and deference, 131, 135, 137
  see also hierarchy
dependants, 134–5, 143, 200

dialogical self, 15, 44, 165
dining, 23, 42
Dinn, Robert, 159
discipline (group), 31, 40, 48–68, 81, 142
discourse, 23, 90, 122
discretion, 85, 202
dispute settlement, *see* arbitration;
	borough court
distraint of chattel, lawsuits of, 54
domestic violence, *see* violence
dress, *see* clothing
Dyer, Walter, citizen, 106, 139, 168
dyes, 29, 55, 183

Earl of Devon, 109
ecclesiastical corporations, 185
education, 110, 188
Eleanor, Duchess of Gloucester, 66
elites, 19, 21, 108
	see also civic elites
Elwell, Hildebrand, citizen, 157,
	170, 172
Elwellsplace, 157
embedded self, 3, 15
emergent self, 8, 95
employees, 137–8
enemies, 95, 97–9, 105, 114, 183
	see also friends; networks
enfranchised, 54, 57, 77
equality, 39
	and arbitration, 80–1, 90
	brotherhood and, 29, 129
	character of groups, 11, 69, 72
	relation to honor, 33, 124–5
	social networks, 115
equity, 50, 54, 63, 80, 86
Erghum, Ralph, Bishop of Bath and
	Wells, 193
exchange, *see* cultural exchanges
experience as a historical category, 7, 9,
	22, 32, 117
expulsion from Community, 56–7,
	59–61, 96
	see also admission to citizenry
external self, 8

factions, 105, 169, 189
faith, 3, 24–6, 52, 76, 111, 130, 179
family, 7, 11, 13, 185, 188–90, 203
	death and, 160–2
	father-centered, 141
	fidelity modelled on, 23–31, 44
	as part of a citizen, 52, 59, 109–10
	surrogate, 61, 96–7, 104, 188
	violence in, 141–2
	see also brothers; Cely; Curteys;
		fathers; wives; women
fathers, 160, 204
	determine family status, 37, 45
	fidelity to, 24–31
	and household identity, 141–2,
		166, 200
Ferrers, John, citizen, 62
Ferrour, Richard, citizen, 97–9, 101,
	103, 106, 132, 141, 180–4
fidelity, 19–20, 122, 197–201
	binding households, 135–7,
		142–3, 153
	Borough Community and, 48, 52, 67
	and commerce, 76, 129–30, 177
	described as master value, 23–32, 36
	relation to honor and hierarchy,
		43–5
	see also enemies; family; friends;
		master values; rebellion
Fifteenth-Century Attitudes, 11, 21
fines, 53–4, 58, 64, 89
fish and meat stalls, 149
fishmonger, 138, 155
Flynn, Maureen, 66
Forbour, Edward, citizen, 62–3, 140
foreigners, *see* burgesses and citizens
fornication, 109
Foucault, Michel, 199
Fox, Richard, Bishop of Exeter, 186
France, 82, 191–2, 202
fraternities and guilds, 17, 96, 152,
	198–9
	civic, 47–50, 52–3
	and court, 55–65, 67, 78
	craft, 113

fraternities and guilds—*continued*
 as an ideal, 29–30, 81, 86, 89–90,
   102, 124
 religious, 48, 96, 141, 156–7, 160–1
 see also Borough Community;
   brothers; court
Freman, John, citizen, 137
Freud, Sigmund, 9, 10
friars, 38, 159
friends
 bequests to, 149, 189
 community and, 48, 51, 169, 199, 201
 craft, 112–25
 expulsion, 56
 identity and, 15, 44
 institutional friendship, 105
 John Godwin's, 169–73
 John Rowburgh's, 177
 lay-clerical, 108–11, 188
 prayers for, 160–2
 Richard Ferrour's, 180, 183
 social networks and, 93–117
 see also enemies; networks
fullers, 134, 177, 183
funerals, *see* death; tombs and burials

Gadamer, Hans-Georg, 23
Galon, John, citizen, 58, 75
Gascoigne, William, citizen, 110, 172
gender, 23, 45, 200–1
 defamation and, 128–9, 153–4
 female, 129, 138
 and group membership, 57, 83
 hierarchy, 39
 and honor, 32, 35
 male social imagination, 38
 sex and, 35–6
 and variable selves, 122
 violence and, 133–44
 see also wives; women
generosity, 75, 151
gentlemen and gentry, 35, 39, 148
 social mobility into, 86, 116,
   170–3, 182
 and towns, 96, 110–11

Giddens, Anthony, 13–14, 23, 197
gifts and gift-giving, *see* cultural
   exchanges
Ginzburg, Carlo, 10
glazier, 167
Gloucester, Humphrey, Duke of, 41–2
glovers, 114
gloves, 52, 167, 178–9
Godwin, Joan, citizen's wife, 173
Godwin, John, citizen, 43, 166–73, 182
Godwin, Matilda, citizen's wife, 167
Goldberg, P.J.P., 7
Goodman, Nelson, 14
gossip, 36, 70, 108, 142, 153
 see also verbal abuse
Gower, John, 108
Gowing, Laura, 35, 129, 143
Green, Richard Firth, 24, 76
Greenblatt, Stephen, 6, 205
Greynton, William, citizen, 63, 102, 104
grocers, 170, 172
Growing up in Medieval London, 8
guilds, *see* fraternities and guilds

Hampton, Thomas, citizen, 130–1, 133
Hanawalt, Barbara, 8, 143
Haselshaw, Thomas, canon of Wells, 109
heads of households, 18
Hegel, G.W.F., 6
Heidegger, Martin, 13
Helmholz, R.H., 123
hermeneutic historiography, 6, 11–13
Herrup, Cynthia, 32
hierarchy, 17, 39–40, 167, 172–3
 and arbitration, 79–81, 85, 88–91
 Chaucer, 40–1
 Dance of Death, 39–41
 ecclesiastical, 109–11, 185–90
 gender, 38–9, 175
 as master value, 19, 23, 36–44,
   197–203
 and overlapping selves, 121–2,
   132–44
 rebellion against, 130–2
 stratification, 40, 44, 70, 94, 143

sumptuary laws, 147–8
variety of, 37
see also degree; gentlemen
Hilton, Rodney, 21, 128
Hobbes, Thomas, 31–2, 136
Hoccleve, Thomas, 41
honor, 94, 197–204
and arbitration, 71, 74–7
community's, 60, 130–3, 172
in the courts, 48, 54–7, 71, 74–7,
89–90, 122–37
defamation and, 122–30
defense of, 122, 133–43
familial, 134–43, 152–4, 191–3
gendered, 35–6, 57, 154
humiliation, 34, 61, 151
as master values, 19, 23, 31–6
relation to hierarchy, 41–2, 44–5
relation to trust, 27, 32, 44
shame, 30, 36, 143
theory of, 31–3
worshipfulness, 33–5, 149, 160–1
Horewode, John, citizen, 149–51
Horn, Robert, citizen, 99, 183
Horrox, Rosemary, 136
Hospital of the Holy Saviour, Wells,
110, 158, 172, 175, 185
human nature, 9–10, 16
Hume, David, 9–10, 12, 15
humiliation, 36, 65–6, 115, 131
humility, *see* honor

Iceland, 129
ideals, 25
ideas, and social self, 21–3, 67–8, 203–6
see also civic values; master values
individual agency, *see* agency
individualism, 5–6, 8–9
individuality, 3–4, 40, 51, 67, 70, 89,
134, 149
see also social self
infidelity, 27, 57
see also fidelity
initiation, 52, 56
see also admission

inner circle (networks), 100–4, 106,
112, 118–19
insubordination, 59, 79
insults, 32, 128–9, 132, 139, 143, 151
see also verbal abuse
Ireland, 191, 192
Isaac, 25, 27, 30, 31

Jesse Tree, 155–6
jewelry, 157
Joan of Arc, 146
journeymen, 66, 111–14, 143, 181
judicial leadership, *see* oligarchy

Kaminsky, Howard, 40
Kant, Immanuel, 12, 94
Kempe, John, 33, 37
Kempe, Margery, 6, 22–3, 191, 203
authority of, 13
cultural centrality, 22–3
evidence for social self, 15, 146, 163
family connections, 26, 140
shame of, 36
slandered, 126
Kermode, Jenny, 8, 17
King, Oliver, Bishop of Bath and Wells,
188, 190
kisses of peace, 63, 205
kneeling, 33, 61
knights, 40, 110, 182
Knyght, Agnes, citizen's wife, 141, 183
Knyght, William, citizen, 141, 182

laborers, 38–9, 41, 140, 154, 175
Langland, William, 95, 122, 158
law
common, 55, 132
courts, 62, 67, 74
fraternities affecting, 50–1
slander and, 124–5
and social regulation, 48, 54, 147
wager of, 73
licenses to prosecute, 53–6, 58–9, 194
licit violence, 135, 143
literacy, 5, 22, 157

literary culture, 22
literary methodology and sources, 10
livery, 57–8, 152
    see also clothes
Locke, John, 121, 123
London, 30–1, 35, 43, 65, 116, 124, 128
lordship, 49, 68, 192, 201
Love, Katherine, sorceress, 66
love-days, 71, 73, 95
    see also arbitration
Lynn, 22, 26, 50, 146

Maddern, Philippa, 21, 135, 142
Magi, 33
male imagination, 38
male-centered household, 139
manumission, 192–3, 201
markets, 26, 51, 65, 77, 113, 149–50
marriage, 153–4, 202
    civic admission and, 52, 57, 169
    Goldberg on, 7
    and hierarchy, 36–7, 136
masculinity, 24, 129, 140, *see* gender
masons, 155–6, 160, 174, 178
Masson, James, citizen, 59, 99
Master of Wells, 107
    compared to mayors, 38–9, 41–3,
        57–8,
    contempt to, 59–61, 127, 130–1,
        133–4
    example, 171–3
    judicial role, 72–3, 76
master values, 19, 23, 31, 36, 48, 53, 68,
        89, 197, 201, 204
    see also Borough Community;
        fidelity; hierarchy; honor
Maundewar, Henry, citizen, 106, 137
Mauss, Marcel, 81
McIntosh, Marjorie K., 7, 21–2, 48
McSheffrey, Shannon, 140
Mead, George, 8
men and women, *see* gender
Mendip Hills, 192
mentality, *see* master values
mercers, 31, 188

merchants
    and arbitration, 72
    as chapmen, 116
    community, 17
    social standing of, 29, 38–9, 41,
        85–6, 148
    worshipfulness and display of, 35, 41,
        149–50
middling groups, 80
middling officers, 77–9, 117
modernization fallacy, 95
monks, 149, 190
Montaigne, Michel de, 5
moral outrage, 58, 129–31
moralists, 19, 21, 25–6, 28, 95,
        122, 126
Morris, Colin, 8
MPs, 50
Muldrew, Craig, 26
multiple communities, 3, 96
mystery plays, 22, 25, 30, 113
mysticism, 203–4

neighbors, 141, 169, 182–3
    see also friends; trespass
Newmaster, John, citizen, 58, 106
Newton, John, citizen, 113, 138
Noah, 139

oaths, 26–7, 52, 56, 58, 60, 75, 130
occupations and trades, 40, 43, 85,
        112–13
    see individual occupations
Ockham, William, 22
oligarchy, 70, 72, 87–90
    arbitration by, 82, 84
    networks, 101, 104–8, 116
    oligarchs, 77, 99, 107, 166–73,
        180–4
    see also borough community
Olson, Sherri, 7, 198
Oriel College, *see* Oxford University
outer circle (networks), 101–4, 118
Oxford University, 2, 48, 111,
        185–9

parish, parochial community, 4
  see also churchwardens; St. Cuthbert's
    Church
parish, the, 4, 30, 179
  see also St. Cuthbert's Church
Partner, Nancy, 9
Pastons, 7
patriarchy, 24, 38, 78, 140
  see also gender
patrons, 67, 102, 113–14, 116
peacemaking, *see* arbitration; borough
  court
peasants, 7, 66, 70, 172, 192
Pedewell, John, citizen, 168, 171
penance, 66, 190
Peres, Richard, citizen, 63, 106, 170
perjury, 26, 58
Pestel, John, citizen, 62, 114, 183
petty burgesses, 77, 79, 88, 101, 117
petty officers, 117
pewterers, 132
philosophical hermeneutics, 10
physical violence, 122, 130–3, 137
  see also verbal abuse
Piggesley, Thomas, citizen, 106,
  114, 168
Pitt-Rivers, Julian, 31, 81, 121
pledges, 114, 174, 177, 179
Pontefract, Cecily, of Wells, 109, 165–6,
  184, 191
Pope, John, citizen, 103, 149
Porter, Philip, citizen, 80, 103,
  169, 170
poverty, 70, 151, 158, 173–6
prayer, 25, 47, 176, 194
pride, *see* honor
private self, 15, 99, 121, 156, 198,
  202–5
  see also social self
processions, 12, 41–2, 112,
  148–50, 153
prosopography, 19
prostitutes, 109, 165–6, 184, 191
psychoanalysis and the self, 9–10
punishment, group, 56–7, 59, 75

reader-response criticism, 10
readmission to Community, 57, 59
real property
  church as, 177, 179
  developing, 157
  housebreaking, 134
  landholding, 172
  and status, 167, 173–5, 181–3
  trespass, 74–5, 97–9, 111, 134
rebellion, 52, 57–8, 60, 65, 131, 135
reciprocity, 19, 62–3, 130
Reformation, 3, 4, 7, 206
region, 155, 186
religious guilds, *see* fraternities and
  guilds
rent collectors, 60, 77, 82–4, 117, 177
reputation
  and arbitration, 87, 105
  court actions and, 64–5, 68, 124–6
  gendered nature of, 36, 125
  making a, 26
  and making of public identity, 13,
    18, 71, 99, 143
  relation to fidelity, 44
  slander, 124–6, 129–32
  and social standing, 85
  and trespass, 74, 99
  for workmanship, 154–5
  see also honor
reverence, 34, 42, 173
Richmond, Colin, 7
Rigby, Stephen, 11–12, 40, 49, 70
rite of institution, *see* ritual
ritual
  and agency, 14, 16
  calendar, 148
  exchange, 89, 141
  funeral, 151
  inclusion and exclusion, 52, 56, 65,
    96, 148
  language of condemnation, 30, 32,
    128–9
  rite of institution, 52, 56, 96
Rowburgh, John, citizen, 176, 178
royal charter, 49, 51

royal courts, 53, 56, 124
royal writ, 56
Rubin, Miri, 9
rumors, 24, 128, 138
rural life, 5, 7, 79, 167, 172, 174
Russell, John, 42, 43.
Rydon, William, citizen, 140

saddlers, 114
Salisbury, 2
Salmon, Joanna, citizen's wife, 174
Salmon, John, citizen, 173–4, 176
sample of burgesses (network), 100,
    102, 104, 117
schedules of values, *see* cultural values
scolds, 65
sculpture, 2, 155
second-order citizens, 57
second-order members, 135, 142
serfs, 192
sermons, 22, 25, 204
servants, 18, 113, 135–44
service, 24, 136–7
    see also servants
sex, 35–6, 109, 112, 139–40, 153–4, 166
    see also gender; women
sexual epithets, 128–9
shambles-keepers, 77, 82, 117
shame, *see* honor
sheep, 69, 75, 97, 99, 137, 182
Shelley, John, mercer of London, 128–9
Shelley, Thomas, mercer of
    London, 128
shops, 41, 93, 141–2, 181
Shrewsbury, Ralph of, Bishop of Bath
    and Wells, 109, 165
sin, 37, 66, 125–31, 204
Skinner, Martin, citizen, 114–15
Skinner, Stephen, citizen, 114–15, 139
skinners, 114–16, 139
slander, *see* verbal abuse
small groups, *see* social groups
Smart, Thomas, citizen, 59, 63, 99, 134,
    178, 183
social capital, 84, 86, 168

social class
    clerical, 148–9
    and development of self, 5–7, 197,
        201, 205
    difference, 69–70, 167
    hierarchical, 36, 38
    interaction between, 110–11
    manifestations of, 148–52
    mobility, 39
    slander and, 124–5
    see also burgesses and citizens;
        hierarchy; social groups
social consciousness, 23, 94
social context, 3–4, 142, 146
social forces, 6, 39
social groups
    cross class relations, 108–11
    group discipline of individuals, 31,
        47–68, 75, 130–2
    in hierarchy, 39–43
    informal and ephemeral, 18, 94–6,
        112–14
    infra (peer), 70–2, 75–80, 85–9,
        102–8, 124–5
    small, 4–5, 18–19, 94, 116, 199, 205
    see also Borough Community;
        burgesses and citizens;
        fraternity; social class; social
        networks; women
    theoretical relation to individuals,
        3–5, 6–8, 11, 14–16
social history, 4–7, 10–11, 14–16, 19,
    21, 36, 70, 165, 197, 201–3, 206
social imagination, 40
social mobility, 41
social networks, 4, 18–19, 95, 115–17, 186
    analysis, 105, 117–19
    density, 20, 102–4, 116–19
    elite, 104–8
    exchanges, 118
    intensity, 102, 117, 119, 202
    modest, 111–15, 115–17
    shape of, 97–103
    town-cathedral, 108–11
    women's, 108

social regulation, 7, 48, 68, 199
  see also Borough Community; social
    groups
social self
  extending social history, 8
  identifying, 3–5
  investigating the, 16–18, 21
  medieval, summarized, 197–200
  master values and, 31, 33–6, 39–41,
    44–5
  philosophical basis of, 11–16
  and private self, 99
  speculations on, 200–6
  variableness, 71
  see also agency; private self
self-expression, 6, 13, 17–18, 162
self-fashioning, 206
social standing, 13, 18, 36, 70–1, 73, 84,
    94, 131, 137–8, 140, 177
sociology, 19, 116, 136
socioreligious fraternity, *see* fraternities
  and guilds
Somerset, 2, 179, 185, 191, 193
Southampton, 54, 55
Sprot, John, citizen, 63, 167
St. Bonaventure, 12
St. Cuthbert's Church, Wells, 106, 150
  burials at, 108, 159–60
  fabric of, 64, 155, 160, 175–7, 179
  fines for, 127
  gifts to, 157–8
  St. James image, 161
  St. Mary's Chapel, 194–5
  St. Nicholas Altar, 161
  Trinity altar, 150, 161
  vicars, 108, 111, 187–9
  see also churchwardens
Stillington, Robert, Bishop of Bath and
  Wells, 186, 188
stocks, 64–5, 155
Stoke, John, citizen, 113–15
Stowell, John, citizen, 155, 174
stratification, *see* hierarchy
streetwardens, 113
structuration, 23, 197

suffragan bishop, *see* bishops
sumptuary regulation, 41, 147, 151
swords of authority, 51
symbolic interactionism, 8

Tanner, Isabel, citizen's wife, 191
Tanner's chantry, 194
tax-collectors, 50
Taylor, Charles, 14, 203
theft, 75, 128–30
theory, 9–16, 31, 170
Thrupp, Sylvia, 21
Tittler, Robert, 7, 9
tombs and burials, 176, 190, 193–4
  Beckyngton's, 1–3, 37
  near site of, 107, 160–1
town council, 77, 106, 107, 131,
    150, 195
tradesmen, 111–12, 114, 171
tradition, 4, 14, 54, 204
Trapp, Nicholas, citizen, 161, 188
treason, 124, 131, 135
trespass, 54, 73–8, 86, 97–8, 132–4
  see also borough court
Trinity Guild of Coventry, 48
trust, *see* fidelity
Tucker, Ralph, citizen, 134, 18

unenfranchised, 111, 138
upper classes, 39
usury, 130

verbal abuse
  backbiting, 124, 126
  defamation and slander, 18, 48, 50, 65,
    75, 123–33, 135, 142, 153, 155
  see also insults
vestments, *see* clothes
vicars-choral, *see* Wells Cathedral
violence, 28, 31, 53, 79, 136
  petty, 122–3, 132–5, 137–43
  see also verbal abuse
Virgin Mary, 141, 159, 193–5
  see also St. Cuthbert's Church
Vowell, Richard, citizen, 130, 172, 182

wager of law, 73
Wakefield, 69
wax, 52, 167
wealth, 39, 201
    arbitrators', 85, 87
    clothes' expressing, 147–8, 150
    and reputation, 129–30
    social standing and, 70–2, 75, 77, 170
    women's and, 190–1, 200
weapons, 28, 132–4, 136, 173
weavers, 133–4, 138, 141, 174
Webbe, William, citizen, 126, 127, 179
Weintraub, Karl, 203
Weissman, Ronald, 8
Wells (general), 2–4, 90–1
    Chamberlain Street, 174
    community quality of, 67–8,
        198–201
    compared to other towns, 48, 62,
        64–5
    evidence from, 16–19,
    High Street, 157, 167, 173–4, 181,
        191–2
    Monierslane (Aungerslane), 157
    New Street, 174, 182
    political history of, 49–50, 60–2
    as smaller town, 44,
    Wetlane, 169–70, 173
    see also Borough Community;
        borough court; burgesses and
        citizens; St. Cuthbert's Church
Wells Cathedral (St. Andrew's), 158
    cathedral officials, 17, 108, 110, 193
    chancellor, cathedral, 188
    dean of, 3, 106, 165, 174, 189
    dean and chapter, 106, 187, 193
    precentor, 185, 189
    school, 108, 188
    vicars-choral, 51, 108, 110, 142, 148,
        184–5
    see canons of Wells

Wells Forum Hundred, 192
Welshot, John, citizen, 110–11,
        159, 188
Weye, William, citizen, 59, 80
White, Hayden, 11
widows, 35, 52, 96–7, 149, 154, 169,
        191–6, 200
windows, 167, 178
wine, 52, 63, 67, 89, 167, 191–2
witnessing, 43, 76, 106–7, 136, 165
Wittgenstein, Ludwig, 13, 123
wives, see women
Woky, 192–4
women, 45, 157, 161, 200
    biographies, 165–6, 173–6, 191–6
    hierarchy and, 38–9, 134–5
    honor of, 33–6, 143, 146, 153–4, 161
    limited community standing, 57, 76,
        78, 83–4
    literacy, 22
    and men, 23–4, 30, 135–6
    and religion, 157, 175–6, 193–6
    social networks of, 107, 112,
    and violence, 128–9, 134–5, 139–41,
        143, 146
    virginity, 146, 154, 200
    wives, 112, 135, 139, 141–3, 151,
        161, 191–6
    see also Margery Kempe
wool, 2, 29, 139, 147
Worcester, William, 110
work, artistic, 155
workmanship, 50, 155
worship, 19, 30–6, 59, 71, 143, 156
    see also honor
Wunderli, Richard, 128
Wyclif, John, 22
Wycliffites and Lollards, 95

yeoman, 182
York, 42, 53, 57–8, 60, 62, 96, 130